PRAISE FOR *READING THE SERMONS OF THOMAS AQUINAS*

Aquinas was both preacher and enquirer. Randall Smith's splendid book takes us closer to understanding the relationship between these two vocations than anyone else has done so far. Aquinas's sermons exemplify a rhetoric structured by arts of memory, so that his listeners' minds were informed by Scripture and their desires focused on Him of whom Scripture speaks.

Alasdair MacIntyre
University of Notre Dame

———————•———————

Randall Smith has written a book that for a very long time has been an urgent *desideratum*. The sermons of Thomas Aquinas arguably are the most under-appreciated and least read part of his theological oeuvre. They are a veritable treasure, but like every true treasure, in need of unlocking. With this excellent book, Randall Smith has finally provided an interpretive key that allows us to receive the treasure of Thomas's sermons. This well-written book is a piece of rigorous scholarship, a must-read for all students of Aquinas's theology, also for all who love Christ-centered, biblical preaching, and last but not least for those who want to understand how preaching worked in the world of medieval universities and among the Dominican preachers.

Reinhard Hütter
Duke University Divinity School

———————•———————

St. Thomas is universally known as a theologian, but few people know that he was also a skilled preacher. His sermons represent an integral part of his work, particularly illuminating for a better understanding of his person and his spirituality. In reading them, one discovers the constant concern of a master theologian to extend his theology through a pastoral practice adapted to the most humble settings. Professor Randall Smith has perfectly grasped this intention. His book, aware of and well informed by the most up-to-date scholarship, will help today's reader to penetrate more deeply into this neglected part of the Thomistic corpus.

Jean-Pierre Torrell, O.P.
University of Fribourg, Switzerland

RENEWAL WITHIN TRADITION

SERIES EDITOR: MATTHEW LEVERING
Matthew Levering is the James N. and Mary D. Perry Jr. Chair of Theology at Mundelein Seminary. Levering is the author or editor of over thirty books. He serves as coeditor of the journals *Nova et Vetera* and the *International Journal of Systematic Theology*.

ABOUT THE SERIES

Catholic theology reflects upon the content of divine revelation as interpreted and handed down in the Church, but today Catholic theologians often find the scriptural and dogmatic past to be alien territory. The *Renewal within Tradition* Series undertakes to reform and reinvigorate contemporary theology from within the tradition, with St. Thomas Aquinas as a central exemplar. As part of its purpose, the Series reunites the streams of Catholic theology that, prior to the Council, separated into neo-scholastic and *nouvelle théologie* modes. The biblical, historical-critical, patristic, liturgical, and ecumenical emphases of the Ressourcement movement need the dogmatic, philosophical, scientific, and traditioned enquiries of Thomism, and vice versa. *Renewal within Tradition* challenges the regnant forms of theological liberalism that, by dissolving the cognitive content of the gospel, impede believers from knowing the love of Christ.

PUBLISHED OR FORTHCOMING

The Culture of the Incarnation: Essays in Catholic Theology
Tracey Rowland

Aquinas on Beatific Charity and the Problem of Love
Christopher J. Malloy

Christ the Logos of Creation: Essays in Analogical Metaphysics
John R. Betz

On Love and Virtue: Theological Essays
Michael Sherwin, O.P.

READING THE SERMONS OF THOMAS AQUINAS

A Beginner's Guide

READING THE SERMONS OF THOMAS AQUINAS

———•———

A Beginner's Guide

RANDALL B. SMITH

EMMAUS
ACADEMIC

Steubenville, Ohio
www.emmausacademic.com

EMMAUS
ACADEMIC

Steubenville, Ohio
www.emmausacademic.com
A Division of The St. Paul Center for Biblical Theology
Editor-in-Chief: Scott Hahn
1468 Parkview Circle
Steubenville, Ohio 43952

Library of Congress Control Number: 2016949315
ISBN: 978-1-941447-97-0

Cover art: *The Apotheosis of St. Thomas Aquinas* (1631) by Francisco de
Zurbarán. Museum of Fine Arts, Seville.

Cover design and layout by Margaret Ryland

To my beloved wife Tamara:
poet, muse, spouse.

"Ignorance of the Scriptures is ignorance of Christ."

St. Jerome, Commentary on Isaiah

"Son: 'All the men who were ordained with me
seemed to think that the faculty of preaching will come to
them as a matter of course.'
Father: 'Then I pity their congregations.'"

Canon Twells, Colloquies on Preaching

"I believe in the existence of the truly great preacher, as I believe
in the existence of Halley's Comet, which comes into sight of this
earth once in about seventy-six years."

Phillip Brooks, Lectures on Preaching

TABLE OF CONTENTS

ACKNOWLEDGMENTS

I am one of those strange people who actually reads "Acknowledgments" pages. I suppose to most people it's like listening to the speeches people give at the Academy Awards. No matter how much you liked the movie, you don't want to hear the actor or director thank everyone and his or her mother. But with books, I find it interesting to see who helped the writer or read earlier versions. This information can be revealing. Probably not so much in this case, but hypothetically it can be.

This book would not exist were it not for the eager support of Matthew Levering, the general editor of the series of which it is a part. His support for the project was immediate and invaluable: like a burst of sunshine after several years of gloomy, overcast skies.

I also owe a debt of gratitude to David Solomon, the founding director of the Center for Ethics and Culture, for his support, especially during the year I spent as the Myser Fellow at the Center, during which time a good portion of the first draft of this book was produced. I am also grateful to Carter Snead, Prof. Solomon's successor for his continued support since that time.

Other than to Matthew Levering, my editor, I owe no greater debt than to John O'Callaghan and the late Alice Osberger of Notre Dame's Jacques Maritain Center, a place where I have spent many happy summers re-searching and revising the manuscript. To my mind, the Maritain Center remains one of the finest research centers in the country, and my time spent there is always fruitful in innumerable ways.

Thanks also go out to Brett Kendall and Chris Erickson for their invalu-able editing work and to the incomparable Susan Needham, to my mind the finest content editor in the business, who read and provided invaluable comments on an earlier, related article.

This book is dedicated to my wife, Tamara Nicholl-Smith, and is also of-fered in memory of the late Ralph McInerny and Alice Osberger of the University of Notre Dame's Jacques Maritain Center. May they rest in peace and pray constantly for those of us who strive to achieve some small portion of what they accomplished on behalf of the Church.

And lastly, I ask for the prayers of St. Thomas and of Our Lady, Seat of Wisdom, for all those who read this book, that they may be led beyond its errors and tangled verbiage, to be able to find their own pathway to the wisdom of those great saints and to Wisdom Itself.

Thomas Aquinas,
a Preacher in an Order of Preachers

It is strange to think that Thomas Aquinas's sermons have garnered so little attention over the years, given that he was a prominent member of the Order of Preachers, a group that identified itself precisely by its members's aptitude for *preaching*, and that moreover, as a Master of the Sacred Page at Paris, one of Thomas's official duties, along with lecturing on the Bible and engaging in disputation, was preaching. All of his extraordinarily valuable commentaries on the texts of Aristotle were, by contrast, largely products of his spare time.

Indeed, according to his earliest biographers, Thomas was renowned as an excellent preacher, not only to educated, "academic" audiences, but also to simple uneducated laymen. William of Tocco—who, in his old age, spoke as a witness at Thomas's canonization enquiry in 1319—testified that he himself had heard Brother Thomas preach and that, on these occasions, "many people came to hear him preach."[1] Another early biographer, Bernardo Gui, says of him that:

> To the ordinary faithful he spoke the word of God with singular grace and power, without indulging in far-fetched reasoning or the vanities of worldly wisdom or in the sort of language that

---

[1] See the testimony of William of Tocco in "From the First Canonisation Enquiry," no. 58, in *The Life of St. Thomas Aquinas: Biographical Documents*, trans. and ed. Kenelm Foster, O.P. (London: Longmans and Green, 1959), 97.

serves rather to tickle the curiosity of a congregation than do it any real good. Subtleties he kept for the Schools; to the people he gave solid moral instruction suited to their capacity; he knew that a teacher must always suit his style to his audience.

The people, for their part, reports Gui:

heard him with great respect as a real man of God. He was a teacher who taught others to do what he himself was already doing, or rather God in him, according to that saying of the Apostle, "I dare speak of nothing except of what Christ has done in me" (Rom 15:18). Hence his words had a warmth in them that kindled the love of God and sorrow for sin in men's hearts.[2]

And yet, although Thomas was known as an excellent preacher, and although it was his constant practice to preach, even so, it is only now, some 133 years since the creation of the Leonine Commission,[3] that a modern critical edition of all of Thomas's extant sermons done by the late Fr. Louis Bataillon, O.P., has finally appeared.[4] We also now thankfully

---

[2] Bernardo Gui, *The Life of St. Thomas Aquinas*, ch. 29, quoted from Foster, *Biographical Documents*, 47–48. Both William of Tocco and Gui suggest that Thomas preached to the faithful in his native Italian, and when in Naples, in South Italian (see Foster, *Biographical Documents*, 74n68). Sadly, none of these sermons have survived, and we have only a precious few of the sermons that Thomas preached in Latin. For more on this, see Fr. Torrell's wonderful introduction to his French translation of Thomas's sermons: *Thomas d'Aquin: Sermons*, trans. Jean-Pierre Torrell, O.P. (Paris: Cerf, 2014), esp. 14–16. Not only does Fr. Torrell provide a superb short introduction to the sermons, his French translation also contains invaluable commentary and notes throughout that would be essential reading for anyone engaged in a more in-depth study of the sermons.

[3] In his letter *Iampridem Considerando* of October 15, 1879, Pope Leo XIII indicated his desire that a new edition of the complete works of St. Thomas might be made available "so that the wisdom of the Angelic Doctor might propagate and be spread as widely as possible." *Iampridem Considerando* was clearly intended to help put into effect the recommendations of Leo's earlier encyclical, *Aeterni Patris*, promulgated just two months before (August 4, 1879), in which he had called the Church to a return to the wisdom of Thomas Aquinas. Within weeks of the publication of *Iampridem Considerando*, the Vicar General of the Order of Preachers, Father Giovanni Maria Sanvito, circulated a letter to the entire order pledging them, in obedience to the initiative of Leo XIII, to publish a new edition of the complete works of St. Thomas. Such were the origins of what is now commonly called "The Leonine Commission."

[4] *Sancti Thomae de Aquino Opera Omnia*, vol. 44.1, ed. L. J. Bataillon, O.P. (Rome: Commissio Leonina, 2014); herafter, for brevity, this volume will be referred to simply as "Leonine 44.1."

have in print an English translation of all of the extant sermons done by Professor Mark-Robin Hoogland, C.P., *Thomas Aquinas: The Academic Sermons*, published in the Catholic University of America Press series "The Fathers of the Church: Mediaeval Continuation."[5]

WHY IS AN INTRODUCTION TO THOMAS'S PARTICULAR STYLE OF PREACHING NEEDED?

This is a book about the sermons of Thomas Aquinas and how to read them with a particular historical and cultural sensitivity and, thus, with greater understanding and a deepened appreciation for the message they were crafted to communicate. This sort of basic preparation is necessary for many, if not most, readers because the medieval style of preaching Thomas employed was so different from most of our modern experiences of preaching, largely because it was so structured and orderly in a very unique way. It had, as I hope to show, its own rhetorical brilliance and beauty, but it was not at all like the brilliance and beauty of a sermon by someone like John Henry Newman or John Donne. It could, therefore, I fear, too easily be mistaken as "dry," "dull," and too given over to "logical categories."

There is, naturally, a matter of taste at work in such judgments, although those of us who make them, especially about writers from the past, are frequently enough unaware of our own cultural and linguistic biases. So, for example, there are any number of people today who consider opera exceedingly dull, dry, and too given over to sentimentalism. It was clearly not so in the time of Mozart or Puccini, when events such as operas or symphonies were exceedingly popular, considered deeply exciting, and attended by large, eager crowds. It seems odd to us now to think that something like a symphony could spark riots in the streets of Paris, as seems to have happened on occasion, perhaps most famously after the first performance of Stravinsky's *The Rite of Spring* (now often a crowd favorite). In our own day, crowds sometimes riot in cities when their sports teams lose; in other cities they riot when their sports teams win. One wonders whether, in two

---

[5] *Thomas Aquinas: The Academic Sermons*, trans. Mark-Robin Hoogland, C.P., The Fathers of the Church: Mediaeval Continuation 11 (Washington, DC: Catholic University of America Press, 2010). I have used Hoogland's fine translation in most cases while preparing the present book, although I have, in every case, checked his English translations against the original Latin text from Leonine 44.1, which resulted in my taking the liberty of making several minor emendations to the English where I thought appropriate.

hundred years, this particular cultural ritual will similarly be greeted with the same sort of confusion as our own current appraisals of the past.

What is clear from the historical record, however, as I point out several times in the pages that follow, is that the *sermo modernus* style of preaching that Thomas and his contemporaries created was not something that was *forced* on the medieval congregations of the time. Rather, it became very popular very quickly, it seems, because there was a demand for it. The newly wealthy, literate, somewhat more educated and sophisticated townsfolk of the thirteenth century seem to have wanted a more structured, more orderly, and more thematic sort of preaching. The older style of doing a kind of line-by-line, free-association commentary on the biblical text was no longer considered sufficient. People increasingly wanted smart, clever preaching; they wanted it to make a point; and they usually wanted "the point" to be something they could apply to their own lives in terms of basic Christian doctrine or morals. It was no longer sufficient in preaching simply to give what, in the schools, would be called a "cursory reading" of the Bible. Nor were the complex imaginative associations manifest in, for example, Bernard of Clairvaux's *Sermons on the Song of Songs* to the taste of the townspeople and of the congregations flocking to hear the preaching of the new mendicant orders during the thirteenth century.[6] If the preacher was going to use the Bible in his preaching—as all preachers knew they must—then it was going to have to be done in a different way and on somewhat different terms. The Bible was going to have to be used in such a way that communicated a fairly clearly delineated message—one that would help them make greater sense of their lives and of their faith.

And yet, even if we respect its basic goals and orientation, the *form* this preaching took will likely still seem rather odd to a modern audience and is, therefore, ripe for misunderstandings. Take, for example, the Bible verse that serves as the foundation of the sermon (the *thema* verse) that stands at the head of the sermon. The medieval preacher of Thomas's day is not going to "preach on" this verse in the sense of providing a line-by-

---

[6] Michèle Mulcahey, for example, notes that John of Wales, a Franciscan master at Paris around 1270, wrote in his *De arte praedicandi* that the older style of homily "did not sit particularly well with modern listeners, who liked to see the clear articulation of a sermon developed from a scriptural *thema*," as was Thomas's practice. Indeed, by 1290, the Italian Dominican Fra Giacomo da Fusignano, prior of Santa Maria sopra Minerva in Rome, would write that the older style was suitable only for preaching to the ignorant; see Michèle Mulcahey, *First the Bow is Bent in Study: Dominican Education Before 1350* (Toronto, ON: Pontifical Institute of Mediaeval Studies, 1998), 403n10.

line commentary on it. Rather, this opening biblical verse will serve, as we shall see, as a mnemonic device providing a structure for the topics covered in the sermon—topics that, from our perspective, will seem to have little or nothing to do with the opening biblical verse other than a series of verbal associations. And, as it turns out, our instinct on this matter will be quite right.

Medieval preachers of the *sermo modernus* style knew that they were *preaching* in a new and creative way and not merely *commenting*. This was acceptable to them and their audiences, however, because everyone involved knew that the sermon was not intended to be an exegesis of the opening biblical verse. Rather, the biblical epigraph at the head of a medieval sermon had largely a structural, mnemonic function. It helped the listeners keep the various parts of the sermon distinct and in order in their minds, while it also helped the preacher develop the topics for his sermon.

The Multiple Benefits of Understanding Thomas's Sermon Style

Exploring how a medieval preacher such as Thomas Aquinas used the Scriptures in his preaching will be revelatory in a number of ways. First, since Aquinas's style of preaching was not *sui generis* but instead, a good example of what was called at the time the "modern sermon" (*sermo modernus*) style of preaching, an added benefit of learning to read Thomas's sermons is that we gain a valuable introduction to the sermons of pretty much any other preacher of the mid- to late-thirteenth century, such as St. Bonaventure, St. Albert the Great, Henry of Ghent, Giles of Rome, and others.[7] And indeed, since the *sermo modernus* style remained popular for several centuries after the thirteenth, learning to read the sermons of

---

[7] For nice short descriptions of the style, see either Mulcahey, *First the Bow is Bent in Study*, 400–19, or Jacques Bougerol, *Introduction to the Works of Saint Bonaventure*, trans. J. Guy De Vinck (Paterson, NJ: St. Anthony Guild Press, 1964), 136–43. Although the first deals with thirteenth-century Dominicans and the second with the Franciscan Bonaventure, there is no substantial difference between them. There is not a "Franciscan" way of composing a "modern sermon" that differs in essentials from the "Dominican" way—not, for example, when one compares the university sermons of Thomas and Bonaventure. On this, compare Aquinas's "academic sermons" treated by Hoogland—which, *pace* the title, were not all delivered to "academics"—with sermons found in *The Sunday Sermons of St. Bonaventure*, trans. T. Johnson, Works of Saint Bonaventure 12 (St. Bonaventure, NY: Franciscan Institute, 2008), the English translation of *Sancti Bonaventurae Sermones dominicales*, ed. J. G. Bougerol (Grottaferrata, IT: Collegio S. Bonaventura, Padri Editori di Quaracchi, 1977).

Aquinas intelligently is to get a good introduction to the sermons of the late medieval and early Renaissance periods in general.[8]

A second benefit of learning how Thomas used the Bible as a structural and mnemonic device in his preaching is that, once he had become a Master of the Sacred Page, one of his duties was to comment on the Scriptures, and for each of these scriptural commentaries he wrote a prologue that was, in effect, a short sermon. So, understanding how Thomas structured and developed his sermons will also serve as a key to understanding how he wrote his biblical prologues, each of which is fascinating and theologically revealing in its own right, and most of which have been better preserved than many of his extant sermons.[9]

How Many Extant Sermons Are There?

The recently released Leonine edition of the sermons contains twenty-three "sermons"; not all of these are considered authentic, however, and some are merely "fragments."

In the 2005 edition of Fr. Jean-Pierre Torrell's definitive biography of St. Thomas Aquinas, *St. Thomas Aquinas: The Person and His Work*, he states in the body of his text that: "Through patient labor, L. J. Bataillon, the unrivalled specialist on this material, has succeeded in establishing a list of 20 authentic university sermons."[10] In the "Brief Catalogue of the Works of Saint Thomas Aquinas" at the back of that same volume, however, assembled by Fr. Gilles Emery, one finds a list of the authentic sermons prefaced with the following comment: "The editions of Thomas's works generally contain a good number of sermons attributed to him, for the most part falsely. We indicate here, in alphabetical order, the list of 19

---

8   For the best recent scholarship on the whole area, see the collection of essays in *The Sermon*, ed. Beverly Mayne Kienzle, Typologie Des Sources Du Moyen Age Occidental 81 (Turnhout, Belgium: Brepols, 2000). Especially instructive for our present purposes are Mark Zier's "Sermons of the Twelfth Century Schoolmasters and Canons" (325–61) and Nicole Bériou's "Les Sermons Latins Après 1200" (363–447). Indeed, the latter of these and Bériou's magisterial two-volume *L'avènement des maîtres de la Parole. La prédication à Paris au XIIIe siècle* (Paris: Institut d'Études augustiniennes, 1998) are undoubtedly the best and most complete treatments of the whole topic.

9   The topic of medieval "prologues" has been given particular attention more recently by the work of Alistair Minnis; see esp. *Medieval Theory of Authorship: Scholastic Literary Attitudes in the Later Middle Ages*, 2nd ed. (Philadelphia, PA: University of Pennsylvania Press, 2010), esp. chs. 1 and 2.

10 Jean-Pierre Torrell, O.P., *Saint Thomas Aquinas*, vol. 1, *The Person and His Work*, rev. ed., trans. R. Royal (Washington, DC: Catholic University of America Press, 2005), 71.

authentic sermons established by L. J. Bataillon, 'Les sermons attribués B saint Thomas: questions d'authenticité,' MM [*Miscellanea mediaevalia*] 19 (1988): 325-41."[11] Why the inconsistency? Is the correct number nineteen, twenty, or twenty-three?

The answer is a bit complicated. It seems that there was one sermon, *Inveni David* (Sermon 16 in the Leonine edition volume) that was identified by Fr. Bataillon *after* he wrote his 1988 article in the *Miscellanea Mediaevalia*. This sermon does *not* show up on the list of sermons (nineteen in total) in the "Brief Catalogue" at the back of Fr. Torrell's biography. And yet there is another sermon, *Lux orta est* (Sermon 17) that *does* show up in the "Brief Catalogue" which is listed as "inauthentic" in the Leonine edition. Such are the difficulties of academic editing, and as this example shows, minor inconsistencies can creep into even scholarship of the first rank.[12]

In his most recent edition of *Initiation à Saint Thomas d'Aquin: Se Personne et Son Oeuvre* (Paris: Cerf, 2015), however—described on its title page as a "*Nouvelle edition profondément remaniée et enrichie d'une bibliographie mise à jour*" (an edition not as yet available in English translation)—Fr. Torrell has revised his account of sermons in accord with the most recent information available in the Leonine edition. Although he lists all twenty-three sermons from the Leonine in the "Catalogue" at the back of the volume, he says of these in the body of his text that, "seventeen of these were certainly or nearly certainly authentic; two, in their present state are inauthentic (Sermon 10, *Petite et accipietis,* and Sermon 17, *Lux orta est*), but they seem to depend on two authentic sermons; two are schemas of sermons reasonably authentic (Sermon 3, *Abiciamus,* and Sermon 4, *Osanna filio David*); one is the prothema of a sermon that may be authentic (Sermon 22, *Sapientia*), and one is a fragment of a sermon nearly certainly authentic (Sermon 23, *Surgere*)."[13] I've retained my description of the difficulties in the 2005 edition simply because it is the version accessible to the bulk of my readers, most of whom will likely not have access to the most recent (2015) French edition. It was only made available to me while I was in the last stages of editing this book. We should simply

---

[11] Ibid., 358. The "Catalogue of Works," however, as noted above, was compiled by Fr. Gilles Emery, O P , whose name appears on p. 330 and whose work on the "Catalogue" Fr. Torrell acknowledges on p. xxi.

[12] For the best account of the authenticity of the various sermons, see Leonine 44.1, esp. 15–22.

[13] See Jean-Pierre Torrell, *Initiation a Saint Thomas d'Aquin: Se Personne et Son Oeuvre* (Paris: Cerf, 2015), 107; 482–3. English translation mine. I am grateful to Fr. Torrell for informing me about the existence of this new, revised edition.

be grateful that *any* of Thomas's sermons have survived, given that, as Fr. Torrell points out, Thomas never undertook any sort of compilation of his sermons as did, for example, St. Bonaventure.[14]

There is, however, another small complication involved in the *numbering* of the sermons. I have, throughout this volume and in the appendix, followed the numbering scheme adopted by Fr. Hoogland largely because I thought this was the place most readers would go if they were going to look up most of the sermons. As it turns out, Fr. Hoogland, likely having an early copy of Fr. Bataillon's work, had simply followed the numbering scheme Fr. Bataillon had created.

This list contains two sermons, however—Sermon 10 (*Petite et accipietis*) and Sermon 17 (*Lux orta est*)—that are *not* considered to be authentic, even though they have at times in the past been attributed to Aquinas. Indeed, Professor Hoogland dutifully notes this fact in his book,[15] as does Fr. Bataillon in the *Tableau des Sermons Édités* on pages 20–21 of the Leonine volume.

Now that the Leonine edition of the sermons has appeared, the problem Fr. Hoogland faced has become clearer. Wishing to follow Fr. Bataillon's numbering system, Fr. Hoogland could not really leave out either Sermon 10 or Sermon 17 because Fr. Bataillon had, for some reason, included them. To leave either of them out would have meant re-numbering the remaining sermons, which would have made his book incongruent with the Leonine volume.

The upshot is this: Although the reader will find a list of twenty-one sermons in the appendix to this volume in the order in which they appear according to the numbering given them in both Fr. Hoogland's translation and the Leonine edition of the sermons, only nineteen of these are currently considered "certainly" or "very likely" authentic, and only sixteen are complete enough to be really helpful.[16]

---

[14] See Torrell, *Person and Work*, 71n70. The collection referred to there is Bougerol's *Sancti Bonaventurae Sermones dominicales*. English translation: *The Sunday Sermons of St. Bonaventure*, trans. T. Johnson (see n. 7 above).

[15] See Hoogland, *Academic Sermons*, 4n4.

[16] The Tableau des Sermons Édités on pp. 20–21 of Leonine 44.1 also lists two more sermons, Sermon 22 (*Sapiencia confortabit sapientem*) and Sermon 23 (*Sermonis fragmentum*, "Surgere"), the first of which is described as merely a "Prothème d'un sermon peut-être authentique," and the second as a "Fragment d'un sermon quasi certainement authentique." Since I am treating only sermons that are "certainly" or "very likely" authentic, I have omitted any discussion of these. In his French translation of the sermons, Fr. Torrell lists the following sixteen sermons as those for which "the manuscripts help ensure they have not been subjected to abbreviation or retouching" (*les manuscrits per-*

Since I intend this volume as merely prefatory to reading the sermons themselves, and since Hoogland's is currently the only complete collection of the sermons in English (although there are other English versions available in print and online),[17] I have maintained the practice throughout of always referring to the sermons both by the number Fr. Hoogland gives them (following Fr. Bataillon) and by the Latin title: for example, Sermon 11 (*Emitte Spiritum*) or Sermon 20 (*Beata gens*).

A word is in order about what I have been calling the "title" of each sermon, which is in fact not a separate *title* but simply the first several words of the Latin text. A quick glance at Sermon 1 in Hoogland's volume, for example, shows that the "title" of the sermon, *Veniet desideratus*, has been taken from the first two Latin words of the verse in Haggai 2:8, on which the sermon is based: "Veniet desideratus cunctis gentibus et implebit domum istam gloria" ("The desired things of all the nations will come, and I will fill this house with glory"). As many readers will know, this practice of using the first several words of a text as the title is merely a vestige of an old tradition among Latin paleographers of listing manuscripts according to the *incipit* ("it begins")—a tradition that persists to this day not only among Latin paleographers working amid their dusty old manuscripts but also among Catholics-at-large, who still refer to official Vatican documents by their first several words in Latin, such as *Gaudium et Spes*, *Evangelium Vitae*, or *Veritatis Splendor*.

DISTINGUISHING "SERMONS" AND "SERMON-CONFERENCES"

A final, necessary bit of background information is in order. Of the twenty authentic sermons listed in the appendix, eleven have an accompanying *collatio*. The Latin word *collatio* is often translated in English as "sermon-conference," but that's largely for lack of a better term. Literally, *collatio* simply means a "gathering," but it clearly came to have a more technical meaning. Similarly, for example, in our own day, the word "retreat"

---

mettent d'assurer qu'ils n'ont pas subi d'abréviations ou de retouches): 1, 2, 4, 5, 8, 9, 11, 12, 13, 14, 15, 16, 18, 19, 20, and 21. Those "too abbreviated to be meaningful" (*trop abrégées pour être significatives*) are: 3, 6, and 7. And finally, those "of more than doubtful authenticity" (*d'authenticité plus que douteuse*) are: 10 and 17. See Torrell, Sermons, 22. Although I have provided analytical outlines of nearly all of these in Appendix 1, the reader will note that I have for the most part drawn my examples to illustrate points about Thomas's style from the first group of sixteen sermons listed by Fr. Torrell.

17 For these, consult the wonderful website maintained by Thérèse Bonin, "Thomas Aquinas in English: A Bibliography" (http://www.home.duq.edu/~bonin/thomasbibliography.html#usermons).

has come to refer to something identifiably religious, such that the people who attend them know that, instead of involving an army moving in the opposite direction from the enemy, a religious "retreat" involves praying and, often, religious instruction of some sort. Indeed, the reader may have experienced the sort of religious "retreat" where a priest or minister combined bouts of prayer with bouts of religious instruction.

When a priest or minister in such a context outside of a Sunday liturgical service makes instructional comments meant to improve the spiritual and moral lives of the people sitting in front of him and help deepen their faith, what would we call that? If it had occurred on a Sunday in the context of liturgical service, we would certainly call it "preaching." When it occurs outside that context, in some instances, it might be called "a teaching" to distinguish it from "preaching"; others call it "instruction" or "an evening of reflection" if it happens later in the day. My point is simply that we do not have a specific, common name for this sort of event in English. "Sermon-conference" fits, but we do not customarily use it.

In St. Thomas's day, this sort of "sermon-conference" would have been called a *collatio*. And when Thomas was a Master of the Sacred Page at the University of Paris in the mid-thirteenth century, preachers who gave university sermons during the day were required by university statute to give a *collatio* at vespers later that same night. The expectation seems to have been that the preacher would expound further on the same topic he took up earlier in the day in his sermon. Modern editions of the Liturgy of the Hours often attempt something similar when they try to match the day's readings from the Gospel at Mass with appropriate readings on the same theme from one of the Fathers or Doctors of the Church. Not all of Thomas's sermons have this accompanying, evening *collatio*, but as we will see, for those that do, Thomas's mnemonic system of delivering his sermon allowed him to preach on a certain topic during the day and then pick up right where he left off later that night without missing a beat. In Hoogland's volume, the *collatio*, when there is one, is included with the sermon itself under the heading *Collatio in sero* or "Sermon-Conference at the Late Hour."

It is also worth noting that these *collationes in sero* done later in the day, generally at vespers, were not the only sort of *collationes* or "sermon-conferences" medieval preachers were called upon to give. So, for example, the list of twenty sermons in the appendix to this volume, it is important to note, does *not* include Thomas's well-known "sermon-conferences" (*collationes*) on the Ten Commandments, the Creed, the Our Father, or the Ave Maria. Indeed, these four are listed separately in Fr.

Emery's "Brief Catalogue of Works of Saint Thomas Aquinas" at the back of Fr. Torrell's biography and are usually published separately from Thomas's sermons.[18] There is, I would argue, good reason for this custom of distinguishing these "sermon-conferences" from the sort of *collationes* that were given later in the day in conjunction with a sermon earlier in the day. Thomas's "sermon-conferences" on the Ten Commandments, the Creed, the Ave Maria, and the Our Father do *not*, for example, follow the same mnemonic, thematic pattern that all of the rest of his acknowledged Sunday sermons do.[19] That is to say, in Thomas's *collationes* on the Ten Commandments, the Creed, the Ave Maria, and the Our Father, what provides the structure for the address is not, as it is in all his sermons, an individual biblical verse, but simply the order of the text upon which he is commenting. As such, they read more like the sort of cursory commentary Thomas would have given on basic biblical texts to novice brothers entering the order or to some other group similarly uninitiated in the basics of the faith.

It is likely, therefore, that we should not consider these *collationes* on the Ten Commandments, the Creed, the Ave Maria, and the Our Father to be in the same category of "preaching" as that which was customarily done in church at a Sunday Mass. As I mentioned above, literally-speaking, "*collatio*" simply means "a gathering" or "a collection," and it is clear from the evidence that these "gatherings" could be of several different sorts. From our modern perspective, using our modern English idiom, perhaps we could say that sometimes a *collatio* (a "sermon-conference") was less of a *sermon* and more of a *conference*, while others were very clearly *sermons*, depending upon the audience and context and, in large part, depending upon whether it accompanied a liturgical service earlier in the day or not.[20]

---

[18] They are not included, for example, in Leonine 44.1. For English translations, see *The Three Greatest Prayers*, trans. L. Shapcote (London: Burns, Oates, 1937; repr., Manchester, NY: Sophia Institute Press, 1997); *The Sermon-Conferences of St. Thomas Aquinas on the Apostles' Creed*, trans. N. Ayo, C.S.C. (Notre Dame, IN: University of Notre Dame Press, 1988); J. B. Collins, *Catechetical Instructions of St. Thomas Aquinas* (New York: J. F. Wagner, 1939; repr., New York: Scepter, 2002); and *The Commandments of God: Conferences on the Two Precepts of Charity and the Ten Commandments*, trans. L. Shapcote (London: Burns & Oates, 1937). Those interested in further study on Thomas's *collatio* on the Ten Commandments should also consult: *Thomas d'Aquin, Sermons sur les dix commandements (Collationes de decem preceptis)*, traduction française, introduction et commentaire de J. P. Torrell (Paris: Cerf, 2015).

[19] The same can be said of Bonaventure's "Sermon-Conferences on the Six Days of Creation" (*Collationes in Hexaemeron*): they do not follow the same pattern as any of the sermons in Johnson, *Sunday Sermons of St. Bonaventure*.

[20] Fr. Torrell notes of the sort of *collatio* that accompanied a sermon later in the day at vespers that, "In this context, there was no other difference between the sermon and

A Comment on the Importance of Considering the Intended Audience

A medieval theologian might have been called upon to deliver, depending upon the need and the circumstances, *collationes* to very different kinds of groups: sometimes they were highly educated, sometimes not. St. Bonaventure's very complex and theologically sophisticated *Collationes in Hexaemeron* ("Sermon-Conferences on the Six Days of Creation") would be an example of a series of *collationes* given to an educated group of students and faculty at the University of Paris in 1273.[21] Thomas Aquinas's *Collationes in Decem Praceptis* ("Sermon-Conferences on the Ten Commandments"), on the other hand, would be an example of a series of talks given to a somewhat less educated, less theologically sophisticated group, perhaps originally in his native Italian.[22] Both of these *collationes* are instructive and have value, but they take very different approaches theologically, and more to the point, each has a very different *style* and *tone*.

We as modern readers should keep in mind the intended audience for any such address, whether it is a sermon (a *sermo*) or a "sermon-conference" (a *collatio*). When we as modern readers *do not* keep in mind the nature of the audience to which the sermon or *collatio* was delivered, we can make the mistake of judging them too harshly: as either overly "scholastic," on the one hand, or a bit too "simple-minded," on the other. Keep in mind, however, when we judge a sermon as being too "scholastic," for example, that it may have been delivered to a group of university scholars and stu-

---

the *collatio* than the name and the moment" (*Dans ce context, il n'y a d'autre différence entre le sermo et la collatio que le nom et le moment. . . .*) See Torrell, *Sermons*, 18. And yet, in every collection and list, the Sunday sermons we are treating here are always listed separately from the *collationes* on the Apostles' Creed, the Ten Commandments, the Hail Mary, and the Our Father. See, for example, Torrell, *Initiation* (2015), 480–483.

21 See *Collationes in Hexaemeron et Bonaventuriana quaedam selecta ad fidem codicum mss*, ed. F. M. Delorme, O.F.M., Bibliotheca Franciscana scholastica Medii Aevi 8 (Florence: Collegium S. Bonaventurae, 1934). In this series of *collationes*, Bonaventure did not employ the *sermo modernus* style we will be discussing below. He did employ it, however, for example, in his *Collationes in Decem Praeceptis*, delivered several years earlier, in 1267; see *Collations on the Ten Commandments*, trans. Paul J. Spaeth, Works of Saint Bonaventure 6 (St. Bonaventure, NY: The Franciscan Institute, 1995).

22 Regarding this *collatio*, Fr. Emery says in his "Brief Catalogue" of St. Thomas's Works: "It is difficult to specify with certitude the date and place of composition of the homilies on the Ten Commandments. Given in Thomas's mother tongue in Italy (1261–1268, or 1273?), they were collected by Peter of Andria" (Torrell, *Person and Work*, 357). See also Torrell, "Les *Collationes in decem preceptis* de saint Thomas d'Aquin. Edition critique avec introduction et notes," *Revue des sciences philosophiques et théologiques* 69 (1985): 5–40 and 227–63.

dents who were used to *dialectical arguments* and who were looking for something more than pious platitudes in preaching. Often enough, one had to gain their respect intellectually before one could gain a hearing with them in a theological or religious setting.

So too, when a sermon or sermon-conference might seem to us a bit too "simple-minded"—say, for example, without the number of literary references to the Bible or to sophisticated theological arguments that we might have expected to be present, especially for someone as well-educated as Thomas Aquinas—we should recall that it was likely being preached to a congregation of the faithful in which many were illiterate and knew only the parts of the Bible that had been read to them each week during the year at the Sunday liturgical services.

What would be more instructive for our purposes than merely disparaging the style of address as having too much of this or too little of that, therefore, would be to compare the sort of beautiful simplicity of one of Thomas's "sermon-conferences" on, say, the Ten Commandments or the Our Father with the amazing intellectual and rhetorical sophistication of his Sermon 5 (*Ecce rex tuus*), with its meditations on the various meanings of "advent," which we will analyze in more detail in chapter 1. Thomas, it seems, could, as St. Paul said of himself, "become all things to all men" (1 Cor 9:22). Depending upon what the occasion warranted, Thomas could provide both "milk for children" and "solid food" for adults (see 1 Cor 3:2 and Heb 5:14).[23] The culture that he was addressing was, of course, very different from our own, so that the sort of "solid food" the adults had a taste for and seemed to demand of their preachers involved a sophisticated art of rhetorical construction that most modern audiences would likely find rather a bit much.[24]

---

[23] It is clear, however, that Thomas's more simple *collationes* on the Our Father, the Ave Maria, the Creed, and the Ten Commandments were more popular and more widely distributed than any of his sermons. Fr. Torrell points out, for example (see Torrell, *Sermons*, 19), that none of the four *collationes* on the major prayers comes down to us in *fewer than* 80 sources, with those on the Creed numbering upwards of 150, whereas none of the university sermons exists in *more than* four manuscripts, with many of them found in no more than one. Things might have turned out differently, however, as Fr. Torrell points out, if Thomas had assembled a collection of his sermons, as did Bonaventure, his colleague at Paris. On these, see Johnson, *Sunday Sermons of St. Bonaventure* (full citation in n. 7 above). Sadly, neither Thomas nor any of his contemporaries thought to leave us such a collection.

[24] In an analogous fashion, I find the elaborate sort of churches that characterized the nineteenth-century French Baroque period—the church of Sacré-Cœur in Paris would be an obvious example—just a bit too much for my tastes. But then, I know a lot of peo-

The ultimate question, therefore, to my mind, is not one of *style*, but of *substance*: Was Christ preached and made present to the people in the sermons of Aquinas? The burden of my discussion in the pages that follow will be to show that Christ was indeed present in Thomas's preaching, and this to a very high degree. I will also argue that Thomas's was a very "biblical" sort of preaching, although it was "biblical" in a way that will seem very foreign to most of us. Let me suggest that reading a medieval sermon for the first time is a bit like reading the poetry of someone like Gerard Manley Hopkins or looking at one of the Cubist paintings of Picasso or Braque for the first time: you may have a sense that something important is going on, but the presentation is so very different from what you are accustomed to that it is sometimes hard to understand not only what the artist is trying to communicate, but also why anyone ever really liked it. It is for this reason that scholars often write introductions. Hopkins's *style* can take some getting used to. It is not always altogether clear on a first reading what the poet is trying to accomplish. So it is too, I would suggest, with Thomas's sermons: the style may be strange and can take some getting used to. But once that hurdle has been crossed, the results for the persevering reader can be not only instruction, but real delight.

An Outline of Things to Come

We begin in chapter 1 with an in-depth examination of a single sermon, one that generally goes by the title *Ecce Rex Tuus*, the first three Latin words of the biblical verse from Matthew 21:5 on which the sermon is based: *Ecce rex tuus venit tibi mansuetus* ("Behold your king comes to you, meek" [and riding on a donkey]). An in-depth analysis of this one sermon will allow the reader to get a fairly quick sense of how a sermon of this sort works—not by going into all the details (which I will do in later chapters), but simply by guiding the reader through an illustrative example of the style.

After a fairly quick overview analysis of this one sermon in chapter 1, I provide a discussion of the basic elements of the medieval *sermo modernus* style in chapters 2, 3, and 4 (for those who are interested in examining the nuts-and-bolts of how the method works). In chapter 2, I offer a general introduction to the "modern sermon" of Thomas's day, especially its most characteristic element, which was the biblical *thema* verse that

---

ple who love them, and clearly, plenty of people at the time thought they were superb, since plenty of French cities, towns, and villages have churches in this same style.

served as a mnemonic structuring device around which the entire sermon was developed.

After stating the *thema* verse for the day, the medieval preacher would "divide" it into several constituent parts that would set the pattern or outline of the sermon he intended to deliver. We will discuss this process of *divisio* and the related art of crafting a "declaration of the parts" in chapter 3.

And finally, after choosing a suitable *thema* verse and making an appropriate *divisio* of it, the medieval preacher had to develop each of these points in the body of the sermon—a process that was known as *dilatatio*—literally, "dilation" or "unfolding." The various methods of *dilatatio* will be the subject of chapter 4. My discussion in these latter two chapters has benefited from illustrations and examples drawn from two popular medieval preaching manuals: the *Forma Praedicandi* by Robert of Basevorn and the *Ars concionandi*, a text that is sometimes published among the works of St. Bonaventure but is almost certainly not by him.

What will become clear as we proceed is the degree to which medieval preachers such as Aquinas took the classical rhetorical tradition handed on to them by writers such as Cicero and Quintillian and not only applied many of those basic principles to the specific needs of preaching to a Christian congregation but also transformed that classical tradition of rhetoric decisively in the thirteenth century by creating a new rhetoric of *preaching* centered on and developed around the texts of the Christian Scriptures.[25]

Having analyzed in detail the nuts and bolts of the process by which medieval sermons were crafted in chapters 2, 3, and 4, we will take a reflective step back in chapter 5 to evaluate some of the strengths and weak-

---

[25] It is worth noting that, since my concern here is largely with the more *formal* characteristics of the *sermo modernus* style, I will *not*, as a general rule, delve into the more *personal* characteristics of Thomas's preaching. As Fr. Torrell points out (Torrell, *Sermons*, 23), Thomas often addresses his listeners directly and engages them personally by, for example, making frequent use of the first person plural: "Let us see"; "We can consider"; "If we consider"; "If we compare." He uses a similar device to recommend virtue and holiness: "[Christ's life] is an example for us"; "Now we must see how [the bad angels] have made ambushes for us"; "Hence we must not be ungrateful for such a great love"; "We must go up to the house of the Lord"; "We must also walk in the way of the Lord." He will also use the second person singular or plural to address his listeners directly: "You should consider that. . ."; "See how great the feast"; "You are wrong if you think that"; "You ought to imitate Jesus Christ so that you may be like him." These are fascinating and important characeristics that would deepen our appreciation of Thomas's sermon style, but I will not have the occasion to examine them in depth in this book. An excellent description can be found in Torrell, *Sermons*, 22–30.

nesses of the *sermo modernus* style of preaching. I have taken as my sparring partner in this chapter the Reverend Charles Smyth, a scholar who had some very interesting and thoughtful things to say about the medieval *sermo modernus* style sermon in his book *The Art of Preaching: A Practical Survey of Preaching in the Church of England, 747–1939*. Although Smyth had some thoughtful, *positive* things to say about the medieval sermon, he also posed what I take to be a series of very serious and important critiques, chief among which was the question of whether the medieval sermon made *inappropriate* use of the Scriptures. Did such sermons, in fact, do a certain kind of *violence* to the Bible? I will argue in reply that, ultimately, medieval preaching—at least as exemplified by its best practitioners, such as Bonaventure and Aquinas—made good use of the Bible. But I take it that the objection to the medieval practice is a serious one, and it will take some space to defend and explain what the medieval preachers understood themselves to be doing.

At the end of the book, in chapter 6, entitled "Summary and Conclusions," I offer some comments about Thomas as a biblical theologian, about what being a "biblical theologian" in the High Middle Ages looked and sounded like, and about the importance of the Bible to medieval rhetoric more generally.

A final note to the reader: Following along with St. Thomas is undoubtedly the best way to learn what this book hopes to teach. Indeed, the author has no greater hope than that the reader will get his or her hands on a copy of Fr. Hoogland's translation of the sermons (see n. 5 above for the reference) and have them at his or her side as he or she reads this book. This book is above all meant to inspire the reader to go back to the texts of Aquinas with greater understanding and increased appreciation for the art, the craft, and the genius of the Common Doctor of the Church.

CHAPTER 1

Ecce Rex Tuus:
Introducing Thomas's Sermon Style

EVEN DEVOTED FANS OF AQUINAS may find the sermons something of an odd read upon first examination. So, for example, when the eager reader opens up Mark-Robin Hoogland's translation of Thomas's sermons and turns, naturally enough, to "Sermon 1," for example, he or she will find that the title of the sermon, *Veniet desideratus*, has been taken from the first two Latin words of the verse in Haggai 2:8, on which the sermon is based: *Veniet desideratus cunctis gentibus et implebit domum istam gloria* ("The desired things of all the nations will come, and I will fill this house with glory"). When this same eager reader turns to the text of Thomas's sermon, however, he or she may be disappointed to find that Thomas is not really going to "preach" on that text in the sense of "explicate it" in any of the usual senses in which we understand that term—as, for example, someone acquainted with the wonderful sermons of John Henry Newman might be led to expect.

In Newman's sermons, one always finds a short biblical passage prefacing the sermon suggesting the theme of what Newman intends to say. So, for example, at the top of Sermon 8 of his *Oxford University Sermons*, on "Human Responsibility, as Independent of Circumstances," one finds this verse from Genesis 3:13—"The serpent beguiled me, and I did eat." In the first paragraph of the sermon that follows, Newman begins thus:

> The original temptation set before our first parents, was that of proving their freedom, by using it without regard to the will of

1

Him who gave it. The original excuse offered by them after sinning was, that they were not really free, that they had acted under a constraining influence, the subtility of the tempter. They committed sin that they might be independent of their Maker; they defended it on the ground that they were dependent upon Him. And this has been the course of lawless pride and lust ever since; to lead us, first, to exult in our uncontrollable liberty of will and conduct; then, when we have ruined ourselves, to plead that we are the slaves of necessity.[1]

And with this, Newman is off and running, and what follows is a masterful exhortation, in Newman's own incomparable style, that we should take personal responsibility for our sins.

St. Thomas, as we will see, does not utilize his biblical epigraphs in the same way at all—although to be frank, Newman's sermon is no more an "exegesis" of Genesis 3:13 than Thomas's use of biblical epigraphs in his sermons. Newman uses the biblical text to suggest a theme; Thomas uses the biblical text as a mnemonic structuring device. Both methods were powerful in their own right for the audiences to whom they were preached, each of which had its own peculiar sort of education and sets of expectations when listening to a public speaker. Newman's audience at Oxford was highly educated, especially in the humanistic letters, and accustomed to hearing public lectures given in a sort of Ciceronian oration style. Many of them had actually read Cicero in Latin at Oxford. Thomas's audience was not as attuned to the sort of grand rhetorical style Newman specialized in, but they did have, it seems, more advanced training in the arts of memory, about which we will have more to say below.

ON THE ODDITY OF THOMAS'S SERMON STYLE: IS HE GUILTY OF READING MEANINGS *INTO* THE TEXT?

Although, in his biblical commentaries, Thomas is noteworthy for his devotion to the literal sense of the text, yet in his sermons, he will often seem to garner all sorts of different interpretations, some of them rather odd, from just one or two words in the biblical text.

So, for example, in Sermon 5 (*Ecce rex tuus*)—a text we will be analyzing in more detail below—it would appear from the opening biblical verse

---

[1] John Henry Newman, "Sermon 8," in *Fifteen Sermons Preached Before the University of Oxford Between 1826 and 1843*, 3rd rev. ed. (repr., Notre Dame, IN: University of Notre Dame Press, 1997).

that Thomas intends to preach on the first words of the passage from Matthew 21:5 that reads: "Ecce rex tuus venit tibi mansuetus" ("Behold, your king comes to you, meek . . ."). The sermon itself was delivered, we know, on the first Sunday of Advent, probably in the year 1271, and so in accord with the season, we find Thomas distinguishing in the body of the sermon the four ways in which we can speak of the coming (the advent) of Christ: the first is the way in which he comes in the flesh in the Incarnation; the second is the way in which he enters the mind of believers; the third is the way in which he comes to the just after death; and the fourth is the way in which he comes to judge all things at the end of time—a fourfold distinction that seems perfectly appropriate in a sermon for the first Sunday of Advent, but which may stretch the reader's credulity upon discovering that Thomas found all four of these senses of Christ's "coming" in the single Latin word *Ecce* ("behold").

One might have thought that Thomas would have made this comment about the four different ways in which Christ "comes" while he was commenting upon the word *venit* ("he comes"), but no, he has other plans for that word. Rather, Thomas reads *venit* together with the next word in the sentence, *tibi* ("he comes for you"), and tells us that these words speak about "the benefits of his [Christ's] coming" (that is to say, the benefits of his coming *for you*), which Thomas lists as: first, to make the divine majesty known; second, to reconcile us to God; third, to free us from sin; and fourth, to give us eternal life.

As before with his comments on *Ecce*, so too here with *venit tibi*, the theological content is certainly appropriate, indeed fairly standard; what strains credulity is the notion that all of this content is somehow *contained within* or *communicated by* the two small, simple Latin words *venit tibi* ("he comes for you").

And even if we could defend finding all four of the senses in which Christ "comes" in the single word *Ecce* or all four of the benefits of his coming in the two words *venit tibi* ("he comes for you"), Thomas will certainly stretch our credulity beyond the breaking point when we find him, in Sermon 16 (*Inveni David*), after beginning with the passage from Psalm 88:21 that reads "I have found David my servant; with my holy oil I have anointed him; my hand will assist him and my arm will make him firm," making the following claim:

> From these words we can learn four praiseworthy things of the holy bishop St. Nicholas: (1) first, his wondrous election; (2) second, his unique consecration; (3) third, the effective execution

of his task; and (4) fourth, his immovable and firm stability. His wondrous election is shown in the words: *I have found David, my servant.* His special consecration is shown where it says: *I have anointed him with my sacred oil.* The effective execution of his task is shown in the words: *My hand will help him.* And his stable firmness is shown where it says: *and my arm will make him firm.*

What Thomas appears to be suggesting here, in other words, is that the Psalmist, whoever he was—a writer who lived roughly a thousand years before the birth of Christ—was referring in this Psalm neither to David (even though the Psalm *says* literally "I have found David, my servant"), nor even to Christ (by means of an allegorical understanding of "David"), but rather to the fourth-century AD St. Nicholas of Myra, a man who lived some 1400 years after the Psalmist's death. At this point, even the most devoted fan of Aquinas may worry that he may be guilty of "eisegesis" rather than "exegesis"—that is, of transporting meanings *into* the text rather than digging meaning *out of* it. Modern biblical exegetes, one hardly need add, would *certainly* be inclined to draw that conclusion.

Let me suggest, however, that such a judgment would be not only hasty, but the result of what philosophers sometimes call a "category mistake"—that is to say, it is the result of an unfortunate misunderstanding of the purposes served by the biblical epigraphs that preface Thomas's sermons. What a diligent reading of Thomas's sermons will show, in fact, is that the biblical verses that appear at the beginning of the sermons are not the texts to be *explicated* in the sermon. Rather, they are *structuring aids* that serve as mnemonic devices, a memory aid, allowing the listeners to remember more easily the material preached in the sermon.

READING THE OPENING BIBLICAL VERSE OF THE SERMON AS A VERBAL MNEMONIC

Let me repeat: The opening biblical verse that prefaces every one of Thomas's sermons is not to be taken as the text he is *preaching on* (in the sense of doing some sort of explication of the text). It is, rather, a structured verbal mnemonic device systematically keyed to the material in the sermon. Allow me to illustrate with an example.

If we turn once again to the sermon *Ecce rex tuus* (listed in Hoogland's translation as "Sermon 5"), we find, as noted earlier, that the sermon is prefaced with the Latin verse "Ecce rex tuus venit tibi mansuetus" ("Behold, your king comes to you, meek" [and riding on a donkey]),[2] a passage from the prophet Zechariah quoted in Matthew's Gospel during Jesus's entry into Jerusalem on Palm Sunday (see Matt 21:6 and Zech 9:9). The casual reader might be tempted to think that: here we have a verse dealing with Jesus's coming into Jerusalem; the sermon is supposed to address Jesus's coming at Advent; so clearly (we assume), the sermon will take its theme from, and perhaps be a commentary on, this biblical verse. Just as Jesus came triumphantly into Jerusalem (we expect Thomas to say), so also will he come triumphantly at the end of time. Indeed, those with some acquaintance with patristic or early medieval biblical commentaries might even be anticipating allegories on, for example, the palm branches, the donkey, the city of Jerusalem as a figure of the heavenly Jerusalem, and the like. But this is not what Thomas does at all.

Rather, after a brief introduction (in Latin, a *prothema*), Thomas repeats the opening epigraph, "Behold your king comes to you, meek," and then tells his listeners that "In these words, the coming of Christ is clearly foretold to us," and we his readers imagine that he is referring to Zechariah's words in the Old Testament "foretelling" the coming of Christ into Jerusalem. But contrary to our expectations, rather than talking about Christ's coming into Jerusalem on Palm Sunday, Thomas does something unexpected. He tells us that there are four different "advents" of Christ: the one in which he came in the flesh in the Incarnation; the one by which he comes into our minds; the one in which he comes at the death of the just; and the one in which he will come at the end of time in the final judgment—none of which, it should be noted, involves the coming of Christ into Jerusalem on Palm Sunday, the obvious literal referent of the text in question. So where does Thomas "find" these four advents of Christ in this simple text about the coming of Christ into Jerusalem? The answer is that he begins by distinguishing four different senses of the word "behold" and then associates with each of them a different "advent" of Christ.

Notice how ingeniously this mnemonic device works. We use the word "behold," says Thomas, in a number of different situations. First, for example, we might be asserting something of which we are certain, as when it says in the Gospel of Luke: "*Behold*, I bring you tidings of great joy, which shall be to all people, for unto you is born this day in the city

---

2   For more on this particular sermon, see Jean Leclerq, "Un sermon inédit de Saint Thomas sur la royauté du Christ," *Revue Thomiste* 46 (1946): 152–66. The Latin text appears as *Ecce rex tuus*, in Thomas Aquinas, *Opera Omnia*, ed. Robert Busa, S.J. (Stuttgart-Bad Cannstatt: Frommann-Holzboog, 1980), 6:45–46.

of David a Savior, which is Christ the Lord" (Luke 2:10–11). "Just as people doubt in some manner concerning the second coming of Christ," says Thomas, "so also some doubted his first coming." But in Habakkuk (2:3), we read that the Lord "will appear at the end, and He shall not lie; if He delays, expect Him because the One coming will come, and He will not delay." And in the Psalms, it assures us: "Surely the Lord will come" (Ps 96:13). Thus, for those who fear that the soul will not survive death, the prophet Zechariah says to assure them of Christ's coming: "*Behold,* your king comes to you."

Next, when we use the word "behold," we might be indicating a determination of time, as when Jesus says: "Behold, my hour is come." So, although Christ's coming at the final judgment is not known to us, says Thomas, because God wished for us always to be vigilant in good works, "yet his coming in the flesh was at a determined time, and thus it [the epigraph from Zechariah] says *behold.*"

In the third place, when we say "behold," we can be indicating the manifestation of a thing, as for example, when John the Baptist points at Jesus and says: "Behold the Lamb of God" (John 1:29). So too, then, although the coming of Christ into the mind is hidden, says Thomas, yet his coming in the flesh was manifest and visible.

And finally, when we use the word "behold," we can be using it for the strengthening of men, and this in two circumstances: first, when they have won victory over their enemies, as when 1 Samuel 24:4 says, "*Behold,* the day has come which I desire: . . . my enemies appear before me"; and second, when they have attained the good, as when it says in Psalm 34:8, "*Behold,* how good the Lord is." Now, since we have obtained both of these things in the coming of Christ—namely, we have peace and victory over the enemy, and we have joy from the hope obtained of future goods—so the prophet says "*Behold.*"

In this way, Thomas systematically associates the four different ways in which Christ "comes" with the four different uses of the word "behold":

1. We say "behold" when there is something of which we are certain ("Behold, it is true"); so too we are certain that Christ will come to us after death.

2. We say "behold" to indicate a determinate time ("Behold, the time has come"); so too the Incarnation happens at a determinate time.

3. We say "behold" when we point out something we wish people to see ("Behold the Lamb of God"); so too, although the

coming of Christ into the mind is hidden, yet his coming in the flesh was visible.

4. And finally, we say "behold" when we have won victory over our enemies ("Behold, the day has come") and when we obtain something good ("Behold how good the Lord is"); so too, with the coming of Christ, we have victory over the enemy and hope for future good.

There is no doubt in each case as to what drives the process: not the particular senses of "behold," but rather the points Thomas wants to make about the four different "advents" of Christ. The word "behold" is used as a mnemonic device to help lend structure to his analysis. Such will also be the case with each word that follows in the opening biblical verse.

Hence, after discussing the different "advents" of Christ in association with the first word in the epigraph, "behold," Thomas turns next to the words in the sentence that immediately follow, in this case *rex tuus* ("your king"), about which he says that they "show the condition of Christ's coming." Now a person's coming is awaited with solemnity for two reasons, says Thomas: either because of his greatness, if for example he is a *king*; or because of a special love we have for the person, if for example he is an intimate friend of ours, which is suggested by the next word in the verse, *tuus* ("your"). And since Christ was coming as both king *and* friend, thus we find the combination "*your king*."

Thomas's practice should be fairly clear by now. He will continue running through each word in the opening biblical verse in order, associating it or different uses of it with the various themes he intends to treat in his sermon. Since Thomas's Latin text has *rex tuus*, whereas in English, we reverse the order and say "your king," Thomas focuses next on the things that follow from Christ being a "king" (*rex*) and then subsequently takes up the things that follow from Christ being our "friend" (which follows from the word *tuus*, "your").

What follows from Christ being a "king"? First, a king suggests unity; second, a king has fullness of power; third, a king has an abundant jurisdiction; and fourth, a king brings equity of justice. As is his custom, Thomas takes up each of these in turn.

With regard to the first, there must be *unity* for there to be kingship; otherwise, if there were many, dominion would not pertain to any one of them. "Thus we must reject Arius," says Thomas, "who was positing many gods, saying that the Son was other than the Father."

Second, Christ is king in that he has fullness of power. Thus laws are not imposed *on* him. Rather, he has authority *over* the law, which is why he can say in the Sermon on the Mount (Matt 6), "You have heard it said of old . . . but I say to you," as if to say, "I am the true king who can establish the law for you."

Third, Christ has an abundance to his jurisdiction because, whereas other kings have dominion over *this* town or *those* cities, all creatures have been made subject to Christ.

Fourth, Christ brings equity of justice. Whereas tyrants submit all things under their authority for the sake of their own utility, Christ selflessly orders all things to their common good. Notice, finally, that all four of these theological points are associated with the single word "king."

And with this, the sermon ends—or at least seems to. But if we have been paying attention, we know that Thomas has not yet finished "explicating" (if that is what we can call it) his opening verse: "Ecce rex tuus venit tibi mansuetus" ("Behold, your king comes to you, meek"). He has only finished "explicating," according to his original plan, the words *Ecce* and *rex*, whereas he still needs to "unpack" the words *tuus, venit tibi,* and *mansuetus.* And indeed, since this is a university sermon and preachers giving university sermons at the University of Paris in the thirteenth century were required by statute to give a *collatio* at vespers later that same night, if we look at the *collatio* that accompanies this sermon, we will find that Thomas begins that *collatio* with the same biblical epigraph from Zechariah with which he began his sermon earlier that morning ("Ecce rex tuus venit tibi mansuetus"). After giving a brief summary of the points he made earlier in that morning's sermon in association with the words *Ecce* and *rex,* Thomas picks up right where he left off without missing a beat with *tuus, "your* king." Notice that Thomas is able to pick up "right where he left off without missing a beat" precisely because his mnemonic device allows him to locate his exact position in the original biblical epigraph and then proceed on with his *collatio* according to his original plan, starting with the next word in the sentence: *tuus* ("your").

Christ is called "your king," says Thomas—namely, the king *of mankind*—for four reasons: first, because of the similitude of image (man is made "in the image of God"); second, because of God's special love for man beyond all other creatures; third, because of God's special solicitude toward man and his unique care for him; and fourth, because of Christ's conformity with our human nature. With regard to the first, says Thomas, although every creature bears the image of God, man is more perfectly and especially created in his image, not according to a corporeal likeness, but according to an intellectual likeness, in respect of the natural light impressed by God on the human mind. Thus, with regard to the second, although Christ loves all things that exist, nevertheless, he specially loves men and has exalted man to the level of and equality with the angels. So too, proceeding on to the third point, though God has care of all things, men are specially subject to divine providence because they are ordered to life eternal. And fourth, Christ is called "your king" because God, not wishing to give mankind a king who was of another kind—that is, of another nature—who would not be our brother, fully took on our human nature.

Christ "comes for you" (*venit tibi*)—that is, he comes voluntarily, not under compulsion, not for his utility, but for our need, for four reasons: first, to manifest to us his divine majesty; second, to reconcile us to God, from whom we were estranged as enemies through sin; third, to liberate us from servitude to sin; and fourth, to give us grace in the present and glory in the future.

And finally, Christ is said to come "meekly" (*mansuetus*), and this meekness is shown in four ways: first, in his conversation; second, in his gentle correction; third, in his gracious acceptance of men (not only the just, but also sinners); and fourth, in the way he accepted his Passion on the Cross (to which he was led "as a lamb").

Note that Thomas has no need here of the final part of the verse in Matthew 21:6—after "ecce rex tuus venit tibi mansuetus," the verse goes on to add, "et sedens super asinam et pullum filium subiugalis" ("and riding on a donkey and on a colt, the foal of one accustomed to the yoke"). He does not need these words to structure any more of the material in his sermon, so he leaves them out. Leaving it out would be a problem if he were *commenting* on the verse, but since the purpose the verse serves is simply as a structuring device, and since he has made the points he set out to make, he stops. And indeed, it is noteworthy that Thomas used this particular passage from Matthew 21:6 and not the parallel passage that appears in John 12:5, which reads: "ecce rex tuus venit sedens super pullum asinae." If Thomas had cited the passage from John's Gospel, he would not have been able to make the points he does in the sermon he actually gives related to the words *tibi* and *mansuetus*: the four ways in which he comes "for us" (to manifest to us his divine majesty; to reconcile us to God, from whom we were estranged through sin; to liberate us from servitude to sin; and to give us grace in the present and glory in the future) and the four ways in which he is said to be "meek" (in his conversation; in his gentle correction; in his gracious acceptance even of sinners; and in his acceptance of death on the Cross). The selection of *that particular biblical verse* was crucial to allow Thomas to make all the points he had set out to make.

Now granted, if we mistakenly thought that Thomas was attempting an exegesis of the biblical verse "Behold, your king comes for you, meek and riding on a donkey," then we would rightly be a bit skeptical that he could have found all that theological content in just this one sentence. We might even be tempted to accuse Thomas of reading the meanings *into* the biblical text that he wants to find there, rather than—as he should— deriving literal meaning *from* the text. But when we come to understand that the opening biblical verse is really an ingenious verbal mnemonic, our perspective changes. Thomas has managed to pack a lot of content into a relatively small space by mapping the points he wants to make onto just a few key words.

It is worthwhile noting as well that, in choosing the particular method of preaching he has, Thomas has managed not to confuse his various roles as a Master of the Sacred Page: he has not mistaken *praedicare* ("preaching") with *legere* ("reading"), nor has he mistaken either of these with *disputare* ("disputation").[3] When engaged in *legere*, the *magister* attempts to teach by giving the students a good first "reading" of the biblical text. When engaged in *praedicare*, on the other hand, the *magister* seeks to teach by imparting knowledge to the congregation in a manner suited to their abilities to recollect it when the need arises. What they retain in their *memory* for immediate recall is merely a passage from Scripture, which, if they are monks or friars, they should be committing to memory anyway. When they call to mind the particular biblical text with which Thomas opens his sermon, then they can more easily *recollect* the entire content of what was preached in proper order. The "order" in this case, however, is not the rational, demonstrative order of a *disputatio*, a disputed question. It is, rather, an order of the mind, particularly of *memory*, directed toward the listener's retention of the material being taught. Indeed, as recent studies have shown, the medievals knew quite a lot about the arts of memory, valued them highly, and spent a great deal of time perfecting them.

---

[3] The three duties of a *magister in sacra pagina* were "preaching" (*praedicare*), "disputation" (*disputare*), and "reading" (*legere*). "Reading" involved reading and commenting upon the Scriptures in class. "Disputation" is what the master did regularly during the periods called *Quaestiones Disputatae* or *Quaestiones Quodlibetales*. And "preaching" is what he did regularly at Mass or Vespers. For more on these three duties in relation to Aquinas's career, see Jean-Pierre Torrell, O.P., *Saint Thomas Aquinas*, vol. 1, *The Person and His Work*, rev. ed., trans. R. Royal (Washington, DC: Catholic University of America Press, 2005), esp. 54–74.

Think about how much we can recollect just by remembering one sentence. "Behold" reminds us of the four manifestations of Christ's coming: in the flesh; into the mind of each person; to the just at the time of their death; and as judge at the end of time. "Your king" reminds us of the condition of his coming: his unity with God the Father; that he has fullness of power; that he has dominion over all; and that he brings equity of justice. The word "your" additionally reminds us of the similitude of image between him and man, his special love for man, his solicitude and singular care for man, and his conformity with our human nature. The words "for you" remind us of the utility of his coming: to manifest to us his divine majesty; to reconcile us to God, from whom we were estranged as enemies through sin; to liberate us from servitude to sin; and to give us grace in the present and glory in the future. And the word "meek" reminds us of the manner of his coming: He showed "meekness" in his conversation, in his gentle correction of others, in his gracious acceptance of men (not only the just, but also sinners), and in his Passion, to which he was led meekly as a lamb. Each word in the sentence is a verbal cue meant to help bring to mind the content Thomas wishes to teach. To recollect the content, one need only bring to mind the one sentence, and the rest will spill out naturally.

On Memory and Recollection

Being able to bring instantly to mind one sentence is a function of "memory"; having the rest "spill out naturally," as I described it loosely above, is a function of what Thomas, following Aristotle, would have called "reminiscence" (*reminiscentia*), or what in English we often call "recollection." An excellent text to help us clarify this distinction between "memory" and the process of "recollection" is Aquinas's commentary on Aristotle's *De memoria et reminiscentia*,[4] in which Thomas distinguishes "remembering," which he describes as "merely keeping in good condition the things that have once been received," from "recollecting," which is "a sort of re-discovery of things that were previously accepted but [are] no longer preserved."[5] "Recollecting," however, is very different from merely "re-learning." Thomas describes the difference between the two thus:

---

[4] For the English text, see Thomas Aquinas, *Commentaries on Aristotle's "On Sense and What Is Sensed" and "On Memory and Recollection,"* trans. Kevin White and Edward Macierowski (Washington, DC: Catholic University of America Press, 2005).

[5] Aquinas, *On Memory and Recollection*, ch. 1 (l. 449b4), in White and Macierowski, *Commentary*, 185.

He who is *recollecting* has the power somehow to be moved to something that is consequent upon a starting-point that has somehow been retained in the memory (for instance, when someone remembers that such and such a thing was said to him but has forgotten who has told him). One therefore uses what he has in the memory to recollect what he has forgotten. But when ones does not arrive at the recovery of a lost notion through a starting-point that has been retained in the memory but through something else that is newly handed on to him by a teacher, that is *not* memory or recollection but *new learning.*[6]

Recollections of this sort can happen naturally, as for example when one hears a tune or smells an aroma that brings back a whole flood of recollections from one's youth. So, too, the sort of mental connections that bring about recollection can be created artificially by means of an association of ideas or images, one to another.

The key to the whole process, though, is having the right sort of starting point from which one can "recall" things not currently available to one's immediate memory. "Just as he who searches through demonstration proceeds from something prior, which is known, from which he is made to come to something posterior, which was unknown," says Thomas, "so too the one who recollects proceeds from something prior, which he remembers, to rediscover what had fallen from his memory."[7] Thus, "recollections come about in the quickest and best manner when one begins meditating from the starting point (*a principio*) of the whole business."[8] It is important, moreover (as we shall see), that whatever one is using as a "starting point" (the *principium*) be "well-ordered." The reason for this, says Thomas, is that "it is according to the order in which the *things* follow each other that their motions are engendered in the soul with this order."[9]

Accordingly, Thomas is able to provide four pieces of advice from the *De memoria* for those who want to want to remember or recollect a large amount of information: the first is "to strive to reduce what one wants to retain into some order"; the second is "to set one's mind upon them deeply and intently" (and by "set one's mind upon *them*" here, I take it that

---

[6] Ibid., ch. 6 (l. 452a4), pp. 217–18.
[7] Ibid., ch. 5 (l. 451b16), p. 212.
[8] Ibid., ch. 5 (l. 451b31), p. 214.
[9] Ibid.

Thomas is referring to the shorter, ordered list to which the original group of items has been "reduced"); the third is to meditate frequently on the list "in order" (*secundum ordinem*); and the fourth is that one should "begin to recollect from the starting point" (*incipiat reminisci a principio*).[10]

This advice from Thomas's commentary on Aristotle's *De memoria et reminiscentia* helps to illuminate his practice in the sermons. Thomas wants his listeners to be able to call to mind what he is teaching them, but he knows that there is likely too much information, too many individual points, for most of the people in his audience to hold it all in their immediate *memory*. So he provides for them a *starting point*—a mnemonic cue—which is both well ordered (such as the order of words in a sentence) and likely to be meditated upon frequently (such as taking a sentence from the Holy Scriptures). As long as the listeners can call to mind the starting point—such as the single sentence from Zechariah with which Thomas prefaces Sermon 5 (*Ecce rex tuus*)—then, with a little training, they will be able to recall all the rest of what was contained in the sermon.

In this regard, we might fruitfully compare what Thomas has to say in his commentary on Aristotle's *De memoria et reminiscentia* with what he says elsewhere, in *Summa Theologiae* (hereafter, *ST*) II-II, q. 49, a. 1, ad 2, where he suggests that "there are four means whereby a man advances in remembering well."[11] The first of these is that "he should get hold of some fitting but somewhat unusual likenesses (*similitudines*), since we marvel more at the unusual and thus the mind is more intensely preoccupied with them." Second, "a man must set out in an orderly fashion in his consideration the things he wants to remember, so that he may easily advance from one object of memory [*ex uno memorato*] to another." Third, "a man must care about and attach his affections to [*sollicitudinem apponat et affectum adhibeat*] the things he wants to remember, since the more something has been impressed on the spirit, the less it slips away. Hence, as Cicero says in his *Rhetoric* (*ad Her.* 3.4): 'care [*sollicitudo*] keeps the shapes of the images whole' [*conservat integras simulacrorum figuras*]." And finally, "one must meditate frequently on the things we want to remember . . . this is why we quickly recollect things that we often think about, as though advancing in a natural order from one item to another."

---

10 Ibid., ch. 5 (l. 451b31), p. 215.

11 Unless otherwise noted, all English translations from *ST* are from Thomas Aquinas, *Summa Theologiae*, trans. The Fathers of the English Dominican Province, 2nd rev. ed., 22 vols. (London: Burns, Oates & Washbourne, 1912–1936); reprinted in 5 vols. (Westminster, MD: Christian Classics, 1981). E-text with facing Latin and English is available at http://dhspriory.org/thomas/summa/index.html.

Since we have already discussed how the order of the words in the opening biblical verse helps both the preacher and his listeners "set out in an orderly fashion" the things to be remembered, "so that he may easily advance from one object of memory to another"—remember the words in the sentence, and the whole sermon can be recollected in its proper order—let me turn our attention now to another of Thomas's recommendations from above (specifically, the third): one must "care about and attach his affections to the things he wants to remember." Consider that, by associating the content of his sermon with a single, memorable passage from the Sacred Scriptures, a book guaranteed to call forth from his listeners the deepest affection and the most profound respect, Thomas is following Aristotle's advice about mentally associating the things to be remembered with things people care about and have affection for. It helps us to remember a series of things—sometimes even a very long series—if they can be associated with something we care about, such as the rooms of our house or the buildings in our neighborhood or the various sites in nature we pass on a pleasant walk. Such was the way classical orators such as Cicero committed his long orations completely to memory: by taking a pleasant walk he knew well and associating each of his points with a different site along the way. In this way, he was able to memorize and then deliver these long orations dramatically in front of a court or the Senate with nary an outline or notes.[12]

And finally we consider another of the recommendations about fostering recollection that Thomas drew from the rhetorical tradition (specifically, the first one listed above): one ought to seek out "fitting but *unusual*" similitudes with which to associate what one wants to be recalled. Thus, although we might consider the associations Thomas makes in his sermons rather odd, even strange—such as, for example, as we saw above, associating the Incarnation of Christ with the word "Behold"—yet, if the classical literature on recollection is right, then the very oddness of the image or the association can help make us recollect more easily.[13] The trick,

---

[12] For a good discussion, see Frances Yates, *The Art of Memory* (London: Routledge, 1966), 20–22, which provides a nice overview of *Rhetorica ad Herennium* 3.16–24 (a text that in the Middle Ages was mistakenly thought to be by Cicero).

[13] On this, cf. *Rhetorica ad Herennium* 3.22, where the author observes that: "When we see in everyday life things that are petty, ordinary, and banal, we generally fail to remember them, because the mind is not being stirred by anything novel or marvelous. But if we see or hear something exceptionally base, dishonourable, unusual, great, unbelievable, or ridiculous, *that* we are likely to remember for a long time. . . . Ordinary things easily slip from the memory while the striking and the novel stay longer in the

on this view—or perhaps it would be better to call it the art—is to find just the right phrase wherein the images suggested by the words are "fitting" (that is, they are *somewhat* similar to the theme you wish to convey) and yet still a bit "unusual" (such as when the single word "behold" is used to remind us of the Incarnation). The other trick is to find just the right phrase with words in just the right order to fit the subject matter you wish to cover. It helps, naturally, to have large sections of the Bible memorized.

In later chapters, I will have more to say about how Thomas selected his biblical *themata*—those opening Bible verses around which he would structure his entire sermon. For now, suffice it to say that Thomas usually chose the biblical verse that would serve as his verbal mnemonic from one of the prescribed readings for liturgy of the day, although this may not have *always* been the case. In the case of the sermon he was required by university statute to give during the ceremony when he was installed as a Regent Master at the University of Paris, Thomas claimed that the verse for the sermon came to him in a vision.[14]

There were, accordingly, I believe, two likely scenarios. The first was that Thomas almost always chose his verbal mnemonic, the biblical *thema*, from the day's readings for the Mass. Indeed, in a process I will describe in more detail in later chapters, it was the order of those words and the associations they suggested that helped a medieval preacher such as Thomas come up with the topics he would then develop within his sermon. If this was the alternative Thomas opted for, the trick of the art, so to speak, would be choosing just the right sentence from the day's reading that would serve his purposes best.

There were clearly certain other occasions, however, in which the biblical verbal mnemonic was not merely "provided" by the readings for the day and Thomas had to choose one from memory. Such was clearly the case, for example, not only with his *principium* sermon at the University

---

mind." "We ought, then," advises the author, "to set up images of a kind that can adhere longest in memory. And we shall do so if we establish similitudes as striking as possible; if we set up images that are not many or vague but active; if we assign to them exceptional beauty or ugliness; if we ornament some of them, as with crowns or public cloaks, so that the similitude may be more distinct to us; or if we somehow disfigure them, as by introducing one stained with blood or soiled with mud or smeared with red paint, so that its form is more striking, or by assigning certain comic effects to our images, for that, too, will ensure our remembering them more readily" (quoted in Yates, *Art of Memory*, 25–26).

14 In his biography of Aquinas, Fr. Torrell affirms that "the story has been transmitted by three different sources, all of which lead back to Thomas himself" (*Person and Work*, 51).

of Paris, but also when he wrote his biblical prologues, most of which, as we shall see, are simply small sermons that employ the same art of the opening mnemonic biblical verse we have analyzed above. Either way, whether Thomas took his *thema* verse from the day's readings or chose one he thought equally appropriate from somewhere else in the Bible, there's simply no getting around the fact that being able to choose just the right phrase to lend structure to a very particular sermon was certainly a tall order. It was a testament to Thomas's remarkable memory and his truly astounding ability to recall just the right text to fit a very particular situation that he so often showed himself up to the task.

ON THE IMPORTANCE OF MEMORY IN MEDIEVAL CULTURE

In her excellent study *The Book of Memory: A Study of Memory in Medieval Culture*, author Mary Carruthers suggests that "medieval culture was fundamentally memorial, to the same profound degree that modern culture in the West is documentary."[15] Indeed, medieval scholars prized mnemonic devices to the same degree that modern scholars prize a thorough index, a good annotated bibliography, or a complete analytical concordance. According to Carruthers, "Ancient and medieval people reserved their awe for memory. Their greatest geniuses they describe as people of superior memories, they boast unashamedly of their prowess in that faculty, and they regard it as a mark of superior *moral* character as well as intellect."[16] "They would not," moreover, she insists, "have understood our separation of 'memory' from 'learning.'"[17] In their understanding of the matter, it was memory that made knowledge into useful experience, and memory that combined these pieces of information-become-experience into what we call 'ideas,' what they were more likely to call 'judgments.'"[18]

Indeed, one of the most renowned and paradigmatic exemplars of this memory culture in the Middle Ages was, as Carruthers notes, our own

---

[15] Mary Carruthers, *The Book of Memory: A Study of Memory in Medieval Culture* (New York: Cambridge University Press, 1990), 1. For good descriptions of the various approaches to memory devices, see particularly Carruthers's ch. 3, "Elementary Memory Design," and ch. 4, "The Arts of Memory."

[16] Ibid., 1.

[17] Although, as we have seen above, Thomas distinguishes both "memory" and "recollection" from new learning in *On Memory and Recollection*. To say that Thomas distinguishes the two, however, is not the same as saying he would have separated them as we do, thinking that somehow "learning" could take place without any "memorization." So, although Thomas distinguishes the two, I take it that Carruthers's point still stands.

[18] Carruthers, *Book of Memory*, 1.

Thomas Aquinas, of whom his Dominican confrere Bernardo Gui wrote at Thomas's canonization hearing:

> His memory was extremely rich and retentive: whatever he had once read and grasped he never forgot; it was as if the knowledge were ever increasing in his soul as page is added to page in the writing of a book. Consider, for example that admirable compilation of Patristic texts on the four Gospels which he made for Pope Urban and which, for the most part, he seems to have put together from texts that he had read and committed to memory from time to time while staying in various religious houses. Still stronger is the testimony of Reginald, his *socius*, and of his pupils and of those who wrote to his dictation, who all declare that he used to dictate in his cell to three secretaries, and even occasionally to four, on different subjects at the same time.[19]

Indeed, his skill in remembering was one he would manifest repeatedly and to similar good effect in all of his works—for example, his *Summa of Theology*, which contemporary sources suggest "was largely dictated from memory, with the aid at most of a few written notes."[20] It is also the skill that made possible Thomas's compilation of patristic texts that served as a kind of running commentary on the Gospels, the remarkable *Catena Aurea*, concerning which Gui reported that Thomas compiled it all "from texts that he had read and committed to memory from time to time while staying in various religious houses."[21] Carruthers insists that, in writing the *Catena*, "Thomas did not look up each quotation in a manuscript tome as he composed; the accounts are specific on this point. The texts were already filed in his memory, in an ordered form that is one of the basics of mnemonic technique. And of course, once the texts were in

---

[19] Quoted in ibid., 3.

[20] Ibid., 6.

[21] Benardo Gui, "The Life of St. Thomas Aquinas," ch. 32, in *The Life of St. Thomas Aquinas: Biographical Documents*, trans. and ed. Kenelm Foster, O.P. (London: Longmans, Green, 1959), 51. See also *Fontes Vitae S. Thomae Aquinatis*, ed. D. Prümmer, O.P., et al. (Toulouse, FR: Revue Thomiste, 1912–1934), for similar comments by Peter Calo (ch. 22) and William Tocco (ch. 17). Tolomeo of Lucca also makes comparable comments in *Historia ecclesiastica* 22, which appears in L. A. Muratori, *Rerum Italicarum Scriptores*, vol. 11 (Milan, IT: Ex typographia Societatis Palatinae in Regia Curia, 1724), 24, and in the partial critical edition by A. Dondaine, "Les *Opuscula fratris Thomae* chez Ptolémée de Lucques," in *Archivum Fratrum Praedicatorum*, vol. 31 (Rome: Istituto Storico Domenicano, 1961).

his memory they stayed there for use on other occasions"[22]—*other occasions*, we might add, such as composing and preaching sermons.

Carruthers is quick to clarify, however, that we should not imagine that Thomas *never* made reference to manuscripts. On the contrary, we know that he did. Indeed, one of the tasks of his secretaries was to copy out manuscripts for his use. And we know that the Dominicans had access to concordances of scriptural verses prepared precisely to help in the preparation of sermons.[23] And yet, Carruthers is also undoubtedly correct when she comments that "the picture we are often given of Thomas pausing while dictating in order to check a reference in a manuscript" is "contrary to the evidence," for "we are told over and over again that Thomas's flow to his secretaries was unceasing."[24] It "ran so clearly," Bernardo Gui reports Thomas's *socius* Reginald of Piperno as saying, "that it was as if the master were reading aloud from a book under his eyes."[25] And indeed *all* of the scribes who wrote from Thomas's dictation, which sometimes numbered three, occasionally even four, to whom he would dictate on different subjects at the same time, appear to have reported much the same thing: "It was as if a great torrent of truth were pouring into him from God." "Nor did he seem to be searching for things as yet unknown to him," reports Gui; "he seemed simply to let his memory pour out its treasures."[26]

What is particularly noteworthy in all these passages is the degree to which it was Thomas's *memory* that so impressed his contemporaries. Even his famous ability to dictate to several scribes at once, which we in the modern world might be tempted to ascribe to his powers of creative genius, was ascribed in his own day to his remarkable powers of memory.

In her book, Carruthers compares Thomas's ability to dictate to several scribes at once with a memory device developed by Hugh of St. Victor to help novices learn several Psalms at once in such a way as to be able to move back and forth easily from any one place in one psalm to any place in any of the others. "The fundamental principle," she says, "is to 'divide' the material to be remembered into pieces short enough to be recalled in single units and to key these into some sort of rigid, easily reconstructable order."[27]

---

[22] Carruthers, *Book of Memory*, 6.
[23] For a good description of these, see D. L. D'Avray's excellent study *The Preaching of the Friars: Sermons Diffused from Paris before 1300* (Oxford, UK: Oxford University Press, 1986), esp. the chapter on "Genres of Preaching Aids," 64-89.
[24] Carruthers, *Book of Memory*, 7.
[25] Gui, "The Life of St. Thomas Aquinas," ch. 16, (Foster, *Biographical Documents*, 38).
[26] Ibid., ch. 32 (Foster, *Biographical Documents*, 51).
[27] Carruthers, *Book of Memory*, 11.

Romans during Cicero's time, as we mentioned above, used a similar practice to memorize long speeches, associating objects they would see while strolling around their house with the various parts of their speech. The sixteenth-century Jesuit missionary Matteo Ricci would later suggest a similar technique to the Chinese (the so-called "Memory Palace") in his famous "Treatise on the Mnemonic Arts." The use of such memory devices, as Carruthers thoroughly documents in her book, had become second nature by the time of Aquinas. Indeed, by that time, their use had become a standard part of the basic medieval pedagogy in the language arts.

It is against the background of this mnemonic culture and the practices that supported it, I suggest, that we must understand the use Thomas makes of his opening biblical epigraphs. Given the intellectual culture in which he lived, Thomas's method of preaching likely would not have struck his audience as oddly as it does many of us today.

THE THEOLOGICAL JUSTIFICATION FOR THIS TEXTUAL PRACTICE: THOMAS'S CHRISTOCENTRIC UNDERSTANDING OF THE BIBLICAL TEXTS

And yet, what rationale could have been offered for such a seemingly odd practice? One rationale, as we have seen, had to do with the nature of human memory: we human beings tend to prefer interesting and evocative *similitudes* arranged in a sensible order to help us recollect things when we have a lot to remember. Using biblical verses as a verbal mnemonic just made sense, therefore, because, if Thomas's audience had not *already* committed the Bible to memory (and many of the young religious brethren to whom he was preaching would have), it would have been at the very least a book from which they had heard verses read to them each week from their youth. It was also a book that was culturally revered and whose words people cared deeply about, making them more easily recalled to the memory.

Indeed, there was a time not too long ago in the English-speaking world when using biblical verses as a mnemonic device would have similarly made sense, given that many people had a storehouse of such phrases flitting about in their minds like various birds in a cage (to borrow an image from Plato's *Theaetetus*).[28] "Yea, though I walk through the valley of the shadow of death, I will fear no evil" (Ps 23:4). "Vanity of vanities, all is vanity" (Eccl 1:2). "This is the day which the LORD hath made; we will rejoice and be glad in it" (Ps 118:24). "Ask, and it shall be given you;

---

[28] See *Theaetetus* 199a.

seek, and ye shall find; knock, and it shall be opened unto you" (Matt 7:7). "The LORD is my shepherd; I shall not want" (Ps 23:1). "Eye hath not seen, nor ear heard, neither have entered into the heart of man, the things which God hath prepared for them that love him" (1 Cor 2:9). These verses and many others used to be part of the common cultural patrimony of church-goers in English-speaking countries. Any of them could have easily been used as a verbal mnemonic the way that the phrase "Every Good Boy Does Fine" is used as a verbal mnemonic to remember the lines on the treble clef: E, G, B, D, and F.

Underlying this mnemonic use of the opening biblical verse, however, is something else as well: a deeper, essentially Christocentric theology. What makes this sort of cross-textual "mapping" conceptually possible in the first place is, I would suggest, a view suggesting that all of Scripture can be (and indeed ought to be) semiotically associated with Christ. Allow me to illustrate what I mean using several examples from Thomas's sermons.

THE IDENTITY OF THE KING WHO WILL COME IN ZECHARIAH 9

In Sermon 5 (*Ecce rex tuus*), as the reader will recall, Thomas opens with the verse from Zechariah 9:9 quoted in the Gospel of Matthew upon Jesus's triumphal entry into Jerusalem:

> As they approached Jerusalem and came to Bethphage on the Mount of Olives, Jesus sent two disciples, saying to them, "Go to the village ahead of you, and at once you will find a donkey tied there, with her colt by her. Untie them and bring them to me. If anyone says anything to you, tell him that the Lord needs them, and he will send them right away." This took place to fulfill what was spoken through the prophet:
>
> > "Say to the Daughter of Zion,
> > 'See, your king comes to you,
> > meek and riding on a donkey,
> > on a colt, the foal of a donkey.'" (Matt 21:1–5; cf. Zech 9:9)

Now, if you take the trouble to look up this verse from Zechariah 9:9 in its original context, you will find that it comes at the end of a prophecy of judgment against the enemies of Judah and in the midst of a series of promises that God will bless Jerusalem. In Zechariah 8, for example, we read of the promised restoration of the city of Jerusalem after the Israelites's long captivity in Babylon, when all the people will be gathered from exile, and the old as well as the young will live in peace as God's people:

> This is what the Lord says: "I will return to Zion and dwell in Jerusalem. Then Jerusalem will be called the City of Truth, and the mountain of the Lord Almighty will be called the Holy Mountain." This is what the Lord Almighty says: "Once again men and women of ripe old age will sit in the streets of Jerusalem, each with cane in hand because of his age. The city streets will be filled with boys and girls playing there." . . . This is what the Lord Almighty says: "I will save my people from the countries of the east and the west. I will bring them back to live in Jerusalem; they will be my people, and I will be faithful and righteous to them as their God." (Zech 8:1–7)

This theme of peace dominates the passages after the verse in Zechariah 9:9 as well. Once "the king" returns, there will be no more need of war:

> I will take away the chariots from Ephraim
> and the warhorses from Jerusalem,
> and the battle bow will be broken.
> He will proclaim peace to the nations.
> His rule will extend from sea to sea
> and from the River to the ends of the earth. (Zech 9:10)

Modern biblical commentators will no doubt insist that these passages refer (in the mind of the original writer, at least) to a hoped-for restoration of the Davidic monarchy over an undivided kingdom with worship at the Temple of Jerusalem at its heart. Whatever truth there may be in such theories, and whether or not such was the original intent of the human author, we can say in retrospect that, as far as the establishment of a *political* monarchy and a lasting *earthly* peace is concerned, it did not happen (or has not happened *yet*).

And yet, whatever the prophet Zechariah himself may have had in mind when he wrote these words, when the New Testament author applied this text to Jesus's entry into Jerusalem, he offered a new perspective and a new possibility for his readers—that perhaps the Holy Spirit had inspired the writing of words the full realization of which would surpass what Zechariah could have imagined or even hoped for when he uttered them. Whatever fulfillment Zechariah might have had in mind when he spoke these words to his fellow Jews returning from exile, the New Testament authors believed that the fullest and final realization of what they promised had occurred only with the coming of Christ, especially with his sacrificial death on the Cross in Jerusalem that revealed a new, very different sort of kingship, one based not on power and conquest, but on love, forgiveness, and service to those in need.

There are other evocative remarks, especially in the second half of Zechariah, that would have had a very different significance for the New Testament authors reading them than they would have had for the original writer and his audience. It sometimes seems as though the prophet himself was aware that the full significance of his words was not apparent even to him. There is, for example, the strange parable in Zechariah 10:12 concerning the good shepherd who takes over the flock and gets rid of the evil shepherds who have been selling the sheep for slaughter. And yet, rather than the good shepherd being welcomed by the sheep whom he has saved, he is rejected by them. So the shepherd takes his staff called "Favor" and breaks it in their midst, revoking his covenant with them and saying: "If you think it best, give me my pay, but if not, keep it," after which we hear the fateful words that will later, in the New Testament, be applied to Judas Iscariot: "So they paid me thirty pieces of silver" (Zech 11:12; cf. Matt 27:9). Since the shepherd in Zechariah knows that taking the money is not right, however, he inquires of the Lord what he should do with it, to which the Lord replies: "Throw it to the potter." And so, says Zechariah: "I took the thirty pieces of silver and threw them into the house of the LORD to the potter" (Zech 11:13). It is of course Judas Iscariot who throws the thirty pieces of silver back into the Temple in the New Testament, whereupon the members of the Sanhedrin, having concluded that it is blood money and cannot be put back into the Temple coffers, buy the "potter's field."

So too, in Zechariah 12:10, we find a prophecy about the one who will be the deliverer of Israel being "pierced" by those whom he has been sent to deliver: "And I will pour out on the house of David and the inhabitants of Jerusalem a spirit of grace and supplication. They will look on me, the one they have pierced, and they will mourn for him as one mourns for an only child, and grieve bitterly for him as one grieves for a firstborn son" (Zech 12:10). What the Gospel writers and theologians of the early Church believed was that these words, beyond whatever else they might signify, signified Christ. Whether or not Zechariah understood the full significance of these words, whether or not he could have known who it was whose side would be pierced by that spear, whether or not he could have known whose "only son" it would be, the Holy Spirit, who writes figuratively with the events of history, did know. Whatever Zechariah had in mind and to whomever he was referring in his own time, this, they believed, would have its ultimate fulfillment in the person of Christ. What the authors of the New Testament and the early Fathers of the Church came to believe, moreover, is that God can *prefigure* not only in words—this much even human authors can do—but in the actual *events of history*. And since, metaphysically and historically, God could use the realities discussed in the Old Testament to prefigure those in the New, so too, textually, many of the things that "lay hidden" in figures in the Old Testament were "made manifest" in the words of the New.[29]

It is to this particular understanding of the relationship between the two testaments that we must look ultimately, I would suggest, to explain why Thomas supposes he can take a verse from the Old Testament and apply it to a sermon on Christ and why, by extension, he considers it fitting to use an Old Testament verse from Zechariah 9:9 ("Behold, your king comes to you, meek, and riding on a donkey") in a sermon on the advent of Christ. Thomas can do this because he believes that, whoever the king is to whom Zechariah is referring, that man is a prefiguration of the "king of kings" who is to come. Thomas has scriptural warrant for this belief, moreover, because he finds Matthew using this text from Zechariah in a similar way in his Gospel: "the king" who enters Jerusalem is not merely a human king like others, he is the incarnate King, the One who is truly "the holy one" and "the most high," and the One who will finally and truly bring peace and justice.

A similar theological association between an Old Testament promise and its ultimate fulfillment in Christ is behind Thomas's comment in Sermon 1 (*Veniet desideratus*). After quoting the passage from the book of the prophet Haggai that says, "He who is desired by all the nations together will come, and he will fill this house with glory" (Hag 2:8), Thomas adds:

the Prophet shows three things [in this sentence], in this order: (1) first, he shows it is God's Son himself who is coming down from the heavens: *he will come*;[30] (2) second, he shows He is the

---

[29] For this oft-quoted comment of St. Augustine's, see his *Questions on the Heptateuch* [the First Seven Books of the Bible] 2.73.

[30] Notice that the first word in Latin is *veniet*, which means "he will come." So, Thomas is justified in saying that the prophet deals with this "first." To render the whole in English translation, however, we have been forced to put "will come" later in the sentence,

one who mercifully fulfills the desires of the Patriarchs: *who is desired by all the nations together*; (3) third, he shows He is the one who freely bestows his pleasing benefit [upon us]: *and he will fill this house with glory.*

Thomas can make this series of associations (even though the prophet Haggai himself clearly did not know that the one who would come would be the Son of God incarnate, the Word made flesh, Jesus Christ) because Thomas shares with the New Testament writers a Christocentric understanding of the relationship between the two testaments.

DAVID AS A PREFIGURATION OF CHRIST AND, BY EXTENSION, CHRISTIAN SAINTS

On the view we have been examining, Christ is seen as the center of all history. The events of salvation history that came before Christ both *prepare for* and *prefigure* his coming, as also the events after Christ *look back to him* to reveal their ultimate source and meaning. Many of us may have experienced something similar in our own lives. As we look back on what at the time may have seemed random, scattered, disconnected events, we see that they were all leading up to some decisive moment when we came to some fundamental realization: "Life does not go on forever, so one ought to value every moment"; "Success should not be gauged in terms of money or career alone"; or "I love this woman, and I want to spend the rest of my life with her." Whatever it is, life after that moment, we know, was different. Not only was it different, but life could never be quite the same again. And life after that point was always to be seen through a new set of perspectives. So too with Christians and Jesus Christ: all of history was leading up to the decisive revelation of God's love in and through him, and after that moment—after that proclamation of divine love—human beings would have to think about their lives and their relationship with God and with their neighbors in fundamentally new ways.

Above, we examined two sermons in which Thomas, following long-standing Christian traditions of exegesis going back to the early Church and the New Testament itself, interpreted several Old Testament references to "the king" who would "come" to set things right in the land as referring ultimately to Jesus Christ. So too, now, we are going to exam-

---

after "who is desired by all the nations," even though the word *veniet* actually comes first in the Latin sentence.

ine an Old Testament passage that Thomas takes not only as a prefiguration of Christ, but also, by extension, as a prefiguration of the saints who
lived after Christ as *alter Christus* ("another Christ") and as faithful members of the Body of Christ on earth. Another way of putting this might be
to say that, as *David* prefigures *Christ*, so too *Christ* prefigures St. Peter,
St. Paul, and St. Ignatius of Antioch, all of whom were tortured and killed
witnessing to their faith in Christ. The problem with that way of stating
the matter, however, would be that Peter, Paul, and Ignatius all believed
that the full meaning of their lives had been revealed in and through the
person of Jesus Christ, not that his life had somehow been a prefiguration
of some higher realization only achieved fully in them. Thus, Christians
would say that kings such as David and Solomon, who lived *before* Christ,
foreshadowed and prefigured the *true* king who was to come, whereas
Christian kings *after* Christ are called upon to look back *to* Christ as the
model for how they should act.[31] In this way, David's power as king over
the land was understood to be a prefiguration of the true kingship over all
things and all history embodied in Jesus Christ. Kings after Christ, however, were meant to look back to him as a revelation of the *true* meaning of
kingship, as something revealed not in conquest and the increase of power,
but in service and sacrifice.

It is from this perspective, I suggest, that we must understand Thomas's striking use of the passage from Psalm 88:21 ("I have found David my
servant; with my holy oil I have anointed him; my hand will assist him and
my arm will make him firm") to refer to St. Nicholas of Myra in Sermon 16
(*Inveni David*), a peculiarity I had occasion to mention near the beginning
of this chapter. The sermon was delivered on December 6, the Feast of St.
Nicholas, and Thomas's mnemonic "unpacking" of the opening biblical
verse from Psalm 88:21 begins like this:

> From these words [namely, the words from Ps 88:2] we can learn
> four praiseworthy things of this holy bishop St. Nicholas: (1) first,

---

[31] One of the best examples of a medieval king who, during Thomas's own lifetime,
thought that imitating Christ in very literal ways was an important part of his office
was Louis IX of France (St. Louis). According to his biographer, Jean de Joinville, Louis
not only bathed the feet of the poor but bid Joinville to do so as well; see Jean de Joinville, *Life of St. Louis*, currently available in print only in *Chronicles of the Crusades*, ed.
and trans. Margaret Shaw (Baltimore, MD: Penguin Classics, 1963), 169.

A modern story based upon this theme—that true "kingship" is revealed not in power and conquest but in service and sacrifice—can be found in Rudyard Kipling's *The
Man Who Would Be King*. The presence of Christ as an ultimate paradigm of the true
king is clearly present in both works.

his wondrous election; (2) second, his unique consecration; (3) third, the effective execution of his task; and (4) fourth, his immovable and firm stability. His wondrous election is shown in the words: "I have found David, my servant." His special consecration is shown where it says: "I have anointed him with my sacred oil." The effective execution of his task is shown in the words: "My hand will help him." His stable firmness is shown where it says: "and my arm will make him firm."

One difficulty in interpreting these lines comes from imagining that Thomas thinks that these words from a tenth-century BC psalm refer *literally* to St. Nicholas, a fourth-century AD Christian bishop. What we first need to realize, however, is that Thomas is merely using this passage from the Psalms as a mnemonic device to help structure his sermon on St. Nicholas, not proposing that these words refer *literally* to St. Nicholas.

And yet, let me suggest that there is a deeper theological point involved here as well. It is important to remember that Thomas lived in an intellectual and spiritual culture where the words of the Psalms were chanted several times a day, and these words were always understood to refer ultimately to Christ. Thomas makes clear that he shares this perspective in the prologue to his own Psalm commentary, where he insists that "all the things which pertain to the faith of the Incarnation are so clearly treated in this book [that is, the Psalms] that it seems almost a gospel, and not prophecy."[32]

So, even with a biblical verse that *says* "I have found David, my servant; with my holy oil I have anointed him" (Ps 88:21), since David was understood to be a *prefiguration* of Christ, Thomas assumed that this text could be applied to Christ and, indeed, that in important ways, it referred to Christ more truly than to David or anyone else. Of whom other than Christ on the Cross would God most truly and most fully be able to say, "I have found my servant"? Who other than Jesus was most truly and most fully "God's anointed one" (in Greek, *Christos*)?

The relationship between David and Christ can also be understood both *analogically* and *pedagogically*. Just as we first know our own human fathers, and then apply the word "father" *analogically* to God, only later to realize that the word "Father" is predicated more truly of God than of our human fathers (since God is the one who created us out of nothing and

---

[32] The Latin and facing English can be found at http://www4.desales.edu/~philtheo/loughlin/ATP/Proemium.html.

who loves us without fail everlastingly), so too we first become acquainted with David and learn *pedagogically* from the Old Testament descriptions of him something about what it means to be God's "anointed one," only later to realize that the order of our learning is the reverse of the order of reality and that the title "[God's] Anointed One" is predicated more truly of Christ than of David. Christ *is* the Anointed One, whereas David *prefigures* the One who is to come by revealing, in a way that we can more easily understand, one of the categories we will need to comprehend if we are to appreciate who Christ is when he comes. Such categories, limited as they are, having primarily a pedagogical role in preparing us for a reality that goes beyond them, both reveal and conceal the reality they prefigure. The prefiguring figures are always utterly surpassed—the limited concepts they entail must all be ultimately broken open—when we enter the presence of their Ultimate Referent: the One whom "no eye has seen, no ear has heard, no mind has conceived."

Once we have come to understand how a passage that begins "I have found David, my servant" can apply to Christ, then by extension, we can also come to understand how Thomas can use the same passage to refer to one of the saints. To the extent that St. Nicholas succeeded during his life in getting his false, sinful self out of the way—thereby allowing his *true* self, the self he was meant to be as he was made by God, to shine forth—to that extent he had become, as the Church Fathers used to say, *alter Christus* ("another Christ"). As such, Nicholas became the visible symbol of Christ's presence, especially for the other members of his diocese. He had, as Paul says, "put off his sinful self," and by "putting on Christ," he had become a new man *for* them. It is for these reasons that passages that are interpreted Christocentrically can be applied, by extension, to the saints, such as St. Nicholas. Since St. Nicholas is one who had very clearly "put on Christ," we can, by extension, apply the Scriptures that apply to Christ to St. Nicholas as well.

To sum up, it is Thomas's Christocentric understanding of the biblical texts that provides the theological justification for what might otherwise seem a rather odd or illicit use of Old Testament texts as epigraphs for his sermons. Just as it is not unimportant for readers to see how Thomas uses his biblical epigraphs as a mnemonic device around which to organize his sermons, so too it would not do for readers to imagine that what Thomas is doing with these epigraphs amounts to nothing more than fiddling around with words. The words offer themselves up for this use because they are understood to witness ultimately to the Word himself, the incarnate God, Creator, and Source of all things. Just as the things of creation point to their Creator who is their origin and end, and thus their ultimate fulfillment that gives them their ultimate meaning, so too the words of Scripture, as the created things of the world, point us back ultimately to the Word who is their origin and end, and thus their ultimate fulfillment, that gives them their ultimate meaning.

"Mixing Memory and Desire": A New Pattern for Preaching

I have mentioned "Mixing Memory and Desire" in the title of this final section because, for one thing, it is part of a famous line from the beginning of T. S. Eliot's poem *The Waste Land*,[33] a reference that I thought might make the title more memorable for some modern readers. But I have used it also because I believe there is something Thomas understands about delivering sermons that many who preach tend to forget: to have a lasting impact on the life of the listener, the substance of the sermon must be remembered past the moment when the sermon is delivered. Many can dazzle with displays of rhetorical fury; few can preach in such a way as to impress the thoughts in a lasting way on the mind of the listener like a seal imprinted into soft wax, as Plato describes it in the *Theaetetus*.[34]

Dom Jean LeClerq entitled his famous book on monastic culture *The Love of Learning and the Desire for God*.[35] It has often been said of the biblical sermons of St. Bernard that they were excellent at enkindling in listeners the "desire for God." St. Thomas's way of preaching is different, no doubt, but no less biblical. And as examples of how to mix learning and the desire for God, his sermons are, I would suggest, no less effective. Friar Thomas was one of the pioneers of a new rhetoric—a rhetoric of the mind—a rhetoric attuned not so much to the rhythms and cadences that stir the passions as to the patterns and structures that inform the memory. The result was a profound—and decidedly *Dominican*—way of mixing memory and desire.[36]

---

[33] T. S. Eliot, *The Waste Land*, lines 2–3 in section 1, "The Burial of the Dead."

[34] See Plato, *Theaetetus* 190e5–196c6.

[35] Jean Leclerq, *The Love of Learning and the Desire for God: A Study of Monastic Culture*, trans. Catharine Misrahi, 3rd ed. (New York: Fordham University Press, 1948).

[36] On the specifically *Dominican* character of Thomas's preaching, see Torrell, *Sermons*, 30–42, a section entitled "*Un prédicateur théologien dominicain.*" Of special note is Fr. Torrell's insistence that Thomas "the preacher is truly the same person as the theologian" (*le prédicateur es vraiment la même personne que le théologien*) and that, for Thomas, in accord with the Dominican motto "*Contemplata aliis tradere*" ("Hand on

The details of how this method works is the subject to which we will turn our attention in the following three chapters.

---

to others [the fruits of one's] contemplation), the contemplative dimension of religious life (centered on the risen Christ) is paramount and is what gives life to one's teaching and preaching.

CHAPTER 2

Thomas Aquinas and the *Sermo Modernus*

THOUGH MANY OF US in the modern world might find Thomas's sermon style a bit odd, yet, by the same token, for those who prefer short, compact, and yet doctrinally-rich sermons to long, flowery speeches that go on for an hour or more, Thomas's sermons might seem like a gift from heaven. Sit and listen for ten minutes, and you still go out with enough food-for-thought to keep you busy reflecting for weeks. From this perspective, perhaps even we, living as we do in the ever-busy world of constant multi-tasking, might understand why these sorts of sermons gained in popularity among the denizens of the cities and towns over the longer sort of monastic homily that characterized previous generations. If done well, these sermons exhibited the skills of a speaker who had to be smart, clever, and highly efficient—characteristics the townspeople who had to listen to them understood and respected. It is not that the busy townspeople of the Middle Ages did not want holiness; it is simply that, as a general rule, they wanted their holiness delivered in packages that were smart, clever, and highly efficient.

THE THIRTEENTH CENTURY "HOMILETIC REVOLUTION" AND THE *SERMO MODERNUS*

Be that as it may, Thomas's sermon style was actually thoroughly "modern" for its time. Indeed, this style of sermon was actually called a "modern sermon"—a *sermo modernus*—and it became very popular in the twelfth and thirteenth centuries. In this regard, it is important to understand, as author James J. Murphy points out in his definitive work *Rhetoric in the Middle Ages*, that "By the year 1200 . . . the Christian Church had produced only four writers who could by any stretch of the imagination be called theorists of preaching." The only systematic treatments of preaching were in St. Augustine's *De doctrina christiana*, Pope Gregory the Great's *Cura Pastoralis* (sometimes called "the Pastoral Rule"), Guibert de Nogent's 1084 work entitled *A Book About the Way a Sermon Ought to be Written* (*Liber quo ordine sermo fieri debeat*), and Alain de Lille's 1199 work *On the Preacher's Art* (*De arte praedicatoria*). And yet, "within twenty years of 1200," notes Murphy, "a whole new rhetoric of preaching leaped into prominence, unleashing hundreds of theoretical manuals written all over Europe." The developments were so quick and so vast that it constituted what can only be called, according to Professor Murphy, a "homiletic revolution." "How did this come about so rapidly?" he asks. "The plain truth is that we do not yet know the complete answer. However, the growth pattern is quite obvious. The genre was well established by 1220. By the middle of the thirteenth century it was fully developed, complete with a technical vocabulary and a stabilized pattern of organization."[1] A key moment in this development seems to have occurred with a series of sermons preached to the university community at the University of Paris in the academic year 1230–1231, where the new homiletic practice may have begun in earnest.[2] Thomas's preaching career fell well in the middle of this new "homiletic revolution."[3]

How did this "modern" style differ from what proceeded it?[4] Thomas Waleys, an Oxford Dominican, who wrote a widely-circulated tract "On the manner of composing sermons" (*De modo componendi sermones*) in the

---

[1] See James J. Murphy, *Rhetoric in the Middle Ages: A History of Rhetorical Theory from Saint Augustine to the Renaissance* (Berkeley: University of California Press, 1974), 309–10.

[2] One can find these sermons in M. M. Davy's *Les sermons universitaires parisiens de 1230–1231 : contribution à l'histoire de la prédication médiévale* (Paris: J. Vrin, 1931).

[3] Beginning with the year 1230, the Mendicants, too, entered the field with treatises on preaching: Etienne de Bourbon (d. 1260), *Tractatus de diversis materiis praedicabilibus*; Humbert of Romans (d. 1277), *De eruditione praedicatorum*; and Thomas of Wales (d.1274), *Ars praedicandi*. Fr. Thomas Charland has compiled a list in *Artes Praedicandi: contribution à l'histoire de la rhétorique au moyen âge*, Publications de l'Institut d'Etudes Medievales d'Ottawa 7 (Paris/Ottowa: J. Vrin/Institute of Medieval Studies, 1936), 17–106.

[4] For good introductory material, see the works cited in n. 8.

early fourteenth century, described the difference in terms of what served as the basis of the sermon. While the "modern" sermon made use of a brief *thema* or Bible verse around which the entire sermon was built, the "ancient" sermon involved a verse-by-verse commentary on the entire Gospel reading for the day. According to Waleys, the older style was still in use in some places—Italy, for example—even in his time. "Although a brief *thema* is used when preaching to clerics," says Waleys, "nevertheless, in some parts, for example in Italy, commonly, when preaching not to clerics but to the people, a brief *thema* is not used; rather the whole Gospel which is read in the Mass is taken for the *thema*, and the whole is expounded upon, and many beautiful and devout things are said."[5] Interestingly, Waleys considers this older style to be the best when it comes to preaching to the people, declaring: "And, in my judgment, this manner of preaching to the people is not only easier for the preacher, but also more useful for the listener among all the modes of preaching. And such was the ancient manner of preaching of the saints, as is clear in their homilies."[6] Indeed, Waleys goes on to decry those who preach to the uneducated in the manner appropriate to clerics: when they fill their sermons with such theological subtleties, says Waleys, they make it all but impossible that multiple errors and "unfitting phantasies" (*phantasiae ineptae*) will not arise in the minds of their listeners. "Better simply not to preach to the people at all than to preach to them in this way," suggests Waleys.[7]

Waleys, it seems, however, was swimming against the tide. Michèle Mulcahey, for example, notes that John of Wales, a Franciscan master at Paris around 1270, wrote in his *De arte praedicandi* that the *sermo antiquus* style homily "did not sit particularly well with modern listeners, who liked to see the clear articulation of a sermon developed from a

---

[5] "Licet autem sic accipiatur them breve, quando praedicatur clero, tamen, in aliquibus partibus, puta in Italia, communiter, quando praedicatur non clero sed populo, non accipitur breve them; sed totum evangelium quod legitur in missa accipitur pro themata, et totum exponituui, et in ejus expositione multa pulchra et devota dicuntur"; see Thomas Waleys, *De modo componendi sermones*, in Charland, *Artes praedicandi*, 344.

[6] "Et, me judicio, iste modus praedicandi populo non solum est facilior ipsi praedicatori, sed etiam utilior auditori enter omnes modos praedicandi. Et iste fuit antiquus modus praedicandi sanctorum, ut patet in eorum homeliis" (ibid.).

[7] "In aliquibus vero partibus, ita subtiliter et curiose praedicatur mulierculis sicut clericis, et ita profundae materiae theologicae tractantur coram eis in sermonibus sicut coram clericis in scholis, ut melius judicarem eis simpliciter non praedicare quam taliter praedicare, quia non est possibile quin inter eas surgant multi errores et phantasiae ineptae" (ibid.).

scriptural theme." And the Italian Dominican Fra Giacomo da Fusignano, prior of Santa Maria sopra Minerva in Rome (1290) wrote that the old style was suitable only for preaching to the ignorant. To other, more intelligent and literate listeners, this sort of exposition, he thought, was unnecessary.[8] The type of sermon "more common to modern preachers" (*modernis praedicatoribus communior*), adds Giacomo, was one in which a theme was divided into various parts. This method, as we will see below, is precisely what characterized the style of the "modern sermon" (the *sermo modernus*).[9]

BASIC CHARACTERISTICS OF THE *SERMO MODERNUS*: THE *THEMA*

So what was this new "modern sermon" style like? Not to belabor the point, it was very much like what we have seen in Aquinas's sermons. Thus in fact, by learning how to read a sermon by Thomas Aquinas, the reader has also learned how to read what would become the most popular sermon style in the Middle Ages.[10] The defining characteristic, according to the preaching manuals of the thirteenth and early fourteenth centuries, was the *thema*, the opening biblical verse.[11] As Mulcahey points out in her work on early Dominican education before 1350, "The theme [that is, the *thema*] of a *sermo modernus* was often likened by the authors of preaching manuals to the root of the tree which was the sermon, or similarly it was the trunk from which sprung the various branches."[12] What characterized

---

[8]　See Michèle Mulcahey, *First the Bow is Bent in Study: Dominican Education Before 1350* (Toronto, ON: Pontifical Institute of Medieval Studies, 1998), 403n10, quoting Bologna, Collegio di Spagna, MS Lib. sacr. 50, n. 2, fol. 124r: "Est autem hoc satis populo rudi utilis. Ceteris literatis et intelligentibus auditoribus populariis exposicio non est necessaria."

[9]　For more on the developments in the *sermo modernus* style, see Richard and Mary Rouse's chapter on the evolution of sermon-form in the thirteenth century in *Preachers, Florilegia, and Sermons: Studies on the Manipulus florum of Thomas of Ireland*, Studies and Texts 47 (Toronto, ON: Pontifical Institute of Medieval Studies, 1979), 65–90. See also David D'Avray, *The Preaching of the Friars: Sermons Diffused from Paris before 1300* (Oxford, UK: Oxford University Press, 1985), 163–203.

[10]　Although the first deals with thirteenth-century Dominicans and the second with the Franciscan Bonaventure specifically, as I pointed out above (see n. 7), there is no substantial difference between their method of composing a sermon.

[11]　On the *thema* generally, see Charland, *Artes praedicandi*, 111–24.

[12]　Mulcahey, *First the Bow is Bent in Study*, 404–05, quoting a passage from the manuscript in Anger, Bibliothèque municipale, MS 1582, fol. 132: "Unde, quia thema est quasi radix totius sermonis et per ipsum fundamentum totius aedificii fabrica consurgit."

the *sermo modernus* style was that the preacher would state his *thema* verse and, after a brief introduction or *prothema* (about which we will say more in a moment), divide it into two or more parts, each part of which was in turn associated with a separate section or "member" of the sermon. "This announcement of the skeleton of the sermon at the outset," says Mulcahey, "is very much the signature of the thirteenth- or fourteenth-century preacher."[13] And indeed it is, as we have seen, precisely one of the defining characteristics of Thomas's sermons.

How was the *thema* chosen? According to Mulcahey: "This verse was sometimes taken from the liturgical readings for the day, it seems, but they were also taken from anywhere else in the Scriptures if the occasion warranted it, regardless of whether the passage was from the liturgical readings for the day or not."[14] Her general observation is borne out by a review of Aquinas's sermons. Of the nineteen extant sermons, in half of them, Thomas seem to have taken the *thema* from within the lectionary reading for the day. One finds the same practice in the Sunday Sermons of St. Bonaventure.[15] Both of these great masters, as far as we can tell, generally took their *thema* from the day's readings when they were preaching at Sunday masses, but allowed themselves to select from elsewhere on special feast days, such as All Saints or on the feast of a particular saint such as St. Nicholas. The reader will find in the Appendix to the present volume a listing of all Thomas's sermons alongside the assigned reading from the lectionary assigned for that day.

It is not generally well known that in the Middle Ages the Dominicans and the Franciscans had a somewhat different cycle of readings during the liturgical year so that, for example, on the Fourth Sunday of Advent, while the Dominicans were reading Philippians 4:4–7 and John 1:19–28, the Franciscans were reading 1 Corinthians 4:1–5 and Luke 3:1–6.[16] There was still a great deal of commonality between the two lectionaries, but not only would Thomas and Bonaventure not always have

---

13 Ibid., 405.

14 Ibid., 404.

15 *The Sunday Sermons of St. Bonaventure*, trans. Timothy J. Johnson, The Works of St. Bonaventure 12 (St. Bonaventure, NY: Franciscan Institute Publications, 2008). This volume is certainly worth perusing. Bonaventure is an absolute master at the *sermo modernus* style, and his sermons have been preserved mostly intact, while Thomas's have not.

16 For a complete calendar of the readings for the year for both orders, see Maura O'Carroll, S.N.D., "The Lectionary for the Proper of the Year in the Dominican and Franciscan Rites of the Thirteenth Century," *Archivum Fratrum Praedicatorum* 49 (1979): 79–103.

had the same lectionary reading to preach on, even when they *did* have the same biblical text, they might not have chosen the same verse as their *thema*. Thus, even when Thomas and Bonaventure were faced with identical readings, such as on the Sunday within the Octave of Epiphany, when the Gospel reading for both Dominicans and Franciscans was taken from Luke 2:42–52, Thomas chose Luke 2:52 as his *thema*, whereas Bonaventure chose Luke 2:48.

Since, during the Middle Ages, there were readings assigned for each Sunday, one from one of the Epistles and one from one of the Gospels, it follows that any time we see a *thema* from the Old Testament it is likely that Thomas chose that verse at his own discretion. It is interesting to note in this regard, however, that on one of the First Sundays of Advent, Thomas chose as his Haggai 2:7 *thema*, whereas Bonaventure chose the immediately following, 2:8, for that same Sunday. Why we find this rough similarity remains unclear. In addition, since we have no record of what Psalms were chanted at each Mass, it is impossible to say whether, when Thomas chose as his *thema* a verse from one of the Psalms, it might have been chanted during that day's Mass, but it is at least a possibility.

As Mulcahey points out, "However he ultimately decided upon his *thema*, the most important thing a preacher had to bear in mind when selecting it was that it should contain latent within it the whole of the sermon he imagined, to be drawn out through a complex yet organic development."[17] With our review of Thomas's sermons and biblical prologues above, we have at least gotten a taste of how this "organic development" worked in practice.

THE *PROTHEMA*

Structurally, though, immediately after the announcement of the *thema*, which in written versions will generally appear at the top of the page, making it seem as though this is the verse being preached on, what follows will often be (but not always) something known as a *prothema*: an introductory passage that stands as a preface to an opening prayer. The presence of this *prothema* verse can often be confusing to the reader because after the original statement of the *thema*, one expects the author immediately to begin developing the ideas contained in the theme. But when there's a *prothema*, the author seems to go off in an entirely new direction—and indeed does, for roughly a paragraph. And while the *thema* verse is always taken

---

[17] Mulcahey, *First the Bow is Bent in Study*, 404.

from some passage in the Bible, the *prothema* is generally built around a separate verse from the Bible, but in the case of a shorter introduction, the content might be associated with a quotation from one of the Fathers or, in some cases, even one from a pagan author.

So, for example, after the statement of the *thema* in Thomas's Sermon 17 (*Lux orta est*), taken from Psalm 97:11—"A light has gone up for the just, and joy for the upright of heart"—Thomas immediately quotes another biblical verse, James 1:17—"Every very good [*optimus*] endowment and every perfect gift from above is coming down from the Father of lights." Based on this verse, Thomas "unfolds" the following idea:

> Temporal things are a good [*bonus*] endowment. The things that belong to us naturally, like the body and the soul are a better [*melior*] endowment. Eternal glory and the goods bestowed by grace are the best [*optimus*] endowment. Every very good [*optimus*] endowment—we understand this as grace—comes from the Father of lights. Grace is called the best [*optimus*] gift, given to us so that we may perform meritorious works. . . . So, because the grace of God is so effective a gift for working the good in the present and for arriving at eternal glory in the future, let us ask at the beginning that the Lord may give us grace.[18]

In the prologue to Thomas's Sermon 6 (*Celum et terra transibunt*), by contrast, right after the statement of the *thema* from Luke 21:33 ("Heaven and earth will pass"), we find a quotation from Aristotle's *Ethics* (10.7): "All delights are at some point cut off. The greatest, however, is the delight that is in accordance with the operation of wisdom, and the most delightful operation is the one that is in accordance with the operation of wisdom." "Because of this," says Thomas, "we will ask at the beginning of this homily, our Lord Jesus Christ, the fountain of all wisdom . . . to illumine our understanding, to kindle our hearts, and to make my mouth eloquent for the honor of his name in accordance with the Gospel teaching and the edification of our souls." In this case, the text from Aristotle does not serve as a mnemonic structuring device. Thomas does not divide it into two or three parts so as to associate each part with material that follows.

---

[18] All English translation of the sermons comes from *Thomas Aquinas: The Academic Sermons*, trans. Mark-Robin Hoogland, C.P., The Fathers of the Church: Mediaeval Continuation 11 (Washington, DC: Catholic University of America Press, 2010), although I have emended the translation occasionally after consulting the Latin text in vol. 44.1 (2014) of the Leonine edition (see nn. 3–5 for further discussion).

But in both cases, what is clear is that the *prothema* is part of a bridge that serves as an invocation to an opening prayer: "Let us ask at the beginning that the Lord may give us grace" (as in Sermon 17); "We will ask the one who makes even the mute speak abundantly that he may give me words to speak" (as in Sermon 11).

According to Mulcahey, "Pragmatic Dominican master-general Humbert of Romans saw another use for the protheme: it could help the preacher mark time while waiting for the late-comers to arrive and quieten down."[19] I love this suggestion, but given how short Thomas and Bonaventure's *promthemata* tend to be, taking up no more than two or three minutes if read aloud, it is hard to imagine they were ever used for this purpose. Either way, Humbert seems to have viewed the *prothema* as "an embellishment which could be dispensed with under most circumstances."[20] Mulcahey suggests that "many of the sermon collections produced by Dominicans do indeed omit this part of the sermon."[21] And yet, whatever the general practice among Dominicans may have been, of the twenty extant sermons we have by Thomas Aquinas, at least fourteen have a *prothema* that finishes exhorting the congregation to prayer.[22]

These *prothemata* should be carefully distinguished, however, from simple introductory sections (in other sermons) that do *not* lead to prayer. Consider, in this regard, Sermon 1 (*Veniet desideratus*), which, immediately after the opening statement of the *prothema* from Haggai 2:7 ("He who is desired by all the nations together will come, and he will fill this house with glory"), begins thus:

> It is as Augustine says to Optatus: "Nobody is freed from the damnation that came through Adam but through faith in Jesus

---

[19] Mulcahey, *First the Bow is Bent in Study*, 406.

[20] Quoted from ibid., 406n20; see also Humbert of Romans, *De eruditione praedicatorum* 7.44, in *B. Humberti de Romanis opera de vita regulari*, ed. J. J. Berthier (Rome: Typis A. Befani, 1888–1889), 2:481–83. The Latin text is actually somewhat difficult to find. Much more easily obtained is the English translation, *Treatise on Preaching*, trans. the Dominican Students of the Province of St. Joseph, ed. Walter M. Conlon, O.P. (Westminster, MD: Newman Press, 1951); see esp. 156–60, where the English varies from that of Mulcahey quoted above (the Domincan Students English translation can be found also at http://www.op.org/sites/www.op.org/files/public/documents/fichier/ treat_on_preaching_humbert_en.pdf).

[21] Mulcahey, *First the Bow is Bent in Study*, 406n20.

[22] The sermons that very clearly have a *prothema* are Sermons 4, 5, 6, 8, 9, 11, 13, 14, 15, 16, 17, 18, 20, and 21. Those that do not appear to have a *prothema* are 1, 2, 3, 7, 12, and 19—although we should remember that some of these, like Sermon 7, remain fragmentary.

Christ." This is sufficiently proven by the Apostle in Hebrews 11 (6), where he shows that no one has ever been able to please God without faith. From this it follows that at all times after a lapse faith has been a necessity for recovery, for there is no other medicine for the weakness of original or actual sin. And therefore all the saints always, from the beginning of the world, longed for and desired the coming of the Savior.

There is no indication in the text that Thomas finishes this comment with an introduction to prayer—although it remains a possibility. After "And therefore all the saints always, from the beginning of the world, longed for and desired the coming of the Savior," he might have simply added, "And so, now, we too should call upon the Savior to come to us in this place." But there is no evidence of this in the text. Rather, after "And therefore all the saints . . . longed for and desired the coming of the Savior," the very next sentence begins, "And this is shown well and plainly in the saying mentioned [in the opening *thema*]." And with this, Thomas has drawn the listener's attention back to the opening *thema*, and he will immediately reveal how he has chosen to divide it and then undertake to develop the various elements. So, while every sermon has a *thema* on which it is based, not every sermon has a *prothema* inviting the congregation to prayer. Sometimes they do; sometimes they do not.

Indeed, one can find an interesting example of the dual practice in the collection of St. Bonaventure's University Sermons.[23] In the introduction to his edition and translation of the sermons, Timothy J. Johnson reports that, in the opinion of Jacques Bougerol, "Bonaventure composed almost the entire corpus of the *Sunday Sermons de novo* without ever having actually preached them in a public setting."[24] If this is true, then what is interesting for our purposes is that, among these sermons, some have the *prothema* and some do not. Thus, not only did Bonaventure seemingly create nearly an entire cycle of sermons to cover the whole liturgical year from Advent to Lent and back again, perhaps very few of which were actu-

---

[23] Johnson, *Sunday Sermons of St. Bonaventure.*

[24] Ibid., 25, esp. n51, in which Johnson notes: "In *The Preaching of the Friars*, 97, D'Avray claims the *Sunday Sermons* are taken from sermon texts Bonaventure had previously preached 'live' in a number of places, but this is not the case according to Jacques Bougerol since the schemas of only nine previous sermons are identifiable in the *Sunday Sermons*." By "D'Avray," he is referring to *The Preaching of the Friars*. On this, see also the introduction by Jacques Bougerol to *Sancti Bonaventurae Sermones Dominicales* (Grottaferrata, IT: Collegio S. Bonaventura, Padri Editori di Quaracchi, 1977), 27–29.

ally preached "live," but he also re-created the practice whereby one would sometimes include the *prothema* and sometimes not.

Take, for example, Sermon 4 in Bonaventure's *Sunday Sermons*, a sermon on "Sunday within the Octave of the Nativity." After the opening statement of the *thema*, which in this case is Luke 2:34 (the assigned Gospel reading for that day being Luke 2:33–40), Bonaventure turns immediately in his "protheme" to another biblical verse, Ecclesiasticus (Sirach) 48:1: "The prophet Elijah rose like a blazing fire." In what follows, Bonaventure does what the reader will often find in these *prothemata*: he uses his *prothema* verse as a mnemonic device in its own right to help structure the elements of the introductory material in the "protheme." "The passage proposed," says Bonaventure (and by this, he is referring to the passage from Ecclesiasticus), "brilliantly expresses the qualities proper to one who preaches the divine word. First, he must be withdrawn or removed from worldly concerns." And this first quality of the good preacher he associates with the phrase "Elijah arose." Second, the good preacher must be illuminated by evangelical truth, which Bonaventure associates with the phrase "prophet." And third, the good preacher must be "inflamed by charity toward God and neighbor," which Bonaventure associates with the phrase "like a blazing fire." We do not get any explanation or expansion on these associations—the audience, it seems, is just supposed to "get" them—because Bonaventure immediately goes on to invoke the prayer of his audience that he too might become a preacher exhibiting these three qualities. "Dearly beloved," he begins:

> let us at the beginning of our sermon before anything else, humbly implore the source and principle of mercy that is the paternal light, that through his gracious condescension, he might separate us from the love of worldly prosperity, illuminate us with the splendor or knowledge of evangelical truth, and inflame us with the fervor of fraternal charity; so that withdrawn from love of the world, illuminated by the splendor of the gospel, and inflamed with love of God and neighbor, we might then offer something worthwhile to the praise and glory of God's blessed name and for the well-being and consolation of our souls. Amen.[25]

This is a classic *prothema*. The *prothemata* of later preachers will sometimes get very long and complicated, but in Thomas's and Bonaventure's sermons, they tend to be short and simple.

---

[25] Johgnson, *Sunday Sermons of St. Bonaventure*, Sermon 6, no. 1 (p. 108).

By the same token, consider Sermon 23 in Bonaventure's *Sunday Sermons*, for the Second Sunday after Easter. The *thema* for this sermon is taken from John 10:11 (the assigned Gospel reading for the day being John 10:11–16): "I am the good shepherd. The good shepherd lays down his life for his sheep." In this case, however, there is no *prothema*. Instead, Bonaventure starts right in on his topic for the day: "Our Lord Jesus Christ, the shepherd of the triumphant and militant Church, like any good shepherd, when the lamb of humanity was missing, placed the angelic flock in the desert of divine pleasure, put on the vestment of human flesh and visibly sought after the long lost lamb." And almost immediately, he is back to his opening *thema*, engaged in what is called "the declaration of parts," the division of the biblical verse into its constituent members that serve as the structuring device for the sermon. And so, St. Bonaventure continues immediately to unfold the content of his sermon, saying:

> But since it is proper for the good shepherd to have toward his herd, first vigilant solicitude in guarding, then benevolent affection in sustaining or nurturing, and later prudent discretion in expanding what is necessary for the sheep proper; the proposed words [and by this he means the *thema* verse] show us the good shepherd, Christ, who is . . . commended for solicitous vigilance in the performance of the pastoral office, when it says *Good shepherd*, for the goodness of the shepherd is displayed when he keeps vigil and guards his flock; second, he is commended for benevolent breadth in the exposure of his own body, when it adds: he *lays down his life*, for there is no greater sign of love and benevolence . . . than to expose his own body to death; . . . third, he is commended for prudent discretion in the defense and liberation of his flock, not that of another, when it adds: *for his sheep*.[26]

Note that Bonaventure *could* have prefaced the "declaration of parts" with a short, introductory *prothema*, as he does in most of his other Sunday sermons, but in this case, he does not. Nor is there an invocation to prayer.

---

[26] Ibid., Sermon 23, no. 1 (pp. 278–79; translation and punctuation altered minimally).

THE BASIC STRUCTURE OF THE *SERMO MODERNUS*

With all these provisions and caveats in mind, we can say that the basic structure of the typical medieval sermon of the *sermon modernus* style looked something like this:

A) First, we get the opening "statement of the *thema*."

B) Next, we will usually get some introductory comments and, in some cases (but not always), a *prothema* with its own structuring verse, its own "declaration of parts," and an invocation to prayer.

C) Next, we return to a re-statement of the opening biblical *thema* and what is called the "declaration of parts," in which the author divides the original *thema* verse into two, three, or four parts that will serve to structure the preacher's comments to follow.

D) Finally, the preacher will expand or "dilate" upon (*dilatatio* in Latin) each of these parts in turn, keeping the order of his presentation clear by continuing to return to the words of the opening biblical *thema*.

Mulcahey provides the following example from a sermon for Sexagesima Sunday by Dominican conventual preacher Jacopo Passavanti.[27] First, we get the "statement of the *thema*," which in this case is taken from Luke 8:8—"Cecedit in terram bonam quia ortum fecit contuplum" ("[Some seed] fell on good ground, and bore fruit a hundredfold"). "After a short introduction," says Mulcahey—by which I take it she means he does *not* provide a *prothema*—Passavanti divides his opening *thema* as follows:

Cecedit // in terram bonam // quia ortum fecit contuplum.

The word *cecedit* ("some fell") Passavanti associates with the fleeting and defective condition of our human frailty. The words *in terram bonam* ("on good ground"), then, he associates in turn with "the commendable and promotive disposition of our mortality." And finally, the words *quia ortum fecit contuplum* ("for it bore fruit a hundredfold") he associates with "the delightful and refreshing perception of our happiness."

Indeed, we have seen much the same sort of division and development in each of Thomas's sermons. It was the hallmark of the *sermo modernus*

---

[27] See Mulcahey, *First the Bow is Bent in Study*, 406–07.

style. For any reader who doubts that medieval preachers could keep up this sort of division and development of a single biblical verse over and over again, sermon after sermon, for an entire year or more, there is no better example of this than Bonaventure's *Sunday Sermons*. In that volume, the reader will find fifty sermons total for the entire liturgical year, each of which fits the basic *sermon modernus* pattern we have outlined above. The conclusion is unavoidable: this was simply the way medieval preachers of the thirteenth century went about the process of preaching. They developed the art and the style until it became second-nature to them. After they had developed the skill, in fact, as we will see in later chapters, they began applying it elsewhere as well, such as all circumstances where they had to provide their listeners or readers with prologue-type materials. We will have more to say on this in due course.

DEVELOPING THE SERMON: *DIVISIO* AND *DILATATIO*

There are two separate processes involved in the development of a medieval sermon: the first is the "division" (*divisio*) of the parts, and the second is the "dilation" (*dilatatio*) of the various members set forth in the *divisio*. The preaching manuals of the thirteenth and early fourteenth centuries identify a number of possible ways in which both the original *divisio* and the subsequent *dilatatio* can be done. The lists vary somewhat, but the methods contained in these lists are usually basically the same.[28] The renowned medieval scholar Étienne Gilson claims, in his article on medieval sermons entitled "Michel Menot et la Technique du Sermon Médiéval," that it was a treatise called the *Ars concionandi* (from the Latin *concionor*, *concionari*: to deliver a public speech or, in an ecclesiastical context, to preach) that provided him with his basic insights into the methodology of the medieval sermon.[29] This particular treatise, the *Ars concionandi*,

---

[28] In this regard, one might fruitfully compare the "Thomistic" tract on preaching translated by Harry Caplan and published as "A Late Medieval Tractate on Preaching" in *Studies in Rhetoric and Public Speaking in Honor of James Albert Winans* (New York: Century, 1925), 61–90, with either of the "Franciscan" tracts we will discuss in more detail below: either the *Forma praedicandi* of Robert of Basevorn or the "Bonaventuran" *Ars concionandi*. Both the Caplan "Thomistic" tract and Robert of Basevorn's text are from the early fourteenth century, while the *Ars concionandi* is likely earlier—from sometime in the late thirteenth century.

[29] Étienne Gilson, "Michel Menot et la Technique du Sermon Médiéval," *Les Idées et Les Lettres* (Paris: Vrin, 1932), 109–54; although it was published earlier in a journal that did not survive long and is now often somewhat difficult to find, *Revue d'Histoire Franciscaine* 2.3 (1925): 301–60.

has an interesting textual history, the description of which I will relegate largely to a footnote.[30] Suffice it to say for the moment that the treatise

---

[30] The basic facts are as follows. The first two parts of the treatise were discovered in a manuscript library in Assisi by Fr. Giovanni Sbaraglia (otherwise known as Joannes Hyacinthus Sbaralea, a historian of the Franciscan Order who lived between 1687 and 1764). The introduction to the treatise indicated that it should contain three parts: the first and second dealing with *divisiones*, and the third with *dilatationes*. Unfortunately, Fr. Sbaralea could find only the first two of the three in Assisi, but the two he did find were subsequently published in 1772 by Fr. Benoit Bonelli as part of the *Supplement to the Complete Works of St. Bonaventure* (*S. Bonaventurae operum omnium supplementum*), vol. 3, col. 385. In his introduction to the treatise, Fr. Bonelli expressed regret at the imperfect quality of its second section and the complete absence of the third, but he nonetheless felt certain that the whole treatise should be traced back to St. Bonaventure himself: "de hoc S. Bonaventurae foetu genuino nullum esse dubitandi." Bonelli had no textual evidence for this claim, but he judged that both the doctrine and the style of the treatise were similar to other of Bonaventure's works and, more importantly, that it was consistent with Bonaventure's practice in his sermons. I have no comment on the first two—issues of doctrine and style—but the consistency with Bonaventure's practice in the sermons is not surprising, since he composed sermons pretty much the way everyone else did. Bonaventure's way of developing a sermon would be found very similar not only to the *Ars concionandi*, but also to Robert of Basevorn's early fourteenth century treatise on preaching and to the early fourteenth century "Thomistic" treatise translated by Harry Caplan as well (see nn. 84 and 88). These methods were common.

Subsequent to the 1772 publication of Bonelli's *Supplementum*, however, the Franciscan Fr. Fedele de Fanna (1838–1881), according to his own account, searched just about every library in Europe, going through an immense number of manuscripts of all types and from all time periods ("percorso quasi tutta l'Europa, rovistato quasi tutte le biblioteche, esaminato un'ingente quantità di codici manoscritti, e di altri documenti d'ogni specie e d'ogni temp") looking for texts relevant to his order. During this search, Fr. Fanna turned up not only a number of previously undiscovered sermons by Bonaventure, but other copies of the *Ars concionandi* containing all three parts. The only problem was that all of the manuscripts of the *Ars concionandi* Fanna uncovered were anonymous: none of them could be traced to Bonaventure himself.

What was an editor to do? Here is what the Quaracchi editors did. In 1901, when it came time to publish volume 9 (*Sermones de Tempore, de Sanctis, de B. Virgine Maria et de Diversis*) of the *Opera Omnia S. Bonaventurae* (Florence, IT: Quaracchi, 1901)—the one with all of Bonaventure's sermons—they collated together the Assisi text published by Bonelli with the newly discovered manuscripts brought back by Fanna, the former of which they published under the title "*Ars concionandi*" but placed it in an introductory section of the volume with an editor's note explaining why they considered it to be of dubious authenticity. First of all, only the Assisi manuscript contained the name of Bonaventure, while all the others were anonymous. In the experience of the Quaracchi editors, the testimony of a single manuscript attestation was often found to be unreliable. So although there was nothing to rule out Bonaventure's authorship, they could not attest to its authenticity either.

appears in the preface to volume 9 of the Quaracchi edition of the *Opera Omnia* of St. Bonaventure, although for reasons too complicated to get

---

When Charland undertook to write *Artes praedicandi: Contribution à l'histoire de la rhétorique au Moyen Age* (published 1936), he reviewed the Quaracchi volume (see Charland, *Artes praedicandi*, 30–32) and concluded that the *Ars concionandi* was not written by Bonaventure. Charland noted that the manscripts Fr. Fanna had uncovered were not written until the fourteenth and fifteenth centuries, while the manuscript uncovered in Assisi by Fr. Sbaralea was from the thirteenth. Charland speculated that perhaps the third part of the treatise had been written by a different author much later than the first two, which would account for Fr. Sbaralea finding only the first two parts in Assisi. Be that as it may, Charland doubted that any of it had been written by Bonaventure.

No authority since Charland has given a detailed defense of the treatise as authentic. Gilson published "Michel Menot et la Technique du Sermon Médiéval" originally in 1925, before Charland's book came out. In that article, he remained neutral on the question of authorship. Bougerol remained entirely silent on the issue in his 1964 *Introduction to the Works of Saint Bonaventure*. The lone defender of the authenticity of the text may well be Harry Charles Hazel, Jr., who wrote a PhD dissertation on the *Ars concionandi* in 1972—one containing, more importantly for our purposes, *an English translation of the text*. In this dissertation ("A Translation, with Commentary, of the Bonaventuran *'Ars Concionandi,'*" Washington State University, 1972), young Mr. Hazel concluded that: "a definite connection exists between Bonaventure and the first two parts of the *'Ars concionandi.'*" "Although the authenticity of the third part is more doubtful," he admits, "it is the methodological outgrowth of the first two." And yet, even Hazel was forced to add this caveat: "Whether Bonaventure actually wrote all or part of the *"Ars concionandi"* remains debatable" (17). His argument for a Bonaventuran authorship in a nutshell is this: "The strongest arguments for maintaining that the tractate accurately reflects Bonaventure's ideas on preaching are drawn from McKeon and Bonelli. McKeon underscores the consistency between Bonaventure's concept of speech and the manual on preaching. Bonelli emphasizes the correlation between Bonaventure's sermons and the Assisi manuscript. These two arguments and the uncontested fact that only Bonaventure's name is linked to most of the treatise support the claim that the famous Franciscan is primarily responsible for the treatise and that it legitimately deserves to be designated 'Bonaventuran'" (17–18). Dr. Hazel (who after graduation from Washington State went off to teach at Gonzaga University, where he still seems to be a prominent member of the graduate faculty) published a 1972 article based on his dissertation, but without the nice English translation of the treatise; see Harry Hazel, Jr., "The Bonaventuran *'Ars Concionandi,'*" *Western Journal of Speech Communication* 36.4 (1972): 241–50.

Like Gilson, I prefer to remain neutral on the issue of authorship. It would, of course, be convenient for my purposes if it could be proven that the *Ars concionandi* had been written by Bonaventure because it would show a direct connection between that text and the sermon practices of the thirteenth century mendicant friars in and around Paris. But sadly, we simply cannot be certain. As I explain above, the *Ars concionandi* serves for us merely to help illustrate the various practices. I am not arguing for a direct influence on either Thomas or Bonaventure.

into here, they considered it as being of dubious authenticity—that is to say, *not* written by Bonaventure.[31]

By the same token, whether they consider the *Ars concionandi* to be written by Bonaventure himself or not, all major scholars agree that its description of how to "divide" and "dilate" the various parts of the opening biblical *thema* correspond to Bonaventure's actual practice in his sermons. Indeed, it is interesting to note that the third part of the *Ars concionandi*—the one that will be of interest to us in what follows—is in many respects nearly identical to chapter 39 of Robert of Basevorn's influential early fourteenth century treatise, the *Forma praedicandi* (the earliest manuscript is dated 1322), the difference being that the section on the eight methods of *dilatatio* in the *Ars concionandi* is actually longer than the one in Basevorn's treatise. From a quick glance, Basevorn's chapter 39 reads as though it were a condensed, edited version of the third part of the *Ars concionandi*.[32]

Determining which text is prior and which is derivative is not essential for our present purposes, however, since I am not arguing that the *Ars concionandi* had a direct influence on Thomas's sermons. Robert of Basevorn's *Forma praedicandi* certainly had no influence on either Bonaventure or Thomas, since it was not published until some fifty years after their deaths. Rather than any direct connection, I am suggesting that these modes of *dilatatio* were commonly known among the Parisian masters of the late thirteenth century. A quick comparison of the Sunday sermons

---

[31] *Ars concionandi* (Quaracchi edition, vol. 9, 1901), 8–21. For the editor's comments on the manuscript, see in particular 7–8. For an English translation of the text, as described in the previous note, see Hazel's dissertation.

[32] Not much is known about Basevorn. The only reason we know his name at all is that he says in the introduction to his treatise: "Should anyone wish to know who and of what status is that friend to whom this work is dedicated, and who I am and what is my status . . . let him look at the capital letters [at the commencement of each chapter throughout the book] and he will learn." Those capitals spell out: *Domino Willelmo abbati de Basingweek Robertus de Basevorn* ("To Lord William, Abbot of Basingwerk, [from] Robert of Basevorn.") Unfortunately, Basevorn did not reveal his status, as was promised, so we do not know much more about him other than his name. Basingwerk was a Cistercian abbey located at the northern end of modern-day Wales, not far south of Liverpool. Basevorn was familiar with both the "Method of Paris" and the "Method of Oxford" (as he calls them), but interestingly, he does not express a preference for one over the other. For the Latin text of Robert of Basevorn's *Forma praedicandi*, see Charland, *Artes Praedicandi*, 233–323. For an English translation, see Robert of Basevorn, *The Form of Preaching*, trans. Leopold Krul, O.S.B., in *Three Medieval Rhetorical Arts*, ed. James J. Murphy (Berkeley: University of California Press, 1971), 109–215 and ch. 39, which contains the eight methods of *dilatatio* and appears on 180–84.

of Bonaventure and Thomas would show this to be the case. It is clear from the manuscripts such as the *Ars concionandi* and the *Forma praedicandi*, among others, that there were very detailed manuals instructing young preachers how to engage in *all* these methods by *at least* the early fourteenth century. Whether preachers such as Thomas and Bonaventure had manuals of the same complexity as the *Ars concionandi* and the *Forma praedicandi* in their own day, to which they could refer in order to learn the various methods of *divisio* and *dilatatio*, remains unclear.

For our present purposes, the methods of "dividing" and "dilating" a sermon we find in both the *Ars concionandi* and Robert of Basevorn's *Forma praedicandi* will serve merely as a convenient way of organizing examples from Thomas's sermons. What we are really interested in showing is how Thomas undertook to develop a whole sermon out of a single scriptural verse or two. Examining the various methods of *divisio* and *dilatatio* will show us how the medieval preacher approached his task. Going through the methods in this way will show the reader that these practices were not "accidental"—they did not "just happen"—rather, they were quite deliberate. Students will often ask teachers of poetry, for example: Did the poet actually do those things (whatever *those* things are) *consciously*, or did they just *happen* to turn out that way? Although critics can sometimes over-interpret texts and suggest too much intentionality to the author, by the same token, our study of medieval preaching techniques will show that these methods were definitely known and were either done consciously or done out of a *habitus* of practice and skill that had become second nature.

The ultimate goal of the analyses in the following two chapters, therefore, is to help the reader appreciate the artistry of Thomas's sermons by delving a bit more deeply and showing the "nuts and bolts" of how a medieval preacher was trained to develop his sermon. For this purpose, I have utilized a fairly common list of methods that appear to have been widely known and utilized in the Middle Ages in order to provide the reader with the resources to read Thomas's sermons with a certain awareness of the methods by which such works were commonly crafted.

CHAPTER 3

Divisio: Approaches to Dividing the Opening Thema

WE WILL BEGIN IN THIS CHAPTER with what is logically the first of the two processes, the *divisio*, because it is only after the opening biblical *thema* has been "divided" into its constituent parts that the "dilation" or "unpacking" of each of the parts can begin. The suggestions for how to divide a *thema* are contained in section 1 of the *Ars concionandi* and in chapter 33 of Robert of Basevorn's *Forma praedicandi*. In this chapter, we will be referring primarily (unless otherwise noted) to the material in Basevorn's *Forma praedicandi* because it is usually clearer and better organized than the parallel treatment in the *Ars concionandi*. Indeed, whereas the strength of the *Ars concionandi* is that it is filled with example after example, a feature that likely made it extremely useful for preachers (even though the examples are not always organized as effectively as one might wish), the strength of Basevorn's work is its brevity and clarity of organization, characteristics that make it especially suitable for our present purposes.[1]

---

[1] So as not to multiply footnotes needlessly, let me stipulate here that, in the sections below where I have cited examples from Robert of Basevorn's *Forma praedicandi* of the various methods of doing the *divisio*, I will be referring to material from the *Forma praedicandi*, chapter 33. On the various methods of doing "the declaration of parts," I will be using material from chapter 34. This material can be found in Latin in Thomas Charland, *Artes Praedicandi: contribution à l'histoire de la rhétorique au moyen âge*, Publications de l'Institut d'Etudes Medievales d'Ottawa 7 (Paris/Ottawa: J. Vrin/ Institute of Medieval Studies, 1936), 233–323 (the whole of Basevorn's work), and in English in Robert of Basevorn, *The Form of Preaching*, trans. Leopold Krul, O.S.B., in

Identifying Words that Fit the Occasion

According to Robert of Basevorn, the first thing the preacher should consider is the force of the words in the *thema* in relation to the topic for the day. So, for example, if the *thema* has been taken from Proverbs 14:35 ("The intelligent minister is acceptable to the king"), and if the sermon is about a learned man—say if it were the feast day of one of the Doctors of the Church—then, says Robert, one might divide the *thema* as follows: "intelligent" might be referred to his *mental perfection*; "minister" might be taken to refer to his *spiritual humility*; and "acceptable to the king" might be taken to refer to his *brotherly kindness*. What one must *not* do, however, is to select words for the *divisio* that are too similar to the words in the *thema*. So, for example, it would *not* be right to divide the *thema* above so that "intelligent" is associated with the saint's *intellectual perfection*; so that "minister" is associated with *ministerial humility*; and "acceptable to the king" is associated with *fraternal acceptance*. To repeat the words in this way, claims Robert, would show a lack of artfulness and also drain the words of the *divisio* of their force and communicative power.

We should remember that, although the medieval preacher may have *on certain occasions* been able to choose his *thema* verse from anywhere in the Bible, it seems to have been the practice among Thomas, Bonaventure, and their confreres to take the *thema* for a Sunday sermon from among the readings specified in the lectionary for that day's Mass. This would *limit* the preacher's options, but he would still have to choose just the right short verse from among all the verses for that day. The first task, it seems, was to look at the various words in each verse in order to see which ones in particular might be especially suggestive of the topic the preacher wanted to cover.

As we have seen in the case of the Sermon 5 (*Ecce rex tuus*), Thomas chose a verse that contained words that were especially fit for the occasion, Palm Sunday, words such as "king" (*rex*), "he comes" (*venit*), and "meek" (*mansuetus*). Granted, he was able to employ the other words in the verse as well—"behold" (*ecce*), "your" (*tuus*), "to you" (*tibi*)—and turn each to his purposes. But it is hard to imagine structuring a sermon around nothing more than these extraneous words: an interjection (*ecce*), a possessive adjective (*tuus*), and a dative personal pronoun (*tibi*).

So too, in Sermon 2 (*Lauda et letare*), another sermon on Advent, the key words from Zechariah 2 that obviously drew his interest were "praise"

Three Medieval Rhetorical Arts, ed. James J. Murphy (Berkeley: University of California Press, 1971).

(*lauda*), "I come" (*venio*), and "I will dwell in your midst" (*habitabo in medio tui*). And thus he divides the *thema*—"Praise and rejoice, O daughter of Zion, for behold I come, and I will dwell in your midst, says the Lord" ("Lauda et letare, filia Syon, quia ecce ego uenio et habitabo in medio tui, ait Dominus")—according to the following threefold division:

> Here the prophet does three things: (1) First, he shows the affection of the holy fathers who preceded the coming of the Saviors, continually persisting in their praises of him, where he says: "Praise and rejoice, O daughter of Zion." (2) Second, he shows the Son of God himself coming down from the heavens: "Behold I come." (3) Third, he shows him humbly appearing in human flesh: "And I will dwell in your midst."

Consider also, in this regard, the *thema* Thomas chooses for Sermon 16 (*Inveni David*), a sermon delivered, we are told, on the Feast of St. Nicholas. The *thema* is taken from Psalm 88:21: "I have found David my servant; with my holy oil I have anointed him. My hand will assist him and my arm will make him firm" ("Inueni David seruum meum, oleo sancto meo unxi eum, manus mea auxiliabitur ei et brachium meum confirmabit eum"). Now, at first glance, this particular verse might not seem especially well-suited for use in a sermon about St. Nicholas, since the verse is about King David. But as I shall discuss in more detail further on, since David is an Old Testament "type" of Christ, and Christ, similarly, is a paradigmatic "type" or "model" for all the saints, Thomas can relate David's election as a servant of God with Nicholas's election as a servant of Christ. The key words for Thomas, considered from this standpoint, therefore, seem to have been: "David, my servant" (*David servum meum*); that he is "anointed" (*unxi*) by God; that God's hand "will assist him" (*auxiliabitur*); and that his arm "will make him firm" (*confirmabit*). Thomas's *divisio* of the opening *thema* is as follows:

> From these words we can learn four praiseworthy things of this holy bishop [St. Nicholas]: (1) first, his wondrous election; (2) second, his unique consecration; (3) third, the effective execution of his task; and (4) fourth, his immovable and firm stability. His wondrous election is shown in the words: "I have found David, my servant." His special consecration is shown where it says: "I have anointed him with my sacred oil." The effective execution of his task is shown in the words: "My hand will help him." His

stable firmness is shown where it says: "and my arm will make him firm."

Note, moreover, that Thomas generally avoids repeating the words of the *thema* in his *divisiones*. So, for example, instead of associating the words "I have found David, my servant" from the *thema* verse with Nicholas "finding" God, Thomas associates "I have found David, my servant" with his *wondrous election*. So too, instead of associating the words "I have anointed him with my sacred oil" in the *thema* verse with Nicholas's "sacred anointing," he associates it with his "special consecration," and so on. Nicholas's *effective execution* of his office is shown in the words "My hand will help him." It is not that Thomas *never* repeats a word from the *thema* verse in his statement of the *divisio*, but he does generally seem to shy away from doing so, in accord with the general principles of the art.

MOVING FROM THE ORDER OF THE WORDS IN THE *THEMA* TO THE ORDER OF THE TOPICS IN THE SERMON

After the preacher has located a verse that contains several key words that will fit the occasion or the subject on which he has been assigned to preach, what then? He has to take these key words or phrases—whatever they are—and begin to turn them into an ordered discourse. The handbooks for preaching contain suggested methods and strategies for beginning this process of shaping the sermon as well.

According to Basevorn, for example, the *divisio* can be done in one of three ways: (A) according to the order of the thing done or to be done, or (B) according to the order of the constitution, or (C) according to the order of the delivery. To illustrate, he takes a *thema* from Proverbs 14:35, "an intelligent minister is acceptable to the king," and shows how the *divisio* can be made in either of the first two ways. Let us say that the three key words or phrase we have identified in this phrase are: "intelligent," "minister," and "acceptable to the king." As words in a sentence, these three have a *syntactical* order. The question is how to turn these three into a series of topics for preaching that follow some sort of *logical* order.

Divisio *According to the Order of the Thing Done or to be Done*

Consider first how a *divisio* according to the *order of the thing done or to be done* might be made. First we have the *knowledge of doing good*; this can be associated with the word "intelligent." Next, from this knowledge of the good, there may follow *suitable conversation*, that is, occasions for speaking of the good to others; this can be associated with the word "minister." And finally, from these two—knowledge of the good and suitable conversation—there will follow *gratifying remuneration*: one is enabled to gain one's heavenly reward. This last notion can be associated, finally, with the words "acceptable to the king."

Before moving on, it is worth noting that Basevorn has followed his own first piece of advice here: he did not repeat the key word of the *thema* in the statement of each member of the *divisio*. Recall that the key words were "intelligent," "minister," and "acceptable to the king." These three were *associated*, not with themselves, but with "the knowledge of doing good," "suitable conversation," and "gratifying remuneration."

Now, the first question we are likely to ask about this method of developing the content of the sermon is this: Which comes first, the key words or the order of topics one wants to treat? So, for example, in the case cited above, we might wonder how *suitable conversation* came to be associated with the word "minister." Did the preacher look at the word "minister" and say to himself, "suitable conversation," or did he look at all three and then try to force each word into an order of topics beginning with "knowledge of the good" and ending in our heavenly salvation wherein we become "acceptable to the king"? It is hard to know for certain. But it seems likely the associations worked both ways: the key words in the sentence suggested certain things to the preacher, and the various methods of *ordering* them would have suggested others. Indeed, we can imagine a preacher going back and forth several times, trying out one order and then another until he felt he had produced the list of topics he wanted to cover in the day's sermon.

What we can say is that this process had as one of its consequences the sort of odd, interesting, and creative associations we have already seen in Thomas's sermon *Ecce Rex*—say, for example, the four different circumstances in which we use the word "behold" (*ecce*). It takes a certain creativity, for example, to associate the word "minister" with the notion of *suitable conversation*. Certainly, not all ministers engaged in "suitable conversation," even in the high Middle Ages. But the relationship, although oblique, is just close enough, I would argue, to suggest the mental association, and more to the point, to make the association *memorable*. The irony involved in associating "minister" with "suitable conversation" might be just funny enough to make the congregation remember it.

Divisio *According to the Order of Constitution*

How else, then, might we have taken our three key words or phrases—in this case, "intelligent," "minister," and "acceptable to the king—and turned them into an order of topics for preaching? Another method, suggests Basevorn, is by following what he calls "the order of constitution." Let us say, for example, that one has studied the work of Maimonides and has read that "purity of life is a proximate disposition to knowledge and prophecy, and likewise to grace." The preacher might, in this case, begin with the words "minister" and "intelligent" and associate them with (1) innocence of life ("minister") and (2) the concomitant knowledge associated with this innocence ("intelligent minister") and finish by discussing the "gratifying satisfaction" that follows from both (a "satisfaction" that comes from having become "acceptable to the king").

Notice again that Basevorn has never repeated the word from the opening *thema* verse in his statement of the *divisio*. This rule clearly *forces* the preacher to make creative associations and not merely repeat the exact words of the Bible verse—in this case the words of Proverbs 14:35—over and over again. But notice as well the way in which two words can be creatively associated with one another. In our first *divisio* above, the two words "intelligent" and "minister" were not tied to one another. In this second *divisio*, however, they are.

We have seen this sort of "combination" of two topics in Thomas's sermon *Ecce rex tuus* as well, for example, when Thomas associated the two words "your" and "king" (*rex tuus*). He did not, however, associate the words "Behold the king" (*Ecce rex*) as, in other circumstances we might have expected him to do. For example, he could have said that we "behold the king" in one way when we see him in the flesh in his Incarnation, and in another way when we see him in his resurrected body, and in a third way in the Eucharist, and in a fourth way when we see him "face to face" at "the right hand of the Father" in heaven. The *sermo modernus* "rules," as we are seeing, while making some very helpful, specific *suggestions*, still also allow the individual preacher plenty of room to mix and match as he sees fit.

Divisio *According to the Order of Delivery*

What about the third type of *divisio*—according to the *order of delivery* (by which he means the order of delivery *from God*, not the delivery by the preacher in his sermon)?

Robert of Basevorn gives this example. Let us say that the *thema* in this case is taken from Psalm 118:66: "Goodness and discipline and knowledge, teach me" ("Bonitatem et disciplinam et scientiam doce me"). Obvious key words in this verse are "goodness," "discipline," "knowledge," and "teach." One possibility is to make a *divisio* into four parts, associating each word with a separate idea. But let us say, instead, that the preacher finds four parts to be too many. He might instead make the *divisio* into three parts, all three of which are things that need to be "taught" to us. Why not merely say: "goodness, discipline, and knowledge need to be taught us"? But that would be to violate the fundamental rule that the preacher should not repeat the words of the *thema* in his statement of the *divisio* because to do this would be to associate the words in the *thema* merely with themselves. Again, the rules of construction *forces* a certain creativity and *rules against* merely repeating the words of the verse in lieu of actually *preaching*. On this view, merely repeating words such as "Jesus saves us" or "I am washed in the blood of Jesus Christ!" over and over again may be dramatic—there are certain contemporary evangelical preachers who have an undeniable knack for this sort of thing—but it is not really *teaching* the congregation anything, at least from the medieval point of view. Medieval congregations clearly wanted something more.

So, the preacher starts with "goodness," "discipline," and "knowledge." What then? Well, suggests Basevorn, let us say that the preacher knows that, according to St. Augustine, grace precedes all good works and that with grace comes good will and the perfection of knowledge. The preacher could then associate each of the three elements of the *thema* with these three "stages of delivery": "goodness" is associated with *prevenient grace*; "discipline" brings to mind *obedient humility*; and *the reception of perfect truth* is associated with the word "knowledge." All three of these are what we are asking God to "deliver" to us—that is, to "teach us": *goodness* (prevenient grace), *discipline* (obedient humility), and *knowledge* (perfect truth). Notice again that, in obedience to the first rule, Robert does not associate *disciplined humility* with the word "discipline" in the *thema* verse or *knowledge* with the word "knowledge" in the *thema* verse. Instead, he associates "obedient humility" with *discipline* and "perfect truth" with knowledge. Any repetition of the words of the opening *thema* would be considered artless and sound to the congregation something like having played a false note on a musical instrument.

THOMAS'S USE OF THE THREE MODES OF *DIVISIO*

Thomas, for his part, is adept at each of these three methods of doing the *divisio*. Take, for example, the first, division according to the *order of the thing done or to be done.* Thomas makes use of this sort of *divisio,* for example, in Sermon 3 (*Abiciamus opera*), for which we have, unfortunately, only a summary. Enough survives, however, to show us the *divisio* of the opening *thema,* which is taken from his Latin version of Romans 13:12: "Abiciamus opera tenebrarum et induamur arma lucis" ("Let us throw off the works of darkness and put on the armor of light"). This was likely a somewhat simpler sermon (although, again, we do not know because we do not have the complete text) because, instead of the three or four divisions Thomas often employs, in this case, he divides his opening *thema* verse into two, dividing the verse at the obvious place: right at the conjunction. "With these words," says Thomas, the Apostle Paul disposes us to two things: we must gain, first, a "liberal abhorrence of all worldly stains and vices" and, second, "an honorable love or pursuit of heavenly virtues." The flight from vice logically comes in order before the pursuit of virtue. The first of these, the flight from vice, Thomas associates with the phrase "Let us throw off the works of darkness," and the second, the pursuit of virtue, he associates with the phrase "and let us put on the armor of light." This is a *divisio* according to the *order of the thing done or to be done.*

The second sort of *divisio* is made according to the *order of constitution or construction of a thing.* There is perhaps no better example of this method of *divisio* than Thomas's Sermon 11 (*Emitte Spiritum*), a sermon that, although preached on Pentecost, contains a long section on creation, and for which the *thema* is taken from the famous line in Psalm 104:30 that says, "Emitte Spiritum tuum et creabuntur et renovabis faciem terrae" ("Send forth your Spirit and they shall be created, and you will renew the face of the earth"). Now, if Thomas had set out to deliver a fairly simple sermon, as may have been the case (as I speculated above) with Sermon 3 (*Abiciamus opera*), which was divided into two parts at the conjunction "and," so too here, he might have chosen to divide this verse similarly into two parts: "Send forth your Spirit and they shall be created" as part one, and "you will renew the face of the earth" as part two. Or alternatively, he might have made a threefold division at each of the conjunctions: "Send for your Spirit" as part one, "and they shall be created" as part two, and "you will renew the face of the earth" as part three. But Thomas has another order of things in mind that causes him to divide the verse into *four* parts, breaking the line at some rather unexpected places: "Send out" as part one; "your Spirit" as part two; "and they will be created, and you will renew" as part three, and "the face of the earth" as part four.

Why such a strange division at such unexpected places? The answer is that Thomas has a certain *order* in mind. In this case, it is the four Aristotelian causes: the formal, final, efficient, and material causes. "We can consider four things in these words," says Thomas:

> first, the special character of the Holy Spirit; second, his mission; third, the strength of the One sent; and fourth, the receptive *materia* of this strength. For it [the opening biblical *thema*] says: "Send out"—behold, the mission; "your Spirit"—see, the Person sent; "and they will be created, and you will renew"—lo, the effect of the One sent; "the face of the earth"—see, the receptive *materia* of this effect.

The four Aristotelian causes are not stated explicitly here, but they are implied.[2] Consider the following:

1. What is the efficient or moving cause? The Spirit.
2. What is the formal cause, that is to say, "the special character" of the Spirit? "Being sent."
3. What is the final cause, that is to say, the "mission" or "purpose" of the Spirit? To create and to renew.
4. And what is the *materia* that is to be created and renewed by the Spirit? "The face of the earth," which Thomas associates with the human mind.

Dividing a *thema* verse according to the four Aristotelian causes is, I would suggest, a very compelling example of a *divisio* according to the *constitution* of a thing.

And yet, it is important that we not miss the deeper *theological* point here as well. By whom is the earth created? Thomas's answer is: by the Holy Spirit. By whom are we renewed—that is to say, by whom are we re-created? Thomas's answer is: by the same Holy Spirit who created us in the first place. This basic *theological* insight is what has caused him to include a long section on *creation* in this sermon, although it is a sermon preached on the Feast of Pentecost.

Thomas's desire to make this *theological* point explains as well why he has divided the opening *thema* verse according to the order of the four

---

2 This is usefully noted in *Thomas Aquinas: The Academic Sermons*, trans. Mark-Robin Hoogland, C.P., The Fathers of the Church: Mediaeval Continuation 11 (Washington, DC: Catholic University of America Press, 2010), 139n2. All English translation of the sermons comes from Hoogland, although I have emended the translation occasionally after consulting the Latin text in vol. 44.1 (2014) of the Leonine edition (see nn. 3–5 for further discussion).

Aristotelian causes (an order of constitution), rather than, say, according to the *order of the thing done or to be done*, which he might have done had he divided it thus: first, God "sends forth his Spirit," second, "we are created," and third, "the face of the earth is renewed." Now, since the words of the opening *thema* are never allowed in the statement of the *divisio*, the *divisio* would have had to be something along these lines: first, we receive God's prevenient grace ("God sends forth his Spirit"); then we persevere in the life of virtue ("and they shall be created"); and finally, together we establish the kingdom of heaven in his holy Church ("the face of the earth is renewed"). I include this alternative *divisio* simply to show that Thomas might have availed himself of alternative approaches. And of course, on other occasions, he does. The *sermo modernus* style allows him this sort of creativity. Even if the opening *thema* verse seems an obvious choice for a sermon preached on Pentecost, beginning as it does with "Send forth your Spirit," Thomas still has plenty of options for how to proceed when it comes to choosing how he will make the *divisio*.

The third type of *divisio*, as we saw above, was the *divisio* according to *the order of delivery* from God. A nice example of this third sort of *divisio* can be found in Thomas's Sermon 21 (*Beatus vir*), a sermon delivered on the Feast of St. Martin of Tours, for which the *thema* was taken from Psalm 83:5–6: "Beatus vir cuius est auxilium abs te; ascensiones in corde suo disposuit in ualle lacrimarum in locum quem posuit" ("Happy the man whose help is from you; he has set his heart on ascending while in the valley of tears, in the place which he has built"). As we have seen in our examples above, Thomas is creative enough, and the *sermo modernus* style allows him freedom enough, to divide this verse into two, three, or four parts, or more, depending upon the circumstances. In this case, he chooses a threefold *divisio*: (1) "Happy the man whose help is from you"; (2) "he has set his heart on ascending while in the valley of tears; and (3) "in the place which he has built."

Why this particular *divisio*? As we have seen in the example directly above (the sermon *Emitte Spiritum*), the *divisiones* are not always made at the obvious syntactical divisions in the sentence. The preacher can divide the *thema* verse in any number of ways, employing any particular grouping of words or phrases he chooses, depending upon the order of topics he wishes to cover in his sermon. So what is the order here?

Since this sermon was preached on the Feast of St. Martin of Tours, and since Martin, as a saint, is recognized as one who has been raised to the kingdom of heaven, and thus to the highest happiness, Thomas divides the *thema* verse according to the *order of delivery* of that happiness from God:

> First, we can consider the beginning of his happiness; second, the progress; and third, its endpoint. The origin or cause of his happiness was divine help, which is mentioned when it is said: "Happy the man whose help is from you." He has made progress in ascents: he advanced from one virtue to another, which is mentioned when it says: "He has set his heart on ascending." The endpoint of his happiness is the gain of eternal happiness, which is mentioned when it says: "in the place which he has built."

So step one is that Martin received divine help. And in fact, as the sermon continues, we discover that, according to Thomas, the origin or the cause of arriving at the special sort of dignity that the saints enjoy can only be divine help. Thus, in an important way, the entire sermon turns out to be about the various means by which God imparts divine help to us: He chides us, he instructs us, and finally, he takes us up into union with him. And thus, as a result of God's gracious gifts, Martin was inspired to greater and greater virtue (having been chided and instructed in faith, hope, and love) and was finally taken up into divine glory. This is a *divisio* based on the order of delivery of God's gracious gifts, culminating in his ultimate gift of union with him in the communion of saints.

DIVISIO: The Art of Relating the Parts and the Whole

Every sort of *divisio* will entail some principle of *order*. We have examined three basic methods, although there were likely others. What was important, as Robert of Basevorn informs his readers, is that the division one chooses should be so ordered that the preacher makes clear how the parts are ordered to a whole and that the division should be exhaustive and complete.[3]

---

[3]   In this regard, the reader might fruitfully compare the medieval method of *divisio* employed in the *sermo modernus* style of preaching with the method of *divisio* commonly used in the exegesis of texts. A useful article on the topic is John F. Boyle's "The Theological Character of the Scholastic 'Division of the Text' with Particular Reference to the Commentaries of Saint Thomas Aquinas," in *With Reverence for the Word: Medieval Scriptural Exegesis in Judaism, Christianity, and Islam*, ed. J. D. McAuliffe, B. D. Walfish, and J. W. Goering (Oxford, UK: Oxford University Press, 2003), 276–83. I will have more to say on this article below, but at present, it is worth noting that,

Let us say, for example, that we take the *thema* verse Robert was working with above from Proverbs 14:35, "the intelligent minister is acceptable to the king," and divide it as follows: first, "the splendor of truth by which God is celebrated in the power of one's vision" (associated with the word "intelligent"); next is "the course of purity by which one lives with affection" (associated with the word "minister"); and finally, "hope for the sweetness of charity" (a hope inspired by the purity by which one lives) by which one is actually rewarded (and thus becomes "acceptable to the king"). Notice that, in this *divisio*, the powers of vision and feeling—that is, reason and will—are the two basic parts of a whole—namely, the soul. Similarly, the preacher could point out that it is *faith* that disposes us to the knowledge of truth; *hope* that adds certitude to the life of purity; and *charity* that is the reward of the king that brings us to our ultimate end with him in heaven. What is crucial is that the preacher make his *divisio* in such a way that the parts clearly "fit" into a structured "whole" and that the list of parts is complete. If, for example, the preacher had mentioned only faith and hope, the congregation would be asking, "Where is charity?" Similarly, one could make a *divisio* according to the three sides of a triangle or according to the four corners of the earth—north, south, east, and west—but what one *could not* do is mention only two sides of a triangle or only three of the directions: north, south, and east.

So, for example, if we were to take the same *thema* verse and make the same threefold *divisio*, the preacher might then go on to describe this threefold *divisio* using the following visual analogy. The knowledge of truth is first because it is, as it were, the *foundation* from which doing good works begins. The cleanliness of purity and humility are, as it were, *the walls* by which the spiritual edifice grows. And the satisfaction of sincerity is, as it were, *the roof* by which the eternal reward is completed. The relation of part to whole is clear: foundation, walls, and roof. It would be a mistake, however, if the preacher were to mention only the foundation and the walls. For, the question hanging in the air in the minds of his listeners

---

as Boyle points out, a scholastic "division of the text" always involves the articulation of a "theme that provides a conceptual unity to the text" and always "begins with the whole and then continues through progressive subdivisions, every verse stand[ing] in an articulated relation not only with the whole but ultimately with every other part, division, and verse of the text" (276). "For the scholastic division of the text to work," he adds, "the unity must be an intrinsic conceptual unity; there must be a unifying idea in the light of which the whole can be seen and, still more important, each part can be understood" (277). In other words, the parts must fit together correctly and the whole they come together to form must be *complete*.

would be: "Where is the roof?" The effect would be a bit like getting up to the "Amen" of a hymn and singing only the "A," then trailing off before closing the loop with the "men." The result would leave the listeners feeling very unsatisfied.

A nice example of this sort of insistence on "completeness" can be found, for example, in Thomas's Sermon 1 (*Veniet desideratus*), a sermon for Advent, for which the opening *thema* verse has been taken from Haggai 2:8: "Veniet desideratus cunctis gentibus et implebit domum istam Gloria" ("He who is desired by all the nations together will come, and he will fill this house with glory"). How will Thomas decide to divide it? There are two clauses, but three verbs. Thomas chooses to make the *divisio* into three parts: (1) "he will come"; (2) "he" is the one "who is desired by all the nations," (note that in the Latin original *veniet*, "he will come," appears in the sentence before *desideratus cunctis gentibus*, "he who is desired by all the nations"); and finally (3) "he will fill this house with glory."

What order does he choose to use? In this case, it is the *order of delivery from God*. Here is what he says:

All the saints always from the beginning of the world longed for and desired the coming of the Savior. And this is shown well and plainly in the saying mentioned [the *thema*] in which the Prophet [Haggai] shows three things, in this order: (1) first, he shows it is God's Son himself who is coming down from the heavens: "he will come"; (2) second, he shows He is the one who mercifully fulfills the desires of the Fathers [patriarchs]: "who is desired by all the nations together"; (3) third, he shows He is the one who freely bestows his pleasing benefit [upon us]: "and he will fill this house with glory."

If we take a step back from our discussion of the technical process of *divisio* for a moment and look at what Thomas has just said about the verse from Haggai, we can see that it makes plenty of sense from the standpoint of a Christian exegete. The verse states: "He who is desired by all the nations together will come, and he will fill this house with glory." Who, from the Christian standpoint, is the one "desired by all the nations" who has "come" to "fill this house [the Temple] with glory"? That, of course, would be Jesus Christ, the Messiah, the one hoped for by all the patriarchs and prophets, whose promises he fulfills. Indeed, Christ's body now fully realizes the Temple's foreshadowing role of making God's glory *present* and *visible* to his people. From the point of view of the Christian exegete, therefore, we might re-state the passage from Haggai this way: Christ, the one whom all the patriarchs hoped for and desired to see, has come and has filled his people (the Church) with his gracious gifts. This is not an especially odd message for a Christian preacher to be delivering in a sermon during Advent.

But Thomas is not yet finished with his opening *thema* verse. Along with this first *declaration of the parts*—a technical term about which we will have more to say in a moment—he offers two others, the first of which is ordered *according to the constitution of the thing*, and the second ordered *according to the thing to be done.*

We will begin with the first, the order *according to the constitution of the thing*, in which Thomas covers, in turn, the "lowliness" of the manner of Christ's coming ("he will come"), the "necessity" of his coming in view of the human race ("he is desired by all the nations"), and finally, the "utility" of his coming (namely, to "fill this house with glory"—that is to say, to bestow upon his people his gracious gifts).

But building upon these first two *declarations of the parts*, Thomas adds a third. Once we have recognized that Christ is the one who has "come," sharing with us our lowly condition, and that he is the one who was "desired by all the patriarchs" and prophets because his presence and work among us is "necessary" for us to be reconciled with God the Father, and that the "utility" of his coming is that he offers us his gracious gifts leading to God's glory, then, given this threefold recognition, we must *respond* in ways that are fitting. "We should," says Thomas, "prepare a warm welcome for him," of which we are reminded by the words "he will come." Second, we should "focus our desire on him," of which we are reminded by the words "he who is desired by all the nations." And finally, we should "receive the benefit offered," of which we are reminded by the words "and he will fill this house with glory."

Thus we have two more threefold divisions following the first. We get, first: (1) the lowliness of his coming; (2) the necessity of his coming; and (3) the utility of his coming. This is actually an example of a method we will discuss in more detail below: dividing according to participles. The second set of divisions involves the images of (1) welcoming the Lord, (2) focusing our desire on him, and (3) receiving the benefit offered by him. Notice that, in all of these divisions, there is a nice sense of completion: here is the one who comes; here is why he comes; and here is what he achieves. Or we welcome him; we focus our desire on him; and we receive his benefits. Thomas never leaves the listener hanging with a series of divisions that seems incomplete. He never chooses to divide his *thema* so that the result is a series where we get only steps one and two—Christ comes; Christ dies—without finishing the triad somehow. Step three is "Christ rises" or "Christ bestows his gifts" or "we gain our heavenly beatitude."

THE "DECLARATION OF THE PARTS"

With this set of considerations, however, we have moved from the rules of *divisio*, which are covered in chapter 33 of Robert's *Forma praedcandi*, to the rules covering what is called "the declaration of parts," treated in his chapter 34.[4] The difference between the two can be a bit confusing. Strictly speaking, *divisio* is simply choosing where to divide the opening *thema* verse and deciding how to take this order of words or phrases and turn it into an order of topics on which to preach. The "declaration of parts" is when the preacher actually states or announces those topics. Thus, strictly speaking, in every example of a *divisio* we examined above, what we were *reading* was "the declaration of the parts." There was an art to formulating these parts verbally, just as there was an art to choosing the right *thema* and making an appropriate *divisio* of it to serve the purposes of the occasion.

Phrases Used to Introduce the Declaration

The simplest part of the art of "declaration of the parts" was choosing the appropriate phrase to introduce them. One finds a list of such expressions in the *Forma praedicandi*, among which are simple passive verbs such as "it is noted," "it is implied," "it is taught," or "it is suggested." If the reader will take the time to look over the Appendix at the back of this volume, he or she will find that Thomas rarely uses expressions quite this simple, but they are similar. In Sermon 1 (*Veniet desideratus*), for example, he begins his "declaration" with the words "this is shown well and plainly in the saying mentioned in which the Prophet shows three things"; in Sermon 2 (*Lauda et letare*), we get, "Here the prophet does three things"; in Sermon 3 (*Abiciamus opera*): "The Apostle [Paul] . . . with these words, or in these words, disposes us to two things"; in Sermon 4 (*Osanna filio David*): "In these words we can consider three things to the praise of our Savior;" in Sermon 5 (*Ecce rex tuus*): "We can see four things in the verse mentioned

---

[4] As noted above, so as not to multiply footnotes needlessly, I am simply going to stipulate in advance that all the material employed below from the *Forma praedicandi* is taken from chapter 34.

above"; in Sermon 6 (*Celum et terra transibunt*): "Our most providential and meek Savior commended these words"; and so on. In some cases, our English translator, Fr. Hoogland, has chosen to translate what are passive constructions in the original Latin in the active voice in English. The use of the passive voice—"it is noted," "it is commended," "it is expressed"—is very common in these declarations, however.

Parallelism of Construction

Next, however, after finding an appropriate introductory phrase (e.g., "in these words, three things are expressed by the prophet"), what comes next is the listing of the topics to be associated with each of the various parts of the opening *thema* verse. The rules for "declaring" these parts were not entirely dissimilar from the rules governing "parallelism" in English grammar today. Most readers will know that it is appropriate in English to say, for example, "He likes running, hiking, and swimming," but *not* "He likes running, hiking, and *to swim*." Nor is it acceptable to say, for example, "He likes to run, to hike, and swimming." The individual phrases in the list must be "parallel" in their construction.

So too, in the "declaration of parts," a medieval preacher had to formulate each of the parts according to an acceptable pattern of parallel verbal constructions. A common way of achieving the necessary parallelism was to set up a pattern based on employing similar constructions using one of the parts of speech: adjectives, verbs, adverbs, nouns, participles, or prepositions. According to Robert, pronouns, conjunctions, and interjections did not normally work well (although Thomas was able to do pretty amazing things with "Behold" in Sermon 5).

Using a List of Dual Adjectives

So, for example, one way of "declaring the parts" of the *divisio* would be by using a series of adjectives, such as (to use Robert of Basevorn's example) if the preacher were to say, "In these words we are taught, first, *honorable excellence*; second, *compensative patience*; and third, *ineffable friendship*." The use of a descriptive set of adjectives was recommended and seems to have been common: not just *excellence*, but *honorable excellence*; not just *patience*, but *compensative patience*, and so on.

One can see a good example of this sort of "declaration of the parts" in Thomas's Sermon 7 (*Ecce ego mitto*), which, although we have it only in partial form, has a fully preserved *divisio*. The *thema* for this sermon on the Second Sunday of Advent is taken from Matthew 11:10—"Ecce ego mitto angelum meum ante faciem tuam" ("Behold I send my angel before your face"). "In these words," says Thomas, "three aspects of the gracious arrival of the Savior are described: (1) the *marvelous estimation* of God the Father—in the words 'Behold, I send'; (2) the *obliging ardor* of the precursor—in the words 'my angel'; and (3) the *marvelous kindness* of the Savior—in the words 'before your face.'"

So too, in Sermon 6 (*Celum et terra transibunt*), another of Thomas's sermons for which we have only a summary, in "the declaration of the parts" Thomas takes the opening *thema* verse, "Heaven and earth will pass away [but my words will not pass away]," and makes a threefold *divisio* focusing on the three key words: "heaven," "earth," and "will pass away." Here, then, is how he formulates his "declaration of the parts":

> By the noun "heaven," the *marvelous loftiness* of the heavenly man is mentioned; (2) by the noun "earth," the *deserved lowliness* of the worldly person is mentioned; and (3) by the verb "will pass," he carefully refers to a distinctive quality of each.

Notice in both this example and the one above from Sermon 7 that it does not matter whether the word in the opening *thema* verse was a noun, an adjective, or a verb. When Thomas formulates the "declaration of the parts," the rules of parallelism demand that each of the words or phrases in the "declaration of parts" must be the same part of speech (in these examples, all were dual adjectives).

Using a Series of Verbs or Prepositional Phrases

Another way of crafting the "declaration of parts" may involve employing a series of verbs, such as (to use Robert of Basevorn's examples): "The first perfects oneself as oneself; the second draws the love of others; and the third makes one happy with God." Another verbal series is: "The first commands the beginning by which there is a start; the middle by which there is progress; and the third, the end by which there is an exit." These are general examples, of course, into which the preacher can plug his own content.

We have already seen an example of Thomas making use of a "declaration of parts" based on a series of verbs in Sermon 1 (*Veniet desideratus*) above. As we saw, Thomas takes his opening *thema* verse from Haggai 2:8, "He who is desired by all the nations together will come, and he will fill this house with glory" ("Veniet desideratus cunctis gentibus et implebit domum istam Gloria"), and makes a threefold *divisio*: (1) "he will come" (*veniet*), (2) "he" is the one "who is desired by all the nations" (*desideratus cunctis gentibus*), and finally, (3) "he will fill this house with glory" (*implebit domum istam Gloria*). As we also saw, Thomas takes this threefold *divisio* and uses it as the basis for three distinct "declarations of the parts." In the first "declaration," Thomas employs three verbs: first, it is God's Son himself who *is coming down* from the heavens; second, he is the one who mercifully *fulfills* the desires of the Father; and third, he is the one who freely *bestows* his pleasing benefit. In the second "declaration," however, he will use a series of descriptive nouns rather than verbs: "In the first part the *lowliness* of the coming one or of the coming is shown; in the second the *necessity* of the coming in view of the human race; in the third the *utility* of the coming in view of the gift offered." And then, finally, in the third "declaration" that follows immediately after the first two, he goes back to using *verbal phrases* again: "The first brings to the fore that we should *prepare a warm welcome* for him; the second that we should *focus our desire* on him; the third that we should *receive the benefit offered* from him.

There is also a hint here in this last declaration of another method of declaring the parts: using *prepositions*. Robert of Basevorn provides a simple example based on the famous verse from *Ecclesiasticus*, "Vanity of vanities, all is vanity." One can formulate the declaration of parts of this *thema* verse in this way, says Robert: "All things were subject to vanity, namely those which were made *for* man; in those which were made *by man*; and in those which were made *in* man." In this example, Robert keeps the verb constant throughout while varying only the prepositions. In that last "declaration of parts" from Sermon 1 (*Veniet desideratus*) above, Thomas varied both. Allow me to re-write it here with the italics on the prepositional phrases rather than the verbs: "The first brings to the fore that we should prepare a warm welcome *for him*; the second that we should focus our desire *on him*; the third that we should receive the benefit offered *from him*." Which of the two sorts of *divisio* would have come to the fore would have depended a great deal, one imagines, upon the verbal delivery of the preacher and the words he decided to emphasize or not.

Thomas's Sermon 1 (*Veniet desideratus*) thus provides us with a fascinating and instructive example of the different sorts of content a preacher can cover with the same *divisio* by employing different ways of constructing the "declaration of the parts." As the reader may recall, I used the sermon *Veniet desideratus* above as an example of the general principle that a *divisio* must be "complete," that it must include all the parts and relate each of them conceptually to the central theme or unified whole. What is especially interesting in this regard, now that we have been able to examine the sermon in terms of its "declaration of parts," is not only that he uses three different "declarations of the parts" in the *same sermon*, but that he is also able to relate all three of them to the same *divisio* in such a way as to keep a coherent message going throughout. For readers who prefer diagrams, I have summarized the content of the sermon and the complex interlocking relations between its various parts in the following table.

Thema (Haggai 2:8)	He will come	Desired by all nations	He will fill this house with glory
Divisio according to order of delivery	God's Son himself is the one coming down from heaven	He mercifully fulfills the desires of the patriarchs	He freely bestows his pleasing benefits
Divisio according to constitution of the thing	The lowliness of his coming is shown	The necessity of his coming in view of the human race	The utility of his coming in terms of the gift offered
Divisio according to the thing to be done	We should prepare him a warm welcome	We should focus our desire on him	We should receive the benefit offered

In all the examples we have examined thus far, the "declaration of parts" has involved a very identifiable parallelism: a series of adjectives in the first set of examples and a series of verbs and/or prepositions in the second. I take it that by now the reader will have gotten the basic idea of what is involved, so I will not belabor the point further by supplying similar examples of parallel sets of adverbs and participles.

There are two other, somewhat more complex, methods of formulating the "declaration of parts," however, that do *not* involve the same sort of obvious parallelism according to parts of speech. The first employs various parts of speech and is sometimes described as the "who, what, when, where, and why" method. The other is based on the properties of the noun or nouns in the *thema*, a method that, although it at first might seem as though it would be as simple as using a series of adjectives or verbs, turns out to be, as we shall see, an especially complicated way of formulating the "declaration" and one that can yield some of the most fascinating results. We will begin in what follows with the first. Getting a taste of the second will require a bit more space—and a great deal more mental concentration.

Using Various Cases: Who, What, When, Why

As we have seen, the most common method of formulating the "declaration of parts" involves using a series of phrases using words all of one type, whether it be verb, adverb, adjective, or participle. Take, for example, the *thema* we were considering above from Robert of Basevorn's *Forma praedicandi* taken from Proverbs 14:35: "The intelligent minister is acceptable to the king." Let us say, furthermore, that we make the following threefold *divisio*: "minister," "intelligent," and "acceptable to the king." We could then formulate the "declaration of the parts" either as a series of descriptive nouns—"minister" might be taken to refer to a person's *spiritual humility*; "intelligent" might be referred to his *mental perfection*; and "acceptable to the king" might be taken to refer to his *brotherly kindness*—or, alternatively, as a series of nouns with a modifying adjective: in which case, "minister" might refer to an *innocence of life*; "intelligent" might refer to the greater *knowledge following from this innocence*; and "acceptable to the king," finally, might be taken as referring to the *gratifying satisfaction* that follows from both.

But we could also do the *divisio* this way: we could describe the order in terms of categories such as who, what, when, why, and the like. We can say what kind of man a priest ought to be (namely, *intelligent)*, what he should do for others (*minister)*, and whom he should please by this ("acceptable to the king," that is, to Christ).

We have already seen a good example of this approach in chapter 1 above with Thomas's Sermon 5 (*Ecce rex tuus*). As the reader may recall, Thomas took the opening *thema* from Matthew 21:5, "Ecce rex tuus venit tibi mansuetus" ("Behold your king comes to you, meek"), and divided it as follows: the manifestation of Christ's coming is associated with the word "Behold" (*what)*; the one who is coming is associated with the words "your king" (*who)*; the benefit of his coming with the words "he comes for you" (*why)*; and the way of his coming with the word "meek" (*how)*.

Notice that this sort of *divisio* is not quite the same as the "declaration of the parts" made according to an *order of delivery* using a series of *verbs* and accompanying *adverbs*, which it would have been if Thomas had said, for example: first, Christ *comes humbly* in the flesh; second he was *crucified cruelly* and *rose gloriously* to the right hand of the Father; third, from there he *delivers us mercifully* from sin; and finally, he *raises us up exaltedly* to eternal life. Thomas would have been relatively free to make this sort of *divisio* had he wished. But for whatever reason, he decided to emphasize, during that particular Advent sermon, the different senses of Christ's "coming": his coming in the Incarnation; his coming into our hearts and minds; and finally, his coming at the end of time. As I have tried to make clear, the medieval preacher had plenty of options, even when he was dealing with a single biblical verse.

Making Use of the Properties of Nouns

Along with a series of adjectives, verbs, and adverbs, however, a preacher could also utilize the properties or attributes of *nouns*. Robert of Basevorn's example of the method is designed for a sermon on the Trinity, for which the preacher might employ the following declaration of parts: "In the first [word or phrase from the *thema*], there is a likeness to the *wisdom* of the Son; by the second, we understand the *clemency* of the Holy Ghost; and by the third, the *power* of the Father. The relevant nouns in this example are "wisdom," "clemency," and "power." Notice, moreover, that by linking these three with the Son, the Holy Spirit, and the Father, the preacher has made a nice, complete series, which he is of course supposed to do.

Indeed, according to Robert, it is important that the preacher be attentive to the specific attributes and properties of the nouns he is using. Notice, for example, if one were using the opening *thema* "The intelligent minister is acceptable to the king," that the word in the verse is "intelligent," not "learned"; that it is a "minister," not "*magister*" (teacher); and that it says "*acceptable* to the king," not "rejected." If there were different words in the *thema* verse, this would necessitate a different declaration of parts.

Robert provides further examples based on a *thema* drawn from Ezra 32:7, "I will cover the sun with a cloud." One could set up a threefold *divisio* based on a metaphorical appropriation of the properties of the nouns in this way, says Robert: "First, the sun shines alone with the gravity of law and judges; but later it comes under the cloud by the kindness of the Incarnation; and finally at the judgment it is covered with the equity of the sentence, because it does not respect the person [that is the status] of the man." Clearly, if the *thema* verse had used the image of the moon rather than the sun, or if the sun had not been said to be "covered with a cloud," but was shining hot in the middle of the day, or if the sun were not covered by a cloud but instead eclipsed by the moon, then the declaration of parts would have had to be completely different and the new declaration would likely not be associated with the relationship between the law, the Incarnation, and status of mankind in the same way.

But Robert's are all fairly simple examples, as is appropriate in a textbook for beginning preachers. Let me suggest that if we really want to see the kind of results a preacher can achieve using the properties of the nouns in his *thema* verse, we should turn to one of Thomas's most involved and theologically sophisticated sermons and its accompanying *collatio*: Sermon 18 (*Germinet terra*).

USING THE PROPERTIES OF NOUNS: THOMAS'S PROFOUND REFLECTIONS ON THE BIRTH OF THE VIRGIN AND THE EXALTATION OF THE CROSS

Sermon 18 (*Geminet terra*) begins with a *thema* verse taken from Genesis 1:11, "Germinet terra herbam uirentem et proferentem semen, lignumque pomiferum faciens fructum" ("Let the earth sprout forth the green plant that brings forth seed, and the fruit tree that bears fruit"). Though one might not have guessed it from the *thema* verse alone, this sermon was designed to commemorate two important feasts in conjunction with one another: the Feast of the Nativity of the Blessed Virgin Mary and the Feast of the Exaltation of the Cross. The first half, the sermon during the day, seems to have been delivered on the first Sunday following the Feast of the Nativity of Mary (September 8, which would have fallen on a Tuesday in 1271). It is very clear from the *collatio* delivered at vespers later that same evening, moreover, that the next day was to be the Feast of the Exaltation of the Cross (September 14).[5] The only year during Thomas's time in Paris when September 13 fell on a Sunday was in 1271, which is why this sermon has been dated to that year.[6]

Although these historical details may seem minor (and perhaps a bit onerous), I have included them here because they are necessary to appreciate the diversity-within-an-overarching-unity Thomas achieves by means of his *divisio* of this single *thema* verse. What is truly amazing, as we will see, is how Thomas was able, by means of this rhetorical device, to transition seamlessly from his meditations on the birth of Mary in the morning's sermon into his reflections on the Exaltation of the Cross later that same day at vespers. He accomplishes this transition by "dividing" the

---

[5] For a discussion of the relationship between the sermon and its accompanying *collatio*, see my comments in chapter 1. Suffice it to say for now that this practice was due to a University of Paris regulation. Why this regulation existed is not entirely clear.

[6] See Hoogland, *Academic Sermons*, 261n1.

opening *thema* verse into the two objects that the earth is said to "sprout forth": "the green plant that brings forth seed" (the first clause) and "the fruit tree that bears fruit" (the second clause). "The Most High has raised from the earth two remedies for us," says Thomas: first, "the green plant bringing forth seed," and second, "the fruit-bearing tree." The rest of the morning's sermon will be dedicated to unfolding the first of these, "the green plant bringing forth seed," which we will soon discover refers to Mary. And then, in the evening's *collatio* address at vespers, Thomas will be able to pick up right where he left off that morning with the second of these, "the fruit-bearing tree," which refers, as the reader may already have guessed, to the Cross of Christ.

The Morning's Sermon: "The Green Plant that Brings Forth Seed"

Let us begin with the first of these, "the green plant that brings forth seed," and consider the sort of theological content Thomas is able to adduce from this phrase by associating ideas with the properties of this plant.

Mary is called a "plant," says Thomas, because of her *humility*; she is called "green" because of her *virginity*; and she is described as "bringing forth seed" because of her *fruitfulness*. Of the three, the association of the word "plant" with the virtue of *humility* might seem the most far-fetched. But Thomas explains that, with regard to the properties of plants, we should take note of three things: first, that a plant is short in height compared to bushes and trees; second, that a plant is slender and pliant; and third, that plants bring health.

With regard to the first, says Thomas, "in the littleness of a humble plant the humility of Mary is commended." And if we presume (as ancient doctors did) that "opposites are cured by opposites," since man was condemned by pride, represented here by the "tallness" of the trees, so too it was necessary that the human race should be shown humility—in this instance, by Mary—as part of its cure. In addition, adds Thomas:

> It is amazing that a tree is highly elevated from the earth and yet most firmly fixed in the earth. A plant, however, only clings a little to the earth, and its roots are just under the surface. In a similar way a proud man's heart is pinned to the earth, and he cannot come loose from the earth, although he makes himself very big and is elevated high. On the other hand, a [lowly or] humble man does not have anything on earth; therefore, his heart is easily re-

moved from the earth. So in this way Mary is compared with a plant in regard to her moderation.[7]

Second, a plant is not hard, but pliant. So too, a heart is called "pliant" when it easily gives in. But there are two circumstances in which the heart can "give in": one is when the heart gives in to unnatural vices; the other is when it submits itself naturally to virtue. Mary is pliant in the second way. Indeed, says Thomas, "the natural order requires that a lower thing give in to an action of a higher thing."[8] And since Mary was obedient to God, she is a model of obedience, and thus also of humility.

The third property of plants Thomas associates with Mary, finally, is that they "bring health." So too, Mary "brings health" to a world of sinners. But it is also crucial to remember that the image of the plant was associated with Mary's *humility*, and by extension, as we saw above, with her *obedience* to God's will. And thus it is precisely in her humility and in her obedience to God's will that Mary "brings health" to us. The *strength* of the medicine, ironically, is exhibited in Mary's lowly weakness (in earthly terms) and her willingness to submit herself to higher things while steadfastly resisting the lower "earthly" vices, such as pride, which causes those who suffer its influence to presume to raise themselves high above others, thinking to "overshadow" them, although their roots are planted deeply in the "earth," showing excessive concern for "earthly" affairs and "earthly" regard.

It is worth recalling that this entire encomium of Mary's humility has been generated out of associations Thomas has made with the single word "plant" from the opening *thema* verse from Genesis 1:11: "Let the earth sprout forth the green *plant* that brings forth seed, and the fruit tree that bears fruit." If the reader has been paying attention to how the *sermo modernus* system works, he or she would rightly conclude that there is a lot more of this sermon yet to go. Not only has Thomas yet to finish his associations with the word "green" and the phrase "brings forth seed" from the first part of the sentence, he has the entire second part of the sentence to get through as well, "[Let the earth sprout forth] the fruit tree that bears fruit," which he will do at vespers later that night.

It is also worth noting that Thomas might have used the same *divisio*—"plant," "green," and "bringing forth seed"—and decided instead upon a different sort of "declaration of parts" to achieve a different effect.

---

[7] Sermon 18 (*Geminet terra*), Hoogland, *Academic Sermons*, 261.

[8] Ibid. (Hoogland, *Academic Sermons*, 262).

So, for example, he might have employed a series of dual adjectives and declared that Mary is said to be a "plant" because of her "obedient humility," "green" because of her "perpetual Virginity," and "brings forth seed" because of her "fruitful fertility." This latter sort of "declaration of the parts" likely would have resulted in a much shorter sermon. Using the properties of the nouns allows Thomas to go into greater detail and to make use of more concrete and in many ways more arresting imagery.

Consider, in this regard, the next word in the *divisio*: "green" (*virentem*)—which comes right *after* the word "plant" (*herbam virentem*) in the original Latin. Mary was said to be a "plant" because of her *humility*. She is called "green," says Thomas, because of her *virginity*. As Thomas had three properties of a "plant" that he associated with Mary's *humility*, so too he offers three properties of a *green* plant that suggests Mary's *virginity*.

First, green plants are green, says Thomas, because they have received plenty of moisture (*humidum*). By what is the greenness of Mary's virginity nurtured? "By heavenly love," answers Thomas. The image Thomas uses here is striking. Instead of declaring that the greenness is the result of the plants getting plenty of rain (*pluvia*) falling from heaven to earth, as we might have expected, instead he uses a much gentler image: green plants receive plenty of "moisture" (*humidum*). The word Thomas uses here is not the Latin word for "dewfall," but the image is similar. The sense the listener gets is that of a quiet, hidden coming of dewfall, a "moisture" whose coming is unseen, just as the manna came quietly from heaven to earth during the evening while the Jewish people were wandering in the wilderness, and just as the Savior came quietly to a young virgin in an out-of-the-way town at the edges of the Roman empire (see Exodus 16 and Luke 1).[9] The angel announced to Mary that the Holy Spirit would "come upon" (*superveniet*) her and the power of the Most High would "overshadow" (*obumbrabit*) her, to which Mary replied: "let it be done to me according to your word" ("fiat mihi secundum verbum tuum"; see Luke 1:35,

---

[9] Readers acquainted with the Roman Catholic Mass may recall that, in what is known as the "Second Eucharistic Prayer," there is a beautiful passage during the *epiclesis*—that is, the "invocation" or "calling down" of the Spirit—that reads: "Make holy these gifts, we pray, by sending down your Spirit upon them like the dewfall." A deeper appreciation of this image would involve understanding the profound theological connections within salvation history between (A) the dewfall that falls upon the camp of the Jewish people bringing to them the manna in the desert, (B) the Holy Spirit "overshadowing" Mary at the Incarnation, whereby the Word becomes flesh in Mary's womb, and (C) the "calling down" of the Holy Spirit upon the gifts of bread and wine offered on the altar that will become the Body and Blood of Christ.

38). God's grace and God's love had "watered" the plant quietly for years, preparing Mary for her role and for her profound "yes" to God's plan. "Virginity is the result of God's grace with the freedom of the free decision," says Thomas. And no one exhibited the presence of this grace better than Mary. And thus of her it is said: "Hail Mary, *full of grace.*"

Secondly, in the greenness of green plants, says Thomas, we see a "beauty that delights." And what makes "a beauty that delights"? A proper order and harmony. The proper order of humankind, according to Thomas, is that the flesh should be subject to the spirit. And since, in the Blessed Virgin, nothing was disordered, neither in action nor in affection—since she did not have the first movement leading to sin—she had in her "greenness" *a beauty that delights.*

Finally, in greenness, there is *utility.* As long as a plant is green, there is hope that it will produce fruit. "In a similar way," says Thomas, "someone who is green through virginity produces the fruit of love [*caritas*], but when he shrivels through concupiscence, his works are fruitless in view of eternal life." But since Mary had the "greenness of virginity" in a most excellent way, she produced amazing "fruit"—not only spiritual fruits, such as love, joy, and peace, but also indeed *physical* fruit: the fruit of her womb, Jesus.

Mentioning the "fruit" that Mary's greenness (her virginity) produced allows Thomas to transition smoothly into the last element of his threefold *divisio*: Mary is not merely a "green plant"; she is a green plant that "brings forth seed" (*proferentem semen*). This image from the opening *thema* verse affords Thomas the occasion to ask: What kind of seed is this? As has been his custom so far, he provides a threefold reply. It is (1) holy seed, (2) virtuous seed, and (3) necessary seed. Something is "holy" because it is from God, and since Christ is from God, and indeed *is* God, the seed Mary brings forth is most holy. It is a "virtuous seed" (*semen virtuosum*) because it is compared with the mustard seed that, although it is the tiniest seed, produces a great tree.[10] So also, says Thomas, "the little seed" is Christ who, although he was "little" on the Cross, grew so big that he filled heaven and earth. And finally, Christ is a "necessary seed." For, as St. Peter says, "There is no salvation in anything else, and no other name is given to the people in which we are to be saved" (Acts 4:12).

---

[10] In this particular instance, I think Thomas is using the Latin *virtuousum* not merely in the sense of "good" or "virtuous," but also in the sense of having a power that allows its bearer to achieve "excellence" and actualize the potencies of its nature fully. Recall that the Latin *virtus* is the translation of what, in Aristotle's Greek, would have been *aretē* (ἀρετή), which means "excellence."

Thus has Thomas moved deftly from praise of Mary to praise of the fruit of her womb Jesus, a rhetorical strategy that not only is theologically appropriate but also will serve him well as he makes the transition in his *collatio* address later that evening into a discussion of Christ's Cross in conjunction with the phrase "the fruit-bearing tree" from the opening *thema* verse. The theological point is this: Mary *participates in* Christ's redemptive act—not only does she give birth to Christ, but we will hear about her again shortly in Thomas's *collatio* standing at the foot of the Cross. But Mary is also the beneficiary of the redemptive grace won for mankind by Christ's sacrificial death on the Cross. Her "yes" to God is *made possible by* God's prevenient grace that prepares and nourishes the life within her (her "greenness") to be able to say "Let it be done to me according to your word"—an especially dramatic statement, given that she will in fact bear in her womb *the Word made flesh*. Thus, Thomas's praise of Mary is not merely a praise of her; it is also always a praise of her son, Our Lord Jesus Christ.

"Amazing is this plant, and amazing its offspring," says Thomas in his closing summation, in which he is able to recap nearly all of the major points he had hit upon in the sermon above. What is the "earth" that "sprouts forth the green plant that brings forth seed"? This "earth," says Thomas, "is the human nature destitute of the moisture of grace," thus recalling his discussion above about the "greenness" of the "green plant." The earth was like a desert, desiccated and without life. "Then how could it bring forth a plant?" asks Thomas. Surely it could not—not by its own powers alone, certainly. It has to be "watered" by God's love and God's grace.

So too, this earth was "arid" because of the "concupiscence of sin." Thomas had several times in his sermon contrasted the "fruitfulness" of Mary's love (*caritas*) with the aridity of concupiscence, saying: "just as every plant withers because of fire or the sun, so too the concupiscence of the flesh makes the greenness of the virginity wither." And so too, later, he says, "In a similar way someone who is green through virginity produces the fruit of love (*caritas*), but when he shrivels through concupiscence, his works are fruitless in view of eternal life." Thus, when a man becomes "dry through the fire of concupiscence," he is no longer "useful" for anything but, like the weeds that have been separated from the wheat, to be thrown into the fire and burned. And yet, "because it was arid," says Thomas, "the Holy Spirit has made it moist."

In addition, this earth was the "lowest," says Thomas, because God created heaven above and the earth underneath (Proverbs 25:3). So how has the earth "put forth" the green plant? Here is where Thomas puts our opening *thema* verse back into its original context. In Genesis 1:11, it says "And God said: 'Let the earth put forth the green plant.'" In other words, it is through God's *Word* that the earth "put forth" the plant that bore fruit. "Thus we read in Proverbs 9:1: 'Wisdom has built a house for herself,' namely, in the Blessed Virgin, and he caused her to produce a plant for himself." Indeed, "because the earth was lowest, he gave himself to it and entered it, so as to make it the heavenly seed. Isaiah 55:10 says: 'Just as heavy rain comes down from heaven and saturates the earth and causes it to bring forth, so my word will be.'"

Consider, finally, how many of the images—how many properties of the various words—Thomas employed above in his sermon so that he was able to work into his summation. Allow me, for ease of reference, simply to outline them below:

"Plant" = humility
i.   Little (the opposite of pride)
ii. Pliant (obedient)
iii. Bringing health (not rooted in the earth, like the trees that overshadow the rest)

"Green" = virginity
i.   Moisture (heavenly love and grace)
ii. Beauty (harmony)
iii. Utility (the plant will bear fruit)

"Bringing forth seed" = fruitfulness
i.   Holy seed (from God)
ii. Virtuous seed (little, but fills the earth)
iii. Necessary seed (required for salvation)

Therefore, concludes Thomas in his closing peroration, "if someone is empty through sin, let him ask for this plant, and he will be filled with good things. . . . Likewise, if someone is arid, let him take refuge with that Word, and he will be moistened. . . . Likewise, if someone is downhearted, let him take refuge with that Word, and he will be led back to the heavenly light." Thus does Thomas conclude his sermon on Mary with the Word made flesh and similarly point forward to his *collatio* address later that evening at vespers on the Cross of Christ.

The Evening's Collatio *at Vespers: "The Fruit Tree that Produces Fruit"*

"Let the earth bring forth the green plant bringing forth seed and the fruit tree bearing fruit" ["lignumque pomiferum faciens fructum"]. The Most High has raised from the earth two remedies for us: the green plant and the fruit-bearing tree. We have spoken about the plant, which is the Blessed Virgin. Now it remains to speak about the fruit-bearing tree, the tree of the Cross of our Lord, which is to be venerated.

Thus begins Thomas's *collatio* address at vespers later that same evening after the sermon we have been reading above. In the circumstances, he needs do nothing more than repeat the opening *thema* verse he used that morning and pick up right where he left off with the phrase "the fruit tree that produces fruit." The connection between the two parts is, I would suggest, not merely rhetorical—the diverse elements of the sermon and the *collatio* are obviously united verbally by their association with the words of one Bible verse—the connection is profoundly *theological* as well.

So, for example, the significance is not lost on Thomas that Mary and the Cross both, although in very different senses, "bore" Christ. As such, both were instruments of our salvation—although, as Thomas made clear at the end of his sermon on Mary, the sole means of our salvation, and Mary's too, is Christ. Thus, "it is very suitable to connect these two remedies," says Thomas, "because the green plant has brought forth [*protulit*] our salvation, whereas the fruit-bearing tree has sustained [*sustinuit*] the plant and has exalted it." He then draws his listener's attention to the famous passage in Philippians 2:8–9, where Paul connects Christ's humility both with his nativity, being born "in the likeness of men," and with his death on the Cross:

> Christ Jesus, who, though he was in the form of God, did not count equality with God a thing to be grasped, but emptied himself, taking the form of a servant, being born in the likeness of men. And being found in human form he humbled himself and became obedient unto death, even death on a cross. Therefore God has highly exalted him.

As the reader may recall, two of the important properties of the "green plant"—that is, of Mary—were her *humility* and *obedience*, a "greenness" that was nurtured by the "moisture" of God's grace gently coming upon her from heaven. So too with Christ, it is his humble obedience to the Father that serves as the proper "medicine" to cure the damage done by man's pride.

Recall also that the feast Thomas is preparing for is "The Feast of the Exaltation of the Cross." In this regard we might ask: "Who is it who does the *exalting*?" Primarily, of course, it is God the Father who *exalts* the Son. But by the same token, it is the Son who is *exalted* by his obedient sacrifice. He is, as he tells his disciples, "lifted up," just as Moses "lifted up the serpent in the wilderness" (see John 3:14). And having been "lifted up from the earth," he "will draw all people" to himself (see John 12:32). Because he has been "lifted up," we are able to be "lifted up" with him. In the congregation's exaltation of the Cross, they, with the Father, exalt Christ; and by becoming one with him in the Eucharist, they are made one with him in his Body and share in his exaltation by sharing in his death and Resurrection. And yet, who was it who first participated in Christ's "exaltation" on the Cross? It was Mary, his mother, who not only was nurtured by the grace attained by his sacrifice but also made the first "exaltation of the Cross," as it were, standing at the foot of the Cross of her son (see John 19:25). Hers was indeed the most intimate sharing in Christ's Cross of anyone in history. And so, like her, standing at the foot of the Cross, we must, says Thomas, "look at this tree."

And what do we find if we examine this tree? We find quite a lot, actually. But in the context of this *collatio* address, Thomas's examination will be in terms of the *thema* verse with which he began: "the fruit tree bearing fruit" ("lignumque pomiferum faciens fructum"). And as has been his custom throughout, Thomas will divide this phrase in accord with a threefold *divisio*. When we look at the tree, what three properties do we notice? First, we see its species: that it is wood, the wood of a tree (*lignum*).[11] Second, we notice its adornment (*ornatum*): it is "fruit-bearing" (*pomiferum*). And third, we notice that it is a fruit-bearing tree that actually *produces fruit* (*faciens fructum*)—as opposed to, one imagines, the fig tree Christ encounters on his way to Jerusalem that had leaves but bore no

---

[11] Strictly speaking, the Latin *lignum* means "wood." But it can also be used by extension, as it is here, to indicate something *made out of* wood, such as a *tree*. Thus "tree" is not an uncommon translation of *lignum*, especially in medieval Latin. The double meaning is why, in English, we can say either that Christ hung on "the wood" of the Cross or that Christ was hung on "a tree." This little linguistic detail is worth noting because Thomas will make full use of both meanings of *lignum* in his comments to follow: his "declaration of the parts" will be worked out in terms of the properties of a "tree" in some cases (as in his example of the two "trees" in the Garden of Eden) and of "wood" in others (such as the "wood" out of which Noah made his Ark).

fruit (see Mark 11:12–14 and Matt 21:18–22). It is, of course, crucial that it is a "fruit-bearing tree" rather than one described as barren and without leaves—although the latter would have made an interesting image for his discussion of the Cross if that had been the word in the *thema* verse Thomas had found himself with. A preacher had a great deal of leeway in this style of preaching, but he had also to be as attentive to the characteristics of the words he found in the Scriptures as any exegete, and as careful of the uses he put them to as any poet.

What the reader should notice in particular for our purposes in the summary of the *collatio* that I have sketched below (and diagrammed in the Appendix) is the way in which crafting his "declaration of parts" in terms of the *properties* of the tree allows Thomas to make abundant use of all the so-called "spiritual" senses of Scripture—the "typological" or "allegorical," the "moral," and the "anagogical"—none of which he made any use of in his sermon on Mary's Nativity. Undoubtedly, Thomas had greater latitude to employ the spiritual senses here because he was discussing Christ, who is the exegetical *center* of the Scriptures for Christians: the ultimate *Word* of God that helps clarify the *words* of Scripture. We will have occasion to note the occurrence of the various "senses" when we come across them.

For now, however, we must return to the threefold *divisio* with which Thomas began: there is a "tree" (*lignum*) that is "fruit-bearing" (*pomiferum*) and "produces fruit" (*faciens fructum*). As we will soon see, there are a complex series of subdivisions (and in some cases, sub-subdivisions) under each of these divisions—so many, in fact, that Fr. Hoogland had to make use of a complex numbering system to help the reader keep the sections clear in his translation. If one is looking for evidence of the kind of diversity-within-order that a mind trained in the scholastic *divisio* can achieve in a sermon, there is likely no better example than the *collatio* we are about to examine.

The Species: A Tree of Wood

Thomas begins his examination, naturally, with the first member of his threefold *divisio* and asks: Why *lignum*? That is to say, why "wood" or "a tree"? This wood "befits our remedy," says Thomas, and this for three reasons: (1) it befits the wound, (2) it befits the healing of it, and (3) it befits the healer. As we will soon see, each of these three will in turn be subdivided into three subcategories. (For a clearer picture, the reader might wish to refer to my diagram on p. 67.)

The *wood* "befits the wound," says Thomas, because, as the first man ate from the forbidden wood (the tree in the Garden), so also "the divine Wisdom found the medicine from the wood." Just as "the human race is wounded because of disobedience, since the first man stole a fruit from the forbidden wood," so also "the new man has placed himself, as a salutary fruit so to speak, back onto the wood." Here Thomas is clearly connecting the word *lignum* ("wood" or "tree") in his *thema* verse with the theological content found in Romans 5:12–18, where Paul famously contrasts how death came into the world through one man, Adam, with how life has come into the world through one man, Christ. Especially relevant for our present purposes would be verses 18–19: "Therefore, as one trespass led to condemnation for all men, so one act of righteousness leads to justification and life for all men. For as by the one man's disobedience the many were made sinners, so by the one man's obedience the many will be made righteous."

This *theological* point is made in the sermon by means of using a "typological" comparison between the tree that served as the instrument of our condemnation in the Garden and the "tree" that served as the instrument of our salvation on Calvary. The tree in the Garden is a "type"—a prefiguration—of the Cross on which Christ is crucified. Indeed, the Cross, on this view, is the ultimate *fulfillment* of a mystery that is merely prefigured in the tree of the Garden. What happened with the tree in the Garden is not merely an *event* whose significance lies solely within itself, so that we must say that a tragedy has happened and there is nothing to be done, nothing more to be said. Rather, this event, seen *in the light of the Cross*, can be understood as *pointing forward* to a more profound realization of the loving communion between God and man realized in the sacrifice of Christ on the Cross.[12]

It is also worth noting not only that Thomas is employing the "wood" as a literary "type" but also that the *way* he makes use of it here allows him to hearken back to two important themes from the morning's sermon on Mary: Mary's *humility* and her *obedience*. As Mary was obedient to God's word (and thus ultimately to God's Word), so too was her son (God's Son) obedient to his Father. Indeed, the themes of *humility* and *obedience* will dominate the three subdivisions that follow.

---

[12] There are many events even in our own lives the full significance or meaningfulness of which we can recognize only in retrospect. The classic literary embodiment of this *post facto* realization of the true significance of prior events is of course Augustine's *Confessions*.

Given that the *wood* of the Cross "befits the wound," and that the *wound* has been traced to the *tree in the Garden*, Thomas contrasts in a *typological fashion* the characteristics of the "forbidden tree" (as the cause of sin) with those of the Cross (as the cure for sin). In Genesis 3:6, we find three characteristics of the forbidden tree: it was (a) good to eat from (*bonum ad vescendum*); (b) beautiful to the eyes (*pulchrum oculis*); and (c) desirable to look upon (*aspectuque delectabile*). The Cross, on Thomas's account, provides the proper medicine for each.

The forbidden tree of the Garden was thought to be good to eat from. But if one lives according to the flesh, he will die, as it says in Romans 8:13. The wood of the Cross, by contrast, teaches the mortification of the flesh, and by dying to the flesh, we live in Christ.

Second, there was said to be worldly beauty in the forbidden tree. As might be expected, Thomas turns this around: the paradox is that, while the worldly beauty of the forbidden tree has caused our ruin, the shame of the Cross has "changed into glory." But given that he is preaching to an academic audience—this is, after all, a university sermon—Thomas takes the occasion to incorporate a little academic reminder of Augustine's famous definition of "virtue": "Virtue is a good quality of the mind, by which we live righteously, of which no one can make bad use, which God works in us, without us."[13] Here is what Thomas says in his *collatio*:

> There are some goods which man does not use in an evil way, for instance, virtues. But having the skill of dealing with material things is not the same as having virtues. Some have an abundance of goods in the world and often they use them in an evil way. That wood [*lignum*] had a visible beauty, whereas the wood [*lignum*] of the Cross had the disorder of foolishness. Hence the Apostle says: "We preach the crucified Christ: for Jews yet a scandal, for Gentiles even foolishness" (1 Cor 1:23). But the beauty of the first wood is completely changed into shame. . . . The shame of the Cross, however, is completely changed into glory. Thus it says in Ezekiel 17:24: "I, the Lord, have brought low the lofty wood and I have exalted the low wood."

This last verse from Ezekiel about "the low wood" being "exalted" allows Thomas to bring the minds of his listeners directly back to the sub-

---

[13] Cf., e.g., Aquinas, *Summa Theologiae* (hereafter, *ST*) I-II, q. 55, a. 4, quoting Augustine, *De libero arbitrio* 2.19.

ject of the feast they are celebrating: "See how the wood of the Cross is exalted," he tells them.[14] It is not altogether unlikely that at this point he would have been able to gesture at the cross that the congregation would be venerating the next day. It also allowed him to tell one of the key stories behind the feast day, how in the early seventh century, a portion of the "true Cross" that had been housed in the Church of the Holy Sepulcher in Jerusalem was taken to Persia after the conquest of the city by the Persian king Khosrau II but was later returned (with abundant miracles) to Jerusalem by Byzantine Emperor Heraclius II.[15]

After this brief excursus on Heraclius and the rescue of the Cross from the Persians, Thomas can return very easily to the third element of his *divisio*. Having already examined how the "forbidden wood" in the Garden was "good to eat" and "beautiful to the eyes," it now remains for him to discuss its giving "delight" (*delectabile*). The delight of the flesh is not true delight, says Thomas, "since it has more about bitterness than about delight." If the circumstances had been different and Thomas had not already had so much else packed into this sermon and its accompanying *collatio*, we might imagine him including a threefold examination of how the delight of the flesh is more about bitterness than about delight—perhaps something along the lines of: (A) bodily delight requires pain, as in the

---

[14] I am often impressed when a preacher is able to work some relevant story about the saint whose feast day it is into his sermon while not turning his entire sermon into a biography of the life of the saint.

[15] The legends surrounding the discovery of the "true Cross" are, as the reader might know, somewhat complicated and lacking somewhat in what we might call "historical verifiability," even apart from the question of whether any of the pieces of the "true Cross" that exist today are actually pieces of the Cross on which Christ was crucified. But according to legend, the "true Cross" was supposedly discovered by Helena, the mother of the Roman emperor Constantine, during a pilgrimage she made to the Holy Land in 326. By order of the emperor, the Church of the Holy Sepulcher was then built on the site of the place where Jesus was thought to have been buried. When the church was dedicated nine years later, a portion of the Cross was placed inside it. The date of the feast marks the dedication of the Church of the Holy Sepulcher in 335. This was a two-day festival, and although the actual consecration of the church was on September 13, the cross itself was brought outside the church on September 14 so that the clergy and faithful could pray before the "true Cross" and all could come forward to venerate it. This remains the date of the feast to this day. The feast does not seem to have entered the Western calendar, however, until the seventh century. The legend here is that, in 614, a portion of the cross was carried away from the church by the Persians and had remained missing until it was recaptured by Byzantine Emperor Heraclius in 628. Initially taken to Constantinople, the cross was returned to Jerusalem the following year. Thomas recounts here the second legend rather than the first, likely because it was after this event that the feast entered the Western calendar.

case of delight we experience when we quench our thirst or hunger; (B) bodily delight does not last, and thus leads to frustration and bitterness when it has passed; and (C) indulging oneself with too much delightful food or wine often leads to physical pain and the ruination of one's life.

Thomas did not really have the time in the present *collatio* to go into this kind of detail, however, especially since he had chosen to spend the morning's sermon praising the Virgin Mary. Again, the medieval preacher had plenty of options, but he had to choose wisely. And as with all preachers, he had to concern himself with *time* and *length*. One can only do so much in the time allotted. And because Thomas's main concern is to contrast the "forbidden wood" from which came our ruin with the wood of the Cross, and since he has chosen to take a "typological" approach in this sermon, he does not go into detail about the "sting of bitterness of bodily delight," but reassures his listeners instead that: "this sting of bitterness turns into sweetness, which is signified in Exodus 15:23–24, where it is said that 'the children of Israel arrived at bitter waters: the Lord ordered Moses to throw a piece of wood in, and the waters became sweet.'" The moral lesson is: "If the just suffer adversities, the wood of the Cross makes these sweet. The Cross even makes one glory in adversity."

And with this, Thomas has finished unpacking the threefold sub-sub-division explaining how the wood of the Cross "befits the wound" (on my outline, he has covered section 1a, b, and c under *lignum*), so he moves onto the next topic: how "the wood" befits the healing of the wound. In this section, Thomas continues his "typological" approach, but instead of *contrasting* the wood of the Cross with the beguilements of the forbidden tree in the Garden, he reviews several instances in the Old Testament where *wood* became an instrument of God's salvation. Rather than the typological *contrasting* we saw above, we might call this method the more common typological *prefiguring*.

Why does *wood* befit the healing of the wound? The "first evil of man" occurred, says Thomas, when Adam was banished from Paradise and, as a result, could not approach the "Tree of Life" (see Gen 3:23–24). Instead, "Christ has taken up the wood for us," and the Cross has become for us the new "Tree of Life." The second danger was the flood (Gen 6–8), the remedy for which came by means of the wood Noah used to construct the ark. The third danger, then, was when the people of Israel were oppressed by the Egyptians (Exod 1:8–22), the remedy for which came by means of wood, since with his wooden rod Moses divided the seas to allow the Israelites to pass through on dry ground and then cast his rod again to cause the seas to cover the Egyptians who were pursuing them. The fourth danger, finally, came from the Philistines who fought against the children of Israel. And in the midst of this danger, the Ark of the Covenant, which was made of wood that could not rot, was brought into the camp. And for this reason, says Thomas, "the *wood* befits the wound and the healing."

Finally, *wood* befits the Healer because Christ is exalted by the wood of the Cross. And here Thomas does something rather interesting. He uses both biblical and non-biblical images. So, for example, he says that Christ is "like a warrior" and the Cross is his "triumphant chariot": it is the thing that elevates Christ. In this way, it is also like the sedan chair of Solomon (see Song of Songs 3:9). Echoing what he said about Moses above, he says the wood of the Cross is like the wooden rod that guides the people. And finally, the *wood* befits the Healer—and here there might have been just a hint of humorous irony, given the academic audience—because on it Christ "is exalted as a *magister* in his (wooden) seat of instruction." As Thomas had never shown himself to be a man with any sense of self-importance or awareness of status, one has to imagine this little reference comparing the Cross of Christ to the chair of the university *magister* at the front of the classroom was likely intended somewhat humorously. It is not as though the analogy between Christ "teaching" from the wooden Cross and a *magister* teaching a class of students from his wooden chair does not work—it serves the intended purpose—it is simply that the implied comparison between the task of teaching students and Christ suffering torture on the Cross cannot have escaped them. Was there, one wonders, a small twinkle in his eye to accompany the low chuckle that may have gone across the room?

The Adornment of the Tree: It is "Fruit-Bearing"

Anyone keeping track knows that we have two more words to go from Thomas's opening *divisio*. He has covered what he wants to say in conjunction with the word *lignum* ("wood" or "tree"), so it is time to move on to *pomiferum* ("fruit-bearing") and *faciens fructum* ("making fruit," or "that makes fruit"). It is of course a little odd to talk about a "fruit-bearing tree" that "bears (or makes) fruit." It seems unnecessarily repetitive. And it may be. But this is the biblical text Thomas has before him, so he uses it to his advantage. It allows him to talk about the "fruits" of the Cross in two different ways: one in conjunction with the word *pomiferum*, and the other in conjunction with the phrase *faciens fructum*.

We begin, naturally enough, with the first of these. If the tree (*lignum*) is "fruit-bearing" (*pomiferum*), then what are its fruits? In Deuteronomy 33:13–15, Moses is said to have blessed the tribe of Joseph with three "fruits" (*pomis*): the "fruits of heaven" (*pomis caeli*), the "fruits of sun and moon" (*pomis fructuum solis ac lunae*), and (3) the "fruits of the eternal hills" (*pomis collium aeternorum*). There are, in fact, a good many other things in that blessing (which runs all the way from verse 13 up to verse 17), but there are in fact only *three* of them that involve the Latin word *pomum*. And although Thomas had an amazing memory, given that this is the *only* place in Scripture where the word *pomum* shows up three times in quick succession, one imagines that, in this particular case, he might have made use of a biblical concordance.[16]

Be that as it may, whether Thomas had the amazing power of memory sufficient to recall this threefold use of *pomum* in Deuteronomy or whether he made use of a concordance, the passage served his purposes perfectly: it gave him precisely the threefold sort of *divisio* he wished: (1) the fruits of heaven, (2) the fruits of the sun and moon, and (3) the fruits of the eternal hills. Now the task that remained was to associate each of them convincingly with the subject matter of the *collatio*.

What, then, are "the fruits of heaven"? The members of Christ's body, says Thomas: not only the physical members of Christ's body (his feet, knees, hands, and face), but the members of his Mystical Body, the Church, as well.[17] How about "the fruits of the sun and moon"? These are the *virtues* that Christ showed on the Cross, especially love, humility, and patience. And what, finally, are "the fruits of the eternal hills"? Here Thomas does something really interesting.

His answer to the question is that "the fruits of the eternal hills" are "the writings of the teachers who are imbued with wisdom." This much

---

[16] I am, of course, open to the possibility that he did not, but if he did not, I think we would have to conclude that he had not only a "very good" memory, but an "eidetic" or "photographic" memory, and that he could remember not only sentences, but each and every *word* he had ever read, since he would have first had to distinguish in his mind the word *pomum* from its near relative *fructum* and then recall the exact place where the word *pomum* showed up exactly *three* times.

[17] On this point, Fr. Hoogland's translation contains a fascinating historical note (*Academic Sermons*, 277n72) in which he points out that, "The *Rhythmica oratorio* . . . attributed by some to St. Bernard of Clairvaux (12th century), by others to Arnulf of Louvain (13th century), both Cistercians . . . contains seven meditations of Christ on the Cross, each one focusing on one member or pair of his members: the feet, knees, hands, side, breast, heart, and face. The text had already spread during Thomas's lifetime (cf. the corpus of *ST* III, q. 25, a. 4)." There is no way of knowing whether Thomas was indirectly referring to this *oratorio*, but it is certainly an intriguing suggestion.

is not entirely unexpected. But then he inserts in his sermon a small meditation, as it were, on the famous "last words" of Christ. What do these "teachers who are imbued with wisdom" teach? We might recall that Thomas had, not long before, made a little jest comparing Christ on the Cross with the university *magister* on his chair in front of the class. Consider now the following meditation on the "last words" of Christ in light of that image. What does the wise teacher teach? Like Christ on the Cross, he teaches faith: "My God, my God, why have you abandoned me?" (Matt 27:46). Like Christ on the Cross, he "shows the way to hope": "Today you will be with me in paradise" (Luke 23:43). Like Christ on the Cross, he teaches patience: "Father, forgive them, for they know not what they do" (Luke 23:34). Wise teachers are those who "incite devotion": "Father, into your hands I commend my spirit" (Luke 23:46). And a wise teacher "teaches how to live a human life together," as Christ did when he said to his mother, "Woman, behold your son," and to the beloved disciple, "Behold your mother" (John 19:26–27).

Thomas may or may not have been jesting above when he spoke of Christ "teaching" from the Cross like a *magister* teaches from his chair. But the point must have *really* hit home when he turned that analogy around and suggested to his academic audience that, instead of thinking of Christ in terms of the privileges of their office, they should think of the duties of their office in light of the model set down by Christ on the Cross. I take it that nearly all of the points Thomas hit upon in this sermon have remained relevant to this day, but there are also undeniable clues in the text that he was entirely mindful of the spiritual needs of his particular audience.

The Fruit of the Tree

We have seen Thomas make divisions within divisions—this whole *collatio* address being itself a subdivision of a larger whole. For those following along, Thomas has one more member of his original threefold *divisio* to cover. He has discussed topics in association with *lignum* ("the wood") and with *pomiferum* ("fruit-bearing"). It remains for him to say something about *fructum*: the "fruit" that the tree "produces." But time was likely running short, and he undoubtedly needed to finish up by a certain hour. So instead of developing subdivisions within subdivisions, as he had done above, he finishes with this:

the wood of the Cross has produced a triple fruit: (1) the fruit of cleansing, (2) the fruit of sanctification, and (3) the fruit of glorification—the "fruit of cleansing" because through the Cross we are liberated from sins; the "fruit of sanctification" because man, alienated from God through sin, is reconciled through Christ; and the "fruit of glorification" because although through sin, man was excluded from paradise, through the Cross, heaven was opened, and as Jacob saw the ladder with its top in the heavens on which angels descended and ascended (cf. Gen 28:12), so now "all the saints go up to heavens by the power of the Cross."

It would not be inaccurate, therefore, to say that Thomas's "wrap-up" was mercifully short. He had to complete the *divisio*, or he would have left his audience hanging. So he did complete it—briefly, but profoundly—and then gave them a blessing and sent them on their way.

Within the context of his comments on this brief phrase, "lignum pomiferum faciens fructum," he was able to hit upon any number of typological references (comparing the Cross to the rod of Moses, for example, or contrasting it with the forbidden tree in the Garden), to exhort his listeners with any number of moral lessons (the virtues being something of which one cannot make bad use, with special emphasis placed on faith, humility, and obedience), and to finish finally with an anagogical vision of their heavenly home, the ladder to which has been provided in the form of the Cross of Christ.

Now, as I have done with prior examples, I ask you, the reader, to call to mind the opening biblical *thema*: "Germinet terra herbam uirentem et proferentem semen, lignumque pomiferum faciens fructum" ("Let the earth bring forth *the green plant bringing forth seed* and *the fruit tree bearing fruit*"). As you look over the six relevant words or phrases that made up the morning's *divisio* and the evening's *divisio* that followed—"plant," "green," and "bringing forth seed" in reference to Mary, and "tree," "fruit bearing," and producing "fruit" in reference to the Cross of Christ—do you remember a great deal more than expected out of what was an undeniably vast thicket of material by associating content with each word? Mary is like a "plant" because she is small (humble), pliant, and brings health; she is "green" because she is a virgin who is watered by the moisture from heaven; she is beautiful because of her harmony and order; and her greenness shows that she will bear fruit. The fruit she brings forth is a "holy seed," since her child comes from God, a virtuous seed that, although small, fills the earth, and a necessary seed, because Christ is required for our salvation.

So too, along with Mary, the other instrument of our salvation that "bore Christ" was the Cross. The Cross is "wood," a "tree." But unlike the forbidden tree in the Garden, which was "good to eat from, beautiful to the eyes, and delightful," the Cross teaches us to die to the flesh and live rather in Christ, that worldly beauty will be brought low while the shame of the Cross will become glorious, and that the delight of the flesh is like the bitter water that was made sweet by throwing wood into it. So too, the "wood" of the Cross saves us like the Tree of Life in the Garden, like the wood of Noah's Ark, like Moses's wooden rod, and like the Ark of the Covenant. Thus, the "wood" of the Cross is like the chariot by which Christ is lifted up to do battle; it is like the sedan chair upon which Solomon was lifted up as king; and it is like the wooden rod Moses used to guide the people—not to mention a bit like the wooden chair that a university *magister* teaches from. The Cross is "fruit bearing." So what are its fruits? There are three (as there are usually three). The members of Christ's Body are the first. The virtues shown by Christ on the Cross (especially love, humility, and patience) are the second. And the third? The third can be recalled from the "last words" of Christ:

"My God, my God, why have you abandoned me?" (Faith)
"Today you will be with me in paradise." (Hope)
"Father, forgive them, for they know not what they do."
(Patience)
"Father, into your hands I commend my spirit." (Devotion)

And finally, what are the "fruits" of the tree associated with the phrase "bearing fruit"? As usual, there are three: the fruit of cleansing (of sin), the fruit of sanctification, and the fruit of glorification. Upon entering the Church, the faithful take the cleansing water of baptism from the font, make the Sign of the Cross on themselves as a sign of sanctification, genuflect before the Cross of Christ by which they have been delivered of sin and made holy, and are given access to the communion of saints in heaven.

Even those who are not admirers of this style of preaching would have to admit that Thomas was able to fit quite a lot of theological content into a relatively short sermon and *collatio* by organizing his subject matter according to topics he associated with each member of the *divisio* he made of his opening scriptural verse. There are some readers, naturally enough, who do not find the systematic, logical style of Thomas's *Summa of The-*

ology quite to their tastes. But even many of these would have to admit to a certain admiration for the genius and clarity of its construction. So too, I would suggest, with Thomas's sermons. They may take some getting used to. But once you have begun to see the internal order and harmony of the various parts, they can become infectious, like reading the *Summa* or appreciating all the intricately interrelated parts of a vast medieval cathedral. These were people who knew how to achieve a lot in a relatively small space.

TWO WAYS OF DIVIDING THE SAME *THEMA* VERSE: THOMAS AND BONAVENTURE

As the reader can probably already tell, there were in fact dozens of ways of constructing the "declaration of parts" of a medieval sermon. The "Bonaventuran" *Ars concionandi*, for example, has page after page of examples—so many, in fact, that the vast abundance of them made it less useful for our present purposes. Since I am not producing a preaching manual, but merely trying to give the reader a "flavor" of the basic elements of the art, I judged dozens of examples to be less helpful than one or two good ones.[18]

So too, in the remainder of this chapter, instead of multiplying examples of all the possible methods of crafting "the declaration of parts"— we have not yet covered adverbs, for example, not to mention participial phrases, gerunds, gerundives, and any number of others—I prefer to conclude with two comparisons. In the present section, I compare two different divisions of the same Bible verse—one division is from a sermon by St. Thomas and the other is from a sermon using the same *thema* written by his contemporary, St. Bonaventure. In the final section of this chapter, I will conclude by comparing the divisions Thomas uses in the last three sermons in Fr. Hoogland's list: Sermon 19 (*Beati qui habitant*), Sermon 20 (*Beata gens*), and Sermon 21 (*Beatus vir*).

We begin, however, with our comparison of Thomas and Bonaventure. The reason for comparing Thomas's practice with that of another, contemporary preacher, other than for its own intrinsic interest, is that in all of Thomas's extant sermons he never uses the same *thema* verse twice, even though the lectionary he was drawing upon would have been the same year

---

18 Besides, there is, as I mentioned in the Introduction to the present volume, an analytical outline of each of the nineteen authentic sermons of Aquinas in the Appendix, so the reader who is interested can very quickly scan these pages should he or she wish to get a sense of the different ways Thomas divides and declares the parts of his opening biblical *themata*.

after year. And even if Thomas *had* used a *thema* verse more than once during his career, since so few of his sermons have survived, unfortunately, we simply have no evidence that he ever did. So we will have to look elsewhere for a suitable sermon to use in our comparison.

One interesting possibility for comparison is presented by the publication of the complete collection of *The Sunday Sermons of St. Bonaventure*, which contains a separate sermon for nearly every week of the liturgical year, some fifty in all. Now, in all fifty of Bonaventure's extant Sunday sermons and in the twenty extant sermons of Aquinas, it turns out that they only preached on the same biblical *thema* verse once. This lack of overlap is interesting in its own right because it suggests that medieval preachers had a good deal of leeway about which verse out of the day's readings they would use to construct their sermons. What this comparison of Thomas and Bonaventure shows is that two preachers, though faced with the same biblical passages on which to preach throughout the year, might still never overlap in their choice of *thema* verse. And yet, fortunately for our purposes, Thomas and Bonaventure did use the same *thema* verse at least once, perhaps even in the same year, although likely *not* on the same Sunday (for reasons I will make clear in a moment).

Thomas's Sermon 13 and Bonaventure's Sermon 29 are both structured around the verse from Luke 14:16 that reads: "A certain man made a great dinner, and he invited many" ("homo quidam fecit cenam magnam et vocavit multos"). Neither man uses any of the words before these eight or any of the words after.[19]

---

[19] The Latin original of this sermon can be found in *Doctoris Seraphici S. Bonaventurae Opera Omnia*, vol. 9, ed. R. P. David Fleming (Quaracchi, IT: Collegium S. Bonaventurae, 1901), 357–60. Interestingly, the Quaracchi editor, David Fleming, includes two other sermons on this same *thema* verse, neither of them quite the same as the one found in *The Sunday Sermons of Saint Bonaventure*, trans. Timothy J. Johnson, Works of Saint Bonaventure 12 (St. Bonaventure, NY: Franciscan Institute Publications, 2008), and each has its own *divisio* scheme. So, for example, along with the threefold *divisio* we find in the sermon we are analyzing above—which is listed in the Quaracchi edition as "Sermo I" under the heading "Dominica Secunda Post Pentecosten"—we find in "Sermo II" a twofold *divisio* similar to Thomas's. Bonaventure's "declaration of the parts" in this sermon reads as follows:

> In these words are expressed the maximum generosity of God's goodness toward mankind in two things: in preparing for his satiety, to which from eternity we are preordained; and this is expressed when it says: *A certain man made a great dinner*; and in inviting or calling together to this dinner which he so studiously prepared; which is expressed when it says: *and he called many*.

"Sermo II" is actually a very short sermon, filling slightly more than a single column in

Bonaventure's sermon of this title was likely written, translator Timothy J. Johnson tells us, sometime between 1267 and 1268.[20] Thomas's sermon, by contrast, was likely preached, we are told, during his second Paris regency, which is to say, sometime between 1268 and 1272.[21] So, whether or not the two sermons were crafted in the same year, they are from roughly the same period in these two great preacher's lives, so that we do not have a situation where one is from an early, less mature period and the other from a later, more advanced period. Both were preachers with substantial years of experience behind them.

Now, although it is somewhat possible that these two sermons were crafted in the same year, what is likely *not* the case is that they were preached the same week, and this for two reasons. The first is simply because, if Johnson is right, "Bonaventure composed almost the entire corpus of the *Sunday Sermons de novo* without ever having actually preached them in a public setting."[22] Now, even if this judgment turns out not to be entirely accurate (although I currently have no good reason to doubt it), it is still the case that the Dominicans and Franciscans in the thirteenth century each used their own lectionary, each with its own cycle of readings. So, although the reading from Luke 16:14–24 was the Gospel reading for the Second Sunday after the Feast of the Trinity in the Dominican calen-

---

the Quaracchi volume. The last sermon in this series, "Sermo III," is different again in that, for this sermon, Bonaventure makes use of the *entire* passage for the day (Luke 14:15–24)—that is to say, he uses *all* the elements of the parable—and "declares the parts" of his sermon thus:

> In this whole Gospel [passage], we can note four things: the preparation of the dinner, where it says: *A certain man made a great dinner.* Second, the calling of the guests: *and he called many.* Third, the excuses of the ones called: *they all began to excuse themselves.* And fourth is the bringing in of others: *call the poor, the feeble, the blind, and the lame.* In the first is shown the greatness of heavenly glory; in the second, the dispensing of divine mercy; in the third, the reproof of human malice; in the fourth, the differentiation of grace.

So, although there are three sermons in the Quaracchi volume, each of which uses the same Gospel passage, I continue to maintain that Sermo I (the sermon we are analyzing above from the *Sunday Sermons of Saint Bonaventure*) remains our best sample for comparison because (A) Sermo II is so much shorter and abbreviated and (B) Sermo III uses the longer form of the *thema* verse. I trust the point has been made clear to the reader from all of this that medieval preachers had a great deal of flexibility in *how* they decided to divide and develop the same *thema* verse.

[20] Johnson, *Sunday Sermons of Saint Bonaventure*, esp. 22–25.
[21] Hoogland, *Academic Sermons*, 171.
[22] Johnson, *Sunday Sermons of St. Bonaventure*, 25, esp. n51.

dar—the Feast of the Trinity falling on the first Sunday after Pentecost, which meant this Sunday was the third after Pentecost—that same reading showed up on the Franciscan calendar a week earlier, on the second Sunday after Pentecost.[23]

Whenever they were preached, if Bonaventure's sermon was preached publicly at all, they were both composed using the *sermo modernus* style, and they are based on the same Gospel verse: "A certain man made a great dinner, and he invited many." Let us see now how each man chose to divide it.

Thomas settled on what appeared to be a simple twofold *divisio* according to the "order of delivery from God": "Just as the body cannot be maintained without physical refreshment, so also the soul is in need of spiritual refreshment for its maintenance," he begins. "Concerning this spiritual refreshment," says Thomas, "in today's Gospel, we can see two things: first, the preparation of this refreshment (*preparacionem huius refeccionis*), where he says, 'A certain man made a great dinner'; second, the announcement of the feast (*conuiuii communicacionem*) when it is prepared, where he says, 'and he invited many.'" The parallel constructions Thomas employs in both instances are an accusative noun and a genitive: "preparation of the refreshment," and "announcement of the feast."

The first of these, "the preparation of the refreshment," Thomas takes up in the day's sermon, in which he "unfolds" the verse "A certain man made a great dinner." The second, "the announcement of the feast when it is prepared," is the subject for the evening's *collatio* at vespers, which is based on the second phrase: "and he invited many." This twofold *divisio* seems simple enough at first, but this sermon will get much more complicated as Thomas works his way through it, as we shall soon see. Whereas each of the sermons we have seen thus far has followed a fairly standard outline or pattern, Thomas is about to exhibit some fairly complex interweaving of themes and sub-themes. The result will make it clear that, while the beginning preachers of his day were writing the literary equivalent of a simple three part harmony, Thomas was crafting complex overlapping polyphonies. They were writing outlines; he was crafting symphonies.

Now, although Bonaventure was capable of an equal degree of complexity—anyone who doubts this has simply to glance at his *Breviloquium*,

---

[23] On this, see Maura O'Carroll, S.N.D., "The Lectionary for the Proper of the Year in the Dominican and Franciscan Rites of the Thirteenth Century," *Archivum fratrum praedicatorum* 49 (1979): 79–103, esp. the table on 85–103 and, for this particular verse, 96.

the *Itinerarium Mentis in Deum*, or any of his *collatios* on, say, the Six Days of Creation or the Seven Gifts of the Holy Spirit—yet in this case, Bonaventure chose to craft a sermon that was a model of straightforward simplicity and clarity. Instead of a twofold *divisio*, dividing the verse at the conjunction "and" ("A certain man made a great dinner *and* he invited many"), he divides it in three, starting with the subject, "A certain man," then taking the first verb and object, "made a great supper, and finally addressing the second verb and object, "and invited many." Here, then, is how he structures his "declaration of the parts":

> Our Lord, moreover, is commended for three things in the pro-posed verse, which render any supper complete and perfect: first for the excellence of his singular dignity [*ab excellentia singularis dignitatis*]; second, for the affluence of his abundant bounty [*ab affluentia abundantis copiositatis*]; third, for the benevolence of his courteous welcome [*a benevolentia invitantis curialitatis*] or charity. First, therefore, he is commended for a singular excel-lence and dignity [*a singularitate excellentiae et dignitatis*], when it says: *A certain man*; this certain man said to be singular is Christ because of his incomparable and excellent dignity. Second, then, he is commended for a liberality of his affluence and boun-ty [*a liberalitate affluentiae et copiositatis*] when it adds: *made a great supper*. And third, he is commended for the courtesy of his benevolence and charity [*a curialitate benevolentiae et caritate*], when it adds: *and invited many*.[24]

The parallel constructions Bonaventure uses to construct his declara-tion are three matching prepositional phrases, each of which is made up of an ablative adjective followed by two genitives: for example, "for the excel-lence of singular dignity" (*ab excellentia singularis dignitatis*). Even when he changes each phrase slightly in his second iteration of the threefold di-vision, he retains this structure while simply rearranging the order of the words to give a slightly different emphasis. So, for example, he transforms his statement that Christ is commended "for the excellence of his singular

---

[24] I have altered Johnson's translation somewhat here to make clear that what is being "commended" in the sermon is not the meal, but Christ. I have also tried to translate so as not to obscure the three prepositional phrases Bonaventure employs to make his "declaration of parts." Translating these phrases in any other way risks obscuring the parallelism within the "declaration of parts," and as we have seen above, this sort of parallelism is crucial to the art of the *sermo modernus* style.

dignity" into one in which Christ is commended "for the singularity of his excellence and dignity" (*a singularitate excellentiae et dignitatis*); and Christ commended "for the affluence of his abundant bounty" (*ab affluentia abundantis copiositatis*) is re-stated as a commendation "for the liberality of his affluence and bounty" (*a liberalitate affluentiae et copiositatis*). In each case, the underlying verbal construction remains the same; the order of the words has simply been rearranged. (For example, someone might say, "He is a highly witty man with tremendous talent," and then, pausing for a moment, ask in jest, jumbling the original words, "Or is he a highly talented man with tremendous wit?" The difference between the two is largely irrelevant, but it is the kind of wordplay that certain people enjoy.)

Notice that both Thomas and Bonaventure take the "certain man" (*quidam homo*) who prepares the "great dinner" (*cenam magnam*) to be Christ, even though, in Luke's Gospel, Christ is the one who is telling this parable to one of the Pharisees and the "certain man" is clearly meant to represent God the Father in the parable. And yet, since neither man is engaged in direct *commentary* on this verse and both are simply *using* this text as a mnemonic structuring device, it is entirely acceptable for both preachers to specify that the *man* is Christ, the one who has "prepared a great meal" and "invited many"—the two are united on this point. Where they differ is in the associations each one makes with the image of "the great meal" and the "many" are who are invited. But again, since neither is doing *commentary*, these associations depend entirely on the points each man wishes to make in his sermon.

So, for example, for Thomas, the basic theme of his sermon is this: "Just as the body cannot be maintained without physical refreshment, so also the soul is in need of spiritual refreshment for its maintenance." Christ, as we will discover, is the source of that spiritual refreshment; he is "the great dinner" to which the many are invited.

For Bonaventure, the basic focus is somewhat different: "Under the veil of these words," he says, "is mystically signified and enfolded the celestial glory, which the Lord will offer to his elect at the end of the world. Thus this meal, which is at the end of the day, is called supper." Thus, while Thomas's focus in his sermon is largely *sacramental*—on the "spiritual refreshment" Christ provides for us *now, in this life*—Bonaventure's concern is with the benefits that Christ provides to those who achieve union with him in the life to come.

I have placed outlines of the two sermons beside one another at the end of this chapter on pp. 108–111 to illustrate the relative complexity of each. For our present purposes, I do not wish to go much into the details of how each man "dilates" each of his *divisiones*; this will be the subject of the next chapter. For now, I would ask the reader simply to focus on how each preacher uses his divisions to set up the accompanying subdivisions within his sermon.

The point of this comparison is simply to suggest to the reader that there was a great deal of flexibility afforded the preacher in the *way* he chose to make his *divisio*. And depending upon how he chose to divide his opening *thema*, he could take his sermon in any number of directions. Since the preacher was not doing a simple *commentary* on a single verse, the results could vary dramatically from preacher to preacher, even among those who had chosen the same *thema* verse.

When each preacher is trying to achieve little more than provide his audience with a fairly simple and straightforward re-statement or "reading" of a biblical text, one can expect sermons to be fairly similar from preacher to preacher. With the *sermo modernus* manner of using the biblical text, however, one Bible verse could, for good or for ill, give birth to a much wider variety of sermons.

On the Various Ways of Employing the Word "Blessed" in a Declaration of Parts

Our final exploration into the art of *divisio* will involve a comparison between three of Thomas's sermons, all of which are based on *thema* verses that begin with some form of the word "blessed" (*beatus*)—Sermon 19 (*Beati qui habitant*), Sermon 20 (*Beata gens*), and Sermon 21 (*Beatus vir*)—all three of which deal in some way with a saint or the saints. Sermons 19 and 20 were both delivered on the Feast of All Saints, and Sermon 21 was delivered to commemorate the Feast of St. Martin of Tours. All three sermons take their *thema* verse from one of the Psalms. Indeed, Sermons 19 and 21 use verses next to each other in the same Psalm. In the Latin Vulgate of Psalm 83:5–7, we find:

> 5 Beati qui habitant in domo tua, Domine; in sæcula sæculorum laudabunt te.
> 6 Beatus vir cujus est auxilium abs te, ascensiones in corde suo disposuit,
> 7 in valle lacrimarum, in loco quem posuit.[25]

---

[25] *Biblia Sacra Vulgata*, 5th ed. (Stuttgart: Deutsche Bibelgesellschaft, 1983).

Verse 5, beginning *Beati qui habitant*, provides the *thema* verse for Sermon 19 on the Feast of All Saints, while verses 6–7, beginning *Beatus vir*, provides the *thema* for Sermon 21 on the Feast of St. Martin. Even taking into consideration these similarities, the way Thomas chooses to make his *divisio* of the opening *thema* verse allows him to take different approaches to the "blessedness" of the saints and cover a variety of topics. Sermon 19 (*Beati qui habitant*) is a special case, however, and makes use of a more complex and creative structure, so I propose to review these three sermons in reverse order, beginning with Sermon 21 (*Beatus vir*).

Sermon 21

Sermon 21 takes its *thema* verse, as we have seen, from Psalm 83(84):6–7: "Beatus vir cuius est auxilium abs te; ascensiones in corde suo disposuit in valle lacrimarum in locum quem posuit" ("Happy the man whose help is from you; he has set his heart on ascending while in the valley of tears, in the place which he has built"). Although Thomas does not always make divisions of three in his sermons, since this verse has three verbs, he chooses to make the opening division in accord with the three phrases that make up the Bible verse: (1) "Happy is the man whose help is from you" ("Beatus vir cuius est auxilium abs te"); (2) "he has set his heart on ascending in the valley of tears" ("ascensiones in corde suo disposuit in valle lacrimarum"); and (3) "in the place which he has built" ("in locum quem posuit").

The question now is what sort of order he will decide to set up between or among these three. In this case, he opts for an order of progression: beginning, middle, and end. On this day, says St. Thomas, "St. Martin is promoted to the highest dignity and the highest place, namely, to the kingdom of the heavens. Therefore, Mother Church commemorates his happiness." Concerning his happiness "three things must be considered based on the words proclaimed. First, we can consider the beginning of his happiness; second, the progress; and third, its endpoint." Very literally, we have here a beginning (*principium*), middle, and end (*finis*).

The "origin or cause of Martin's happiness," says Thomas, was "divine help," which he associates with the words "Happy the man whose help is from you." The "progress of his happiness" consisted in "ascending" from one virtue to another, which is suggested first by the words ("He has set his heart on ascending while in the valley of tears"), and second by the next verse in the Psalm (83:7): "For the lawgiver shall give a blessing, they shall go from virtue to virtue." And finally, the "endpoint of his happiness" consists in gaining eternal happiness, which Thomas is able to

associate with the words "in the place which he [namely God] has built."
Two things are notable about this particular *divisio*. The first is that
it depends upon Thomas dividing the verse and construing it differently than modern editors have. In modern editions, the natural division is
made between *diposuit* and *in valle lacrimarum*, so that verse 6 reads (in
the Douay translation), "Blessed is the man whose help is from thee: in
his heart he hath disposed to ascend by steps," which is followed in verse 7
with, "In the vale of tears, in the place which he hath set." Read in this way,
"the valley of tears" (*valle lacrimarum*) is the place where "the blessed man"
has been "posited" or "set" (*disposuit*)—not, as Thomas reads it, "the place
which God has made," by which he means "heaven."

Note also that, if the Psalm verse had been written differently (say, for
example, "The man in the valley of tears who set his heart on ascending
will receive help from you—a dwelling in the place which he has built"),
then Thomas would have had to set up a different order, beginning, perhaps, with a discussion of the nature of the "valley of tears," followed by
how we "set our heart on ascending," perhaps with a discussion of the need
to turn our hearts from worldly things to heavenly things and develop the
virtues, especially of temperance. He might have discussed the "help" we
receive from God next, and then finally the heavenly home God has in
store—making this a fourfold *divisio* rather than threefold, as it is now.

I mention this as a *logical* possibility, but it might be of interest to
compare Thomas's Latin text with the Greek Septuagint version of this
Psalm, which reads (using the punctuation of a modern edition):

6 μακάριος ἀνήρ, οὗ ἐστιν ἡ ἀντίλημψις αὐτοῦ παρὰ σοῦ, κύριε·
ἀναβάσεις ἐν τῇ καρδίᾳ αὐτοῦ διέθετο
7 ἐν τῇ κοιλάδι τοῦ κλαυθμῶνος εἰς τόπον, ὃν ἔθετο.[26]

Since a good translation of this verse into Latin or English is not our concern at the moment, merely the order of the words, allow me to offer an
awkward word-for-word rendering of the Greek:

6 Blessed the man in whom is the assistance to him from you,
Lord;
ascending in his heart he ordained;

---

[26] *Septuaginta*, ed. Alfred Rahlfs and Robert Hanhart (Stuttgart: Deutsche Bibelgesellschaft, 2007), available at https://www.academic-bible.com/en/online-bibles/sep-
tuagint-lxx/read-the-bible-text/.

7 into the valley of the place of weeping; into the place which he put

This is nonsense, of course, so an actual translation into English would look something like this:

6 Blessed is the man whose help is of thee, O Lord;
in his heart he has purposed to go up
7 to the valley of weeping, to the place which he has appointed

This translation is not too far from the Vulgate Thomas was using, although "O Lord" for κύριε seems to have been left out, and it is still not entirely clear whether the "the place appointed" in verse 7 is "the valley of weeping." If the valley of weeping is "the place he has appointed," then it clearly cannot be our heavenly homeland, as Thomas interprets it in his sermon.

But other than these few small issues, the basic structure of Thomas's sermon could have remained the same—with three parts: (1) "Happy the man who help is from you [O Lord] [μακάριος ἀνήρ, οὗ ἐστιν ἡ ἀντίλημψις αὐτοῦ παρὰ σοῦ, κύριε]; (2) to ascend in his heart he has purposed into the valley of weeping [ἀναβάσεις ἐν τῇ καρδίᾳ αὐτοῦ διέθετο ἐν τῇ κοιλάδι τοῦ κλαυθμῶνος, which is not far from *ascensiones in corde suo disposuit in valle lacrimarum*]"; and finally (3) "in the place which he has set up [εἰς τόπον ὃν ἔθετο, which is not too far from *in locum quem posuit*]." If St. Jerome had chosen what is sometimes called among contemporary scholars a more "dynamic" style of translation in the Latin Vulgate, things might have been very different.[27] But in this Psalm, at least, he stuck fairly close to the Greek.[28]

---

[27] For a general overview of Jerome and his work, see H. F. D. Sparks, "Jerome as Biblical Scholar," in *The Cambrige History of the Bible*, vol. 1, *From the Beginnings to Jerome*, ed. P. R. Ackroyd and C. F. Evans (Cambridge, UK: Cambridge University Press, 1970), 510–40.

[28] Here, for the sake of comparison, are the same two verses from Jerome's later *Versio juxta Hebraicum* (AD 405), which was not as widely used as his earlier version based entirely on the Greek Septuagint: "beatus homo cuius fortitudo est in te semitae in corde eius transeuntes in valle fletus fontem ponent eam." The modern Nova Vulgata has: "Beatus vir, cuius est auxilium abs te, ascensiones in corde suo disposuit. Transeuntes per vallem sitientem in fontem ponent eam." Both versions of Jerome's translation of this Psalm, the so-called "Gallican" version and the version *iuxta Hebraicum* can be found side-by-side in the Stuttgart edition of the Vulgate.

The sermon Thomas developed based on the division he makes of this *thema* is fairly straightforward. Thomas seems to have run out of time at the end of the *collatio*, however, and so was not able to finish all of what he had intended to say about the endpoint of St. Martin's happiness—the subject of his third division. So he concluded very simply with one sentence: "So, because the saint we celebrate today has well prepared his ascent in the progress of happiness, he has arrived at the endpoint of happiness, which is eternal glory, to which may we be led by him who with the Father and the Holy Spirit, etc." And with this, he brings his *collatio* to its close.

Sermon 20

Thomas seems to have had a similar problem finishing all he set out to do when he delivered Sermon 20 (*Beata gens*). For this sermon, he took the *thema* from Psalm 33:12: "Beata gens cuius est Dominus Deus eius, populus quem elegit in hereditatem sibi" ("Happy the nation whose Lord is its God, the people whom he has chosen for his inheritance"). Whereas in Sermon 21 Thomas based his *divisio* on three verbs, here in Sermon 20, there are only two verbs, but Thomas will still make a fourfold *divisio* based on verbal associations with the noun *gens* ("the nation"), the phrase *cuius est Dominus Deus eius* ("whose Lord is its God"), the noun *populus* ("the people"), and the verb *elegit* ("he has elected" or "he has chosen"). Here happiness is not the primary topic, although it comes up in passing in the second section, on "whose Lord is its God." Instead the primary topic is, in accord with the celebration of the day, a fourfold praise of the saints: first, based on their dignity, which he associates with the words "Happy the nation"; second, based on their leader, which he associates with the words "whose Lord is its God"; third, based on how they are arranged, which he associates with the word "people"; and fourth, based on their election, which he associates with the words "whom the Lord has chosen for his inheritance."

According to Thomas, the *dignity* of the saints consists in three things: (1) they have arrived at the place for which we strive, the eternal Kingdom; (2) they possess everything we desire and even more; and (3) they are invested above what we can understand. When we come to the second section, in which Thomas calls to mind *their leader*—that is to say, because their "Lord is God"—it is here that we get his extended discussion of happiness. At first, Thomas sets forth arguments as to why our happiness can lie only in God: (1) it would be miserable to be subordinate to someone inferior or to a villain; (2) the highest perfection of a thing is to be subordinate to what is more perfect than it; (3) as *materia* is not perfect unless it is subordinate to a *forma*, so the soul is not perfect unless it is subordinate to God; (4) thus, our happiness lies in being subordinate to God. Next, he takes up and refutes several counter-arguments: first, "but there were and are some people who have said that our happiness is in earthly things"; second, "so too there were and are some, like the Stoics, who say that happiness is found in internal goods such as virtues and knowledge"; and third, "still others say that happiness is found in things that are next to us" (i.e., "they put their trust in humankind").

After responding to each of these objections in turn, Thomas takes up the meaning of the word "its" in the phrase: "Happy the nation whose Lord is *its* God." According to Thomas, this "its" (*eius*)—which you will notice is the last word in the Latin phrase and is thus treated last in the morning's sermon—means that God is to be: (1) known, both by a clear and direct vision and by a perfect similarity to Him; (2) possessed; and (3) enjoyed.

In these final two sections of the morning's sermon and continuing in his evening vespers we see Thomas incorporating into his sermon, albeit rather awkwardly, the Beatitudes from Christ's Sermon on the Mount. (He does a better much job of this in Sermon 19, as we will see shortly.) In the final two sections of the morning sermon, he is able to mention four of the Beatitudes in association with topics he is covering: (1) "Blessed are the poor in spirit"; (2) "Blessed are the meek"; (3) "Blessed are those who hunger and thirst for justice"; and (4) "Blessed are the merciful." Later that evening at vespers, he repeats "Blessed are the poor in spirit," "Blessed are the meek," "Blessed are those who hunger and thirst for justice," and "Blessed are the merciful," before adding "Blessed are the peacemakers" and "Blessed are the pure in heart," leaving out "Blessed are the persecuted" and "Blessed are those who mourn," both of which he is able to fit, with all the rest of the Beatitudes, into Sermon 19.

In the *collatio* at vespers, Thomas was supposed to dilate upon the final two sections of his opening *divisio*: how the saints are arranged, which he associates with the word "people," and their election, which he associates with the words "whom the Lord has chosen for his inheritance." In practice, things seem to have turned out somewhat differently.

Thomas began the vespers *collatio* as planned, dilating upon *populus* ("people"), which calls to mind how the saints are arranged—namely, as a people. A "people," says Thomas, quoting St. Augustine, is "a multitude of men and women together, united by a consensus of law and by a common purpose."[29] From this definition, Thomas generates his next three topics for development: (1) first, the saints are a "multitude"; (2) second, they are arranged in "an ordered manner" according to the Beatitudes; and (3) third, they enjoy a "harmonious union."

The problem is that, after discussing the saints as a "multitude," Thomas seems as though he is going to forego discussing the second and third of these—the order among the saints and their harmonious union—and proceed right on to his fourth division, "the election of the saints," which he associated in his opening *divisio* with the final part of his *thema* verse: *quem elegit in hereditatem sibi* ("whom he has chosen for his inheritance"). He says at this point in the *collatio* (if the scribe and/or the manuscript are a reliable witness): "We must speak about the election of the saints." But he does not go on to speak of their election. Instead, he goes on as planned to discuss the "ordered distinction" among the saints according to the Beatitudes. But during this discussion, he also makes a lengthy digression in which he argues against those who claim that, since virginity involves a total renunciation of sex, it cannot be a mean. After disposing of this objection by pointing out that virtue is a mean according to reason, but not always according to quantity, he continues his discussion of the "ordered distinction" among the saints in terms of the remaining Beatitudes.

If Thomas had stuck to the structure laid out in his earlier *divisiones*, he would have moved on to discuss "the harmonious union among the saints" and finally their election. But it is clear from the manuscript that he did not have time. So, after a quick (and incomplete) summing up of his previous comments—"It is clear now how the poor have acquired the kingdom; the meek, the earth; the mourning, consolation; those who hunger after justice have received satisfaction; the merciful gained mercy; the clean, the vision of God; and the peacemakers are called children of God"—he concludes. We have no idea why Thomas had to cut the *collatio* short. Perhaps the digression on virginity took him longer than he thought. Perhaps it was some external factor at work. We can imagine even the best preachers run short on time now and then. Closer to our present concerns,

---

[29] The reference is to Augustine's *De civitate Dei* 19.31, a section in which Augustine is similarly attempting to demonstrate the superior happiness of the saints in the eternal City of God over the limited sort of happiness that can be obtained by dedicating oneself completely to any earthly commonwealth, such as Rome. For a good discussion, see Veronica Roberts, "Augustine's Ciceronian Response to the Ciceronian Patriot," *Perspectives on Political Science* 45.2 (2016): 113–24. For another interesting perspective, see R. A. Markus, *Saeculum: History and Society in the Theology of St. Augustine* (Cambridge, UK: Cambridge University Press, 1970), 65–71.

however, is the realization that we can *know for sure* Thomas was forced to cut his comments shorter than he had anticipated precisely because he had not finished working through all the sections of his opening *divisio*.

The benefit of setting up a clear structure at the beginning of the sermon is that it allows the congregation to follow along in an orderly fashion; the drawback is that it is very apparent when the speaker does not have sufficient time to finish everything he set out to do. One wonders how embarrassing this might have been for the preacher, not to mention how much it would have left the listeners wondering what the preacher *would have said*.

Sermon 19

We turn, finally, to Sermon 19 (*Beati qui habitant*), another sermon for the Feast of All Saints. Here Thomas takes Psalm 84:4 as the *thema*: "Beati qui habitant in domo tua, Domine, in secula seculorum laudabunt" ("Blessed are those who dwell in your house, O Lord; they will praise you forever and ever"). Having seen Thomas's practice in Sermons 21 and 20, our first question might be: Will he divide the topic of the happiness of the saints (*beati*) in a progression as he did in Sermon 21, or will he set up a series of topics of the "who-what-when-where" type as he did in Sermon 20? The answer is that he does neither.

This sermon is odd, which is why I have left it for last, in that the overall structure is *not* the usual one for a sermon of the *sermo modernus* style. It is also especially ingenious. In a "modern sermon," the "declaration of parts" is supposed to come immediately after the opening *thema* or immediately after the *prothema*, if there is one, or right after a brief introduction. Given the *thema* verse he has chosen, we might have expected Thomas to make a twofold *divisio* in accord with the two phrases that make up the whole: (1) "Blessed are those who dwell in your house, O Lord"; and (2) "they will praise you forever and ever." Not only does he *not* do that, he does not set forth a clear "statement of the parts" at all. As I explain in my analytical outline of this sermon in the appendix, one can discern a rough outline, but the relevant part of the *thema* verse will appear at the end of a section rather than at the beginning.

The subject of the entire sermon is related to the first word in the *thema* verse, *Beati*, which can be translated "blessed," but which is sometimes translated "happy." Thus, the entire sermon involves a series of reflections on happiness or "blessedness" (*beatitudo*). At points in that discussion, Thomas mentions the saints, but not throughout.

If we take "blessedness," which he associates with the first word of the *thema* verse, *Beati*, to be the subject of the entire sermon, then we can discern three major sections related to the remaining words in the verse. In the first section of the sermon, Thomas discusses three ways in which people err with regard to happiness. (1) Some people err, says Thomas, regarding the abode of happiness, a discussion he relates to the words *qui habitant in domo tua* (those "who live in your house"). (2) Others err, he says, concerning the duration of happiness, which he relates to the next words in the Latin verse, *in secula seculorum* ("forever and ever"). (3) And finally, there are those who err concerning the occupation or operation of the happy ones (the *beati*), which he relates to the final word in Latin, *laudabunt* ("they will praise"). As I mentioned above, this structure is not stated clearly at the beginning of each section; it is stated at the end, as though providing an answer to the question posed by the discussion.

In the second section of the sermon, Thomas discusses how we can arrive at the sort of true happiness enjoyed by the "blessed" (the *beati*, the happy ones). This section is organized around the three types of happiness—worldly, political, and contemplative—and the answer to the question of how we can arrive at happiness is given in terms of the eight Beatitudes from the Sermon on the Mount recounted in Matthew 5:3–11, each of which begins in Latin with the word *beati*, "blessed [are]," (the poor, the meek, those who mourn, etc.).

In the third section of the sermon, then, Thomas brings together the three types of happiness from the previous section—worldly, political, and contemplative—with each member of his original threefold division of the *thema* verse. Thus we can say of the happiness of the saints (the *beati*) that: (1) compared to earthly happiness, the happiness of the saints has an abundant abode (hence it says: "Happy are those who live in your house"); (2) compared to the happiness that belongs to the political life, the saints have continuity, for the ruler of a city ought to apply himself to preserve the good of the city all the time (hence it says: "forever and ever"); and (3) compared to the happiness that belongs to contemplation, the saints live with the divine things, since contemplative happiness consists particularly in contemplation, which the saints do (hence it [the opening *thema* verse] says: "They will praise you").

The structure of the whole is remarkably ingenious. While it employs the opening *thema* verse as a structuring device, it does so in a novel and fascinating way. And along the way, Thomas is able to incorporate flawlessly not only all eight Beatitudes but also a discussion of earthly, political, and contemplative happiness in relation to the happiness enjoyed by the saints. It is a fascinating sermon, filled with invaluable instruction for the faithful and profound insights about the nature of the blessedness. The overall structure is well ordered and the coordination of the parts ingenious. It just was not fully in accord with the canons of the *sermo modernus* style, however important or unimportant that might have been.

Perhaps there is a valuable lesson in this variation from the standard pattern, however. Perhaps it is important to understand that the "rules" and examples that we find in treatises such as the *Ars concionandi* and Robert of Basevorn's *Forma praedicandi* are idealized examples of patterns that were often much more ragged in actual practice than these manuals might suggest. Anyone who has used a manual for nearly any activity—say, auto repair—knows that things do not always look the same as the manuals say they will or work the same way that the manuals say they should. Spark plugs are sometimes of a different sort than the manual says you will find, and although the manufacturer may have used regular screws, *somebody* may at some point have replaced them with Philips-head screws. Finding exceptions is the rule. Such was likely also the case with "modern sermons" of the thirteenth century. This fact appears to be one among the many things we can learn from unfinished Sermons 21 and 20 and the ingenious but uncharacteristic organization of Sermon 19.

We have reviewed the general principles because I believe they will help the reader to appreciate these medieval sermons and, by knowing what to look for, read them more easily. I wish I could say this system will always work. But it will not. I'm told that there's an old dictum among pharmacists and physicians about medicine that goes something like this: Some things work some of the time; a few things work a lot of the time; but nothing works all of the time. So too with the guidelines one finds in manuals: some of it applies a lot of the time, but none of it will apply in absolutely every case. So, be forewarned: sometimes you just have to read and do your best.

The value of recognizing when a sermon does not fit the general pattern, however, is that then one can inquire why this is so. Did the author simply not have the time or talent to craft the sermon correctly? Or did he, having learned the rules, decide to break them purposefully for effect? Our goal here was simply to compare and contrast three sermons, all using a Psalm verse as the opening *thema*, all having as their first word some version of the Latin word *beatus*, but all very different in content and execution. In one (Sermon 21, *Beatus vir*), Thomas expounded upon the relationship between happiness and the life of virtue. In another (Sermon 20, *Beata gens*), the topic was the happiness of the saints in heaven. And in a third (Sermon 19, *Beati qui habitant*), a sermon we might have expected would have dealt primarily with the happiness of the saints ("Blessed are they who dwell in your house"), he dealt instead primarily with the errors that lead people to *unhappiness*.

As I have tried to show throughout this chapter, the forms and patterns of the *sermo modernus* style did not restrict the flexibility or creativity of the medieval preacher adept at its use. Rather it provided a basic structure—a "tree trunk," as it was sometimes describe, from which he could follow various branches large and small to reach the fruit of his choice. The patterns of the style were no more stifling to Thomas's preaching than the notes on the scale and the rules of composition were to Mozart's concertos or Bach's cantatas. These formal patterns seem to have provided, instead, various avenues through which to channel their amazing genius.

From *Divisio* to *Dilatatio*

The classical scheme of the rhetorical art made famous by writers such as Cicero and Quintilian suggested that a speech should have six parts: the *exordium* or introduction; the *narratio* or statement of the case; the *divisio* (or *partitio*), the statement of the arguments to be used in the case; the *confirmatio*, or proof of the case; the *confutatio*, or refutation of opposing arguments; and finally the *peroration*, or conclusion. Listing the parts in this way, however, can make the classical speech seem highly rigid, which in practice it was not. Both Cicero and Quintilian encouraged writers to rearrange the parts when it would help their case. In addition, *inventio* and *dispositio* were understood to be dynamic, interrelated activities. The practice of formulating one's arguments (*dispositio*) could often result in the discovery of new arguments (*inventio*). An orator's task was to refine his speech until the arguments and their organization were just right for the situation at hand.

Just as the two first parts of the classical rhetorician's art were *inventio* (the discovery of arguments) and *dispositio* (the arrangement of arguments), so too, I would suggest, for the medieval preacher, the first two parts of his art after selecting a biblical verse for his *thema* were *divisio* and "declaration of the parts." A medieval preacher's choice of which biblical verse to use for his sermon might have been limited by the cycle of lectionary readings for the day, but he still had a great deal of creative room in which to maneuver in crafting how he would approach his topic. Choosing how to craft the *divisio* and how to make the declaration of parts was as important a part of the rhetorical art of the *sermo-moder-*

nus-style preacher as *inventio* and *dispositio* were for the art of the classical rhetorician.

And yet, just as for classical rhetoricians, after *inventio* and *dispositio*, there was still plenty of work to do in crafting the body of the speech, along with plenty of rhetorical devices that the skilled speech writer could employ, so too after *divisio* and *declaratio*, the medieval preacher still needed to develop his theme. These methods of "developing" a theme were included under the general heading of *dilatatio*, "dilation." And it is for this reason that, if we are to understand how a medieval sermon was constructed, the common methods of *dilatatio* must be our next subject of investigation.

AQUINAS, SERMON 13: *HOMO QUIDAM* [SEE FULLER OUTLINE IN THE APPENDIX]

Homo quidam fecit cenam magnam et vocavit multos. (*Luke* 14:16)
A certain man made a great supper and invited many.

Just as the body cannot be maintained without physical refreshment, so also the soul is in need of spiritual refreshment for its maintenance. . . . Concerning this spiritual refreshment, we can see two things in today's Gospel: first, the preparation of this refreshment ("**A certain man made a great dinner**"); second, the announcement of the feast when it was prepared, ("**and he invited many**").

I. "A certain man made a great dinner"— We must consider: First, the man who made the dinner; second, the kind of dinner it is; and third, how it is great.

A) Who made the dinner? ("a certain man")

1. The man is the Son of God, who is truly a man in view of his assumed human nature,

2. It indicates a "certain" man, as if to say some particular things are in him not in others:

a) The fullness of divinity;

b) The fullness of truth;

c) The fullness of grace

B) What kind of dinner it is and its greatness ("made a great dinner") — a triple refreshment:

1. Sacramental refreshment (since Christ has the fullness of grace)

2. Intellectual Refreshment (since Christ has the fullness of truth)

3. Refreshment for our affection (since Christ has the fullness of divinity)

BONAVENTURE, SERMON 29: *HOMO QUIDAM*

Under the veil of these words is mystically signified and enfolded the celestial glory, which the Lord will offer to his elect at the end of the world. Thus this meal, which is at the end of the day, is called supper. Our Lord, moreover, commends three things in the proposed verse, which render any supper complete and perfect: first the excellence of the singular dignity ("**a certain man**"); second, the affluence of abundant bounty ("**made a great supper**"); third, the benevolence of welcoming cordiality ("**and invited many**").

I. *A certain man*: Christ is commended for excellence of singular dignity.
   A) By reason of his purity and innocence in avoiding all sins
   B) By reason of profound wisdom in the revelation of divine mysteries
   C) By reason of forceful power in the working of many miracles

II. *made a great supper*: Christ is commended for the affluent abundance or overflowing bounty
   A) Three characteristics of the supper:
      1. Pleasure of exultant happiness due to the reflection of divine clarity
      2. The bounty of satiating refreshment due to the overflowing of immense goodness
      3. The eternity of continual duration due to the lack of all defects
   B) Thus the soul is:
      1. Pleased by the clarity of splendor with regard to the rational power
      2. Satiated by the bounty of refreshment with regard to the concupiscent power

Collatio *(at vespers)*

II. "He invited many"
  A) Two kinds of calling:
    1. Interiorly (God directly)
    2. Exteriorly (servants who say "Come!")
  B) Who are called?
    1. Those who were invited (received the privilege of a divine office) but did not come because of a triple hindrance:
      a) Pride
      b) Concupiscence of the eye
      c) Concupiscence of the flesh
    2. The weak, the blind, and the lame, who failed in:
      a) Knowledge ("blind")
      b) Virtue due to sin ("weak")
      c) Rectitude ("lame")
    3. Strangers—("There is still room"): Unbelievers, of three types:
      a) Those in the dark roads: those with no faith
      b) Those in the scattered roads: the Jews, who share the Old Testament.
      c) Those in the hedges: heretics (because hedges divide and their thorns sting)
  C) How are they called? There is a triple manner of calling:
    1. The ones invited by simple summons
    2. The poor and downtrodden must be *led* inside
    3. The unbelievers and heretics must be compelled

   3. It is secured by the eternity of duration with regard to the irascible power.
C) Threefold dowry of glory:
   1. Unobstructed vision
   2. Quiet enjoyment
   3. Firm security

III. *and invited many*: Christ is commended by the benevolence of his welcoming charity

CHAPTER 4

Dilatatio: Methods of "Unfolding" a Sermon

DILATATIO IS LITERALLY "AN EXPANDING" (as in the English "dilation"), a process I have described above as a kind of "unpacking" or "unfolding" of the *thema* verse, although the term is also sometimes translated as "amplification." We will once again in this chapter be making use of Robert of Basevorn's *Forma praedicandi* to help provide us with a general picture of how *dilatatio* was done.[1] I will remind the reader that Robert's text was likely not written until 1322, long after Aquinas's death in 1274, so it could not possibly have had any direct influence on him. We are using Robert's text merely to help us organize our approach to Thomas's sermons and to help provide us with categories of analysis that are roughly contemporaneous. So, for example, when we discuss medieval preaching, we cannot simply apply the classical rhetorical categories of *inventio*, *dispositio*, *elocutio*, *memoria*, and *actio*. It is not that they do not apply *at all*, but these are not the categories that medieval preachers themselves used. When they thought about crafting a sermon, instead of *dispositio*, they thought in terms of *divisio*, which we examined in the previous chapter, and *dilatatio*, which will be our subject in the present chapter.

---

[1] Robert of Basevorn, *The Form of Preaching*, trans. Leopold Krul, O.S.B., in *Three Medieval Rhetorical Arts*, ed. James J. Murphy (Berkeley: University of California Press, 1971); ch. 39, which contains the eight methods of *dilatatio* and appears on 180–84 (see n. 88 for more detail). This material can be found in Latin in Thomas Charland, *Artes Praedicandi: contribution à l'histoire de la rhétorique au moyen âge*, Publications de l'Institut d'Etudes Medievales d'Ottawa 7 (Paris/Ottowa: J. Vrin/Institute of Medieval Studies, 1936), 233–323 (the whole of Basevorn's work).

As for the methods of *dilatatio*, chapter 39 of the *Forma praedicandi* and section 3 of the "Bonaventuran" *Ars concionandi* are, as I mentioned above in my discussion of these two texts in chapter 2, nearly identical. I did not there, and will not here, hazard a guess as to which text came before the other. Both are useful for our purposes, but in the present case, the *Ars concionandi* not only has more examples but is also (in this case, as was not true for its discussion of *divisio*) nicely organized.

Both the *Ars concionandi* and Robert's *Forma praedicandi* list eight methods of *dilatatio*. According to both manuals, the eight ways the various parts of a *divisio* set forth in a "declaration of parts" can be "dilated" or developed in a sermon are these:

1. By proposing a discussion based on a noun as it occurs in definitions or classifications (*proponendo orationem pro nomine, sicut fit in diffinitionibus seu quibuscumque notificationibus*).
2. By subdivisions of the original *divisio* (*per divisionem*).
3. By reasoning or argumentation (*ratiocinando vel argumentando*).
4. By "chaining" together concordant authorities (*per auctoritates concordantes*).
5. By setting up a series running from the positive through the comparative and arriving finally at the superlative in the manner of "good, better, best" (*ut ponendo superlativum curratur ad positivum et comparativum*).
6. By devising metaphors through the properties of a thing (*excogitando metaphoras per proprietetem rei*).
7. By expounding the *thema* in diverse ways accordingly to the literal, allegorical, tropological, and/or anagogical senses (*exponere thema diversimode: historice, allegorice, moraliter, anagogice*).
8. By a consideration of causes and their effects (*per causas et effectus*).

As might be expected, Thomas is adept at each of these methods and makes frequent use of nearly all of them at one point or another, even in the few sermons of his that still survive. Allow me to illustrate with examples of each.

METHOD 1: PROPOSING A DISCUSSION BASED ON A NOUN AS IT OCCURS IN DEFINITIONS OR CLASSIFICATIONS

Let us say that the *thema* for the sermon is to be taken from Wisdom 10:10, which says that Wisdom "led the just man in the right paths, and showed him the reign of God, and gave him the knowledge of holy things." And let us say that the preacher divides this passage by saying that, in this text, Wisdom does three things for the just man: first, "she *led the just man in the right paths*"; second, she "*showed him the reign of God*"; and third, she "*gave him the knowledge of holy things*."

Our question now is how the preacher can "develop" or "dilate" each of these three. For our present purposes, let us focus on only the first of these three, in which Wisdom is said to have "led the just man in the right paths." According to the nearly identical instructions in both the *Ars concionandi* and Basevorn's *Forma praedicandi* (which henceforth I will simply refer to as "our manuals"), one could "dilate" this phrase, first, by defining the "just man" as "he who gives everyone his proper due." Then the preacher might further develop this thought by expounding upon how "giving everyone his proper due" applies, first, to God, second, to one's neighbor, and finally, to oneself.

Or, alternatively, the preacher might choose to define "justice" and then develop the idea by expounding upon those things that are *contrary to* justice, such as vices of various sorts or surrender to the passions. Or one might discuss the virtues *related to* justice, such as prudence, temperance, and fortitude. For example, one might suggest that: *prudence* is "the ability to discern good things from evil"; *fortitude* "the sustaining of difficulties because of love"; and *temperance* "the firm command of sensual desires." The preacher would then introduce this discussion or conclude it using words such as these: "Therefore, prudence consists in *discerning*, fortitude in *enduring*, temperance in *checking illicit passions*, and justice in *giving to each one his proper due*."[2] And with this, the preacher would be off and running. Using this method, he would have succeeded in taking one word from his *thema* verse—in this case "just"—and turning it into a discussion about not only justice, but about all of the cardinal virtues. And given that the original context proposes that it is "Wisdom" who is "leading the just man," the preacher might discourse on the relationship between Wisdom and the virtues, or on how God's "Wisdom" is the Holy Spirit, then devel-

---

[2] *Ars concionandi* 3.33. All Latin quotes of this work are taken from the 1901 Quaracchi edition (see n. 86 for more detail). All English translation is from Harry Charles Hazel, "A Translation, with Commentary, of the Bonaventuran *'Ars Concionandi'*" (PhD diss., Washington State University, 1972).

oping the relationship between the virtues and the Gifts of the Holy Spirit. The possibilities are nearly endless—so much so that the *Ars concionandi* bids the aspiring preacher to notice "how an expansion can be made in the oration by using a noun, not only by indicating what is contained in the [word] itself, but also by indicating other things which can be drawn from it."[3] Indeed, I would be willing to guess that this tendency to "draw into" the sermon subjects not mentioned in the opening biblical verse may be one of the characteristics of medieval preaching that modern readers will find most disconcerting.

And yet, medieval preachers were also warned that there were limits— that they "should not attempt to take up definitions or descriptions of everything indiscriminately."[4] How well any particular preacher is judged to have observed those limits—that is, how "indiscriminate" he might appear to be in the definitions and descriptions he has added to a particular sermon—will likely depend to a large degree upon each reader's taste and tolerance for such things. Readers who just want to "get to the point and be done with it" will likely find these "dilations" on various related topics annoying. Others, like me, who enjoy word games and word associations and seeing the connections between ideas, may find the method rather more delightful. Like any word game, though, the method can be confusing and thus a bit frustrating at first. But once you get the hang of it, the results can be not only intellectually satisfying, but great fun.

A simple example of this first method of "dilation" within Thomas's sermons can be found early on in Sermon 4 (*Osanna filio David*), a sermon delivered during Advent, in which Thomas dilates upon the word "Hosanna" in the opening *thema* from Matthew 21:9: "Hosanna, the son of David; blessed is he who comes in the name of the Lord." Thomas begins with a threefold *divisio* of his opening *thema*. "In these words we can consider three things to the praise of our Savior: first, the task of our Savior [which he will associate with the word "Hosanna" for reasons we will discuss in a moment]; second, the privilege of his origin [which Thomas associates with the words 'the son of David; blessed is he who comes in the name of the Lord']; and third, the highest point of his power [which Thomas associates with the last part of the verse: 'Hosanna in the highest']."[5] No-

---

3   Ibid.
4   Ibid.
5   All English translation of material from Aquinas's sermons is, again, taken from *Thomas Aquinas: The Academic Sermons*, trans. Mark-Robin Hoogland, C.P., The Fathers of the Church: Mediaeval Continuation 11 (Washington, DC: Catholic University of America Press, 2010), although I have emended the translation occasionally after con-

tice that crafting the *divisio* in this manner has allowed Thomas to take a simple exclamation of praise, "Hosanna to God in the highest," and turn it into an outline for a long sermon that incorporates key points of Christology and soteriology.

And yet, making a suitable *divisio* is merely as a promissory note for things to come. Thomas's task now, however, is to "develop" or "unpack" each of these topics that he has introduced in this opening section. How does he do it? In this case, he begins with the word "hosanna" and sets up a discussion based upon its definition. "Hosanna," he says, "is the same as 'hosyanna' which means 'Save, I beseech.'" Now, if the reader is concerned that Thomas has, in this instance, made use of, say, one of St. Isidore's less reliable etymologies, he need not be. As it turns out, Thomas is quite right. The most recent entry in the Oxford English Dictionary, for example, indicates that the Latin *osanna* or *hosanna* is related to the Greek ὡσαννά or ὠσαννά, which was the Greek way of representing the Hebrew *hōshaʿ-nā*, an abbreviated form of *hōshīʿāh-nnā*, meaning "save, pray!"

So much for the definition. How does one develop a section of a sermon based on a definition? Thomas says, as we have seen, that "the task of the savior is mentioned because it [the *thema* verse] says 'Hosanna,'"—that is to say, we humans are "in need of salvation." And this provides Thomas with the opening he needs: "The human race was in need of salvation for three reasons," says Thomas: "the perversity of sin, the oppression of enemies, and the rejection of the glory of the world." And this is how a medieval preacher such as Thomas can use the definition of one word, in this case "hosanna," to set up three distinct topics for discussion.

Another example in the *Ars concionandi* suggests that, if the name "Jacob" should appear in the *thema*, the preacher might mention, for example, that Gregory the Great interpreted the name "Jacob" as *wrestler* or *supplanter* because he fought with an angel. Then from this definition, he might continue in this vein, saying: "every faithful man should *supplant* vices and *wrestle* with the conniving soul."[6]

Thomas does something similar in Sermon 2 (*Lauda et laetare*). He begins with a threefold *divisio* of his opening *thema* verse from Zechariah 2:10, "Praise and rejoice, O daughter of Zion, for behold, I come, and I will dwell in your midst" ("Lauda et laetare filia Sion quia ecce ego venio

---

sulting the Latin text in vol. 44.1 (2014) of the Leonine edition (see nn. 3–5 for further discussion).
6   Ibid.

et habitabo in medio tui").[7] "Here the prophet does three things," says Thomas:

(1) First, he shows the affection of the holy fathers who preceded the coming of the Savior, continually persisting in their praises of him, where he says: "Praise and rejoice, O daughter of Zion." (2) Second, he shows the Son of God himself coming down from the heavens: "Behold I come." (3) And third, he shows him humbly appearing in human flesh: "And I will dwell in your midst."

With regard to the first, "the joy of the holy fathers," Thomas "dilates" by creating a subdivision—a method we will discuss in more detail shortly—and in that first subdivision, he says that "three things are required for perfect gladness": first, "that the mind is elevated to a divine benefit," which is indicated where it says "Daughter of Zion"; second, "that the affection is enlarged by spiritual joy," which is indicated where it says "rejoice"; and third, "that the tongue is excited to the favorable gift of the divine praise," which is indicated where the text bids us to "praise." Now, the latter two associations—"affection enlarged by spiritual joy" with "rejoice" and a "tongue excited to give divine praise" with "praise"—will likely make sense to the reader. But what about associating the mind's *elevation* with the phrase "daughter of Zion"? How is that possible? The answer is that the word "Zion," says Thomas, can be interpreted to mean "watchtower"[8] and the image of a "watchtower" suggests the notion of a mind *elevated*. Thus, "understood in a spiritual way," says Thomas, the phrase "Daughter of Zion" signifies the soul of someone contemplating, watching patiently, just as the night watchman on the watchtower looks forward eagerly to the coming dawn. This is the image Thomas wants his listeners to have of the fathers who preceded the coming of the Savior: minds elevated as the watchman is elevated above the city, waiting patiently but expectantly for the coming of Christ as the watchman awaits patiently but eagerly the coming dawn.

Sometimes, instead of defining a word, Thomas will list out some of what he takes to be its essential properties, each of which he will then ex-

---

[7] Fr. Hoogland cites this verse as being from Zechariah 2:14, but I can find it in only Zechariah 2:10.

[8] It was interpreted thus at least from the time of St. Jerome (e.g., his *Commentary on Jeremiah* 6:2–4a and the *Commentary on Isaiah* 24:23) up to the time of Erasmus (e.g., his *Paraphrasis in Lucam* 19:40–2). One can find it additionally in Augustine's *Expositions of the Psalms* 134:21.

pand upon. Consider, for example, how Thomas dilates on the word "king" in Sermon 5 (*Ecce rex tuus*), as we saw in chapter 1, by suggesting that the four things that characterize a king are: first, that he must be the *only* king; second, that he possesses fullness of power; third, that he has full jurisdiction; and fourth, that he exhibits equity of justice. He then applies each of these to the way in which Christ is "king." In each case, the content is created by expanding upon various descriptions or characteristics implied by a noun, "king" (*rex*), in the opening *thema*.

We find a similar example in Sermon 11 (*Emitte Spiritum*), a sermon on the Feast of Pentecost, in which Thomas begins with the famous "Holy Spirit" prayer from Psalm 104:30—"Send forth your Spirit and they shall be created, and you will renew the face of the earth" (*"Emitte Spiritum tuum et creabuntur et renouabis faciem terrae"*). Although there are three clauses in this verse—(1) send forth your Spirit; (2) they shall be created; and (3) you will renew the face of the earth—Thomas chooses to make a rather unexpected fourfold *divisio*: (1) "send out"; (2) "your spirit"; (3) "and they will be created and you will renew"; and finally, (4) "the face of the earth." Thomas's "declaration of parts," then, reads as follows:

> We can consider four things in these words, namely, (1) the property of the Holy Spirit, (2) his mission, (3) the strength of the One sent, and (4) the receptive *materia* of this strength. For it says: "Send out"—behold, the mission (2); "your Spirit"—see, the Person sent (1); "and they will be created, and you will renew"—lo, the effect of the One sent (3); "the face of the earth"—see, the receptive *materia* of this effect (4).

In Thomas's discussion of the "effects of the One sent"—that is, the Holy Spirit—he suggests that one of the "effects" of the Spirit is *peace*. Now there are "two sorts of peace," he says: one in the present in which, although we live peacefully, we still struggle against vice; and the other that we will have in the future where there is no struggle. "But which of these is true peace?" asks Thomas. Although the answer, "the future peace where there is no struggle," seems pretty obvious, Thomas has more to add, and he does so precisely by "dilating" on a definition of "peace" he finds in a sermon of St. Augustine, that "Peace is serenity of mind, tranquility of soul, simplicity of heart, a bond of love [*amor*], and the company of love [*caritas*]."[9] Thomas is then able to expand upon this definition in

---

[9] See Aquinas, *Catena Aurea in John,* ch. 14, lec. 7: "Augustinus de Verb. Dom.: 'Est autem pax serenitas mentis, tranquillitas animi, simplicitas cordis, amoris vinculum,

the paragraph that follows, claiming (based on Augustine's definition of "peace") that:

> True peace is threefold: in relation to yourself, to your neighbor, and to God. As for peace with yourself, it is required that your reason not be infected by errors or obscured by passions, and in view of this, he [Augustine] says: "Peace is security of mind." There also needs to be quietness in one's affection, and in view of this he [Augustine] says: "quietness of soul." Furthermore, there ought to be simplicity in one's intention, and in view of this he [Augustine] says: "simplicity of heart." Peace with your neighbor is "a bond of love [*amor*]," and the peace through which we have a bond with God is "the company of charity [*caritas*]."

Notice that, at this point, Thomas *could* have chosen to take up each of these categories in turn, starting with why it is important that "reason not be infected by errors or obscured by passions" and moving on from there to show how the virtues of temperance or humility are necessary for "quietness of soul" and "simplicity of heart." This is not, in fact, what he does here, choosing instead to move on to the question "Is peace, then, very necessary for us?" But notice that the power of the *sermo modernus* style is that, once the preacher has set up the definition and distinctions as Thomas has here, the possibilities for developing each of these points in turn are nearly endless.

The power and flexibility of the method come from the fact that one word can suggest another word or a series of distinctions, all of which provide potential topics that can be developed in their turn in a process not

---

consortium caritatis.'" The work entitled *De verbis Domini* (short for *De verbis Domini et quibusdam sententiis Pauli Apostoli*) was one of the most popular collections of Augustine's sermons in the Middle Ages. It contained almost one hundred pieces and seems to have been conceived by its compilers as constituting a commentary on the Gospels and the Pauline epistles. Modern scholarship suggests at least some of the sermon material in this collection may have been spurious. This particular text can be found in Sermon 97 (*PL*, 39:1931), in a section containing sermons that even the Migne editors considered inauthentic. Indeed, an exhaustive search of Augustine's extant works in Latin did not turn up this particular quotation or any vestiges of it. I have altered Fr. Hoogland's translation here a bit in accord with the original Latin. For some reason, he seems to have translated *serenitas mentis* as "security of mind," perhaps because he had a slightly different Latin text. Thomas's point is that the mind should not be "infected by errors or obscured by passions." I take it that a "serenity of mind" is what would allow our minds to avoid being obscured by *passions*. The difference, however, is minor.

entirely unlike the process of *reminiscentia* we described above in chapter 1. Once the author has a key word and decides how to "dilate" it, then the rest "spills out" rather naturally through the natural connections of words and concepts. The preacher is not struggling at each step to dream up new content *ex nihilo*. Rather, he begins with the divine words and lets *them* bring to his mind associations and connections of the sort that his theological training has provided for him. He did not need to remember chapter after chapter of the *Summa* to do this—although Thomas was more than capable of that, as we know. Rather, one key word was often enough to begin the process of recollecting. More material is available in our "deep memory" than in our short-term memory (what we might call, on the model of the computer, our "random access memory"). Getting the process of *recollection* going is one of the ways of accessing those deep memories. It is also one of the ways the preacher can help *create* accessible memories in the minds of his listeners. An ordered discourse allows for ordered memories.

There is also a unique synthesis here of three of the five steps in the classical art of rhetoric. Those classic five steps were:

1. *Inventio*: the "finding" of an appropriate topic and the suitable approach to the topic.
2. *Dispositio*: the arrangement of the arguments and various parts in a persuasive order.
3. *Elocutio*: perfecting the presentation and pronunciation of the speech.
4. *Memoria*: the memorization of the speech.
5. *Actio*: the actual delivery of the speech.

The *sermo modernus* method, involving as it did the art of choosing an appropriate *thema* verse, *divisio*, and *dilatatio*, combined (1) *inventio*: it helped the medieval preacher find his topic; (2) *dispositio*: it gave him a method for creating content and arranging the various parts in a suitable order; and finally (3) *memoria*: it provided a built-in way of aiding not only his memory, but the memory of his audience—the latter of these being something even the classical rhetoricians did not consider fully.

We will have more to say on the *sermo modernus* style as a uniquely new rhetorical art in the next chapter. For now, however, we must turn to the next method of "dilating" a sermon, one at which Thomas is especially adept: namely, creating subdivisions—and at times, even subdivisions on subdivisions.

METHOD 2: CREATING SUBDIVISIONS

After the original division of the opening biblical *thema*, a preacher would sometimes make further subdivisions within one or more of the "members" of his opening *divisio*. Thomas loves this method. If you take a look at one of the early sections of Sermon 1 (*Veniet desideratus*), for example, you will find a complex series of divisions and subdivisions—so complex, in fact, that, as I had mentioned in the last chapter, Fr. Hoogland saw fit to insert a complex numbering system into his English translation to try to help the reader keep things straight.

The *thema* for the entire sermon is taken from Haggai 2:8: "He who is desired by all the nations together will come, and he will fill this house with glory" ("veniet desideratus cunctis gentibus et implebo domum istam gloria").[10] Thomas divides the *thema* into three parts. With regard to the first, "he will come," he proposes that it is God's Son himself who comes down from the heavens. In the second, "who is desired by all the nations together," he shows that Christ is the one who mercifully fulfills the desires of all the patriarchs. And in the third, "and he will fill this house with glory," he shows how Christ freely bestows his pleasing benefit. So far, so good; this is nothing more than a basic threefold division of the *thema*—pretty standard fare so far.

But when we come to Thomas's *dilatatio* of the first part, "he will come" (*veniet*), here is what he says: "I interpret 'he will come' insofar as it is absolutely necessary for us." That is to say, when someone says "he *will* come," one means that it *will* happen and, thus, there is a certain sort of "necessity" involved. He continues (with Hoogland's numbering inserted):

> Well, the coming of the Savior was necessary for three reasons: first, because the world was imperfect in many ways; second, because man was cast down from his rightful honor in a foul way; and third, because God was offended by man in a wondrous way. Therefore, he came (1.1) in order to grant to the whole world the highest grade of dignity; (1.2) in order to lead man back to his proper human state; and (1.3) in order to take away the offense of man against God.

But with this, Thomas is only warming up. For he continues:

---

[10] Fr. Hoogland cites the source of this verse as Hag 2:7. I found it in a modern Vulgate edition, however, in Hag 2:8; *Biblia Sacra Vulgata*, 5th ed. (Stuttgart: Deutsche Bibelgesellschaft, 1983)—all citations are from this edition.

Now the grade of dignity [note the notion of "dignity" in 1.1 above] in the world fell short in three respects: (1.1.1) one grade of *union* is more wonderful than the others; (1.1.2) one way of generation is more sublime than the others; and (1.1.3) one way of perfection is more excellent than the others. Yet, when Christ came into this world, he accomplished a new *union* [cf. 1.1.1], he took on a new *generation* [cf. 1.1.2] and he brought along a new *perfection* [cf. 1.1.3].

So, as it turns out, what we will discover in the section that follows (which is a subsection of why Christ's coming was "necessary") is how Christ has "granted the whole world the highest grade of dignity"—and this in three ways: a new sort of *union*; a new sort of *generation*; and a new sort of *perfection*. These specific categories allow Thomas to communicate some serious Christology.

Allow me to quote the relevant passages that follow in full, along with my own subdivision system (parenthetical capital letters) added on top of Fr. Hoogland's numbering system (numbers with periods). In each case, Thomas is going to propose several different species of, first, *union*, second, *generation*, and third, *perfection*, but only the last of which will apply to Christ. Here are the next three paragraphs of his text in outline form. Recall that these paragraphs follow directly after Thomas says that "Yet, when Christ came into this world, he accomplished a new *union*; he took on a new *generation*; and he brought along a new *perfection*." The outline of the paragraphs follows:

(1.1.1) So in the world one grade of *union* was lacking, the one more wonderful than the others. For in our world there are four kinds of union:

(A) The first is the union of something corruptible with something corruptible, as in natural things.
(B) The second is the union of something corruptible with something incorruptible, as in human beings.
(C) The third is the union of something incorruptible with something incorruptible, as in spiritual things: a union of *essentia* and *potentia*.
(D) The fourth, however, was lacking: the union of something temporal with something eternal. Well, this union was made when "the Word became flesh and dwelt among us," as

it says in John 1.14; "when he emptied himself (and took on the form of a slave; made in the likeness of human beings he was, through his way of life, found a man)."

(1.1.2) Also, the one way of *generation* was lacking that is more wonderful than the others. For there are four kinds of generation in the broad sense of the word:

(A) The first is from the Father without a mother, the generation that occurs eternally.

(B) The second is without a father and without a mother, in the beginning, as with the first parents.

(C) The third is from a father and a mother, the generation that occurs all around us.

(D) The fourth did not exist before, namely, the generation from a mother without a father in time. Well, this generation was made when the Virgin conceived, when, as we read in Isaiah 10, "the stone is hewn from the mountain without hands.". . . The stone hewn from the mountain [without hands] is Christ, born from the Virgin without a human action. . . .

(1.1.3) Also lacking was the one grade of *perfection* that is more excellent than the others, although anything that is connected with *its end is* perfect. Hence, a creature is most perfect when it is united with its Creator. Well, with a triple connection a creature is conjoined with its Creator:

(A) The first is a union in respect of strength, by reason of a dependency that is in all things. . . .

(B) The second is in respect of the [human] species: through the grace that is in just people, since according to Dionysius love [*amor*] is a unifying force.

(C) The third union concerns the thing itself, by essence. This did not exist before, but it came into being when the human nature was taken on by the Son of God in unity of supposit or person. In taking on the human nature in a certain way the whole world was taken on, because, according to Gregory, "in a way every creature is a human being."

Recall that all of these subdivisions were in service of showing how Christ has granted the whole world the highest grade of dignity (1.1).

After he has finished his "dilation" of this section, he must still take up, according to his announced intentions, in section 1.2, how Christ leads man back to his proper human state and, in 1.3, how he takes away the offense of man against God. Each of these subsections will have further subsections, just as we saw with section 1.1 above. And *all of this*, please recall, is simply in service of Thomas's "unfolding" of the first phrase in his *divisio*: "he will come."

Consider how unlikely it probably would have seemed in a sermon that began with the verse "He who is desired by all the nations together will come, and he will fill this house with glory" that Thomas would be able to work into that sermon a discussion of how Christ achieved, first, the union of something temporal with something eternal, second, the generation from a mother without a father in time in the Virgin Birth, and third, how "the human nature was taken on by the Son of God in unity of supposit or person" in Christ and that "in taking on the human nature, in a certain way the whole world was taken on."

After Thomas has finished with all these subdivisions and sub-subdivisions under the heading "he will come," it still remains for him to "unfold" the material that he is going to associate with the second part of his opening *thema* verse, the phrase "he who is desired by all the nations together," in which he intends to show that "Christ is the one who mercifully fulfills the desires of all the patriarchs." And finally, he will have to "unpack" the last part of the *thema* verse, "he will fill this house with glory," in order to show how "Christ freely bestows his pleasing benefit."

Anyone who knows the infinite orderliness and elasticity of Thomas's mind will realize how capable he is of dividing his divisions into further subdivisions, all the while mentally keeping track of each and every one of them. A sermon as complex as this one exhibits a sophisticated orderliness of parts to whole on par even with that of Thomas's *Summa of Theology*.

In making these subdivisions, Thomas generally follows some of the same methods we reviewed above in the chapter on *divisiones* and the "declaration of parts": he will "dilate" the parts based on, for example, a repetition of nouns, adjectives or verbs, or based on a series of otherwise interrelated categories. In other words, in making subdivisions, Thomas generally follows the methods he follows for making his opening *divisiones*.

The reader will note in the passage quoted above from Sermon 1 (*Veniet desideratus*), for example, that the two subdivisions listed there are based on cause-effect relationships. "The coming of the Savior was necessary for three reasons," says Thomas: first, because the world was imperfect; second because man was cast down; and third, because God was offended by man. In other words, man's sin was the *cause* of our need for a Savior. Why did the Savior come? He did so, first, to grant the whole world the highest grade of dignity, second, to lead man back to his proper state, and third, to take away the offense of man against God. In other words, these were the *effects* of Christ's coming.

Thomas does not always make subdivisions based on cause-and-effect. Sometimes he likes to set up a hierarchy, as he does in the subdivision in the very next paragraph. Taking up in order the first of his contrasting pairs—namely, that the world was imperfect (cause of our need for Christ) and that Christ restored to the whole world the highest grade of dignity (effect of Christ's coming)—Thomas makes this further subdivision: "Now the grade of perfection in the world fell short in three respects: one way of generation is more sublime than the others; one grade of union is more wonderful than the others, and one way of perfection is more excellent than the others." This is a *divisio* based on adjectival comparisons: "more sublime," "more wonderful," "more excellent."

Sometimes, as we have seen, Thomas likes to make subdivisions based on combinations and permutations of categories, as for example when he identifies the four kinds of *generation*: (1) from the Father without a mother; (2) without a father and without a mother; (3) from a father and a mother; and (4) from a mother without a father. He likewise later identifies the four different sorts of *union* in the world: (1) the union of something corruptible with something corruptible; (2) the union of something corruptible with something incorruptible; (3) the union of something incorruptible with something incorruptible; and (4) the union of something temporal with something eternal. Thomas seems to appreciate these sorts of subdivisions that show the similarities and differences between things. Indeed, his subdivisions within the body of the sermon are often even more expressive than his opening *divisiones* of the *thema*, and in each of Thomas's sermons, the reader will find abundant examples of this method throughout.

In Sermon 4 (*Osanna filio David*), for example, the reader will find no fewer than the following six subdivisions of divisions:

(1) "Note that the human race was in need of salvation for three reasons: first, because of the perversity of sin; second, because of the oppression by enemies; and third, because of the rejection of the glory of the world."

(2) "See Jesus is drawing near to three kinds of people: to those who make peace with him; to those who are devoted to God; and to those who are kind to their neighbors."

(3) "See that in these messengers we can consider three characteristics: their courage, their power, and their justice."

(4) "Now see that a human being ought to humble himself in three ways: he ought to humble his mind, his body, and his affection."

(5) "See that David bears the image of Christ in three respects: first, as for the royal sovereignty; second, as for the victory of wars; and third, as for grace."

(6) "Hence, our salvation consists in: the stability of eternity; in the beauty of light; and in the enjoyment of delight."

And finally, if the reader will take a moment to glance back at the outline of Aquinas's Sermon 13 (*Homo quidam*), he or she will see how detailed Thomas's divisions and subdivisions can get. In particular, the reader should note the way in which he can make use of a subdivision more than once—that is to say, in more than one way. Perhaps one of the most complicated examples of this method can be found in his dilation of his second *divisio* from the morning's sermon. As a reminder, the original *thema* verse was taken from Luke 14:16, "A certain man made a great dinner, and he invited many." Thomas's first division is twofold so that he can treat "the preparation" of the spiritual refreshment of the Lord in the morning in association with the words "A certain man prepared a great dinner," after which, at the evening *collatio*, he can take up the "announcement of the feast after it was prepared" in association with the words "and he invited many."

After making this original, twofold "declaration of parts," Thomas immediately begins his dilation of the first part by subdividing it. "Regarding the preparation [of the great dinner], there are three aspects that must be considered: (1) first, who this man is who made the dinner; (2) second, what kind of dinner it is; and (3) third, how great it is." The first of these—"who the man is who made the dinner"—is a question Thomas is able to dispose of rather quickly: "the man" is Christ, and he possesses the fullness of (a) divinity, (b) truth, and (c) grace. It is with the second and third parts of this *divisio*—concerning what kind of dinner it is and how great it is—that Thomas's overlapping subdivisions can get confusing.

"As for the second aspect," says Thomas, "we must look at what kind of dinner it is that this man has prepared. I say that he has made a triple spiritual refreshment: (2.1) one has to do with the sacrament, (2.2) another with the intellect, and (2.3) a third with our affection." Then, after a few words about the "sacramental" character of the meal, Thomas sets out his next subdivision: "See that this dinner was great and in what way it was great. I say that the dinner is called "great" because of (3.1) the magnificent provision, because of (3.2) the greatness of the delight in taste, and (3.3) because it results in a great virtue. These characteristics were in that refreshment."

In what follows, Thomas is going to analyze each type of "spiritual refreshment"—sacramental, of the intellect, and of the affections—by using each of the categories describing in what ways the dinner was "great": (a) magnificent provision, (b) greatness of delight in taste, and (c) greatness of virtue is the result. The result is so complicated that, in Fr. Hoogland's English translation, he has had to resort to a *very* sophisticated numbering system in an attempt to give the reader the sense of what is going on. I offer here sections 2.1–3 from my own outline in an abbreviated form.

2.1 Sacramental Refreshment (because Christ, who is "the certain man" possesses fullness of grace): this "meal" is provided by the Eucharist

3.1) *Great* because of the magnificent provision: it is bread from heaven.

3.2) *Great* in giving delight: delight is caused by three things:
a) By the memory of things past: What is more delightful to call to mind that man is redeemed by Christ?
b) By the hope of future things: sacramental sign giving hope of future happiness.
c) By experience of things present: the thing signified that is contained in it is the body of Christ.

3.3) *Great* in the virtue that results, because it unites us with God and makes us live in God.

2.2 Refreshment of Our Intellect (because Christ possesses the fullness of truth): the "meal" is provided by the Sacred Scriptures

3.1) *Great* because of the magnificent provision: Scripture deals with
(a) the highest things,
(b) beyond human comprehension, and
(c) most useful.
3.2) *Great* in giving delight: there is sweetness to the highest extent in the words of Sacred Scripture.
3.3) *Great* in the virtue that results: it gives life.

2.3 Refreshment of our Affections (because Christ possesses the fullness of divinity)
3.1) *Great* because of the magnificent provision: enjoy Christ himself in his essence.
3.2) *Great* in giving delight: something gives delight to the extent it is good; Christ is the highest good.
3.3) *Great* in the virtue that results: eternal life in communion with the saints.

Now it might be worth remembering at this point as we conclude this section that all of the material Thomas has preached in this sermon about the nature and value of the "spiritual refreshment" Christ offers us was generated—"dilated"—out of five simple Latin words: "Homo quidam fecit magnam cenam" ("A certain man made a great dinner"). Such is the power and flexibility of the *sermo modernus* method.

METHOD 3: ARGUMENTATION

The famous medieval scholar Étienne Gilson is reported to have said that "the place for disputes is the School, the place for the sermon is the church" ("la place des disputes est à l'École, celle du sermon est à l'Église").[11] In this, he was simply echoing a warning made by thirteenth-century preaching manuals that a sermon should not sound like a disputation: that is, it should not proceed by setting forth premises from which a conclusion is then deduced.[12] Clearly, such advice would only have become necessary

---

[11] Étienne Gilson, "Michel Menot et la Technique du Sermon Médiéval," *Les Idées et Les Lettres* (Paris: Vrin, 1932), 134.

[12] Cf. *Ars concionandi* 3.40, where the text warns that certain precautions should be taken "lest preaching seem like a disputation" ("Ne praedicatio videatur esse disputatio, oportet, quod sic fiat, quasi non esset argumentatio, ut scilicet non praemittantur propositiones, et postea inferatur conclusio").

once preachers were gaining the sort of education in logic on offer at universities such as those at Paris, Oxford, and others. And yet, to say that a sermon should not proceed in the manner of a disputation was not the same as saying that a sermon should not make use of arguments, since "argumentation" was universally recognized as a method of *dilatatio*.

According to the *Ars concionandi*, the type of argument that is especially fitting for a sermon involves reasoning by opposing two contraries, one of which will be approved and the other of which will be the subject of approach, "thereby demonstrating a type of cause." The *Ars concionandi* suggests, for example, that to prove that continence should be fostered, the preacher should speak about riotous living and show that it destroys the body, the soul, possessions, and reputation. Continence, on the other hand, does the reverse. Therefore, it follows, one ought to "practice continence."

So too, for example, in Sermon 11 (*Emitte Spiritum*), Thomas proposes a set of contraries: "Everything man knows he knows either because he finds out or because he learns it." "So how is man led to the knowledge of God?" he asks. It cannot be that he *learns it* by his own powers. Therefore, he must *find out* these things having been told by God's own divine revelation to him." And similarly, elsewhere in the same sermon, he posits the general principle that stipulates that "all things that are moved to a certain end must have something that moves them to that end." Now, the things that are moved to a natural end are moved by something in nature. But things moved to a supernatural end cannot be moved by something in nature, says Thomas, so they must have a "supernatural mover."

We find a similar sort of argument that operates by excluding a contrary position in Sermon 9 (*Exiit qui seminat*), where Thomas posits that every virtue "is derived from the Son of God, just as an example is from the exemplar." Thomas then "dilates" upon the point by imagining the following objection: "But you could say: 'This does not apply to me, for I cannot see the Word in its eternity.'" That is to say, how can the virtues "be derived from the Son of God as an exemplar" when, as the theologians tell us, we cannot see God in his essence? We cannot imitate what we cannot see. Yes, replies Thomas, but this is precisely why we have been given the Incarnation, whereby, as St. Augustine says: "God's wisdom itself is made an example in a man whom it has taken on: an example for mankind of returning above and abiding with the angels."

We will also often find Thomas asking rhetorical questions—as in these examples from Sermon 11: "But how has God created all things?"; "But what is the first movement of the will?"; or "What then is the reason for the mission of the Holy Spirit?" In this sermon, he also gives voice to objections he suspects may exist in the mind of his listener, such as "You will say: 'You must not summon such people nor lead them to religious life," or "You will say: 'It is good for boys to preach, so that they let go of the secular world and come to Christ in religious life, but it is not good to attract or allure them with temporal benefits,'" or again: "You will say: 'It is allowed to attract boys to religious life but not to let them take vows.'" Why not? "You will say: 'Because many who had taken vows returned [into the world].' I then will say what the Apostle says: 'Will the unbelief of those make the faith empty?' (Rom 3:3)."

Thus, although Thomas resists the temptation to turn the sermon into another version of a disputed question, he also understands that simple *arguments* are not foreign to a good sermon, especially with an audience accustomed to hearing logical arguments. After all, one would not wish for one's educated audience to imagine that things like *thinking* and *logic* and *clarity of thought* were somehow foreign to the Christian faith and that the faith was only about one's pious *feelings* or about merely repeating scriptural verses thoughtlessly. There is no danger of making this foolish error with one of Thomas's sermons.

What is needed in these matters, obviously, is a certain balance. When a preacher employed any of these methods, but perhaps especially with complex subdivisions and arguments, it was important that he possess a good sense of his audience and their level of education. The trick was to reveal just enough dialectical skill in argumentation to suggest to the congregation that there was some serious intellectual reflection that had gone on and that all sorts of good arguments might be brought to bear to support the preacher's remarks, even though the congregation was not being burdened with the task of listening to an involved theological disquisition.

Thus, although arguments were not at all *foreign* to preaching in the thirteenth century, they were certainly not the single most essential element of preaching either, as some might have mistakenly supposed if they had read nothing but medieval *quaestiones disputatae* or any of the great *summae*.

METHOD 4: CONCORDANCE OF TEXTS OR THE "CHAINING" OF AUTHORITIES

Although medieval preachers occasionally used arguments in their sermons, the truth is they loved to quote Bible verses every bit as much as any modern-day evangelical preacher. Indeed, a medieval sermon of the *sermo modernus* style would be noteworthy to any modern audience precisely because of its dual nature. On the one hand, it would *sound* extremely "scholastic" because of its definitions, distinctions, and arguments. But it would also sound extraordinarily "biblical," given that one does not go more than a sentence or two without getting another biblical verse. As the historian of early Dominican life Michèle Mulcahey notes, "the use of [biblical] *auctoritates* by some preachers became so extensive that a whole sermon was sometimes virtually no more than an uninterrupted sequence of quotations." "The problem facing the preacher," she suggests, "was how to connect all his *auctoritates* in a logical and pleasing fashion. The usual method was to build up 'chains' of authorities by concording them all either *verbaliter*, verbally, with a key word of the member under discussion, or *realiter*, that is, by means of analogous ideas, or both."[13] This practice, sometimes described as the "chaining" of authorities was, as Mulcahey notes quite accurately, "a device universally employed by the preachers of the thirteenth and fourteenth centuries."[14]

Like other medieval preachers, Thomas loved this method of "expanding" a sermon. And given his prodigious memory and wide knowledge of the Scriptures, he was extremely adept at finding several Bible verses to support not only every argument, but nearly every passing remark.

Take, for example, Sermon 18 (*Germinet terra*), the sermon in praise of the Virgin Mary that I spent some time analyzing in detail in the previous chapter. As the reader may recall, the *thema* verse was taken from Genesis 1:11: "Let the earth put forth the green plant that brings forth seed and the fruit-bearing tree that yields fruit." In his dilation of the word "plant," Thomas begins with three properties of a plant: "a plant is short in height, pliant in slenderness, and health-bringing through strength." With regard to the first, shortness of height, Thomas suggests that it represents Mary's humility. Note the concatenation of thoughts and related scriptural verses as Thomas dilates upon Mary's humility, as opposed to the pride of others, in the following section of his sermon:

> First I say that a plant is short in height. If we compare a plant with a tree, we see that a plant grows upwards a little bit, whereas a tree grows very high. Now, by the height of the tree pride is signified [see Dan 4:1–24]. Thus the Psalmist says: "I have seen the godless

---

[13] Michèle Mulcahey, *First the Bow is Bent in Study: Dominican Education Before 1350* (Toronto, ON: Pontifical Institute of Medieval Studies, 1998), 410.

[14] Ibid., 409.

exalted and lifted up like a cedar of Lebanon" [Ps 37:35]. "I have seen the godless," that is, the proud, because "pride is the origin of godlessness" [Sir 10:12]; "exalted" in the prosperity of the world [see Ps 37:35 above]. Against them the Apostle says: "Tell the rich of this age not to be wise in a lofty way" [1 Tim 6:17] and "lifted up" in their thoughts [see Ps 37:35 again], because a proud man elevates himself above himself in his thoughts. As we read in Job 20:6: "If he ascends to heaven and his pride and his head touch the clouds, in the end he will be lost like a dunghill." Thus you see that "the godless" is "exalted" in the prosperity of the world and "lifted up" in his thoughts "like the cedars of Lebanon" [Ps 37:35 again]. Hence it says in Amos 2:9: "The height of cedars is his height." So a plant does not grow very high, but is short, in which humility is signified. The Psalmist says: "He put forth a plant for the servitude of the people" [Ps 104:14].

Short plants suggest their opposite, high trees. High trees suggest pride. The cedars of Lebanon are high trees, and this suggests the verse about "the godless" being exalted and lifted up "like a cedar of Lebanon." "Godlessness" and "pride" are then connected by the verse about pride being the origin of godlessness—which is, one has to admit, a fascinating addition in that the "humility" being praised is that of the Virgin Mary, who as the "Mother of God" is the very opposite of "godless." Thomas then continues his use of the image of "height": "Tell the rich not to be wise in a lofty way" and "lifted up" in their thoughts, which is what a proud man does. In the end, such men, though they presume to lift themselves up to the clouds will be brought low like a dunghill. Mary, however, is the very opposite. She is a lowly "plant": the plant put forth "for the servitude of the people."

In the same vein, consider also, for example, this passage from Sermon 1 (*Veniet desideratus*), a sermon for the First Sunday in Advent, in which Thomas repeats the standard argument for the necessity of the Incarnation that holds that, "since man had trespassed, he offended God and had to die"—an argument one finds repeatedly in the Christian tradition, perhaps nowhere more famously than in St. Anselm's *Cur Deus homo*, St. Athanasius's *On the Incarnation* before that, and of course, in St. Paul's Letter to the Romans before them both (see Rom 5:2). Here, then, is the manner in which Thomas addresses this classical question of "Why a God-man?" in the rhetorical setting of a sermon during Advent:

Thus a certain case, so to speak, was set in motion from the beginning of the world for the coming of the Lord. For truth required that man would die, because it is written in Numbers 15:30: "A soul that sins through pride will be cut off from his people." But mercy required that man would be set free. The Psalmist says (Ps 77:8–9): "Will God reject in eternity (so that he would not remember) that he was more favorable until now, or will he until the end (abandon his grace)?" Justice, however, required in the end that he be condemned, because Genesis 2:17 reads: "On whatever day you will eat from it, you will die." And Deuteronomy 17:12 says: "A person who will be so proud as to disobey an order of the wise one will die by decree of the judge." But peace requires that a settlement be arranged and the disposition be changed. The Psalmist says (Ps 85:6): "Will you be angry with us in eternity (or do you extend your wrath from generation to generation?" And therefore Isaiah asked (Isa 16:1): "Send out the lamb, Lord, the rulers of the earth." And Moses says (Exod 4:13): "I beseech you, Lord, send the one whom you will send." But since God is "good and merciful: (2 Macc 1:24), he could "not deny himself" (2 Tim 2:13), but he answers through Jeremiah (Jer 31:20): "My inner parts are stirred up because of him; I will show him great mercy." And Hosea 11.8: "My heart is turned within me; my penance has turned likewise." Thus the Lord has sent someone to settle [the debt]: not a human being, not an angel, but God's Son, who satisfied through mercy so that it did not fall short of justice in anything. And so it happened that there was in the same man justice to the full and infinite mercy, and so "mercy and truth have met one another; (justice and peace have kissed one another" (Ps 85:11).

That, if the reader was not yet clear on the concept, is "chaining." What we have here is essentially the core argument of Anselm's *Cur Deus homo* (see especially I.11–15, 24–25; II.6–11) summarized in one paragraph, enunciated almost entirely by the chaining together of biblical verses. This is the way to give a fairly sophisticated theological argument in preaching, not in the terms and tropes of Greek philosophy, but speaking almost entirely in the language of Sacred Scripture.

It is worth noting that this method of "chaining" biblical authorities was to remain very influential in subsequent centuries, even after many of the other methods of the *sermo modernus* style had lost their widespread popularity. So, for example, Charles Smyth concludes from his survey of centuries of preaching in *The Art of Preaching: A Practical Survey of Preaching in the Church of England, 747–1939*, that "The citation of concordant texts of Scripture has an important place in all expository preaching," and indeed that this is "the characteristic method of the Homilies of the Church of England."[15] As evidence, he cites a wonderful passage from a sermon by John Donne on the text from Psalm 6:2–3, "O Lord, heal me, for my bones are vexed: my soul also is sorely troubled," where Donne discusses five sorts of *Troubles*" (*turbatio*). There is, says Donne:

> *Turbatio timoris*, A trouble out of fear of danger in this world, Herod's trouble; *When the magi brought word of another king, Herod was troubled, and all Jerusalem with him*. There is *Turbatio confusionis*, The mariner's trouble in a tempest; *Their soul melteth for trouble*, says David. There is *Turbatio occupationis*, Martha's trouble; *Martha thou art troubled about many things*, says Christ. There is *Turbatio admirationis*, The Blessed Virgin's trouble, *When she saw the angel, she was troubled at his saying*. To contract this, there is *Turbatio compassionis*, Christ's own trouble, *When he saw Mary weep for her brother Lazarus, he groaned in the spirit, and was troubled in himself.*[16]

Let me suggest that a complex passage of this sort would have been impossible, indeed literally unthinkable, without the influences of the medieval *sermo modernus* style—in particular the first method of *dilatation* we discussed above, "proposing a discussion based on a noun as it occurs in definitions or classifications," and the "chaining" of concordant biblical authorities.

Finally, "chaining" is a common feature of Thomas's biblical commentaries as well. Indeed, it is so common that one can rarely go more than a few sentences in most of his commentaries without running into another example of the practice. Allow me here, then, if I may, merely for purposes of illustration, to cite just two: one from his *Commentary on Galatians*, the other from his *Commentary on the Psalms*.

---

[15] See Charles Smyth, *The Art of Preaching: A Practical Survey of Preaching in the Church of England, 747–1939* (New York: MacMillan, 1940), 46.

[16] Quoted from ibid., 46–47. See also John Donne, *The Sermons of John Donne*, ed. George Potter and Evelyn Simpson, vol. 5, no. 17 (Berkeley: University of California Press, 1959), 357 (also available on-line under the title "Preached upon the Penitentiall Psalmes" at the Brigham Young University Harold B. Lee Digital Library Collections web site).

In his *Commentary on St. Paul's Epistle to the Galatians*, commenting on Galatians 5:22, which states that "the fruit of the Spirit is charity, joy, peace, patience, benignity, goodness, longanimity. . . ," Thomas says the following:

> Now a man is perfected and directed inwardly both as to good things and as to evil: "By the armor of justice on the right hand and on the left" (2 Cor 6:7). With respect to good things a person is perfected, first of all, in his heart through love [*amor*]. For just as in natural movements there is first an inclination of a nature's appetite to its end, so the first of the inward movements is the inclination to good, i.e., love [*amor*]; accordingly, the first fruit [of the Spirit] is *charity* [*caritas*]: "The charity of God is poured forth in our hearts by the Holy Ghost Who is given to us" [Rom 5:5]. And through charity the others are perfected; wherefore, the Apostle says in Colossians (3:14): "But above all these things have charity, which is the bond of perfection."[17]

Thomas performs a similar sort of "chaining" of authorities when it comes to the next two "fruits of the Spirit" Paul lists in this verse: *joy* and then *peace*.

> But the ultimate end that perfects man inwardly is *joy*, which proceeds from the presence of the thing loved. And he that has charity already has what he loves: "He that abideth in charity abideth in God and God in him" (1 John 4:16). And from this springs joy: "Rejoice in the Lord always; again I say, rejoice" (Phil 4:4).

> But this joy should be perfect, and for this two things are required: first, that the object loved be enough to perfect the lover. And as to this he says, *peace*. For it is then that the lover has peace, when he adequately possesses the object loved: I am become in his presence as one finding peace" (Cant 8:10). Secondly, that there be perfect enjoyment of the thing loved, which is likewise obtained by peace, because whatever else happens, if someone perfectly enjoys the object loved, say God, he cannot be hindered from enjoy-

---

[17] *Commentary on Galatians*, ch. 5, lec. 6, trans. F. R. Larcher, O.P. (Albany, NY: Magi Books, 1966); both this English translation and the original Latin can be found at http://dhspriory.org/thomas/SSGalatians.htm#56.

ing it: "Much peace have they that love thy law and to them there is no stumbling block" (Ps 118:165). In this way, therefore, joy connotes the fruition of charity, but peace the perfection of charity. And by these is man inwardly made perfect as to good things.

This is clearly the "chaining" of concordant biblical authorities based on single words (in this case, "charity," then "joy," then "peace") much like Thomas does in his sermons. There were, of course, actual biblical *concordances* available to preachers and biblical commentators at this time to facilitate this sort of thing. The question is not *how* this was done, but *why*.

Were the biblical citations simply "padding," so to speak, something to fill up space? Or are they serving as "proof texts" to support the commentator's point? I suggest neither is the case. But if not, then why were they added? There are a number of possible reasons, but let me suggest three.

The first involves the issue of rhetorical beauty and effect. Adding the biblical verses transforms what might otherwise sound like a dry doctrinal treatise into something more "literary," something more "alive." Consider, in this regard, how the first paragraphs above could have been shortened had Thomas *not* added the concordant biblical verses:

Now a man is perfected and directed inwardly both as to good things and as to evil. With respect to good things a person is perfected, first of all, in his heart through love [*amor*]. For just as in natural movements there is first an inclination of a nature's appetite to its end, so the first of the inward movements is the inclination to good, i.e., love [*amor*]; accordingly, the first fruit [of the Spirit] is *charity* [*caritas*], and through charity, the others are perfected.

That shortened version is perhaps easier *to read*, but consider now how much more dramatic it would *sound* if a preacher with the right sort of deep intonation were to make this same point about charity, but do so in the following way:

Now a man is perfected and directed inwardly both as to good things and as to evil; thus, as it says in 2 Corinthians 6:7, we must be protected "by the armor of justice on both the right hand and on the left."

Now clearly a person is made perfect by *good* things, not evil. But first of all, a person must be perfected and directed *inwardly* to the good *in his heart*—through love [*amor*]. Why? Because in all natural movements, there is first an inclination of the appetite to its end—as, for example, when we *hunger*, we are naturally inclined to seek out *food* to nourish our bodies. So too in us, the first of our inward movements is the [natural] inclination to [some] good.

Since *every* movement to the good begins in the love of some good, so we say that the first fruit [of the Spirit] is *charity*—as we read in Romans 5:5: "The charity of God is poured forth in our hearts by the Holy Ghost Who is given to us." And it is through *charity* that the other gifts are moved to their perfection. Thus the Apostle Paul tells us in Colossians 3:14: "But above all these things have *charity*, which is the bond of perfection."

I have taken some liberties with Thomas's wording here, but the point of doing so was merely to make more patent the overall rhetorical effect. Thomas's sermons may at first reading seem to some like dry, dull stuff, full of abstract scholastic categories. But I ask the reader to imagine those last three paragraphs coming from the mouth of any of the great Protestant Bible preachers of the past two hundred years. It is possible, is it not? It is possible because the great Protestant Bible preachers often used the Bible in much the same way. The Bible verses are not merely extraneous words added to fill up the space; nor are they "proof texts" meant to authoritatively demonstrate a point. The first purpose they serve, I would suggest, is as verbal devices added to increase the rhetorical power and beauty of the prose. Adding the Bible verses is precisely what keeps the commentary, as well as the preaching, from sounding too much like a medieval disputation, even when the commentary or the sermon makes use of some of the same categories and distinctions.

A second reason that might justify the frequent use of the method, moreover—one not entirely unrelated to my reference to Protestant Bible preaching in the paragraph above—has to do with inspiring and instilling a certain biblical literacy in a largely illiterate audience. Very few people in the Middle Ages knew how to read at all, and even those who did would very rarely have had *all* the books of the Bible at their disposal. Thus, if a preacher was going to instill in his congregation any knowledge of the texts of the Bible not explicitly covered in the weekly lectionary, he was likely going to have to do it by repeatedly incorporating verses from other books into his sermons.

I have known any number of Protestants who were proud, and not without justification, of their familiarity with the entire Bible. Not infrequently, however, their familiarity was much as it would have been for Thomas's audience: that is to say, they possessed in their random-access, easily-accessible memory an impressively large number of key Bible verses, not all of which, however, had been memorized *in their original context*. Bible verses remembered in this way often seem to serve a role similar to the one proverbs serve: they are tidbits of wisdom that provide a certain kind of guidance. What is more, they set the terms of debate and discussion within which the mind operates. It is not unimportant for a person to think about the fundamental questions of life in terms of a suitable "faith, hope, and love" or about living a "righteous life in accord with God's law," as opposed to thinking about such matters in terms of "maximizing utility" or "expressing one's autonomy" or "acting in accord with a rationally defensible maxim that can be applied universally to all agents."

This set of considerations about the *words* listeners find familiar in everyday discourse because they have heard them used repeatedly and which *associations* these words bring to their minds when they hear them brings us to a third, not entirely unrelated reason for the method of using concordant biblical authorities. Let me call this the "Oxford English Dictionary" approach to understanding key biblical terms. As is generally well known, what has classically distinguished the Oxford English Dictionary from others is that it proceeds by citing the *uses* of a word *in actual English works of literature*, not merely by listing synonyms or crafting abstract definitions. So too, we might ask how we are to understand the meaning of a key word in Scripture—let us say, a word like "charity" or "faith" or "justification." One way would be to begin to catalogue how that word was used in other key places in the Scriptures. In practice, the process might sound something like this:

> What moves all things to their ultimate end is *love*. Now love, as St. Paul tells us, is "the bond of perfection." But love is not something we produce simply on our own. No, as it says in 1 John 4: "We love because God has loved us first." And as we read in Romans 5:5, it is by the Holy Spirit that "love is spread abroad in our hearts." Indeed "our hearts are restless until they rest in thee," says St. Augustine in his *Confessions*. And so it is. For now we have "hearts of stone," (2 Cor 3:3) and have "hardened our hearts against him,"

(Exod 4:21), "each one walking according to the hardness of his own evil heart, without listening to Him" (Jer 16:12). We need his Spirit to make our hearts fleshy again (2 Cor 3:3)—soft so that God can write his law not merely on tablets of stone as he gave to Moses on Sinai, but now with his Spirit he writes on the "fleshy tablets of our hearts" (see Jer 31:33; 2 Cor 3:3).

Such paragraphs are not difficult to write once one gets the hang of it. I crafted the one above very quickly merely drawing upon passages from memory. (Full disclosure: I had to look up the chapter and verse numbers in order to add them afterward.) A biblical concordance would have made the process even easier, and it would have made available a much wider collection of verses than I am capable of calling upon given my rather limited mental storehouse of Bible passages.

Be that as it may, I ask the reader to glance at the entries for any key word in a good biblical concordance if he or she has not done so recently. Let me suggest that the effect can be much like the effect one has looking over the literary examples listed in any good dictionary, such as the full *Oxford English Dictionary*, the full *Lewis and Short Latin Dictionary*, or the full *Liddell-Scott Greek Lexicon*. Indeed, the inspiration behind what is known as the *Index Thomisticus*, essentially a concordance of all the words in all the works of Aquinas, was that, by looking over the list of Thomas's *uses* of a word or a phrase, one could more accurately determine its *meaning*.

"Chaining" biblical passages together repeatedly in sermon after sermon goes a long way, I would suggest, to giving one's listeners a "concordant" sense of the meanings of terms as they are used in the Scriptures as a whole. It also helps introduce listeners into what is sometimes called a "linguistic community."[18]

It is important for our purposes to distinguish the notion of "introducing one's listeners *into*" a linguistic community, which is what a mother does with her children or a preacher does with his congregation from week to week, from what we might do with modern students in a classroom

---

[18] I have in mind here something like John Gomperz's famous definition of a "speech community" as "any human aggregate characterized by regular and frequent interaction by means of a shared body of verbal signs and set off from similar aggregates by significant differences in language usage"; see J. J. Gomperz, "The Speech Community," in *The International Encyclopedia of the Social Sciences* (New York: Macmillan, 1968), 381–86; reprinted in *Linguistic Anthropology: A Reader*, ed. Alessandro Duranti, 2nd ed. (Oxford, UK: Wiley-Blackwell, 2009), 66–73.

setting, namely "introducing them *to*" a linguistic community that is *not their own*. To be introduced *into* a linguistic community, in the sense of *being made a part of it*, is precisely to become one whose linguistic usage will henceforth become characterized by the meanings made possible by a "shared body of verbal signs." In this case, one no longer merely "understands" these signs by "translating" them, as it were, into one's *own* linguistic categories. Rather, the words and phrases and categories of the linguistic community *become one's own*. These are the categories with which and by means of which one understands the world.

When, at any mention of the word "faith," a person not only *can* call to mind, but automatically *does* call to mind (perhaps cannot help *but* call to mind) the notions that "Abraham believed, and it was credited to him as righteousness," that "faith is the substance of things hoped for, the evidence of things not seen," that "by grace you have been saved through faith, and this is not your own doing, it is the gift of God," and that "faith by itself, if it does not have works, is dead," then this fact suggests one has been effectively *introduced into* a biblically-influenced linguistic community. Such a linguistic community would be very different from one in which the mention of the word "faith" would bring to mind associations such as "the opiate of the masses," "a crutch for weak minds," "opinions unsubstantiated by evidence," or "believing six impossible things before breakfast every morning."

To use the language of Scripture—its words, its phrases, its passages—as the default "language" within a sermon, as the language to which the preacher knows he must constantly return and within whose categories he knows he must express whatever it is he wishes to express, whether arguments or praise or warnings or exhortations, such as happens with "chaining," is precisely the sort of practice that facilitates the creation of such a linguistic community, one centered, in this case, around the language of the Bible.

METHOD 5: SETTING UP A SERIES: GOOD, BETTER, BEST

The short, one-sentence description in Latin of this method is harder to understand than the method itself. The rather complicated way the *Ars concionandi* describes the method is to say that the *dilatatio* is carried out "through those words which have the same meaning and which agree in root, although they carry incidental differences. Therefore, if a superlative has been proposed, one can proceed to the positive and comparative."[19] This is a complicated way of saying that the preacher should set up a series along the lines of "good-better-best." The example the *Ars concionandi* gives is as follows. Suppose the division of the *thema* verse has left the preacher with this bit of the verse from Psalm 44:4, "Bind your sword around your thighs, strongest one." This verse can be dilated by suggesting that: those people who are *strongly* bound by the sword are those who are married; those who are even *stronger* are the continent; and those who are *strongest* are the virgins. Or again, take the passage from the Song of Songs 5:1, which reads, "I have drunk, dearest one." One might dilate this verse by suggesting that those are *dear* who live in charity, although of an imperfect type; those are *dearer* who can endure adversity for the sake of Christ but with some annoyance; and those are *dearest* who laugh in the midst of their humiliations.[20]

Thomas will, on occasion, employ this method in its simplest form. So, for example, in Sermon 10 (*Petite et accipietis*), he dilates on the verse from James 1:17, "every very good present and every perfect gift [is from him]," saying: "A *good* present is the good of prosperity like riches; a *better* gift is a gift of nature, like physical strength or health; the *best* is the gift of grace, like the virtues; the *perfect* gift is the gift of glory." God gives all these gifts. And again, in Sermon 17 (*Lux orta est*), Thomas begins his sermon with a very similar procession of "goods," saying that:

> Temporal things are a good [*bonus*] endowment. The things that belong to us naturally, like the body and the soul, are a better [*melior*] endowment. Eternal glory and the goods bestowed by grace are the best [*optimus*] endowment. Every very good [*optimus*] endowment— we understand this as grace— comes from the Father of lights. Grace is called the best [*optimus*] gift, given to us so that we may perform meritorious works. Hence it says in John 15:5: "Without me you cannot do anything." Likewise, we call grace the *perfect* gift, given to us so that we may receive the good of glory. And this grace comes from the Father of lights.

And yet, although Thomas certainly knows how to organize hierarchies based on "good-better-best," he rarely (if ever) will do so based on one

---

[19] *Ars concionandi* 3.42: "per ea eiusdam sunt cognitiones, quae scilicet conveniunt in radice, licet diversitatem habeant. Posito igitur superlative, discurraatur ad positivum et comparativum."

[20] Ibid.

stem word, such as "dear, dearer, dearest" or "strong, stronger, strongest."

What Thomas will do more often, however, is to dilate by cataloguing the three ways in which something is, for example, a "better" sort of happiness or a "more excellent" sort of virtue. In Sermon 1 (*Veniet desideratus*), for example, Thomas praises Christ in three respects, claiming that his "grade of union is more wonderful than the others," his "way of generation is more sublime than others," and his "way of perfection is more excellent than others." He is then able to dilate upon each of these three. So too, as we have already seen in Sermon 13 (*Homo quidam*), the sermon on "a certain man" (that is, Christ) who "made a great dinner," Thomas stipulates that the dinner is called "great" for three reasons: (1) the greatness of the provision, (2) the greatness of the delight in taste, and (3) the great virtue that results.

There is, however, another interesting example of this method in Sermon 9 (*Exiit qui seminat*). The sermon itself is on the Parable of the Sower from Luke 8: the farmer who sows his seed in thistles, on rocky soil, and on good soil. Having dealt with the first two—the problems and hindrances that arise when God's word is sown among thistles and in rocky soil—Thomas finally comes to the sowing on good soil. "If it comes to pass," he says, that the earth in which the seed is sown is good, then it produces a triple crop: "thirty-fold, sixty-fold, and a hundred-fold" (referring now to a statement in Matthew's account of the same parable in Matt 13:8). Thomas dilates upon these three levels of productivity, starting with the smallest, the thirty-fold crop. These are the simple converts, he says, who "pursue the fruit that [converted people] necessarily bring forth." Why thirty? Because "the number thirty comes from multiplying three by ten." Thus, if you have faith in the Trinity and the Ten Commandments of the Law—as Matthew 19:17 says, "If you want to enter into life, follow the Commandments"—then you produce a thirty-fold crop.

Others "go further," says Thomas, "and convert to the highest state of perfection through a way of penitence after having committed sins, and thus produce a sixty-fold crop." Why sixty? Because, he says, the number sixty comes from multiplying six by ten, and "the six counsels must be added to the Ten Commandments." Do this and "you will produce a sixty-fold crop." Some, finally, produce "an even greater crop." These are not converted "by way of penitence," but rather arrive at the state of perfection "by way of innocence." Only these are the ones who produce the "hundred-fold crop."[21]

---

[21] This technique of interpreting numbers as having a specific significance is something Christian exegetes like Origen learned from the first-century Jewish scholar Philo of

Note that it is possible for there to be overlap among the methods we are examining. So, for example, as we have seen, it is not only possible, but likely, for a medieval preacher to create a threefold subdivision by setting up a series based on "good, better, best"—or as is more common in Thomas's sermons, a series based on the three reasons something is "more excellent" or "more perfect" than others. In either case, the goal is usually not simply to *state* the series. What the preacher is really after is providing a series of topics that can be developed further in the paragraphs that follow.

Method 6: The Use of Metaphors

Dilating by way of the metaphorical meanings of terms is, along with subdivision, one of the most common techniques in Thomas's sermons. Thomas seemed to have preferred this technique over *defining* a noun and then dilating on the definition. Instead, he tends to list the properties of a word from his *thema* and then apply those properties metaphorically to the topic he wishes to discuss. There are about as many different ways of doing this as there are different ways of giving various metaphorical meanings to terms.

So, for example, in Sermon 4 (*Osanna filio David*), Thomas suggests that our salvation consists "in the stability of eternity." As a ship whose safety is threatened in a dire storm is not considered "safe" or "saved" until it has arrived at its destination in a stable harbor, "in the same way," says

---

Alexandria. Among the many possible examples that might be cited, see Philo's *On the Creation of the World* 3.13–14: "And he says that the world was made in six days, not because the Creator stood in need of a length of time (for it is natural that God should do everything at once, not merely by uttering a command, but by even thinking of it); but because the things created required arrangement; and number is akin to arrangement; and, of all numbers, six is, by the laws of nature, the most productive: for of all the numbers, from the unit upwards, it is the first perfect one, being made equal to its parts, and being made complete by them; the number three being half of it, and the number two a third of it, and the unit a sixth of it, and, so to say, it is formed so as to be both male and female, and is made up of the power of both natures; for in existing things the odd number is the male, and the even number is the female; accordingly, of odd numbers the first is the number three, and of even numbers the first is two, and the two numbers multiplied together make six. It was fitting therefore, that the world, being the most perfect of created things, should be made according to the perfect number, namely, six: and, as it was to have in it the causes of both, which arise from combination, that it should be formed according to a mixed number, the first combination of odd and even numbers, since it was to embrace the character both of the male who sows the seed, and of the female who receives it" (trans. C. D. Yonge, Bohn's Library [London: H. G. Bohn, 1854–1855]).

Thomas, "a human being is not saved during his life on earth [*in via*], but only in our heavenly homeland [*in patria*]."

So too in Sermon 6 (*Caelum et terra transibunt*), we find a fairly straightforward *dilatatio* by metaphor based on Luke 21:33, which reads: "Heaven and earth will pass." Dilating upon the word "heaven," Thomas says that this word describes the situation of the just man in four ways: (1) because heaven is of great brightness; (2) because it has a splendid appearance; (3) because it is in motion; and (4) because it is high in location. Each of these characteristics, then, can be applied metaphorically, says Thomas, to the just man, for: (1) the just man should "shine brightly," in that he ought to be full of the light of heavenly wisdom; (2) he ought to be "like a circle by a wide mercy or like an orbit by a broad devotion and perfect love"; (3) he should be "set in motion" always by a "spiritual carefulness"; and (4) the just man ought to be "high" by excelling others in holiness.

This is certainly not allegory, which always refers to Christ. Nor is it dilation based on the *definition* of a noun, as in method 1 above. "Great brightness," "splendid appearance," and the rest are not parts of a *definition*. Rather, in this method of *dilatatio*, we take the *properties* of a thing in the biblical *thema* and apply them metaphorically to something the preacher wishes to speak about, whether it is the virtues of the just man, the vices of the unjust man, the nature of Christ, or the circumstances of the Incarnation. Note, in fact, that the metaphorical relationship need not be as obvious as the relationship between "the just" and "heaven." Indeed, sometimes the relationship can be rather creative—which is to say, not entirely obvious at first glance.

Indeed, we have already seen two very distinctive uses of a *dilatatio* based on the use of metaphors in Sermon 5 (*Ecce rex tuus*), where Thomas dilates by beginning with the properties of a "king," on the one hand, and the circumstances in which we use the word "behold," on the other, and then applying these metaphorically to Christ. "There are four characteristics required for calling someone a king," says Thomas, as the reader may recall: first, he is the *only* king, and there are no others; second, he must have full power; third he must have full jurisdiction; and fourth, he must exhibit "equity of justice." Thomas then proceeds to show how each of these properties belongs superlatively to Christ. (For the details, see the discussion in chapter 1.)

Some readers will recognize in these words a classic example of how analogous predication applies most properly to God. That is to say, when we are beginning to try to understand God, we must start with those things better known to us, such as the things that we can see and experience all around us. To begin to understand what sort of relationship God has with us, we begin by saying God is like a "father" to us. Like our human fathers, God gave us life; like our human fathers, God cares for us; and like our human fathers, God wills our good. At this stage, we begin with our human father and come eventually to some understanding of God. But as our knowledge and understanding of God increases, we come to understand that, in reality, God is the prime analogate and our human fathers are merely "fathers" by participation and in a secondary sense. God is totally responsible for our being, whereas our human fathers are only partially responsible. God cares for us always and everywhere, no matter where we are, for ever and ever *in saecula saeculorum*, whereas our human fathers care for us only partially and only for a short time until they (or we) die. So too, God cares for us and wills our good perfectly, whereas our human fathers have neither the power nor the moral goodness to will the good of their children perfectly. Thus, God is most truly and most perfectly our Father, whereas our human fathers are only "fathers" by participation.

So too, in Sermon 5 (*Ecce rex tuus*) with the word "king," we start with the characteristics of human kings and apply them *analogically* to Christ. And yet, when we are finished, we realize that Christ is "king" more fully and more perfectly than any human king could ever be. And yet, we do not have in this case an *allegorical* reading of the text. "Allegory" is, as St. Augustine says in *De doctrina christiana* (1.2), when one "thing" represents another "thing"—the other "thing" usually being Christ. In this case, we have the properties of a word—in this case, "king"—being applied analogically to Christ. The difference is subtle but not unimportant. It would be an "allegory" if King David were being taken as a "type" of Christ. It is subtly different if we start with the properties of any king and apply them analogically to aid our understanding of Christ.

The differences will perhaps become a little clearer if we glance again at our other example of dilation by means of metaphor in Sermon 5 (*Ecce rex tuus*)—one somewhat more "creative," shall we say, Thomas's use of the word "behold." As a quick reminder, Thomas suggests that we use the word "behold" in four circumstances: first, when we want to certify something ("Behold it is true!"); second, when we want to demarcate time ("Behold, my hour is come!"); third, when we want to manifest something ("Behold the man!"); and fourth, when we are attempting to comfort someone, and this in two ways—either because one's enemies have been defeated ("Behold, your enemies have been placed beneath you") or because one has received a benefit ("Behold how good it is"). All of these four circumstances in which we use the word "behold" are then applied metaphorically to Christ's Second Coming: (1) it will certainly happen; but (2) we do not know the time; (3) it will happen openly and not in a hidden way (as now when Christ comes into our mind); and (4) Christ will comfort his people by conquering their enemies and bestowing benefits upon them. This is certainly not allegory. But it is not entirely odd when one begins to recognize the many ways in which medieval preachers such as Thomas can use metaphors for dilating the content within a sermon.

Here are two final examples, the first relatively straightforward and the second relatively more complex, both of them from Sermon 11 (*Emitte Spiritum*), a sermon on Pentecost, for which the opening biblical *thema* is the famous verse Psalm 104:30, "Send forth your Spirit, and they will be created, and you will renew the face of the earth." Dilating upon the first half of the verse ("Send forth your Spirit, and they will be created"), Thomas suggests that the word "spirit" seems to imply four things: first, "a fineness of substance," since "we usually call substances without a body 'spirits'"; second, a "perfection of life," since "as long as animated creatures have a spirit, they live"; third, an "incitement of motion," as when we say of a person that he has an impulsive spirit; and fourth, a "hidden origin," as when someone is disturbed but does not know what is disturbing him, he will often attribute it to a spirit. Each of these properties Thomas will then apply in turn to the Holy Spirit. I will point out once again that Thomas has not *defined* the word "spirit"; he has listed out various properties that he will then apply metaphorically to his description of the character and role of the Holy Spirit (as in the case of the word "father," we might call it an analogical predication). This is a fairly straightforward sort of dilation-based-on-metaphor.

We find a somewhat more complex example later on in the same sermon, in the second half, where Thomas is dilating on the last part of the opening *thema*: "and you will renew the face of the earth." "Who receives this renewal?" asks Thomas. "The face of the earth" is the obvious answer. "The face of the earth," says Thomas, refers in one sense to the whole world, but in another sense it refers to the human mind because, says Thomas, "just as we see with our face in a corporeal way, so we see with the mind in a spiritual way." So, metaphorically speaking, and for the purposes of this sermon, the "face" of the earth is the human mind. What, then, is involved in "renewing the face of the earth" in this sense? Well, says Thomas, making full use of the associations ovne derives from the image of a face, a face is "renewed" when it is: (1) clean, (2) uncovered, (3) directed towards God, and (4) firm (as in the phrase "set your face firmly and truly on God").

Each of these metaphorical ways in which a "face" can be "renewed" is then taken to be a way in which God renews our mind.

Take the first of these, for example: *cleaning* one's face. Thomas quotes the verse in Matthew 6:17 that says, "When you fast . . . anoint your head and wash your face," which he interprets as meaning "wash your face *with the tears of a moved heart*," so that you will be able to receive the renewal of the Holy Spirit. So the metaphorical "chain," if you will, has gone like this: "face of the earth" was metaphorically taken to mean the human mind; renewing the human mind was metaphorically related *back to* the physical human face; the physical human face is "washed by tears"; and so the conclusion is that the Holy Spirit can "renew the face of the earth" when men weep with a humble and contrite heart and thereby open their minds to the Truth.

Some readers may find this chain of associations between the human face and the phrase "renew the face of the earth" to be something of a stretch. And yet, by the same token, most readers, even in a modern audience, will understand the sense of the phrase "something of a stretch" in that last sentence, even though there is no actual physical stretching going on. We use metaphors in speech all the time, often without even noticing that we are doing so. When medieval preachers noticed the *metaphorical potency* of words and used that expressive power of language in their preaching, was it really so different from what poets often do with words? In these sermons, preachers such as Thomas are certainly stretching the expressive power of the words, but then, so do great poets. The trick in making these associations for the purposes of a sermon is that the association should be *close enough* to be suggestive, but also *odd enough* to be interesting and evocative so as to be memorable.

Thomas has the sort of mind that can conceive of "renewing the face of the earth" as metaphorically akin to washing one's face with tears. This fact may help explain how, along with writing his detailed "disputed questions" and his great theological *Summa*, Thomas also had the ability to compose marvelous poetic hymns such as the *Adoro te devote, Lauda Sion*, and *Tantum ergo*.

METHOD 7: A FOURFOLD EXPOSITION ACCORDING TO THE HISTORICAL, ALLEGORICAL, MORAL, AND/OR ANAGOGICAL SENSES OF SCRIPTURE

It is sometimes thought, mistakenly, that the allegorical, moral, and anagogical senses of Scripture were largely abandoned starting in the thirteenth century in favor of a more strictly literal reading of the biblical texts.[22] Although it is certainly true that a new interest in and emphasis on the *literal* sense of the Scriptures arose in late twelfth- and early thirteenth-century biblical commentary, we still find all four of the senses of Scripture in the preaching of the high Middle Ages as means of "dilating" a term or phrase in the opening *thema*. We have already seen ways in which Thomas dilates the literal senses of a word—whether by metaphorical associations or by interpretation of names or by expounding upon the comparative or superlative degree of the term. What remains to be seen is how he develops content based upon the allegorical, the moral, and anagogical senses of a term.

Consider, for example, Sermon 1 (*Veniet desideratus*), where Thomas is dilating the various divisions of Haggai 2:7—"Veniet desideratus cunctis gentibus: et implebo domum istam gloria" ("He who is desired by all the nations together will come, and he will fill this house with glory"). When he reaches the word "house" (*domum*), Thomas distinguishes several senses of the word. In one sense, the "house" filled with glory is the Virgin Mary. In a second sense, the "house" filled with glory is the Church Militant, which Christ has built from living stones. In a third sense, the "house" filled with glory is our final heavenly homeland. God fills the first house—namely, the Virgin Mary—with the glory of divinity in the Incarnation. God fills the second house—namely, the Church—with the Holy Spirit to make it capable of doing his will. The third house, finally—our heavenly homeland—is "filled with glory" when Christ rises from the dead and ascends to the right hand of the Father. The first exposition is fundamentally *allegorical* or Christological: Mary gives birth to Christ. The second is *moral* in that it refers to the means by which we are enabled to live the moral life—that is to say, within the Church. The third is basically *anagogical* in that it concerns our final end in heaven.

Another nice example of a *dilatatio* based on the spiritual senses can be found near the end of Sermon 2 (*Lauda et laetare*), a sermon for Advent, where Thomas is dilating upon the last part of the *thema* from Zechariah 2:10 ("'Sing praise and be glad, daughter of Zion, for behold, I come and

---

[22] There are others, of course, who assume that all the benighted medieval scholars used *nothing but* an allegorical approach to the Scriptures until the Protestant scholars of the sixteenth century or those of the nineteenth century (depending upon your viewpoint) finally restored biblical scholarship to an authentic dedication to the *literal* sense of the text. It was Beryl Smalley's somewhat lonely task to disabuse many twentieth-century biblical scholars of this mistaken notion. For example, see her *The Study of the Bible in the Middle Ages* (Oxford, UK: Blackwells, 1941; latest edition currently available from University of Notre Dame Press, 2007).

I will dwell in your midst,' says the Lord"). Dilating upon the phrase "I will dwell," Thomas suggests that Christ "dwells with us" in three ways. First, he dwells "with all people, in a general way, through the substance of the flesh, as we read in John 1:14: 'The Word became flesh and dwelt among us.'" Second, he dwells with the saints "in a special way, through infused grace, as we read in 2 Cor 5:16: 'I will dwell among them and I will be their God.'" And finally, Christ dwells with the just in heaven "in a familiar way" (*familiariter*) by being present before their eyes, as the Psalmist says (5:12): "Forever they will exult and you will dwell among them." The first of these three sorts of "dwelling" refers to Christ; the second is moral, dealing with how grace makes possible our obedience to the moral law; and the third is anagogical, dealing with the activities of the saints in heaven.

Notice in these examples that when Thomas lists the three spiritual senses, as we have seen here in Sermons 1 and 2, there is usually what I would describe as a "basic trajectory" to the order: he will frequently begin with some reference to the Incarnation (step 1), move to some reference having to do with the Holy Spirit and the moral life made possible by grace (step 2), and arrive finally at some reference to the heavenly glory of the just (step 3). Understood in this way, the three "spiritual senses" correspond to the three basic elements of the Paschal Mystery: (1) Christ's Incarnation, Death, Resurrection, and Ascension (the allegorical level); (2) the sending of the Holy Spirit by which "charity is spread abroad in our hearts," whereby we become *alter Christus*, "another Christ" (the moral level); and finally, (3) Christ's being seated at the right hand of the Father from whence he will come to judge the living and the dead at the end of time (the anagogical level). Within Thomas's exegetical perspective, *every* biblical text speaks ultimately about Christ and finds its ultimate meaning in the central Paschal mystery of Christ's Incarnation, Death, Resurrection, Ascension, sending of the Spirit, and final glorification.

Distinguishing Metaphor from Allegory and Dilatatio *from the "Spiritual Senses" of Scripture*

It is possible to confuse this sort of allegorical *dilatatio* with a *dilatatio* based on metaphors applied to Christ, such as when, in Sermon 5 (*Ecce rex tuus*), Thomas lists four characteristics required for calling someone a king—(1) he must be the *only* king and there are no others; (2) he must have fullness of power; (3) he must have full jurisdiction; and (4) he must exhibit "equity of justice"—and then shows that each of these applies most properly to Christ. This is *analogy*, not *allegory*.

One way to recognize the difference is by noticing whether Thomas provides a list of the *properties* of the noun or verb. If he does, then it is probably a dilation by metaphor—as for example when Thomas takes the word "spirit," lists some properties of spirits, and then applies each of them to the Holy Spirit, or when he takes the word "behold," lists the various occasions when we use the word "behold," and then associates each of these with the various "advents" of Christ.

Notice the difference, however, in Sermon 1 (*Veniet desideratus*). Thomas does not begin by listing out several properties of a house—say, for example, providing comfort, keeping out the elements, and preserving the family from invaders—and then proceed to associate each of these properties with ways in which Christ is our "house": say, for example, he "comforts" our hearts; he "keeps out" the storms of the passions; and he "preserves" the soul from the invasions of the devil." Those would be *metaphorical* associations.

Instead, Thomas says in Sermon 1 that: the first "house" in which Christ dwells is the Virgin Mary; the second "house" in which he dwells is the Church; and the third "house" in which he dwells is heaven. Now, although we might say that the word "house" is understood metaphorically in these three statements, the notion of Christ "dwelling" is not. Christ *dwells* in the womb of the Virgin, not metaphorically, but really. Christ *dwells* in the Church, not metaphorically, but really. And Christ *dwells* in heaven, not metaphorically, but really. These are certainly different senses of the word "dwell," but allegory and the other spiritual senses, although they often *depend upon* the metaphorical meanings of words, go beyond mere metaphor.

Why, then, do we call these three ways in which Christ "dwells" with us that Thomas discusses in Sermon 1 "spiritual senses"? We do so because the original *thema* verse is from the prophet Haggai, and *literally*, the words "he will dwell" refer to the person the prophet Haggai is talking about in Haggai 2.7, Yahweh. Often in such cases, especially with the Psalms, such verses refer to David or to one of the patriarchs. In this case, however, the "person" Haggai is talking about is God (Yahweh), and when Haggai has God say, "I will fill this house with glory" ("implebo domum istam gloria"), the "house" he is speaking about is the Temple in Jerusalem. The first level of signification is crucial because we cannot call Mary "the Temple of the Lord," unless we know what "the Temple" is. Nor can we refer meaningfully to heaven as "the New Jerusalem" if we do not know what "Jerusalem" is.

If we were to diagram the four senses underlying Thomas's interpretation of Haggai 2:7 about God "filling this house with glory" in Sermon 1, they would look something like this:

"I will fill this house with glory":
a) *Literally* refers to the God of the Old Testament (Yahweh) filling the Temple with glory—although, if the circumstances had been different, the Old Testament verse might have referred to any number of other Old Testament figures, such as David or Abraham or Moses.
b) *Allegorically* refers to Christ, the Word made flesh, who fills the womb of the Virgin with glory in the Incarnation.
c) *Tropologically* refers to Christ who fills the Church Militant with glory.
d) *Anagogically* refers to Christ who fills heaven with his glory.

We might better understand the difference between a metaphorical *association* and the attribution of an allegorical *meaning* if we think of it in the terms Thomas Aquinas would have: the basic distinction set out by St. Augustine in his *De doctrina christiana* between "words" and "things."[23] "Words," says Augustine, signify "things." When the word "house" signifies an actual house, this is the *literal* meaning of a text. When, in the Scriptures, those "things" are taken to signify other "things"—for example, when the house referred to by the word "house" is taken to signify Christ or heaven—then we have the *spiritual* senses of the biblical text, as Thomas makes clear in his own discussion of the four senses of the Scriptures in a key section of his *Commentary on Galations* (ch. 4, lec.7). "For signification is twofold," says Thomas:

one is through words [*voces*]; the other through the things signified by the words [*per res quas voces significant*]. And this is peculiar to the sacred writings and no others, since their author is God in Whose power it lies not only to employ words to signify, which man can also do, but things as well. Consequently, in the other sciences handed down by men, in which only words [*nisi tantum verba*] can be employed to signify [*accomodari ad significandum*], the words alone signify [*voces solum significant*]. But it is peculiar to Scripture that words and the very things signified by them sig-

---

[23] See esp. 1.1.2.

nify something. Consequently this science can have many senses. For that signification by which the words signify something pertains to the literal or historical sense ["illa significatio qua voces significant aliquid, pertinet ad sensum litteralem seu historicum"]. But the signification whereby the things signified by the words further signify other things pertains to the mystical sense ("illa vero significatio qua res significatae per voces iterum res alias significant, pertinet ad sensum mysticum").[24]

Metaphor, however, is a type of signification that remains on the *literal* level of meaning, as Thomas also makes clear in his discussion in the same section of the *Commentary on Galatians* (ch. 4, lec.7). "There are two ways in which something can be signified by the literal sense," says Thomas:

> either according to the usual construction (*secundum proprietatem locutionis*), as when I say, "the man smiles"; or according to a likeness or metaphor (*secundum similitudinem seu metaphoram*), as when I say, "the meadow smiles." Both of these are used in Sacred Scripture; as when we say, according to the first, that Jesus ascended, and when we say according to the second, that He sits at the right hand of God. Therefore, under the literal sense is included the parabolic or metaphorical ("sub sensu litterali includitur parabolicus seu metaphoricus").[25]

So when we say, for example, that a ship "cuts through" the water, this is a metaphor (at least on Thomas's understanding of the term). So too, when we say the lawyer "cuts through the red tape," this is another metaphor. The lawyer is not actually *cutting red tape* with a pair of scissors. By the same token, the phrase "the lawyer cuts through the red tape" is not being taken *literally* to signify that he or she is actually cutting through red tape and then applied *allegorically* to what he or she is actually doing. No, the *words* "the lawyer cuts through the red tape" are here being taken

---

[24] Trans. F. R. Larcher, O.P. (http://dhspriory.org/thomas/SSGalatians.htm#4/). For other texts in which Thomas discusses the fourfold sense of Scripture, see hi *Quaestiones quodlibetales* 7.6.1–3, *Quaestiones disputatae de potentia* 4.1, and *Summa Theologiae* I, q. 1, a. 10. For an excellent short introduction to Thomas's understanding of the four senses and biblical exegesis in general, see John Boyle, "Thomas Aquinas and Sacred Scripture," *Pro Ecclesia* 4 (1995): 92–104.

[25] *Commentary on Galatians*, ch. 4, lec. 7.

to signify the *thing* "he is removing the bureaucratic obstacles that stand in our way." Note, however, that the latter phrase is also based on a metaphor related to moving objects. It is, in fact, very difficult to speak literally in English *without* using metaphors of one sort or another.

When Thomas applies the Old Testament phrase "I will fill this house with glory" to Christ in the Virgin's womb, however, he understands this to be allegory. In allegory, although one often *begins* with a metaphor or some sort of equivocal use of a term, we then move *beyond* metaphor. The words "I will fill my house with glory" signifies a *thing*: God filling the Temple in Jerusalem with his presence. Granted, even at this *literal* level, we have a metaphorical or analogical use of the term "house," just as in Thomas's own example from his *Commentary on Galatians* (ch. 4, lec. 7), where he suggests that the statement that Christ "is seated at the right hand of the Father" is literally true, but a "literal" sense making use of a metaphor. God the Father does not have a physical "right hand," nor does he "live in a house" in the same way human beings do. That is to say, God does not have a body and is not physically circumscribed within a particular place. And yet, talking about the "right hand" of God or the "house" of the Lord in this way is not yet allegory. We are still dealing with the *things* signified by the *words*. When it is a case of allegory, that *thing*—the Temple in Jerusalem—is now taken to signify another *thing*: in this case, Christ filling the womb of the Virgin Mary, or Christ filling heaven with his resurrected glory.

When we say that the Temple in Jerusalem is the "house" of God, this is a metaphor. The *thing* signified by the words "house of God" is the Temple in Jerusalem, although the application of "house" to God is metaphorical. When we turn around and suggest that the Old Testament Temple of Jerusalem is a prefiguration of the Virgin's womb, then we are implying not merely a *semantic* relationship of *words*, but an *ontological* relationship of *things*. Indeed, on the Christian understanding, as our "Father" in heaven is more truly a "father" than our human father because God is our Creator and never fails to do good for us, so too the Virgin's womb is *more truly* the "house of God" than even the Temple of Jerusalem was because God was more fully and intimately present there.

Contrast this notion of Mary being *more truly* the "house of God" than the Temple was "the house of God" with the difference between politicians metaphorically "cutting red tape" and young girls in elementary school taking a pair of scissors and cutting red tape. When young girls in elementary school "cut red tape," they are not "cutting" in some secondary way or merely in some participated sense in the sort of "cutting" politicians do. Quite the reverse: politicians are "cutting" only *metaphorically*. What Thomas held, however, following the constant tradition of the Church, was that Mary's womb was more truly the "house of God" than the Temple in Jerusalem—indeed, that once we understand the truth of the matter, we come to understand that the Temple in Jerusalem was only the "house of God" in a secondary way, in some participated sense, as a *prefiguration of* God's presence in the Incarnation in the womb of Mary.

Allegorical meanings are based, like metaphors, on the power of words to signify in multiple ways. But even though the allegorical senses are based on metaphorical associations with the images suggested by words— the "house" of God is something we can understand because we first know what human "houses" are—yet an allegorical sense of a word or phrase goes *beyond* that literal level to suggest another sort of ontological (not merely verbal) association.

The confusion that exists between dilating by means of a metaphorical use of a *word* in a *thema* verse and dilating by means of the allegorical interpretation of a *thing* referred to in a *thema* verse is only one sort of confusion. I have seen some scholars go much further and describe any and all methods of dilating a word or phrase from the opening biblical *thema* verse as an "allegorical reading" of that Bible verse. This is too broad a use of the term "allegorical."

The preacher's manuals of the time made a clear distinction between the process of *dilatio* and discerning the allegorical or spiritual senses of a text. Setting out the "spiritual senses" of a word, phrase, or verse is but one means among many of *dilatio*. *Dilatio* is a way of constructing a sermon; recognizing the spiritual senses of the Scripture is a way of reading and interpreting the text. When a medieval preacher divides his opening biblical *thema* into several parts and then "dilates" each of these in turn in the ways we have been examining, he does not take himself to be "interpreting" that text. Thomas does not, for example, really think that, when Matthew wrote the words "Behold, your king comes to you meek," he consciously used the word "behold" in that place in his Gospel because the word "behold" would signify (1) that we are certain that Christ will come to us after death, (2) that the Incarnation happened at a determinate time, (3) that although the coming of Christ into the mind is hidden, yet his coming in the flesh was visible, and (4) that with the coming of Christ, we have victory over the enemy and hope for future good.

When, by contrast, Thomas reads the words in Psalm 71(72):7–8— "In his days shall justice spring up, and abundance of peace, till the moon be taken sway. And he shall rule from sea to sea, and from the river unto the ends of the earth"—he believes that they are said more truly of Christ then they are of either David or Solomon. As he says in his *Commentary on the Gospel of Matthew* (ch. 1, lect. 5):

> because not only the words of the Old Testament, but also the events signify Christ, sometimes some things are said literally [*ad litteram*] others are referred to [*referuntur*] Christ in so far as they bear some figure of Christ, as is said of Solomon, 'And he shall rule from sea to sea' (Ps 71:8), for this was not fulfilled in Solomon.[26]

And again, similarly, in the prologue to his *Commentary on the Psalms*, he says:

> we read some things about the reign of David and Solomon which were not to be fulfilled in the reign of those men, but were fulfilled in the reign of Christ, of whom those things are a figure, as in Psalm [71:1], "Give to the king thy judgment, O God," which is according to the title, about the reign of David and Solomon; and [yet] something is set forth that exceeds the power of David, namely that "In his days Justice will arise, and abundance of peace, until the moon fails" [Ps 71:7] and again, that "He will rule from sea to sea, from the river to the ends of the earth" [Ps 71:8]. This psalm, then, is explained (*exponitur*) as being about the kingdom of Solomon, insofar as it is a symbol of the Kingdom of Christ in which all the things said there will be fulfilled.[27]

Medieval exegetes such as Thomas believed that they could make such claims because, while human writers can signify only in words, God can signify in the events of history. God, they believed, really was signifying

---

[26] This English translation is my own from the Latin in the *reportatio* of Peter of Andria in Aquinas's *Super Evangelium s. Matthaei lectura*, ch. 1, lec. 5: "Sed quia non solum verba veteris testamenti, sed etiam facta significant de Christo, aliquando dicuntur aliqua ad litteram de aliquibus aliis, sed referuntur ad Christum, inquantum illa gerunt figuram Christi, sicut de Salomone dicitur *et dominabitur a mari usque ad mare* etc.; hoc enim non fuit impletum in eo" (ed. R. Cai [Turin: Marietti, 1951]).

[27] Translation by Hugh McDonald at The Aquinas Translation Project: http://www4. desales.edu/~philtheo/loughlin/ATP/index.html. The alteration in brackets is mine. NB: The Latin text incorrectly cites "Psalm vi"; the actual reference is to Ps 71, which begins "Deus iudicium tuum regi." The subsequent references to Ps 71:7, 8 confirm that this is the correct Psalm.

and prefiguring Christ in these words about Solomon; the relationship is *ontological*, not merely *textual*.

Dilatatio, however, is not like this; it is not in and of itself "allegory" unless the preacher decides to dilate by means of the various spiritual senses. Allegory involves being attentive to how Christ is prefigured in the entire Bible. *Dilatatio* is a method for developing one's ideas in the context of preaching, not entirely dissimilar to the classical rhetorical practice of *inventio* or "discovery" of what one is to say in a speech.

Although both metaphor and allegory are based on the expressive power of words, properly speaking, as Thomas makes clear above, only the Bible can contain the spiritual senses because only God can "write" not only in words, but also in things. Human authors are capable of using metaphors—that is, of having their "words" apply to various "things"— but only God can create "things" as prefiguring other "things." Only God can create David as a prefiguration of Christ. And this is the real reason to press the distinction between "metaphor" and "allegory."

Saying that the word "Behold" signifies the coming of Christ because we say the word "Behold" when somebody comes in the door is a kind of wordplay. But when a medieval preacher claims that Abraham's sacrifice of Isaac prefigures God the Father's sacrifice of Christ on the Cross, this is not merely wordplay; this is an assertion of a historical reality—of a connection made in and through history by God, the author of both the Book of Creation and the Book of Scripture. Human authors cannot signify in this way—only the divine author of all things can.

Dilating Using Only the Moral Sense

Note that Thomas does not feel compelled in all cases to dilate by listing all *three* of the spiritual senses; he can use only one or two if he feels the occasion warrants it. If he is going to dilate upon a word or phrase by making use of just *one* of the spiritual senses, he will generally make use of the *moral* sense. When he does so, however, he always makes reference to the deeds of Christ, so he is not really *bypassing* or *excluding* a Christological reading.[28]

Consider, for example, Thomas's dilation in Sermon 4 (*Osanna filio David*) upon the word "Hosanna," which he takes to mean "Save, I be-

---

[28] Thomas's practice is in accord with his own description of the moral sense in his *Commentary on Galatians* (ch. 4, lec. 7), where he says that the moral sense is "among those things which signify Christ, the signs of the things which we ought to do" ("in his quae Christum significant, sunt signa eorum quae nos facere debemus").

seech." The human race was in need of salvation, says Thomas, because they were looking for salvation in the wrong place: in worldly glory and the things of this world. "So in order to show that this is not the proper way of salvation, the Lord showed us another way of salvation, the way of humility," which he showed, for example, when he rode into Jerusalem on a donkey and when he was willing to bear his Cross. And from his humility, says Thomas, we too should learn to humble ourselves. And "a human being ought to humble himself in three ways: he ought to humble his mind, his body, and his affection." The dilation upon these three points each in its turn takes up roughly a full page of text, but in brief, let me summarize by saying we should humble our *minds* by not becoming puffed up and by following the lives and examples of the great men and women of the Church, accepting the authority and example of the saints. We should humble our *bodies* by means of fasting and vigils. And finally, we ought to humble our *affections* in such a way that we give them completely over to God, not in loving something as "ours" without linking it to God.

Note the way Thomas has delivered this *moral* lesson. He begins with the word "Hosanna" in his opening *thema* verse, then defines its meaning ("Save, I beseech"), and then associates "salvation" with Christ (who, not unimportantly given this *thema* verse, is also a "son of David"), and then, having appealed to Christ as a moral exemplar of humility, he is able to dilate at length on the nature of this virtue. Note that Thomas did not need a text with the word "humility" in it in order to give a sermon on the virtue. The word "Hosanna" served altogether nicely.

We find another, rather more direct approach to getting at the moral sense of the text in Sermon 8 (*Puer Jesus*). The resulting sermon is, as we shall see, however, extraordinarily more complex. For this sermon, Thomas used Luke 22:52 as his *thema*: "The boy Jesus advanced in age and wisdom and in grace with God and man." Now, as we have seen, it is altogether possible that Thomas might have used this verse to preach all sorts of different messages, depending upon the occasion and depending upon how he crafted the "declaration of parts." If it had been a sermon on the saints, he might have focused on the notion of advancing in age, wisdom, and grace, dilating individually upon each. Or if his goal had been to say something about the Incarnation, he might have focused on the words "Jesus," "grace," and "God and man." In fact, in the first part of this sermon, Thomas does provide a brief disquisition on how the Son of God, who "is eternity and from eternity," can be said to "advance" at all. His ultimate goal, however, after settling these theological matters, is basically *moral* instruction. And he crafts the remainder of his sermon to show

how "the progress of Christ is . . . an example for adolescents." As the boy Jesus advanced in age, wisdom, and grace with God and other people, so too should all young men and women.[29] Thus we might say that the entire sermon is a *moral* interpretation of Luke 2:52, and by the "moral sense" of the text, we mean showing *how the things that signify Christ signify the things we ought to do.*[30] We will see how this sort of "signification" works as we proceed.

After his brief discussion of how Christ could be said to "advance" in any way, Thomas returns to his opening *thema* verse about which he had said, "We will find in these words"—that is, the words from Luke 2:52—"four progresses of Christ: first, the progress of age in regard to the body; second, the progress of wisdom in regard to the intellect; third, the progress of grace with God; and fourth, the progress of grace in view of his living together with men." As might be expected, Thomas takes up each of these sorts of progress, dilating upon each in its turn, in the parts of the sermon that follow—two of the four in the morning *sermo* and the remaining two in the evening's *collatio*—in each case contriving to show how Christ's progress in each of these areas can serve as a model for our progress as well.

We need not go through each of these four in detail, but allow me to focus on just one from the evening's *collatio* to illustrate the point that the "moral instruction" Thomas is going to derive from this little comment in Luke 2:52 about the boy Jesus advancing in "age, wisdom, and grace with God and man" is not at all simplistic. This, as we shall see, is a sermon for intellectually and spiritually mature adolescents, not a "youth sermon" for "the kids." It is also a good example of Thomas's use of the "moral sense."

In his morning sermon, Thomas takes up, first, the boy Jesus's progress in *body*, which was largely an exhortation on the necessity of developing the mind and the soul along with the body, and second, his progress in *grace*. The alert reader might notice that Thomas has not observed the order of his *thema* text, which says that Jesus progressed, first, in body,

---

[29] We could almost imagine at this point that the sermon might have been given to a "youth group" of adolescents. As we will see, the sermon itself and its accompanying *collatio* are far too complex for that. In fact, given the many references to passages in the *Catena Aurea* in it, Fr. Hoogland suggests (*Academic Sermons*, 87n1) that it came from the period of Thomas's second regency at Paris (1268–1272). Indeed, the presence of the accompanying *collatio* means that it must have been a university sermon. It might do to recall, however, that most of Thomas's students would have been adolescents, as would many of the Dominican novices at St. Jacques. The sermon, as we will see, is clearly meant for them.

[30] See the passage from Thomas's *Commentary on Galatians* (ch. 4, lec. 7).

second, in wisdom of *intellect*, and third, in *grace*. He in fact apologizes to his listeners for the variance, explaining:

> So the first point of attention is this: that we may grow in mind as we grow in age. But how does a human being grow in mind? Certainly when he grows "in wisdom and grace." And although in the verse that is the point of departure for this homily, wisdom is mentioned before grace, we will nevertheless speak about grace first, since "the beginning of wisdom is the fear of the Lord," according to Sirach 1:14.[31]

Thus, when he begins his *collatio* at vespers later that evening, he is able to repeat his opening *thema* verse and then immediately begin by saying: "Today"—and by that he means earlier that morning—"we have spoken about the double progress of Christ, that is, about (1) the progress of age and (2) that of grace. So it remains that we must speak about the other two progresses, namely, about (3) the progress of wisdom and (4) his life with the people."[32]

So what lessons can we derive from the life of young Jesus with regard to progress in wisdom? Scholars often comment upon the fact that we know very little—next to nothing, in fact—about Jesus's adolescence *other than* this little story found at the very end of Luke 2 about the time when Jesus was twelve and his family went down to the Temple in Jerusalem for the Passover (which, according to Luke, they did every year) and he was left behind. His parents did not realize his absence for a day, and they did not find him for a space of three days, at which time, says Luke, "they found him in the temple, sitting among the teachers, listening to them and asking them questions; and all who heard him were amazed at his understanding and his answers" (Luke 2:46–47). The entire account, the sum total of what we know about Jesus's adolescence, begins at Luke 2:41 and is finished a mere eleven verses later at Luke 2:52. What moral lessons can Thomas derive for his young Dominican confreres from this meager bit of material? Quite a lot, as it turns out, but it will involve not merely attending to the *literal* or *plain* meaning of the text, but also developing meaning from an expressly *moral* exegesis of the text as well.

And so he begins, "just as the progress of grace is shown in peace," which was the message of the final part of his morning's sermon, and continues:

---

[31] Hoogland, *Academic Sermons*, 94.
[32] Ibid., 99.

so the progress of wisdom is shown in contemplation. Therefore, Solomon says in Eccl. 1.16: "I have surpassed all who were before me in Jerusalem"; and he adds why: "My mind has contemplated many things wisely." Someone who contemplates many things wisely advances in wisdom.[33]

So far, Thomas is sticking fairly close to the letter of the text, merely adding the notion of *contemplation* to that of *wisdom*. The culmination of the growth in wisdom is shown in contemplation.

At this point, however, Thomas begins to dilate upon his topic more fully by making use of the *spiritual* meaning of the text—in this case, by incorporating a *figurative* interpretation of the Temple. "Behold," he says, "a building is called a temple by reason of the contemplating that takes place in it, or we speak of contemplation by reason of the fact that it takes place in a temple. So, since the Lord is found in the Temple, he shows us the application to contemplation and that by the Temple contemplation is signified."[34] Note how the physical building, the Temple, is now being taken as a "figure" of contemplation, which, as Thomas has already said, is the means to growth in *wisdom*. Thus, we can "see what Christ has done in the Temple, and on the basis of these things we can know whether someone advances in the Temple."[35] The reader could hardly fail to miss how, in that last sentence, Thomas has conflated "advancing in the Temple" where young Jesus is said to "advance in wisdom" with the notion of how anyone "advances in contemplation" and, thus, "advances in wisdom."

"Now four things are necessary for man in order to advance in wisdom," announces Thomas: "that he (1) listens open-heartedly, (2) inquires diligently, (3) answers prudently, and (4) meditates attentively."[36] Now *here* are clearly the sort of moral lessons that Thomas wants his students and the young novices to learn; these are the virtues he wants them to develop. This is understandable. But how are these four to be related to the text of Luke's Gospel? *This* is his challenge.

Now, although Thomas's usual practice is to *begin* with the biblical verse he wishes to dilate upon, in this case, the reader is going to find the relevant biblical verses at the *end* of each section. Indeed, his treatment here is more subtle than his usual clear-and-distinct *divisio textus*. But

---

[33] Ibid.
[34] Ibid.
[35] Ibid., 99–100.
[36] Ibid., 100. My numbering differs from Fr. Hoogland's, whose number system is keyed to the entire sermon. Mine is done with an eye only to this section.

if we were to outline the relevant lines from Luke 2 and associate them with the "four things necessary for man in order to advance in wisdom," it would look something like this. For a man to advance in wisdom, he must:

(1) *listen open-heartedly*: "And after three days they found him in the temple, sitting in the midst of the teachers, listening to them" ("et factum est post triduum invenerunt illum in templo sedentem in medio doctorum audientem illos").
(2) *inquire diligently:* "and questioning them" ("et interrogantem").
(3) *answer prudently*: "and all who heard him were amazed at his prudence and his responses" ("stupebant autem omnes qui eum audiebant super prudentia et responsis eius").
(4) *meditate attentively*: "and his mother kept all these words in her heart" ("et mater eius conservabat omnia verba haec in corde suo").

It is not without significance that immediately after this last statement about Mary "keeping all these words in her heart," Luke adds the line that serves as the *thema* verse for the entire sermon: "The boy Jesus advanced in age and wisdom and in grace with God and man" ("Puer Jesus proficiebat aetate et sapientia et gratia apud Deum, et homines").[37] But with this, we have only glanced at the basic structure. Allow me to provide a few of the more relevant details, for this section contains a wonderful mini-sermon in itself on how students should approach their education.

First, says Thomas, to advance in wisdom it is necessary that one "listen freely" (*libenter audiat*), or as Fr. Hoogland translates it, "listen open-heartedly." Why? "Because wisdom is so profound that no one is by himself sufficient to contemplate it." So it is necessary that a person *listen freely*, especially to those who are wiser. As it says in Proverbs 1:5: "A wise man who listens to wisdom will be wiser." Indeed "no one," says Thomas, "is so wise that he would not learn anything by listening. Thus his parents found Jesus as he was listening [Luke 2:46]."[38]

"But *how* should you listen?" Thomas asks his students. "Surely, with perseverance" (*perseveranter*), he tells them. "Some want to listen, in passing [*transitorie*], to just one lecture in one science [*scientia*], their heart not in it." But consider Jesus, he tells them. He, by contrast, was three days in

---

[37] The modern Vulgate has a slightly different version of Luke 2:52, without *puer* (boy): "et Iesus proficiebat sapientia aetate et gratia apud Deum et homines."
[38] Hoogland, *Academic Sermons*, 100.

the Temple listening assiduously (*assidue*). "Thus you too ought to listen assiduously."[39]

What else can students learn from young Jesus? Well, says Thomas, just as Jesus was found listening to *many* while sitting in their midst, so too students should not listen to just one teacher only, but to many—an interesting remark coming from a man who was himself a highly-admired teacher with a wide following—because as St. Paul says in 1 Corinthians 12:4, "there are different graces" and "one man has not advanced in all fields." And here he makes a fascinating comment on the different strengths of various Fathers of the Church. "St. Gregory knew the morals very well," he says, whereas "St. Augustine was very good at finding solutions to problems, and St. Ambrose was very good at giving the allegorical meaning of sacred texts." "What you do not learn from one, you learn from someone else." Although Thomas might have made this comment earlier in his career, it is likely not without significance that he wrote this comment *after* he had finished putting together the *Catena Aurea*, with all the research into the various patristic resources that work necessitated.

"Moreover, Jesus was found listening to many people and standing in their midst" (*in medio*). What is the significance of this statement? This, says Thomas, is the position of the just judge. The Latin here is simply "hoc est justi judicis": literally "this is of the just judge." Fr. Hoogland has translated this phrase as "this is the role of the just judge." In both his rendering of the phrase and mine, we have had to supply a word: I supplied "position" and he supplied "role." Both are fine, to my mind, as far as they go, but neither quite communicates what I think Thomas has in mind here. The image I think Thomas has in mind is metaphorical, but the metaphor is based on the vision of a judge (or a king) in the midst of advisors or litigants, listening to each one carefully to get the best information and advice available and then rendering a *just* judgment in accord with what he judges to be the *truth* of the matter. Accordingly, we might (somewhat less literally) render the phrase and what follows it thus: "For this [namely listening attentively] is characteristic of the *just* judge," for the office (or "duty," *officium*) of judge is entrusted to one who listens (*auditori enim committitur officium judicis*) because the just judge "ought to judge justly about the things he hears" ("quia juste debet judicare quae

---

[39] Ibid. I have altered Fr. Hoogland's translation somewhat here, translating *scientia* as "science," rather than "academic field," and *assidue* as "assiduously," rather than "constantly."

audit").[40] Christ was "in the midst" (*in medio*), says Thomas a little further on, "because it says in Sirach 15.5: 'He has opened his mouth in the midst of the Church, and the Lord has filled him with the Spirit of wisdom and understanding.'"

The point here, however, is not so much about judges, but about how students are to be like these just judges. Some students simply follow the opinion of their teachers (*opinionem magistrorum*) because they hear them. But no one, says Thomas, should cherish a friend over the truth. Rather, he should adhere to the truth alone, since, as Aristotle says, disagreements in opinions are not (or perhaps we should say, "should not be") incompatible with friendship.

Fr. Hoogland translates the Latin quite faithfully here: "No one, however, ought to have a friend in truth" ("sed nullus debet habere amicum in veritate"). I think the *sense* of it is rendered more accurately, however, in a translation by Athanasius Sulavik: no one should cherish a friend *over* the truth.[41] The following clauses make clear that one should adhere to the truth *only* and that differing opinions about the truth should not be "repugnant" to true friendship. In this context, it just does not quite make sense to say that "no one ought to have a friend in truth," if by this one means one ought not to be friends *with* truth. The sense in this context is more that "no one ought to have a friend *in place of truth*" or "no one ought to place friendship *above* truth" because, of course, a *true* friendship would be based on a common search for truth. Thus, to place friendship *above* truth would destroy the very foundation of true friendship. So too, placing one's affection for a teacher *above* the truth would destroy the very foundations of the search the teacher and student are supposed to be engaged in together.

So, the student should be like Christ: (1) listening, (2) perseveringly (over three days), (3) to many teachers, (4) in their midst, like a just judge who listens attentively, but then decides upon *the truth*. And these four are suggested by the biblical verse for the day that indicates that Jesus was found listening, after three days, to many, while standing in their midst.

All of this wonderful advice, however, is only what can be found under the *first* subdivision of four, since after (1) "listening freely," the student must also (2) "inquire diligently," (3) "answer prudently," and (4) "meditate attentively."

---

[40] As should be clear, I have altered Fr. Hoogland's translation somewhat here (see *Academic Sermons*, 101).

[41] This translation can be found at http://www.dhspriory.org/thomas/Serm08PuerIesus.htm.

Thus, after (1) "listening freely" (2) "for progress in wisdom," says Thomas, "it is required that someone inquire *diligently*." "Thus they also found Jesus in the Temple as he put questions and sought wisdom, so as to give us an example of seeking wisdom." We must seek wisdom, says Thomas, "because wisdom is more precious than all things that can be desired." This point matches up nicely with the point he has *just* made about friendship not being valued above truth. So it is too with wisdom: it should be valued above all other things. Thus it says in Proverbs 3:15, "Wisdom is more precious than all jewels together; and all the things that people desire do not have value compared to it." And in Wisdom 7:8 says: "I have preferred [wisdom] to thrones and kingdoms." Some people travel vast distances in harsh circumstances over mountains and seas in order to acquire money. "In this way you too ought to labor for wisdom," Thomas tells his students, a nice echo of St. Paul's admonition in 1 Corinthians 9:25 that, if every athlete exercising self-discipline in all things in order to receive a "perishable crown," how much more should Christians do so for the sake of an "imperishable" one.

"But where ought we to seek wisdom and from whom?" asks Thomas. "Surely from three," he tells them. First, one seeks wisdom from a teacher or from those who are wiser, not only those alive now, but also from "the old ones," those "who are not with us anymore" the great "fathers" of the Church such as St. Augustine and St. Ambrose.

Second, he tells them, "it is not only enough that you inquire of people or even these texts, but you ought to seek in the contemplation of creatures as well, for it says in Sirach 1.9: 'God has poured out his wisdom over all his works.'" In the same way we can learn from a piece of art a lot about the wisdom of the artist, so too by investigating nature we can learn something about the wisdom of the Creator.

And finally (third), one acquires wisdom "by communicating with others" (*cum aliis communicando*). Hence, the wise man says: "I have learned without delusion, and I share without envy" (Wis 7:13). No one can advance in knowledge so well, says Thomas, as when he shares with others what he knows himself. Indeed, this is an obligation one owes to others (a *debitum*): to share with others the things one has learned and to allow oneself to be questioned by them to test the firmness of the truth.

This last point about the importance of "communicating with others" and engaging in a spirited dialogue of give-and-take in a common search for the truth leads quite naturally back to the biblical account of young Jesus in the Temple and to Thomas's next point: "Christ gave answers, and all were amazed at his prudence and his responses" (Luke 2:47). It is worth recalling that Thomas's students would have been engaged in a good deal of disputation as part of their studies. Any teacher who leads seminars can tell you that some students have more of a taste for this sort of Socratic give-and-take than others. The more introspective students tend to shy away from it, as they tend to shy away from working in groups. For the most part, they prefer to keep their thoughts to themselves. Such students need to be encouraged to take part—indeed, they need to be given *good reasons* to take part—which is precisely what Thomas has done above with his exhortation about *inquiring diligently* not only from teachers and books but also from nature and by communicating with others openly and freely.

By contrast, the more naturally gregarious students who love disputation and take to it with gusto often need to be tempered somewhat, not only for the benefit of the quieter students, who also have a great deal of "quiet insight," but also because (as was my own case as an undergraduate), their tongues tend to rush ahead of their more prudent thoughts. They are sure of everything. They criticize freely. They dismiss others rashly, not only their fellow students but also some of the foremost thinkers in history, as if they were brushing off a fly. Their energy can be invigorating. But we all know that, at some point, they need to learn a little self-discipline—a little *prudence*—so that they can be more like the young Jesus, about whom it is said that "all were amazed at his prudence and his responses."

"So what makes for a 'prudent' answer'?" an inquiring student might want to know. "In an answer, prudence is required in three ways," Thomas replies. Prudence, for both Thomas and Aristotle, is the intellectual virtue that discerns the "mean," the proper "proportion" between too much and too little. So, for an answer to be "prudent," says Thomas, there must be a threefold sort of proportionality.

First, the answer should be in proper proportion with the one who gives the answer. That is to say, one should not try to answer a question that is beyond one's knowledge and capacities. If you do not know, simply admit honestly you do not know. Trying to impress someone who knows about a subject with words that lack all knowledge of the subject is not the sure road to success.

Second, a prudent answer should be in proper proportion with the listener. As it says in Proverbs 26:4, "Do not answer a fool with the same foolishness, in order to avoid your becoming like him." How can you tell someone is a fool? "When he asks with insolent words," answers Aquinas. It is best not to get entangled attempting to answer such persons. Christ showed the way in this regard, says Thomas: "when some people asked him with which power he worked miracles, he replied to them by asking them another question in return."

And thirdly, a prudent answer should be in proportion to the question asked, "not with elegant ornaments of words" (*cum phaleris verborum*), but "to the point" (*ad quaestionem*), otherwise the answer would be "windy" (*ventosa*). This, of course, is not bad advice for faculty members either.

"The fourth thing that makes prudence complete," says Thomas, "is that someone meditates with attention." Now, the alert reader might have noticed that, above, Thomas said that "prudence is required in three ways," and he has, in fact, listed all three ways. "The fourth thing that makes prudence complete" makes a nice transition, however, to Thomas's fourth and final set of moral lessons related to the comment in his opening *thema* verse that the boy Jesus advanced *in wisdom*. We have learned so far that the student should (1) listen freely, (2) inquire diligently, and (3) answer prudently, so now it remains for Thomas to dilate upon (4) *meditating attentively*. This is interesting because we have no comment among the verses here in Luke 2 that Jesus "meditated" at all, attentively or otherwise. So to make this last point, Thomas turns to the penultimate words in the Gospel reading, to that great paradigm of *meditating attentively*, the Blessed Virgin, who, after all that is said and done in this chapter, is said to have "kept all these words with her in her heart." She now becomes the moral model for Thomas's students. What can they learn from her about the sort of meditation in which they should be progressing?

"Take a look at three things concerning the meditation of the Blessed Virgin Mary," Thomas tells them. There is no explicit *divisio* here, but if Thomas had made one, it would have looked like this: Mary (1) kept (2) all these words (3) in her heart. Consider the three things Thomas mentions concerning Mary's meditation. First, it was "fruitful," he says, but by that he means she kept all these things in her memory. "What is the fruit of meditation?" he asks. "Meditation is the key to the memory of someone who can read and listen to many things, but cannot keep it unless he meditates," he tells them. This reply makes sense in light of the association with the notion that Mary "kept" these things.

Indeed, says Thomas, the meditation of the Blessed Virgin was complete (*integra*) because "she kept *all* the words in her heart." And so too with one who seeks to progress in wisdom, he ought to meditate "on all the things he has heard."

And finally, the meditation of Mary was "profound" (*profunda*). Whereas some meditate only superficially, Mary kept all these things *in her heart*. Thomas finishes with a passage from Psalm 77:7: "I have meditated at night in my heart, and I trained my spirit and kept it focused," which contains a nice pairing of the notion of meditating in one's heart with the notion of training one's spirit and, of course, *staying focused*, not allowing one's mind to stray.

"There is no doubt," Thomas assures his students, "that someone who listens open-heartedly, responds prudently, inquires diligently, and meditates with attention will advance much in wisdom"—just as young Jesus did.

This section of Sermon 8 (*Puer Jesus*) provides, as I have suggested above, as nice an example of Thomas's use of the *moral* sense as one will find, not to mention of how one can dilate in a sermon by using the moral sense. From one short scene dealing with the young Jesus in the Temple, Thomas was able to "unpack" a host of useful moral advice for his listeners, much of it extremely good advice crafted with an eye to their special circumstances as students at the University of Paris.

Note that in the two sermons we have examined where Thomas dilates by means of the moral sense of the text—Sermon 4 (*Osanna filio David*) and Sermon 8 (*Puer Jesus*)—the sort of moral exegesis Thomas gives of the Scriptures is fairly straightforward because the biblical text on which he is preaching deals directly with Christ. A moral exegesis is still possible, however, if the text in question is not directly about Christ—but rather, say, from the Old Testament—if the preacher first makes an allegorical exegesis to show how the text allegorically refers to Christ and *then* shows how what Christ has done teaches us what we should do. For those who are curious about what this sort of exegesis would look like, consider the following example Thomas himself gives in his *Commentary on Galatians* (ch.7, lec. 4):

> For when I say, "Let there be light," if I am referring literally to corporeal light, it is the literal sense. But if it be taken to mean "Let Christ be born in the Church," it pertains to the allegorical sense. But if one says, "Let there be light," i.e., "Let us be conducted to glory through Christ," it pertains to the anagogical sense. Finally, if it is said "Let there be light," i.e., "Let us be illumined in mind and inflamed in heart through Christ," it pertains to the moral sense.

This passage is especially fitting for our present purposes not only because, in it, Thomas lays out so nicely the four different senses of Scripture, but also because one can certainly imagine how a preacher could dilate upon each of these four to expand his sermon.

The Spiritual Senses: Not Merely a Matter of Words

The "spiritual" senses of Scripture are not, then, as is sometimes thought, merely a way of fooling around with words. They are rather, I would suggest, a mode of thinking about the Scriptures, always attentive to the ways in which they manifest Christ and the central Paschal mystery (the allegorical sense), always attentive to the ways in which we are called upon to change our lives in accord with the text (the moral sense), and always attentive to the ways in which the text draws us as a pilgrim people on to our final union with God (the anagogical sense).

There's no doubt that this constant attentiveness to—this constant being-on-the-alert-for—the larger meaningfulness of the text could at times result in some rather strained interpretations, just as a man or woman who is always alert to the sound of danger in the wilderness will sometimes "hear things" that are not there or will, say, interpret the wind as an approaching stranger. I would, however, be willing to contrast favorably the constant medieval alertness to the deeper significance of the biblical text precisely as "Christocentric" with the modern tendency to read it "historically"—that is, as representing nothing more than an antiquated historical artifact in a dead language from a dead people.

When the Bible is read in this manner, two results are to be expected: either the text will be seen as having *no* significance at all for contemporary readers, at least for those who are not themselves historians interested in the hobby of the study of antiquarian languages, peoples, and customs, or else, having been evacuated of all meaning, it will become a blank slate on which can be drawn whatever political program the reader (or preacher) favors—be it liberal or conservative, Marxist or capitalist. What people tend to hear when they read the Scriptures in this way is not necessarily the word of God, but more often than not the mocking echo of their own voice.[42]

---

[42] Cf. Robert Frost's poem "The Most of It," which contains the wonderful lines:

He thought he kept the universe alone;
For all the voice in answer he could wake
Was but the mocking echo of his own
From some tree-hidden cliff across the lake.
Some morning from the boulder-broken beach

METHOD 8: THE CONSIDERATION OF CAUSES AND THEIR EFFECTS

The last method of *dilatatio* we will be examining is the consideration of causes and their effects. Given Thomas's training in dialectic, this method of "dilating" a point comes naturally to him, and he uses it frequently—indeed, he will often "chain" a series of cause-and-effect relationships.

Take, for example, the section from Sermon 11 (*Emitte Spiritum*) in which Thomas is "dilating" on the opening *thema* from Psalm 104:30, which contains the words "Send forth your Spirit." The word "Spirit," says Thomas, implies four things: first, the fineness of substance; second, the perfection of life; third, the incitement of a movement; and fourth, a hidden origin. We discussed this passage above under the heading of "the interpretation of a name." When he comes to the fourth of these considerations—the one in which he suggests that the word "spirit" implies or suggests a "hidden origin"—Thomas "dilates" upon the point by saying that "Faith teaches and reason argues that all visible and changeable things have a hidden cause. What is that cause? That cause is God." "But how has God created all things?" asks Thomas. Not out of necessity, he insists, but out of his own free will. But why, then, did he create the world? "For sure, it is love [*amor*]," answers Thomas, and adds: "We celebrate now the feast of the Holy Spirit, and the Spirit is the principle of being in all things. Thus the Spirit has a hidden origin, the property of which is love [*amor*]."

So too, when it comes to the third of the characteristics implied by the word "spirit"—namely, "the incitement of a movement"—Thomas comments as follows:

For we see in the world different movements, natural and voluntary ones, in people and in angels. Where do these different

---

He would cry out on life, that what it wants
Is not its own love back in copy speech,
But counter-love, original response.

Is not the conviction that the Scriptures contain "counter-love, original response" precisely what distinguishes believers from ostensibly "neutral" observers? Those who listen to someone they love, or perhaps merely a person they view with deep respect, are usually attentive for what this person is really trying to say. Those who listen without such love, by contrast, often enough become like the sort of journalists who do interviews always looking for the "gotcha'" moment. To the latter, the words are not "messages in a bottle" from a living *person*; they become mere "material" to be bent to the writer's own purposes. A reader must decide what he or she believes is the proper way to read a text, let alone to communicate with another human person.

movements come from? They must come from one first mover, evidently from God. The Psalmist says: "you will change them, and they will be changed" [Ps 102:27]. And God moves by his will. But what is the first movement of the will? For certain it is love [*amor*].

Readers of the *prima pars* of Thomas's *Summa of Theology* will recognize the cause-effect relationship sketched ever-so-briefly here as one of the "five ways" of demonstrating the existence of a Creator: reasoning from effect to cause, from the things that are moved to a first, unmoved mover. Readers of the *prima pars* of Thomas's *Summa of Theology* might also notice how different the argument sounds in the context of a sermon. Indeed, in the context of a sermon, Thomas can add this final, important point about the "first mover": He moves out love and is the "first mover" because he *is* love.

But it is not merely metaphysical causality of this sort that interests Thomas. Cause-and-effect relationships are all around us, for both good and ill, some leading us to virtue, some to sin. On the former, see for example this section from Sermon 3 (*Abjiciamus opera*) in which Thomas is "dilating" upon a *thema* from Romans 13:12 ("Let us throw off the works of the darkness and put on the arms of the light"). He divides the verse into its two constituent parts—"Let us throw off the works of the darkness" and "put on the arms of the light"—the first of which is meant to "stir up a liberating abhorrence of all worldly stains and vices," while the second is meant to inspire "an honorable love or pursuit of heavenly virtues." When he comes to the second of these—the love and pursuit of heavenly virtues— Thomas "dilates" upon the phrase "put on the arms of light" by the various effects of grace, saying:

the works of the Gospel and the spiritual gifts of the Holy Spirit are for us the arms against the world, the flesh, and the devil, and that they make us stand firm in the light. Because through the *effects of enlightening grace*, which is like a light, they cause us to recognize the divine secret. In 2 Cor 4:6 it says: "Yet God, who has said that light will shine from the darkness, (has shone his light in our hearts in order to bring to light the knowledge of the glory of God which is on the face of Jesus Christ)." Because *by the effect of reconciling grace*, which is like a light, these [spiritual gifts] make peace when we wage war among ourselves [see Gal 5:22–23]. Proverbs 6:23 says: "The commandment is a lamp and the law a light," etc. Because *through the effect of the grace of honesty*, which is like a light, they make us beautiful, and, in us, the whole universe. John 5:35 reads: "He was a burning and light-giving lamp" [emphases mine].

In so many of these examples I have supplied, notice how these methods of *dilatatio* are frequently used in conjunction with one another. That is to say, a cause-and-effect discussion is often built upon an "interpretation of names" or a guiding metaphor, and each of these will provide opportunities for a concordance of texts and the "chaining" of biblical authorities.

In this regard, consider the following wonderful passage from Sermon 18 (*Germinet terra*), celebrating the Feast of the Birth of the Virgin Mary, where Thomas, dilating upon the opening biblical *thema* from Genesis 1:11, "Let the earth put forth the green plant that brings forth seed and the fruit-bearing tree that yields fruit"—a passage that, let us be honest, is not one that most of us would have naturally associated with a sermon on the Virgin Mary—says that Mary was a "green plant." He explains:

She is a green plant because of her virginity. It says in Jer 12.4: "Every plant of the land will wither," but the Blessed Virgin was a green plant through her virginity. Hence it says in Luke 1.26–27: "The angel Gabriel was sent to the Virgin Mary." See that in the greenness we observe (1) moisture, (2) beauty, and (3) usefulness or necessity. First, I say that in the greenness we see moisture as a cause, since moisture is the cause of greenness. Thus we read in Sirach [Ecclesiasticus] 40.16: "Greenness on all waterfronts." And you should know that, just as every plant withers because of fire or the sun, so the concupiscence of the flesh makes the greenness of virginity wither. It says in Job 31.12: "It is a devouring fire aimed at consummation." But by what is the greenness of virginity nurtured? Surely by heavenly love [*amor*].

In this case, we begin first with a metaphor: Mary is like a green plant because of her virginity. We move next to a consideration of the implications of the "greenness" of a plant: it indicates moisture, beauty, and usefulness. Then we are presented with a cause-and-effect relationship: moisture is a cause of greenness. Next, we get another metaphor: concupiscence of the flesh (lust) is like a fire or like the heat of the sun. Then we get another cause-and-effect relationship: What does fire or heat from the sun do to green plants? It withers them. This consideration leads us back into another metaphor: just as heat withers a green plant, so concupiscence destroys virginity. And we finish (this little section at least) with another cause-and-effect relationship: by what is the greenness of virginity nurtured? It is nurtured by heavenly love, which is metaphorically like water from heaven that causes the greenness of the plant.

Note that each stage of development along the way, each cause-and-effect relationship, provides another lively opportunity for the "chaining" of biblical passages. In this little section, Thomas's metaphorical consideration of "greenness" and "moisture" lead him to the passage from Ecclesiasticus 40:15–16 that reads: "Never a branch will the posterity of the wicked put forth; dead roots they are that rattle on the wind-swept rock. Yet how green yonder rushes grow by the river's bank!" One sentence later, his consideration of heat and the sun leads him to make another concordance-type search—whether he made this search in an actual printed concordance or merely by searching his memory is immaterial at the moment—and this search turns up the passage in Job 31:12, "that fire, once lighted, will rage till all is consumed, never a crop shall escape it." The result is biblical authority associated with a metaphor based on the results of a cause-and-effect analysis that is itself based on another metaphor and an interpretation of a name. Here, as elsewhere, all of these methods of *dilatatio* will frequently overlap and intersect with one another as the author develops the content of his sermon.

I suggest that none of this is just for play—although it is playful. These methods of *dilatatio* are the means by which a medieval preacher can, if he is good, craft an intellectually sophisticated sermon with a serious theological point in such a way that it will be both compelling and memorable to his audience. In Sermon 18 (*Germinet terra*), for example, the serious theological point has to do with the interesting (and somewhat ironic) relationship between the virginity of Mary and her ultimate fecundity (the green plant will bring forth seed; the "seed" is Christ; and the "fruit-bearing tree" is the Cross of Christ, the fruits of which are manifold). But Thomas has also made clear that Mary's "yes" to God—that is, the fecundity of her greenness—was first *made possible by* the grace of God, by the divine love that waters her "greenness" as rain nourishes the green plant.

If our preacher were in addition to have chosen as his biblical *thema*, as Thomas does here, a verse from the book of Genesis dealing with creation, then he might also help confirm in the minds of his listeners the further theological point that the divine Word who created us in the beginning is the same Word who creates us anew by means of his Incarnation, death on the Cross, and Resurrection from the dead. Thomas does not actually have to *quote* the prologue to John's Gospel or *quote*, say, the relevant texts from Athanasius's *On the Incarnation* to make these key theological points for his listeners. Preaching in this way does not involve "dumbing down" or "watering down" one's theology. It does, however, involve spurring interest by making beautiful and memorable rhetorical associations.

Granted, a preacher could just decide to *make* these theological points straightforwardly about the fruits of Mary's virginity, her cooperation in Christ's salvific sacrifice on the Cross, and the prevenient grace and divine love that makes possible her cooperation with the God's salvific act in the dry categories of the theological textbook without any of Thomas's metaphorical associations. Or he could choose, as Thomas has done here, to discuss Mary's virginity and the divine love that makes its "fruit" possible in relation to the greenness of plants and the fecundity of creation itself. I will let the reader decide which of the two is more likely to remain memorable for most audiences.

THE SPECIAL CASE OF *EXEMPLA*: CONSPICUOUS BY THEIR ABSENCE

Another method of *dilatatio* that became common in the late-thirteenth- and early-fourteenth-century preaching, but which we do not find mentioned in either Robert of Basevorn's *Forma praedicandi* or the earlier "Bonaventuran" *Ars concionandi*, was the use of what were called *exampla*: pious little stories meant to exemplify the moral lesson of the sermon. Indeed, there seem to have been whole volumes devoted to cataloguing such *exempla* and indexing them for the preacher's use. If a preacher needed a good moral fable to exemplify the virtues of "temperance" or "courage" or "faith," he could find a half dozen or so for any occasion in such preacher's manuals. Charles Smyth, in his *Art of Preaching: A Practical Survey of Preaching in the Church of England, 747–1939*, playfully compares these medieval collections of *exempla* to modern compositions such as "A Thousand and One Things to Say in Sermons."[43] One of the best known of these

---

[43] Smyth, *Art of Preaching*, 58. One of the key secondary sources on the medieval *exemplum* is J. Th. Welter, *L'Exemplum dans la littérature religieuse et didactique du moyen age* (Paris: Occitania, 1927), but see also, for its wonderful examples, G. R. Owst, *Literature and Pulpit in Medieval England* (Cambridge, UK: Cambridge University Press, 1933). And for a more recent treatment that examines the use of *exempla* manuals, specifically among the thirteenth-century Dominican friars, see David D'Avray, *The*

catalogues, the *Tactatus de diversis materiis praedicalibus* (ca.1250–1261) by the Dominican Stephen of Bourbon, contains nearly 2900 *exempla*, not counting the Bible stories and interesting "facts" (often enough wrong) from natural history.

With regard to these *exempla*, they were of various kinds, as Smyth usefully summarizes for us:

> the Biblical *exemplum*, taken from the Canonical Scriptures or from the Apocrypha: the pious *exemplum* (deeds and sayings of holy men and holy women, such as are to be found in the *Vitae Patrum* and Cassian's *Collationes*, and in certain devotional treatises): the hagiographical *exemplum* (the varied progeny of the *Acta Sanctorum*): the prosopopeic *exemplum* (stories of visions of the next world or of ghostly visitants to the earthly scene): the profane *exemplum* (anecdotes, etc., from the literature of Classical antiquity): the legendary *exemplum* (from the epics of the Middle Ages, from mythologies, Classical and Celtic, and from religious and popular traditions): the *fable* (a story in which the actors are animals) and the *narration* (in which the actors are human beings): the moralised allegory and the natural phenomenon: and lastly, the personal anecdote, which the popular preachers knew well how to turn to good effect.[44]

There was, for example, the popular story of the prostitute who happened upon a church, and venturing inside out of curiosity to see "what this folk do there," she was converted upon the hearing of the hymns and the solid Christian preaching of the pastor. There is also the story of the Dominican who heard the tale of a lady's pet monkey that escaped into the church and swallowed the Host. Forthwith the monkey was burned by its mistress, but the Host was rescued from the animal's stomach unharmed. There were other stories, somewhat less fantastical, such as the one concerning the Franciscan friar who, near death, begged that the lector be brought to his bedside quickly. When asked why, he replied: "Innumerable devils have just come in by window and door and have filled the house, and as I have very little learning they are posing me with hard questions on the Trinity and the Catholic Faith, so run and ask the lector to help me

---

Preaching of the Friars: Sermons Diffused from Paris before 1300 (Oxford, UK: Oxford University Press, 1985).

[44] Smyth, *Art of Preaching*, 55.

and to answer for me." The sick man's Franciscan confrère hurriedly took the cross and put it into the sick man's hands, saying, "Do not be afraid if you cannot answer; this will answer for you till I return," then turned to go for the lector. At which point, the sick brother broke into loud laughter, and when asked why, replied: "As soon as you gave me this champion, all the devils took to flight, and they are crowding out of the windows and doors in such a hurry and confusion that I think they are breaking each other's necks and backs."[45] Such tales were almost never first-person narratives, but were frequently introduced with formulaic pronouncements such as: "This is a story which I learnt from the lips of a certain very truthful and holy man, who asserted that he had himself witnessed the fact which he narrated"; or "A certain trustworthy man of religion, a great preacher and a dependable witness, who learnt this same story from the priest who heard the confession of the woman mentioned in her last infirmity, related it to me."[46] There were also jokes, such as the one about the pastor who was rebuked by the bishop for having buried a wealthy man along with his donkey in the church graveyard. "My lord," replied the priest, "you do not know how much that donkey left you in his will—it was forty shillings." "*Requiescat in pace*," replied the bishop.[47]

Illustrating sermons with these little stories seems to have become increasingly popular during the thirteenth century and after. Scholars Richard and Mary Rouse, for example, did a study of three separate collections of sermons preached at various churches in and around Paris during the years 1230–1231, 1272–1273, and 1274–1302. What they noted from this study was a shift in the preferred methods of dilation. In the earliest sermons, preachers, say the Rouses, "displayed a near single-minded enthusiasm for the *distinctio*," that is, for providing several figurative meanings for a scriptural term, and for each meaning providing a passage of Scripture illustrating the use of the term in the given sense.[48] Later in the century, one finds more and more use of the "chaining" of biblical *auctoritates*, accompanied by the "near disappearance of the *distinctio*."[49] According to the Rouses, the sermons of 1272–1273 contain many more *exempla*

---

[45] See ibid., 62, referencing A. G. Little, *Studies in English Franciscan History* (New York: Longmans and Green, 1917), 145–46.

[46] See ibid., 60, referencing Owst, *Literature and Pulpit*, 171–72.

[47] See ibid., 61–62.

[48] Richard H. Rouse and Mary A. Rouse, *Preachers, Florilegia and Sermons: Studies on the "Manipulus Florum" of Thomas of Ireland*, Studies and Texts 47 (Toronto, ON: Pontifical Institute of Mediaeval Studies, 1979), 69.

[49] Ibid., 74.

than do the sermons of forty years earlier, and those of the latest period, 1274–1302, even more. Indeed, since the sermons studied by the Rouses were intended primarily for university audiences, they speculate that the use of *exempla* would have been even greater in sermons intended for less educated audiences, given that, even Thomas's rough contemporaries in Paris, such as the French cardinal Jacques de Vitry (ca. 1160/70–1240) and his Dominican confrère Humbert of Romans (ca.1200–1277), considered them valuable devices.[50]

I mention the use of these *exempla* in passing, however, because, although they became a major element in later medieval preaching and the contemporary literature on these *exempla* is vast, we will not be saying anything more about them here for one simple reason: Thomas never uses them. They are, as my subtitle above suggests, conspicuous by their absence. As far as I can tell from a quick review of Bonaventure's *Sunday Sermons*, he never uses them either. Whether this absence is due to a conscious choice on their part or the practice simply had not "caught on" yet is not clear. But whatever the reason, they do not use them.

And while I have no desire to deny the value of using concrete "examples" to help illustrate one's points in a sermon—since, as many medieval preaching manuals point out, the unlearned tend to enjoy visual imagery more than abstract reasoning—by the same token, there may be good reasons that Thomas never chose to incorporate any of these little stories into his preaching: they became rather notorious later on. Michèle Mulcahey, for example, repeats the marvelous lines Dante puts in the mouth of Beatrice in *Paradiso* 29.109–117, where she chastises preachers for their increasingly silly use of these *exempla*:

> Christ did not say to his first company:
> 'Go, and preach idle stories to the world';
> but he gave them the teaching that is truth,

---

[50] Some preachers, suggests Humbert, use exclusively one of the three—examples or arguments or authorities—"but to combine the three is far better," he says, "for, where one fails, another will succeed. The combination will form 'a threefold cord,' with a fishhook attached, and which 'is not easily broken by the fish' (Eccl 4:12)"; see Humbert of Romans, *De eruditione praedicatorum* 1.6, found in Latin in *B. Humberti de Romanis opera de vita regulari*, ed. J. J. Berthier (Rome: Typis A. Befani, 1888–1889), and in English in *Treatise on Preaching*, trans. the Dominican Students of the Province of St. Joseph, ed. Walter M. Conlon, O.P. (Westminster, MD: Newman Press, 1951); this English translation can be found also at http://www.op.org/sites/www.op.org/files/public/documents/fichier/treat_on_preaching_humbert_en.pdf. On Jacques de Vitry, see T. F. Crane's study: *The Exempla of Jacques de Vitry* (London: T. F. Crane, 1890).

and truth alone was sounded when they spoke;
and thus, to battle to enkindle faith,
the Gospels served them as both shield and lance.

But now men go to preach with jests and jeers,
and just as long as they can raise a laugh,
the cowl puffs up, and nothing more is asked.[51]

So too she repeats the criticisms of the early thirteenth-century Florentine Dominican friar Jacopo Passavanti (ca. 1302–1357), who admits that some of his fellow preachers were acting more like "jongleurs and storytellers and buffoons" than like the preachers they were supposed to be.

In retrospect, one imagines there were both good *exempla* and bad. Many of us have had the privilege of hearing sermons with interesting and illuminating stories or especially illustrative examples from great literature or the lives of the saints. And yet, by the same token, many of us have also had to sit through mind-numbingly dull personal stories, silly pious tales, and inaptly chosen and incompetently described movie scenes when what everyone in the church came expecting to hear was a sermon. Telling stories—providing *exempla*—can undoubtedly be a good means of preaching and teaching. And yet, by the same token, they can also be overused or poorly used. Thomas, for whatever reason, for good or for ill, does not use them at all in his preaching—at least not in the sermons that have come down to us. Indeed, Thomas remarks, in passing, in a series of responses (*responsi*) to Gerard, the conventual lector of Besançon, that "it is not proper for the preacher of truth to be diverted to unverifiable fables" (*ad fabulas ignotas divertere*).[52] And Thomas biographer Fr. Jean-Pierre

---

[51] *The Divine Comedy of Dante Alighieri: Paradiso*, trans. Allen Mandelbaum (New York: Bantam Books, 1984).

[52] *Responsi ad lectorem Bisuntinum*, in Leonine edition vol. 42 (1979), 355. The text is also more easily found online at the Corpus Thomisticum website under "Responsio de 6 articulis ad lectorem Bisuntinum," Quaestio 3. The question the lector of Besançon poses to Thomas is what form the star that appeared to the magi took: a cross, a man, or a crucifix. It is in his reply to this question that Thomas suggests the preacher of truth should not be diverted to unverifiable fables. Thus, a very legitimate objection might be leveled against my use of this passage, the objection that Thomas is not really referring here—at least not directly in any sense—to the use of *exempla* in preaching. I have added this note (prior to all editorial comment) precisely to point this fact out to my readers. It would be wrong, in my view, to read this one sentence as a blanket condemnation of the use of *exempla* in preaching, and I do not intend it to be interpreted in that vein. What I do think the passage reveals, however, is Thomas's general attitude toward

Torrell informs his readers: "Thomas believes orators need an art that can move feelings, but he refuses to reduce that art to the wisdom of this world. That is why we scarcely find in him those little stories (*exampla*) so valued by so many preachers. He warns us, on the contrary, against what he calls 'frivolities' (*frivolitates*)."[53]

A New Rhetoric of Preaching

Let me suggest, then, in closing, that what we have been exploring is a new sort of rhetoric—one that constitutes a significant development on the classical rhetorical tradition that had been handed down to the Middle Ages. This new rhetoric was in fact a rhetoric of *preaching*. Along with classical categories of *inventio* (discovery), *dispositio* (arrangement), *elocutio* (style), *memoria* (memory), and *actio* (delivery), along with the exordium, the narrative (or *narratio*), the partition (or *divisio*), the confirmation, the refutation, and the peroration, and along with techniques such as accismus, allegory, analogy, anecdote, anticipation, antirrhesis, apophasis, aporia, concession, chleuasmos, diatyposis, epiplexis, and all the rest, the medievals developed a series of rhetorical techniques, such as those we have examined, specifically for preaching.

What was original and unique about these new medieval rhetorical devices is that they were based on Scripture and directed toward the goal of helping people hear the Word of God more effectively so as to live it

---

the use of stories in preaching, which is that they should be *true*. There is so much truth already revealed in Scripture and contained within the tradition—the stories there are already so good and so nourishing to the spirit—that there is really no need to look elsewhere (to be "diverted") in order to use "made-up" material and little "fables." As a general rule, they serve no purpose other than a kind of empty entertainment that flatters both the prejudices of the listeners (when they hear words that neither teach nor challenge them) and the vanity of the preacher (when his listeners congratulate him for the delight he has provided them).

[53] See Jean-Pierre Torrell, O.P., *Saint Thomas Aquinas*, vol. 1, *The Person and His Work*, rev. ed., trans. R. Royal (Washington, DC: Catholic University of America Press, 2005), 72–73. Fr. Torrell does not indicate here where Thomas makes this comment, but he kindly sent me the reference. It is, in fact, on the same page in the *Responsi ad lectorem Bisuntinum* cited above (Léonine, t. 42, p. 355 b, line 54): "nec estimo huiusmodi frivola esse predicanda ubi competit tanta copia certissime ueritatis." Both Torrell and Bataillon have made special note of the conspicuous absence of such *exempla* in Thomas's sermons. See Torrell, *Sermons*, 24: "Parmi les caractéristiques externes, le P. Bataillon signale encore que Thomas diffère de la plupart de ses contemporains dans son utilisation parcimonieuse des *exempla*. . . ." See also L. J. Bataillon, "*Similitudines* et *exempla* dans les sermons du XIIIe siècle," in *Prédication*, Étude 10, 192–193.

more faithfully. The genius of the *sermo modernus* style of preaching was that it turned one or more of the biblical verses specified by the lectionary for a specific liturgical day into the means for *inventio* (for finding and developing one's topic), for *dispositio* (for organizing one's material), and for *memoria* (the remembering of one's material). There was nothing like it in the ancient world of classical rhetoric.

This was a mode of rhetorical practice that had both its beginning and its end in Scripture. The method of rhetorical composition came *from* Scripture and had as its *purpose* the goal of helping people hear the Word of God more effectively so as to live it more faithfully. This was not merely a matter of convincing an audience to undertake some course of action. No doubt the preacher wished that his congregation would live a better life having heard his sermon. But the primary goal of the sermon was to initiate a decisive engagement with a sacred text. The changed behavior was, as it were, a secondary goal. If the behavior of the congregation was to change, it would change first and foremost because of the encounter with the Word, and the changed life was meant to stem from that decisive encounter. This was a rhetoric designed to make a set of authoritative texts part of the living consciousness of its audience. It was the way in which preachers of the Middle Ages set out to help congregations that could not read the Bible for themselves in such a way that they would begin, over a period of listening week after week, to have biblical passages resonating in their minds, helping to form their consciences.

CHAPTER 5

Evaluating the *Sermo Modernus* Style

THE *SERMO MODERNUS*: DECADENT, PEDANTIC, MECHANICAL, UGLY, AND A MISUSE OF THE BIBLE?

THE *SERMO MODERNUS* STYLE—the style Thomas adopts as his own—is likely to seem strange to many modern readers. Indeed, it may even strike some as not only alien, but perhaps a bit pedantic and more than a little questionable in the way it incorporates Scripture into the sermon. So, for example, we find the Anglican scholar Charles Smyth in his exhaustive survey of the history of preaching entitled *The Art of Preaching* at first suggesting about the *sermo modernus* that "upon the very face of it this elaborate pedantry of form bears the ugly stamp of decadence."[1] It is not until roughly a paragraph later that he grants that there may be "something to be said upon the other side."[2] (We will have more to say on "the other side" in a moment.) Some years earlier, moreover, we find the Sorbonne medievalist Charles Victor Langlois concluding his study of "sacred eloquence in the Middle Ages" claiming that, with the elaborate rules for sermon-making that arose in the thirteenth century with the *sermo modernus*, "the era of artistic composition" was supplanted by one "of industrial manufacture."[3] Indeed, even the famous French medievalist

---

[1] Charles Smyth, *The Art of Preaching: A Practical Survey of Preaching in the Church of England, 747–1939* (New York: MacMillan, 1940), 42.
[2] Ibid.
[3] Quoted in ibid. Cf. V. Langlois, "L'éloquence sacrée au moyen age," *Revue des Deux Mondes* 115 (1893): 194.

Thomas-Marie Charland, author of the monumental (and in many ways still unsurpassed) study of medieval preaching, *Artes praedicandi : Contribution à l'histoire de la rhétorique au moyen age*, warns his readers that: "We have to arm ourselves with patience to get to the end of this *exposé* of the rules of university preaching in the Middle Ages. . . . The reader will not have arrived to the end before concluding: *il fallait savoir prodigieusement pour prêcher si mal"* (it was necessary to know a lot to preach so badly).[4] Judgments such as these are likely to be shared by any number of contemporary readers as well. Is there, then, anything to be said "upon the other side," as Reverend Smyth put it?

Let me admit up front that in composing this chapter, I had forefront in my mind a particular set of criticisms about Thomas's use of the Bible. "Ah yes," I could hear my Protestant friends say, "your book merely confirms my suspicion that medieval theologians such as Aquinas did not really *theologize biblically*, and what is worse, they did not really *preach the Bible*." I wanted to defend Aquinas against that potential (and what I saw as very likely) accusation. It is one I have heard not only from my Protestant friends, but from some Catholics as well. Thomas and his contemporaries certainly did not approach "preaching the Bible" the way a contemporary Protestant or Catholic preacher would, where even if one begins with some discussion of textual context, salted here and there (depending upon the preacher's educational background) with bits and fragments of modern historical-critical scholarship, the subject is likely to veer off rather quickly into either moral exhortation or some sort of life lesson.

ENGAGING WITH A FAIR-MINDED CRITIQUE: THE ENDURING VALUE OF SMYTH'S *THE ART OF PREACHING*

Here is where Reverend Smyth's work provides a valuable service. Smyth was a fine scholar in his own right, and although his work has been in some ways superseded by later scholarship, it is still widely cited by both Protestant and Catholic scholars who work on the history of preaching. What we find in Reverend Smyth is not only a Protestant scholar of the first rank, but also someone who, as we will see in more detail in a moment, *actually appreciated certain aspects of the medieval style of preaching*. What is especially impressive is that he was able to appreciate the medieval style even though it was so distinctly different from the sort of preaching

---

[4]   Thomas Charland, *Artes Praedicandi: contribution à l'histoire de la rhétorique au moyen âge*, Publications de l'Institut d'Etudes Medievales d'Ottawa 7 (Paris/Ottowa: J. Vrin/ Institute of Medieval Studies, 1936), 224.

to which he was accustomed as a twentieth-century Anglican cleric. We also find in his work evidence of not only a scholar who took the art of preaching very seriously but also of a cleric who believed that preaching had an important role to play not only in moral exhortation and communicating life lessons but also in Christian pedagogy and teaching key Christian doctrines.

Why not choose someone more contemporary? There are several reasons, one of which was simply seeing no need to pick a fight with any contemporary Protestant scholar. But the key reason was that I have not found anyone else whose work I thought was quite as judicious in his critiques and, thus, quite as good for the purposes of the defense I wished to make of Thomas and his use of the Bible in preaching.

Allow me to begin, then, if I may, by reviewing the engaging suggestions made by Reverend Smyth himself at the end of his chapter on preaching in the medieval period. Having suggested, as I mentioned above, the possibility that the medieval form of preaching was merely "elaborate pedantry" bearing "the ugly stamp of decadence," he does his best, in what I consider to be a rather fair-minded way, to find the positive elements in the style and to suggest those that might be most useful for modern preaching. Reverend Smyth suggests first, for example, that the medieval sermon had an admirable *structure*; second, that in one sense at least, it was firmly anchored in the Bible; and third, that it made use of effective rhetorical devices such as the "rule of three" and internal rhyme. It will be worthwhile considering each of these in turn.

THE VALUE OF *STRUCTURE*

"In the early centuries of the Church," says Smyth, "the holy Fathers preached without any *theme*"—and by that he is referring to what we have repeatedly called here the *thema*—"neither did they arrange the matter of their sermons." "But modern men," he suggests, precisely because they "are not holy" and are not "filled with divine knowledge, ought to arrange the matter of their preaching before they preach."[5] Smyth's delightfully pious attitude toward the Fathers of the Church, along with the notion that *they* did not need to arrange the structure of their preaching as much as modern preachers do because *they* (unlike most of us) were "holy" and "filled with divine knowledge," may seem a bit overstated. But it is certainly true that, even if men with the rhetorical training and skills, not to mention

---

[5] Smyth, *Art of Preaching*, 42.

the personal holiness and breadth of knowledge, of a St. Ambrose, St. Augustine, or St. John Chrysostom, were able on occasion to preach "off the cuff"—although there's not much evidence that they ever did—those of us with much less training, skill, knowledge, and holiness would not likely be anywhere near as successful were we to try.

By the same token, there is undoubtedly also a danger in over-romanticizing the often-disorganized style of much of the preaching that preceded the advent of the medieval "modern sermon." As the noted Cambridge medievalist G. R. Owst suggests in his 1926 book *Preaching in Mediaeval England*:

> We may believe that the art of homiletics has had always a majority of the rambling unpolished speakers among its disciples of the rank and file. The rambling catechetical address was possibly as common and as dull in Augustine's day as were the later "divisiones" [of the Middle Ages].[6]

Indeed, suggests the Reverend Smyth, the sort of structured sermon that came into fashion in the thirteenth century was "probably a welcome improvement on the disjointed, ill-planned efforts that preceded it."[7] "Other things being equal, the halting and indifferent preacher whose sermon is at least constructed on some definite and intelligible plan is likely to preach better, and to edify more, than if he contents himself with 'just saying a few words.'"[8] And "when there is a real demand on the part of laity for 'teaching sermons'"—as, in fact, it seems clear there was in the thirteenth century, especially among the laity in the newly burgeoning towns—"it is more painfully evident that 'the disjointed, ill-planned effort' is as unnecessary as it is indefensible."[9] What is desirable in this regard, concludes Reverend Smyth in a delightful footnote, is that the church should be—or become once again—"a place not merely of devotion, but also . . . of solid, continuous, and methodical instruction" with preachers who have acquired the skill "of interesting an audience profoundly."[10] Amen to that.

---

6   G. E. Owst, *Preaching in Mediaeval England* (Cambridge, UK: Cambridge University Press, 1926), 311–12.
7   Smyth, *Art of Preaching*, 44.
8   Ibid.
9   Ibid.
10 Ibid., 44n2. The actual quotation goes as follows: "The new race of preachers that I have been imagining . . . may acquire the power of interesting an audience profoundly,

I suggest, from the evidence we have of the occasional outbursts of emotion from congregations and from the widespread use of the *sermo modernus* style, that this sort of preaching appears to have both interested and delighted the faithful. This was not a style that was enforced by royal decree or ecclesiastical fiat; it was one that was adopted by widespread popular demand. And as the style was employed by preachers such as Thomas and Bonaventure, we can certainly say that it made the sermon a matter not merely of devotion, but also "of solid, continuous, and methodical instruction."

A Method of *Inventio* Directed to the Ends of Preaching the Bible

What the *sermo modernus* style also provided medieval preachers with, along with an impressive array of structuring devices—namely, all the various methods of *divisio* and *dilatatio*—was a very definite method for discovering a suitable topic on which to speak. In classical rhetoric, this part of the rhetorical process would have been called *inventio*. By keying the structural methods of *divisio* and *dilatatio* to one opening biblical verse, usually one of the biblical verses specified by the lectionary for the day, the *sermo modernus* style provided the medieval preacher a method of *inventio* directed specifically to the needs and demands of the Christian preacher who had the task of teaching Christian doctrine and relating it back continually to the community's authoritative text, the Bible.

Cicero and his contemporaries, by contrast, did not take themselves to be responsible for imparting to their audience a specific set of "doctrines" as defined by a believing community, nor were their orations related specifically to any single text considered authoritatively binding and defining. Thus, although the classical rhetorical methods employed by Cicero could be (and were) useful up to a point, they could not entirely satisfy the needs and purposes of the Christian preacher. The methodical approach of the *sermo modernus* style, by contrast, seemed to have done so and allowed its more accomplished practitioners to deliver a well-ordered, biblically-oriented, Christian pedagogy to what had become by the thirteenth century increasingly more intellectually sophisticated groups of Christian worshippers.

---

and may make the church once more a place not merely of devotion, but also, *as Protestant churches should be*, of solid, continuous, and methodical instruction" [emphasis mine]. With what sort of preaching those of us who are Catholics are supposed to satisfy ourselves, he does not say.

Stultifying Rules?

Having granted the value of an orderly discourse to the art of preaching, Reverend Smyth later makes this criticism, however: "Rules exist for a purpose," he says (quite rightly), "and the criterion of their efficacy—a criterion which must continually be applied—is their capacity to serve that purpose." In the later Middle Ages, he claims, however, the rules became "so elaborated as to stultify their *raison d'être*."[11]

Did they? Perhaps in some cases they did, but in others, they did not. And yet, a broad conclusion of this sort would certainly seem to require a much wider survey of medieval sermons than has been undertaken to date. It may well be, as Owst suggests above, that "the art of homiletics has had always a majority of the rambling unpolished speakers among its disciples of the rank and file." Of that I am not qualified to judge, although it seems not altogether unlikely. Even a quick perusal of classical rhetoric, for example, will reveal that not everyone had the skill of, say, a Cicero. And there were certainly a lot of dull, boring orations coming from England's pulpits when John Henry Newman was delivering his spectacular Oxford University Sermons. Can we stipulate up front that the practitioners of any of the various methods must be either expert craftsmen or dull mechanics? Certainly method alone will not produce interesting, intellectually substantive, and rhetorically compelling sermons.

So the question we must ask is whether the *sermo modernus* style is any worse than any other method. Is it any *more* likely to produce bad sermons than any other method of constructing a sermon?

On the positive side, we can say that the *sermo modernus* required skill and serious preparation. On the negative side, we can admit that it required skill and serious preparation. For those without the skill and those unwilling to take the necessary time to prepare, one imagines the results could be quite horrible. Imagine trying to preach like Newman without Newman's literary skill or his theological insights or his time to write. The result would be endless streams of the sort of stale, hoary rhetorical tropes so characteristic of some nineteenth century preaching. What can be said in favor of the best of the *sermo modernus* manuals is that they coached the skills with good, solid examples and encouraged various methods of preparation. Preachers knew what they were *supposed* to be doing, even if they did not always manage to do it.

One can also question the accusation that the *sermo modernus* imposed rules that were "stultifying." Methods of constructing an ordered

---

[11] Ibid., 44.

pedagogy can either help liberate the mind or serve to constrain it, depending upon the person and the situation. Were the "rules" of construction of the *sermo modernus* style helpful or constraining? Asking that question, however, is a bit like asking whether the "rules" of Ciceronian rhetoric liberate or constrain the orator, and/or whether the "rules" of sonnet construction liberate or constrain the poet? In some ways they constrain, and in other ways the constraint can foster a type of creative liberation—even though, admittedly, such constraints may eventually outlive their usefulness. Such was the case, one imagines, with the "rules" of construction of the academic sermon.

If the Reverend Smyth means to suggest that the rules of the *sermo modernus* style *eventually* became "so elaborated as to stultify their *raison d'être*"—say, for example, by the very late thirteenth or early fourteenth century—then perhaps he has a point. But since we have not surveyed any of the sermons from that period here, I will not deign to make any kind of negative judgment on them without giving them their due. The question for the reader to decide, it seems to me, is whether he or she thinks the rules of sermon construction stultified the preaching of Thomas Aquinas. In the end, however, the question of "rules"—as Reverend Smyth clearly sees—comes down to the *purpose* of a sermon, and this is a subject on which we will have more to say below.

FIRMLY ANCHORED IN THE BIBLE AND DIRECTED TOWARD REMEMBERING THE BIBLICAL TEXT

Another positive element the Reverend Smyth finds in the *sermo modernus* is that, whereas in contemporary sermons it is possible to hear an entire sermon "which does not contain one single text of Scripture," by contrast "the mediaeval sermon was firmly anchored to the Bible."[12] Indeed "elaborate precautions were taken," notes Reverend Smyth, "notably in the Confirmation of the parts of the division, to secure the principle that the preacher must say nothing for which he cannot find a warranty in Scripture." It was necessary "that the theme must be congruous with the matter of the sermon, and that the sermon must be, as it were, an unfolding of the text," as contrasted with those sermons where the text serves merely as "a convenient peg on which to hang a sermon, and, at that, a peg which is sometimes not even selected until after the sermon has been written."[13]

---

[12] Ibid.

[13] Ibid, 45. See especially 45n1, where Reverend Smyth tells the story of the famous Dr. Benjamin Jowett of Oxford, translator of the texts of Aristotle and Master of Balliol

"It is surely the test of a good sermon," suggests Reverend Smyth, "that it should be possible to deduce the text of a sermon from the sermon itself. In the Middle Ages such a task would have presented no difficulty whatsoever."[14] And on this point, he is certainly correct. Indeed, not only would it have been *possible* to deduce the text of a sermon from the sermon itself, it would have been nearly *impossible* to have mistaken it, given that the entire sermon was constructed around the parts of that text, the goal being the remembrance of the whole.

The Reverend Smyth also praises the medieval rule about repeating the text for the day—that is, the biblical *thema*—after the prologue or ante-theme. The value of repeating the biblical verse for the day is not "in our case," says the Reverend Smyth (and, by this, he means Anglican congregations in the 1930s), "for the benefit of late comers," since "one of the characteristic notes of the Anglican piety is decorum"—something that he appears to assume must have been conspicuously lacking in the thirteenth century—"but because the congregation are so busy settling down and adjusting their attention that they often fail to take in the text when it is given out at the beginning of the sermon, especially when it is not given out with a particularly careful and deliberate emphasis."[15]

If the reader is curious what the Reverend Smyth might be referring to when he mentions "late comers" (which are decorously absent from Anglican services), there is in fact a brief comment in a treatise *On Preaching* by Humbert of Romans, a late twelfth-century Master General of the Order of Preachers, in which he advises the preacher to provide a preface (or prothema) after stating the opening *thema* verse in cases "when a large audience is expected, but as yet the people have not all arrived."[16] The context of Humbert's comment makes it clear, however, that he did not expect this problem with "late comers" to be a common occurrence. Nor was it

---

College, who "declared that it was his habit to write his sermons, and then choose a text as a peg on which to hang them." "I am quite free to say," says Smyth in a characteristically Oxbridge sort of comment, "that the study of his sermons will reveal the accuracy of his statement, and show the peril of the method."

[14] Ibid.

[15] Ibid., 45–46.

[16] Humbert of Romans, *De eruditione praedicatorum* 7.15, which can be found in Latin in *B. Humberti de Romanis opera de vita regulari*, ed. J. J. Berthier (Rome: Typis A. Befani, 1888–1889), and in English in *Treatise on Preaching*, trans. Translated by the Dominican Students Province of St. Joseph, ed. Walter M. Conlon, O.P. (Westminster, MD: The Newman Press, 1951). The text is extremely difficult to find in print, but this English translation is also available at http://www.op.org/sites/www.op.org/files/public/documents/fichier/treat_on_preaching_humbert_en.pdf.

his sole reason for recommending a prefatory prothema section at the beginning of a sermon. Here is Humbert's comment in its original context:

> First, let us note that it is sometimes unnecessary to precede the sermon with a preamble or prayer; for example in the Chapters of Religious, only members of the community are ordinarily admitted. In the other case, it will suffice for the preacher to ask a prayer, as is done in parishes where sermons are often given. In other circumstances, it will be necessary to give first an exordium; for example, in the case of solemn sermons, or when a large audience is expected, but as yet the people have not all arrived, or when one speaks unexpectedly, in order to explain the reason for giving the sermon.[17]

Thus the issue is not so much regular "late comers," but a large group at a special event that has not yet gotten settled. Anyone who has come on time, but not a half hour or hour early, to an especially popular Vigil Mass service will understand the problem. People who come on time, but not early, are likely to be searching around for a suitable place to stand in a very crowded church. Notice as well what Humbert goes on to say:

> In these exordia or preambles, we must be brief, for if we weary our listeners, it will prove detrimental to the rest of our sermon. The exordium should be pleasing, so as to prepare our audience to listen with attention, good-will, and docility; just as writers do in the prefaces of the books which they publish. The exordium must always be terminated by asking devoutly for the prayers of the congregation, that God may bless the sermon; for thus did St. Paul, speaking to the Thessalonians: "Brethren, pray for us, that the word of the Lord may run and be glorified" (2 Thess 3:1).[18]

Thus, although it is true that Humbert of Romans did once make this comment about the usefulness of repeating the *thema* for latecomers—and a quick review of the literature on medieval sermons will show that many authors have fixated on this little piece of advice—I still find it unlikely that the prothema or preamble was ever regularly used for this purpose, given how short they tended to be—a brevity that was in fact in accord

---

[17] Ibid.
[18] Ibid.

with Hubert's advice on the matter and of which Thomas's sermons serve as an excellent example. Delivering most of these preambles would have taken no more than two or three minutes. Are we really to take seriously the notion that enough members of the congregation generally arrived in the period after the Gospel reading and within the period of the first few sentences of the preacher's sermon that it was generally considered necessary to repeat the *thema* two or three minutes after the first statement of it? To believe that, we have to imagine that scores of congregants skipped the Scripture readings for the day in order to arrive at church just in time to hear the sermon. It would be easier to believe that scores of congregants skipped the sermon in order to arrive at church just in time for the Liturgy of the Eucharist, or that, after the readings, there was thought to be a need for a pause so that groups of congregants could skip out for a smoke during the homily.[19]

What is more likely, to my mind, is that the opening *thema* verse from the Bible was repeated for precisely the reason the Reverend Smyth proposes: "because the congregation are so busy settling down and adjusting their attention . . . they often fail to take in the text when it is given out at the beginning of the sermon, especially when it is not given out with a particularly careful and deliberate emphasis."[20]

Those of us who have attended church services, no matter what the denomination or faith tradition, can attest to the problem: there are times after the Gospel reading is finished, when one begins to settle in one's seat or pew, feeling the blood run from one's head and the energy drain from one's body, that the troubling realization slowly dawns that one has not retained the slightest memory of the readings for the day one just heard read out in church. Indeed, in my own informal surveys of fellow church-goers, I have found that many of the members of the congregation will not be able to identify what the biblical readings for the day were. If a key goal of preaching is helping to make the Scriptures a *living presence* in people's lives, then this result cannot be good. One valuable lesson that both medieval and patristic sermons can teach us, therefore, is that repetition is the essence of education. Very few people will remember a sentence on the first hearing, or even the second. The medieval "rule of three," therefore, is probably about right.[21]

---

[19] Or the medieval equivalent of the same (obviously tobacco was not introduced to medieval Europe until after the first explorations of the New World).

[20] Smyth, *Art of Preaching*, 45–46.

[21] For an interesting discussion of the medieval "rule of three," see ibid., 48–49, which contains, among other things, these three noteworthy assertions: (1) "Single things said

Medieval Sermons: A "Superficial and Purely Formal" Use of the Bible?

Having thus praised elements of the medieval style of preaching and put aside what he considers less worthy criticisms of it, the Reverend Smyth comes to the nub of the matter. "But the real criticism of the mediaeval sermon scheme goes far deeper," he claims.

> Such preaching may be extremely clever and ingenious, but its connection with the Word of God, though undeniable, is purely superficial and purely formal. There is here no wrestling with the Word, no preaching as of a dying man to dying men. The text from Scripture is supposed to be the preacher's theme: it is in fact merely the peg on which he hangs an academic exercise.[22]

These are important and serious objections worth spending some time examining. Is the use of Scripture in the *sermo modernus* style forced and inappropriate ("purely superficial and purely formal"), and does it use biblical texts out of context and thereby fail to give its audience any real sense of the meaning of the Christian Scriptures?

I will put aside for the moment the rather odd contrast between the Reverend Smyth's *praise* of the medieval sermon (on p. 45 of his text) because of the requirement that the opening biblical *thema* had to be "congruous with the matter of the sermon, and that the sermon must be, as it were, an unfolding of the text," as contrasted with those modern sermons in which the biblical verse serves merely as "a convenient peg on which to hang a sermon, and, at that, a peg which is sometimes not even selected until after the sermon has been written" and his criticism here (on p. 53, a scant eight pages later) that the medieval sermon "is in fact merely the peg on which [the preacher] hangs an academic exercise." Is the biblical verse in the medieval sermon "merely a peg" or not?

To be fair, perhaps the Reverend Smyth means to laud the medieval sermon, on the one hand, because at least the biblical *thema* is clearly se-

---

are soon forgotten. Too many confuse. Arrangement in threes binds them together, and a threefold cord is not swiftly broken"; (2) "I believe that the rule of three . . . is the secret of clear exposition which lies behind all effective preaching. The rule will give pattern and form to the outline of the sermon"; and (3) "that the text should be divisible into three, and to that end should be composed of three significant words, neither less nor more—whether, as Basevorn suggests, because that gives you a sermon of about the right length, or rather because of some deep-seated understanding of the psychology of the man in the pew—is still, I think, suggestive."

[22] Ibid., 53.

lected first and is not merely chosen as an afterthought (as Oxford's Benjamin Jowett bragged about doing; see n. 183 above), whereas he thinks it appropriate to censure the medieval sermon, on the other hand, for not treating the biblical *thema* appropriately after its original statement. To re-phrase his criticism, then, we might say that the medieval sermon *begins* with the Bible and certainly *makes use* of the Bible, which is good, but it uses the Bible *badly* and out of context, which is *not* good.

So, for example, the Reverend Smyth complains of his Cambridge predecessor J. M. Neale (1818–1866), author of *Mediaeval Preachers and Mediaeval Preaching* (1856), that he "was curiously impressed by the profusion and variety of Biblical quotations in these mediaeval sermons: to him, the mediaeval preacher seemed to range at will through all the pages of the Sacred Volume, not quoting merely from those passages which we regard as particularly valuable or important."[23] And yet, what is an object of praise in the medieval sermon for J. M. Neale is precisely the subject for scorn to the Reverend Smyth, who claims that "the use made of these citations is sufficient to indicate that the preacher's selection was governed less by his Biblical piety and learning than by the use of his concordance. In short, nothing could have shown more clearly that the preachers did *not* know their Bible."[24] Would the Reverend Smyth's judgment be altered, I wonder, if he knew that preachers such as Thomas generally did *not* use a concordance and were merely quoting from memory? Would that show to his satisfaction that they *did* know their Bible?

MERELY PROOF-TEXTING?

Perhaps it might. But even if the Reverend Smyth was willing to retract that particular criticism (if only in the case of remarkable men like Aquinas and Bonaventure, although there were undoubtedly others with similar abilities in this culture so dedicated to the arts of memory, as we noted above), there would still be the question of what served to *unify* all these diverse biblical quotations thematically or textually. What purpose was served, for example, by the common medieval practice of "chaining" a long string of biblical quotations? Was there any connection between and among these verses other than the obvious *verbal* one: that a common word appears in all of them? And there is certainly a danger in preaching (as in theology more generally) of selectively "proof-texting" from the

---

[23] Ibid. (referencing the introduction to J. M. Neale's *Mediaeval Preachers and Mediaeval Preaching*).

[24] Ibid.

Bible apart from the proper *context*. Indeed, one imagines the Reverend Smyth might have been especially sensitive to this particular problem if he had been involved in theological arguments with nineteenth-century evangelical, "revivalist" Bible preachers.

But were medieval preachers merely proof-texting from the Bible? To claim they were is to misunderstand the problem of "proof-texting." "Proof-texting" is indeed a problem *if the biblical exegete or theologian is trying to construct an argument*. But Thomas is not doing that. He is not, for example, formulating an argument that women should "cover their heads in church" by selectively quoting 1 Corinthians 11:5–13 apart from any consideration of the historical or cultural context of the time, nor is he selectively quoting Leviticus 18:22 or 20:13 to argue that homosexual activity is a capital crime. Those would be examples of "proof-texting." What Thomas is trying to achieve with the biblical quotations in his sermons, however, is more *rhetorical* than it is strictly speaking *dialectical*.

So, for example, quoting selectively the famous line from act 1, scene 3 of *Hamlet*, "neither a borrower nor a lender be," as evidence of Shakespeare's hatred of business would be an example of unwarranted proof-texting. The character who speaks this line is not some paragon of wisdom, after all, but Polonius, the pompous blowhard who is constantly intruding himself into everyone's affairs, a habit that finally gets him killed when Hamlet mistakes him for the king hiding behind a curtain. And yet one hears people quote this line as a rhetorical trope all the time, as people often quote notable lines from many places in literature: "No man is an island, entire in himself"; "Ask not for whom the bell tolls, it tolls for thee"; "If you can meet with Triumph and Disaster / And treat those two impostors just the same"; "If we had but world enough and time"; "But at my back I always hear, Time's winged chariot hurrying near"; "Ay, there's the rub"; and "Methinks the lady doth protest too much." This last line is commonly quoted even though Queen Gertrude's actual line in *Hamlet* is the reverse: "The lady doth protest too much, methinks." So too, when someone in a hurry or overburdened with too many tasks says, "Ah, were there but world enough and time," it is usually not relevant at all, nor will the speaker necessarily call to mind the fact that this line is part of a poem of seduction ("To His Coy Mistress" by Andrew Marvell) and that the actual poem reads, "Had we but world enough and time, / This coyness, lady, were no crime"—after which the poet goes on to point out that there *is not* all that much time, so her coyness should give way to his romantic advances. Indeed, rarely, if ever, when I have heard someone use the line "Had we but world enough and time" has it *ever* been in the service of seduction. People use such lines for rhetorical effect all the time, and when they do, they are usually intending to tap into a deep well of mental associations and images related to a literary tradition that has become part of the cultural heritage of a people or a nation.

So too, I would suggest, Thomas is not "proof-texting." He is merely tapping into a vast well of biblical associations and images that have already become part of the cultural heritage of his audience, or that he wishes to make part of their heritage. To quote such lines and verses is not merely to make reference to a forgotten, semi-mythical past; it is to be an instrument of making that linguistic tradition living and present for one's listeners *now*.

So, the charge made by Reverend Smyth that medieval preachers "did *not* know their Bible" is, I think, unfounded, as is the claim that their use of biblical passages suggests "that the preacher's selection was governed less by Biblical piety and learning than by the use of his concordance." [25] One can use a concordance precisely as a *tool* of biblical piety, after all, just as one can use a concordance to look up the precise wording of beloved passages from Shakespeare or Kipling or Donne. I assume that preachers of all denominations have used biblical concordances for this purpose for generations, even if some of them have done it badly or awkwardly.

A SYLLOGISTIC EXERCISE?

Besides, it is unclear whether Reverend Smyth finds the medieval use of the Bible intolerably ignorant or whether it was, rather, in various respects *too sophisticated*. For, after complaining of their ostensible biblical illiteracy, he then goes on to suggest that:

> In these Scholastic discourses, there is more to impress the people than to edify them. The preacher displays his intellectual gymnastics instead of ministering the Word of God. Divine Truth is buried beneath the *minutiae* of logical divisions and distinctions. Preaching, and even prayer, becomes regarded as a syllogistic exercise in which the end is forgotten in the means. [26]

There are always, in such matters, questions of *taste* and how much of one approach or another one's audience can tolerate. John Henry New-

---

[25] Ibid.
[26] Ibid., 53–54.

man's congregations tolerated a length and a literary style that many of us love to read but few people would really be willing to sit through and listen to. Reverend Smyth may find the medieval *sermo modernus* "a bit much" with regard to its dialectical divisions and distinctions, but it is fairly clear that medieval congregations appreciated them and clamored for more.

Besides, medieval preaching manuals and medieval preachers who wrote about preaching were always very careful to warn against the temptation to merely "impress" rather than "edify." So, for example, in commenting upon 2 Corinthians 4, Thomas remarks that:

> Evil is avoided in doctrine when the Lord's word is proposed in the proper way. . . . This is explained in two ways. First, not mixing false doctrine with the doctrine of Christ . . . Secondly, not preaching for gain and for one's own glory. The first of these is a wolf and the second a hireling, but one who preaches the truth and for the glory of God is a shepherd. Hence Augustine says: "The shepherd should be loved and the wolf avoided, but the hireling must be tolerated for the present."[27]

One will find many such warnings in Thomas's corpus. So too, for example, in the *Liber contra impugnantes Dei cultum et religionem*, he tells his reader that "although an elegant style of preaching is at times commendable, it is likewise under certain circumstances reprehensible. It is reprehensible when it is used from motives of vainglory, or when beauty of language or a show of learning are esteemed as the chief essentials in preaching."[28] And he warns a bit further on in this same section against "those who consider eloquence and fluency of speech to be the chief essentials of preaching" precisely because these preachers "strive to attract attention to themselves, rather than to the truths they utter."[29] And again later, he writes:

---

[27] See *Commentary on the Second Epistle to the Corinthians*, ch. 4, lec. 1, trans. Fabian Larcher, O.P. (available at http://dhspriory.org/thomas/SS2Cor.htm#41).

[28] *Liber contra impugnantes Dei cultum et religionem* 3.5, in *An Apology for the Religious Orders*, trans. John Procter (London: Sands, 1902; reprint, Westminster, MD: Newman Press, 1950); available at http://dhspriory.org/thomas/ContraImpugnantes.htm#35, which can be located, along with everything else of Thomas's available in English online, through Thérèse Bonin's invaluable website: "Thomas Aquinas in English: A Bibliography" (http://www.home.duq.edu/~bonin/thomasbibliography.html).

[29] Ibid.

It is commendable to use eloquence and learning in preaching when the primary motive in so doing is not elegance of diction, but the more profitable teaching of Holy Scripture, in whose service eloquence is used. When we act thus, we fulfil the words of St. Paul, "bringing into captivity every understanding unto the obedience of Christ" (2 Cor 10:5).[30]

And again, still later in the same treatise, he says: "it is praiseworthy to make use in preaching of a harmonious and learned style, provided this is done, not from ostentatious motives, but in order to instruct our hearers and to convince our opponents."[31]

Indeed, it seems to me difficult to maintain credibly that the medieval preachers sought "more to impress the people than to edify them" (as Reverend Smyth suggests they did), given that the style of the discourse is so often taken to be so dry. One would have thought that a style such as theirs was designed precisely *not* to impress in terms of its eloquence and rhetorical beauty, choosing to err instead on the side of pure edification rather than delight.

But perhaps by "impress," Reverend Smyth is referring to what he describes as the "intellectual gymnastics" of the medieval sermon, where, according to him, "Divine Truth is buried beneath the *minutiae* of logical divisions and distinctions. Preaching, and even prayer, becomes regarded as a syllogistic exercise in which the end is forgotten in the means." In this regard, Reverend Smyth quotes (actually paraphrases) Cardinal Newman: "you cannot convert people with a smart syllogism." There is certainly an element of truth in this statement, but you also cannot convert intelligent people with a logical mess of contradictory propositions or with mere bits of emotional fluff.

For the record, what Newman actually says in *The Grammar of Assent* is this:

If I am asked to use Paley's argument [from design] for my own conversion, I say plainly I do not want to be converted by a smart syllogism; if I am asked to convert others by it, I say plainly I do not care to overcome their reason without touching their hearts. I wish to deal, not with controversialists, but with inquirers.[32]

---

[30] Ibid.
[31] Ibid.
[32] John Henry Newman, "Revealed Religion," in *An Essay in Aid of a Grammar of Assent* (London: Longmans and Green, 1903), 425.

And elsewhere, regarding syllogisms, he says much the same: "Logic makes but a sorry rhetoric with the multitude; first shoot round corners, and you may not despair of converting by a syllogism."[33] And yet, note that, on this account, if medieval preachers had merely been trying to *impress* the masses, they would not have made use of logic, which, as Newman suggests, "makes but a sorry rhetoric with the multitude."

What Newman *goes on to say* in *The Grammar*, immediately after the passage quoted above, however, is this:

> I think Paley's argument clear, clever, and powerful; and there is something which looks like charity in going out into the highways and hedges, and compelling men to come in; but in this matter some exertion on the part of the persons whom I am to convert is a condition of a true conversion. They who have no religious earnestness are at the mercy, day by day, of some new argument or fact, which may overtake them, in favour of one conclusion or the other. And how, after all, is a man better for Christianity, who has never felt the need of it or the desire? On the other hand, if he has longed for a revelation to enlighten him and to cleanse his heart, why may he not use, in his inquiries after it, that just and reasonable anticipation of its probability, which such longing has opened the way to his entertaining?[34]

In other words, Newman does not deny the value of a certain sort of logic *for those who are already believers*, such as would have been the audience to which Thomas and his contemporaries would have been preaching. What he denies, in the context of *The Grammar*, is that some sort of neutral, all-encompassing logic can *convert* or *compel*, on purely rational grounds, non-believers into becoming believers, for what Newman *also* denied was that a neutral, dis-interested reason could ever really convince anyone of anything or bring the certitude of assent to anyone. So, perhaps we should admit that quoting Newman's remark about not converting people with a smart syllogism is, in this context, with regard to preaching to a congregation of already-converted believers, a bit of a rhetorical red herring.

---

[33] See Letter 6 in his *The Tamworth Reading Room: Letters on an address delivered by Sir Robert Peel, Bart., M.P., on the establishment of a reading room at Tamworth* (London: J. Mortimer, 1841).

[34] "Revealed Religion," 425.

The Reverend Smyth may have been preaching to Anglican congregations of British men and women in the 1930s and 40s among whom there may have been a good many who were present for no other reason than that it was culturally "the thing to do" in England at that time and, so, were in need of preaching that would help convince and truly *convert* them to the Christian faith of the house of worship they were dutifully attending for reasons other than faith. It is not as clear that the congregations that *Thomas* was preaching to in the thirteenth century were as much in need of this sort of apologetic discourse. What these people seem to have yearned for, given the widespread popularity of the *sermo modernus* style, was preaching that was both substantial and intelligent, as well as (and perhaps above all) *clearly organized*. Sloppiness in structure was not something they seem to have been willing to tolerate in sermons any more than sloppiness in grammar and syntax were things that congregations during Newman's day seem to have been willing to abide. In current American practice, by contrast, we seem willing to tolerate sloppiness in both logic *and* rhetoric, as well as in fundamental grammar and syntax as well.

Be that as it may, the charge that medieval sermons were largely a "syllogistic exercise" is, I think, not entirely fair, especially given that many major medieval preaching manuals agreed on the point that technical syllogistic arguments were not to be used in preaching, as for example, in the *Ars concionandi*, where the author warns that "preaching should not sound like a disputation," advising to contrary that "the speaker can avoid making the sermon appear like an argument by omitting propositions and then inferred conclusions."[35] So too, Humbert of Romans warned, in his treatise *On Preaching*, against preachers who "use too many subtleties in their discourse for the sake of elegance. At one time they seek those novelties which the Athenians delighted in; at another time they produce arguments drawn from philosophy which, they imagine, improve their speech." On the contrary, advises Humbert, "good preachers study principally what is useful and, building their sermons on this, they exclude what is less profitable."[36]

---

[35] Cf. *Ars Concionandi* 3.41: "Since preaching should not sound like a disputation, the speaker can avoid making the sermon appear like an argument by omitting propositions and then inferred conclusions." All Latin quotes of this work are taken from the 1901 Quaracchi edition (see n. 86 for fuller details). All English translation is from Harry Charles Hazel, "A Translation, with Commentary, of the Bonaventuran '*Ars Concionandi*'" (PhD diss., Washington State University, 1972).

[36] Humbert of Romans, *De eruditione praedicatorum* 1.6.

Is Divine Truth Buried Beneath Logical *Minutiae* in Thomas's Sermons?

But apart from the issue of one's tolerance (or lack thereof) for "syllogistic exercises," a serious question remains. In medieval preaching, was Divine Truth "buried beneath the *minutiae* of logical divisions and distinctions," as the Reverend Smyth claims, and did this style of preaching constitute a *misuse* of the Scriptures? For certainly, the "Divine Truth" the Reverend Smyth is talking about that is supposedly getting "buried" is the Divine Truth of Sacred Scripture.

With regard to the use of logical divisions and distinctions in preaching, St. Thomas mounts his own extended defense of this method in his *Liber contra impugnantes Dei cultum et religionem*, in a chapter on the "attacks brought against religious on account of their systematic (*ordinate*) method of preaching." It seems that Reverend Smyth's accusation against the mendicant's new manner of preaching was nothing new. Thomas faced it in his own day, undoubtedly from those who thought that the new sort of ordered discourse that characterized the *sermo modernus* had no place in Christian preaching. Thomas concludes, to the contrary, not only that "it is commendable to make use of human eloquence and wisdom in the Divine service," but also "that they who blame others for so doing resemble blind men who envy those who can see, and ignorant men who blaspheme against what they cannot understand."[37] He then goes on to cite no less an authority than St. Augustine to claim that "those whose duty it is to expound the Holy Scripture must be careful to speak eloquently and fluently [*eloquenter et ornate loquatur*], for the greater advantage of those who hear them."[38]

Although Augustine, early on in his life, as he reports in the *Confessions*, found the Christian Scriptures to be sadly lacking in learning and eloquence, fairing rather poorly in comparison to the classic works of Cicero, later on in his life, by the time he wrote book 4 of *De doctrina christiana*, he had come to realize that the Christian Scriptures had their own sort of eloquence and learning—indeed that they had both a simple message

---

[37] *Liber contra impugnantes Dei cultum et religionem* 3.5.

[38] Ibid. (Procter, *Apology*, 3.5.2; note that Fr. Procter's system for numbering his paragraphs differs from the one in the Latin text—I have provided both for ease of reference.) Cf. also Augustine, *De doctrina christiana* 4.5.8. Thomas is not quoting directly here, but summing up the general tenor of Augustine's comments. Indeed, a quick glance at this entire section of book 4 of the *De doctrina* will show that it was a gold mine of texts for medieval theologians who wished to defend the use of learning and rhetoric in preaching, as it is for St. Thomas in the *Contra impugnantes*.

for the unlearned and ever-deeper layers of meaning for those who would search for it.[39] Thus, in book 4 of *De doctrina*, Augustine exhorts his readers to "acknowledge then that our canonical writers are not merely learned, but likewise eloquent, making use of an elegance of style befitting them." [40]

Thomas made use of this text of Augustine's to argue that a good preacher, in imitation of the canonical authors, "must in order to induce his hearers to do what is right, not merely instruct and delight them, but he must likewise convince them."[41] Thomas writes:

He [St. Augustine] shows, by eloquent passages taken from the Fathers, how those holy men instructed, charmed and convinced their hearers. Hence it becomes plain that he who has to preach or to expound the scriptures must make use both of eloquence and secular learning. The same lesson is taught by St. Gregory and St. Ambrose, who are both remarkable for elegance of diction. St. Augustine, likewise, Dionysius, and St. Basil have interspersed their works with many passages culled from secular authors. Nay, St. Paul himself makes use of a heathen authority in his preaching, as may be seen in the eighteenth chapter of the Acts of the Apostles, and in the first chapter of the Epistle to Titus.[42]

He goes on to quote the authority also of St. Gregory the Great, who argued that "As they who are wise with the wisdom of God make use, in Holy Scripture, of the wisdom of the world, so God Himself, the Creator of mankind, uses for the benefit of mankind our human language." "This passage is a further proof," says Thomas, "that the teachers of Holy Scripture may lawfully employ human eloquence and learning."[43]

The analogy here is, I would suggest, both fascinating and theologi-

---

[39] See Augustine, *Confessions* 3.5.9: "I resolved, therefore, to direct my mind to the Holy Scriptures, that I might see what they were. And behold, I saw something not comprehended by the proud, not disclosed to children, something lowly in the hearing, but sublime in the doing, and veiled in mysteries. Yet I was not of the number of those who could enter into it or bend my neck to follow its steps. For then it was quite different from what I now feel. When I then turned toward the Scriptures, they appeared to me to be quite unworthy to be compared with the dignity of Tully"; trans. J. G. Pilkington, A Select Library of the Nicene and Post-Nicene Fathers of the Christian Church, ed. Philip Schaff (New York: Scribner's, 1907).

[40] Cf. Augustine, *De doctrina christiana* 4.7.21.

[41] *Contra impugnantes*, pt. 3, ch. 5, corp. (Procter, *Apology*, 3.5.4).

[42] Ibid.

[43] Ibid. (Procter, *Apology*, 3.5.5), here quoting Gregory's *Moralia in Job* 9.11.12.

cally profound. Preachers should think of themselves, on this view (as all artists ultimately should), as working in imitation of the Creator of all things. As God deigned to communicate himself to mankind by means of human language, so too preachers must have the wisdom to embody God's Truth in a language that can be understood by their congregation. How does God communicate himself to man? Through the Word made flesh. How, then, must preachers preach the Good News about the Word made flesh? In and through words that give witness to, and are guided authoritatively by, God's Incarnate Word and God's self-revelation in the Scriptures.

But we must not forget that human language functions by means of its own proper modes of signifying. Not just any order of words will do. If they are to learn, human beings require an ordered discourse. So, for example, while he is commenting on John 12:4, Thomas declares that two things "are necessary for preachers if they are to lead others to Christ." The first is "clear, orderly speech." And the second is "virtue manifested in good actions."[44] In other words, the effective preacher must possess and express both a rectitude of life and a rectitude of speech; and quite naturally, they must be in agreement both with each other and with the ultimate measure of the "rightness" of things: the eternal Word and Reason (*Logos* in Greek; *Ratio* in Latin). Rectitude or proper order in language, like rectitude in action, is made necessary by (and patterned on) the ultimate rectitude and order of *things* in the cosmos as revealed definitely in and through God's eternal Word. One's *words* must be ordered because, ultimately, God's *creation* is ordered, and God's creation is ordered because it is the production of God's "Word."

Thus, neither an orderly discourse nor an orderly life *alone* will do for the one whose vocation is to be a *preacher*. Preachers must *preach*: they must use *words*. They are not called to proclaim Christ with their deeds only, but also with human *language*. And just as there are virtues that order human life rightly, so too there are skills of eloquence and wisdom that order human speech rightly so that it may have the intended effect. We might say of preaching what the Second Vatican Council's *Dogmatic Constitution on Divine Revelation* (*Dei Verbum*) says about God's divine revelation: the deeds should manifest and confirm the teaching and realities signified by the words, while the words proclaim the deeds and clarify the mystery contained in them.[45]

---

[44] *Commentary on the Gospel of St. John*, ch. 12, lec. 4, Marietti no. 1634 (available at http://dhspriory.org/thomas/John12.htm).

[45] *Dei Verbum*, §2.

Pope Benedict XVI made a similar point about logic and language in his famous *Regensburg Address* when he described the "inner rapprochement between Biblical faith and Greek philosophical inquiry" that occurred when John began the prologue of his Gospel with the words "In the beginning was the *logos*." "*Logos*," as Pope Benedict pointed out, "means both reason and word—a reason which is creative and capable of self-communication, *precisely as reason*" [emphasis mine]. "From the very heart of Christian faith," said Pope Benedict, "and, at the same time, the heart of Greek thought now joined to faith," we can say, with Byzantine Emperor Manuel II Paleologus, that "Not to act 'with *logos*' is contrary to God's nature." And so too, insists the Pope, although God remains infinitely beyond our ability to grasp him by means of our finite categories, "yet not to the point of abolishing analogy and its language."

Certainly, love, as Saint Paul says, "transcends" knowledge and is thereby capable of perceiving more than thought alone (cf. Eph 3:19); nonetheless it continues to be love of the God who is Logos. Consequently, Christian worship is, again to quote Paul, "*logikei latreia*," worship in harmony with the eternal Word and with our reason (cf. Rom 12:1).

Thus, as Pope Benedict perceived, worship must make use of logic because logic reflects in language the ordered nature of the cosmos.[46]

USING ARGUMENTS IN PREACHING

It may be good to recall, in this context, Thomas's discussion in the *Summa of Theology* (hereafter, *ST*) on "whether sacred doctrine uses arguments" (*utrum sit argumentativa*). In reply, Thomas quotes Titus 1:9, where Paul tells Titus that a bishop should "embrace that faithful word [*fidelem sermonem*] which is according to doctrine [*secundum doctrinam*], that he may be able to exhort in sound doctrine [*doctrina sana*] and to convince [*arguere*] the gainsayers." Given the connection between "sermon" (*sermonem*), "teaching" (*doctrina*), and "arguing" (*arguere*) in this passage,

---

[46] See "Faith, Reason, and the University: Memories and Reflections, Meeting with the Representatives of Science," Lecture of the Holy Father given at the Aula Magna of the University of Regensburg on Tuesday, September 12, 2006 (http://w2.vatican. va/content/benedict-xvi/en/speeches/2006/september/documents/hf_ben-xvi_ spe_20060912_university-regensburg.html).

Thomas is convinced he has the backing of St. Paul for his position and practice. Thomas argues here, as he does frequently, that:

> as other sciences do not argue in proof of their principles, but argue from their principles to demonstrate other truths in these sciences: so this doctrine [*sacra doctrina*] does not argue in proof of its principles, which are the articles of faith, but from them it goes on to prove something else; as the Apostle from the resurrection of Christ argues in proof of the general resurrection (1 Cor 15).[47]

How then, in the final analysis, do we know that the use of arguments is permissible? According to Thomas, we know because we have the example of St. Paul, who makes use of arguments in his epistles. Paul is the paradigmatic preacher. Paul uses arguments. Therefore, the use of arguments in preaching is licit, indeed praiseworthy.

Contrary to the modern view, however, wherein we generally think "arguments" have a place with unbelievers but not believers, both Thomas and Newman were convinced that one cannot argue with interlocutors who do not share one's first principles. And since the first principles of the theological science are provided by divine revelation, those who do not accept divine revelation are unlikely to be "argued into" belief, whether by the arguments of William Paley or any other. "It is to be borne in mind," says Thomas, that:

> In regard to the philosophical sciences . . . the inferior sciences neither prove their principles nor dispute with those who deny them, but leave this to a higher science; whereas the highest of them, viz. metaphysics, can dispute with one who denies its principles, if only the opponent will make some concession; but if he concede nothing, it can have no dispute with him, though it can answer his objections. (*ST* I, q. 1, a. 8, corp.)

The case of arguments in theology is the same. Since Sacred Scripture "has no science above itself," a Christian can "dispute with one who de-

---

[47] *ST* I, q. 1, a, 8. All English translations from *ST* are from Thomas Aquinas, *Summa Theologiae*, trans. The Fathers of the English Dominican Province, 2nd rev. ed., 22 vols. (London: Burns, Oates & Washbourne, 1912–1936); reprinted in 5 vols. (Westminster, MD: Christian Classics, 1981). E-text with facing Latin and English is available at http://dhspriory.org/thomas/summa/index.html.

nies its principles only if the opponent admits some at least of the truths obtained through divine revelation; thus we can argue with heretics from texts in Holy Writ, and against those who deny one article of faith, we can argue from another." If one's opponent does not accept the authority of the Scriptures, however, and "believes nothing of divine revelation," then says Thomas, "there is no longer any means of proving the articles of faith by reasoning, but only of answering his objections—if he has any—against faith. Since faith rests upon infallible truth, and since the contrary of a truth can never be demonstrated, it is clear that the arguments brought against faith cannot be demonstrations, but are difficulties that can be answered."[48] With unbelievers, this is the best reason and arguments can achieve.

With believers, on the other hand, reasoning and arguments can play an important role in helping to clarify belief or to increase one's understanding of what is believed. In theology, we start from biblical first principles and argue to other truths. So too in a sermon, the preacher starts from biblical propositions and, using logical entailment, argues to other truths. Thus, just as *theology* can make use of arguments, so too can preaching. Preaching, on this view, is a properly *theological* enterprise, not merely an exegetical one. Though it *begins* in Scripture, it does not *end* there. And so, concludes Thomas:

> sacred doctrine makes use even of human reason, not, indeed, to prove faith . . . but to make clear other things that are put forward in this doctrine. Since therefore grace does not destroy nature but perfects it, natural reason should minister to faith as the natural bent of the will ministers to charity. Hence the Apostle says: "Bringing into captivity every understanding unto the obedience of Christ" (2 Cor 10:5).[49]

It is interesting to note that Thomas uses this exact same passage (2 Cor 10:5) in his argument in *Contra impugnantes* against those who are attacking the mendicants for their style of preaching. There, he says:

> It is commendable to use eloquence and learning in preaching when the primary motive in so doing is not elegance of diction, but the more profitable teaching of Holy Scripture, in whose ser-

---

[48] Ibid., corp.
[49] Ibid., ad 2.

vice eloquence is used. When we act thus, we fulfil the words of St. Paul, "bringing into captivity every understanding unto the obedience of Christ" (2 Cor 10:5). It was in this manner that the Apostle [Paul] himself made use of eloquence.[50]

"Bringing into captivity every understanding unto the obedience of Christ" is, of course, the New Testament version of the analogy, used frequently by Patristic-era writers, of Christians appropriating the thought of Greek philosophy in the way the Jewish people appropriated "the wealth of the Egyptians" as they began their journey to Sinai. So, for example, in book 2 of his *De doctrina christiana*, St. Augustine argues that:

If those who are called philosophers, and especially the Platonists, have said anything that is true and in harmony with our faith, we are not only not to shrink from it, but to claim it for our own use from those who have unlawful possession of it. For, as the Egyptians had not only the idols and heavy burdens which the people of Israel hated and fled from, but also vessels and ornaments of gold and silver, and garments, which the same people when going out of Egypt appropriated to themselves, designing them for a better use, not doing this on their own authority, but by the command of God, the Egyptians themselves, in their ignorance, providing them with things which they themselves were not making a good use of; in the same way all branches of heathen learning have not only false and superstitious fancies and heavy burdens of unnecessary toil, which every one of us, when going out under the leadership of Christ from the fellowship of the heathen, ought to abhor and avoid; but they contain also liberal instruction which is better adapted to the use of the truth, and some most excellent precepts of morality; and some truths in regard even to the worship of the One God are found among them. . . . These, therefore, the Christian, when he separates himself in spirit from the miserable fellowship of these men, ought to take away from them, and to devote to their proper use in preaching the gospel.[51]

---

[50] *Contra impugnantes*, pt. 3, ch. 5, corp. (Procter, *Apology*, 3.5.5; note that Fr. Procter's English text has misstated the biblical reference as 1 Cor 10:5, rather than the correct reference, which is 2 Cor 10:5).

[51] *De doctrina christiana* 2.40.60. Cf. also Augustine, *Eighty-Three Different Questions*, q. 53.

So it seems that the sort of criticism the Reverend Smyth poses against the medieval preachers has an even longer patrimony than we first might have imagined: not only does it occur among Thomas's contemporaries who were critical of the mendicants for using logic and their own brand of "eloquence" or orderly discourse in preaching, but it is in fact a species of a critique that goes back to the earliest Church and the criticisms that Christians should not be making use of Greek philosophy.

Again we see Thomas looking for inspiration—and justification—to the model of St. Paul. He notes in *Contra impugnantes* that, according to St. Augustine, St. Paul "did not hesitate to declare that he possessed learning" because, without it, "he could not have been the doctor of the Gentiles."[52] Commenting on Paul's words "although I be rude in speech, yet not in knowledge," Thomas remarks: "This is a proof that in a teacher learning is more profitable than eloquence," to which he then adds the caveat "[but] we cannot assume that St. Paul made no use of eloquence in preaching. All that we can conclude is that he did not, like rhetoricians, make fluency and elegance of style his main object in preaching."[53]

Consider what medieval preachers would likely have learned from reading and meditating upon this statement from St. Paul, considered the paradigmatic preacher: "although I be rude in speech, yet not in knowledge." Might they not have concluded that, although learning is always good, when it came to eloquence, the preacher should be careful not to overdo it. Medieval sermons were crafted with an emphasis on learning; they were not meant to be crafty in their rhetorical expressiveness. They were meant to teach, not to impress by making "fluency and elegance of style" the main object in preaching.

One would have thought it more likely to accuse Newman or any of the great nineteenth-century preachers with the fault of rhetorical show-manship rather than Aquinas, Bonaventure, or any of the great practitioners of the *sermo modernus* style of preaching. While I think Newman

---

[52] *Contra impugnantes*, pt. 3, ch. 5, ad 3 (Procter, *Apology*, 3.5.5). Cf. Augustine, *De doctrina christiana* 4.7.15, to which Augustine adds the comment: "And certainly if we bring forward anything of his as a model of eloquence, we take it from those epistles which even his very detractors, who thought his bodily presence weak and his speech contemptible, confessed to be weighty and powerful" (trans. J. F. Shaw in "St. Augustin's Christian Doctrine," in *A Select Library of the Nicene and Post-Nicene Fathers of the Christian Church*, ed. Philip Schaff, vol. 2 [New York: Scribner's, 1907]). St. Paul shows up again here as the model preacher—not in the sense that every preacher must preach exactly as Paul did, but in the sense that they should learn to incorporate human learning as he did.

[53] *Contra impugnantes*, pt. 3, ch. 5, ad 3 (Procter, *Apology*, 3.5.5).

could certainly be defended, it is more than a bit ironic to hear an Anglican clergyman from Oxford in the early twentieth century complaining about *medieval* preachers preaching merely to show off their erudition and rhetorical fluency. Perhaps Reverend Smyth was a bit more sensitive on this score, given his own personal experiences with the preaching he was hearing from week to week in churches in and around him at Oxford.

USING PHILOSOPHICAL CATEGORIES IN PREACHING OR BEING DOMINATED BY THEM?

To be fair to Reverend Smyth, however, there is another, even deeper issue at stake here. When philosophical categories (or any other categories from "secular" learning) are used in either theology or preaching, do they help foster theological understanding, or is theological understanding being subordinated to secular categories of discourse? If, with the Church Fathers, we speak of Christians using pagan philosophy as akin to the Israelites using the "spoils of the Egyptians,"[54] the gold and silver which they took with them to use in the service of God when they fled their captivity in Egypt, then we might ask whether, when we appropriate the gold of the Egyptians, the bright allure of the golds end up dominating rather than the demands of the covenant. It is one thing to *talk* about "bringing into

---

[54] This use of the image of the "spoils of the Egyptians" goes back in the Christian tradition at least to Origen: see "A Letter from Origen to Gregory," nos. 1 and 2 in *Ante-Nicene Fathers*, vol. 4, ed. Philip Schaff (Edinburgh: T&T Clark), 393–394:

> But I am anxious that you should devote all the strength of your natural good parts to Christianity for your end; and in order to this, I wish to ask you to extract from the philosophy of the Greeks what may serve as a course of study or a preparation for Christianity, and from geometry and astronomy what will serve to explain the sacred Scriptures, in order that all that the sons of the philosophers are wont to say about geometry and music, grammar, rhetoric, and astronomy, as fellow-helpers to philosophy, we may say about philosophy itself, in relation to Christianity.
>
> Perhaps something of this kind is shadowed forth in what is written in Exodus from the mouth of God, that the children of Israel were commanded to ask from their neighbours, and those who dwelt with them, vessels of silver and gold, and raiment, in order that, by spoiling the Egyptians, they might have material for the preparation of the things which pertained to the service of God.

Cf. also, for a source clearly available to Aquinas, Augustine's *De doctrina christiana* 2.40.60: "The wisdom of the classical philosophy could be used by Christian thinkers, just as the 'spoils of the Egyptians' were taken with them by the Israelites when they fled from their captivity in Egypt" (see n. 221).

captivity every understanding unto the obedience of Christ" (2 Cor 10:5), but it is also possible to bring our obedience to Christ into captivity to our limited human understanding.

What should be the goal, then, when it comes to preaching? Thomas expresses the ideal in characteristically *sacramental*—that is to say, *Eucharistic*—terms, reflecting his basically *liturgical* understanding of preaching. He says in the *Contra Impugnantes* that:

> When one substance is wholly transformed into another, there no longer exists a mixture. In a true mixture, one of two substances is converted into a third. Hence when a preacher, in expounding Holy Scripture, makes use of human learning subject to the truths of faith, the wine of Holy Scripture is not adulterated; it remains pure. Adulteration of the Scripture would consist in adding something to it which would destroy its truth. The Gloss observes: "He who, instead of correcting his hearers by means of the Scriptures, makes the Scriptural precepts subservient to their auditors does, by his teaching, adulterate the wine of truth.[55]

Here, then, it strikes me, is the real issue and the way we should be asking the question at hand. The question should not be posed as, "Do the medieval preachers use logic and rhetoric in preaching?" Of course they do. Every effective preacher does to one extent or another. The proper question is this: "Does the use of logic and its mnemonic style of rhetoric in the *sermo modernus* style make the Scriptures *subservient* to human truth? Does it adulterate the Scriptures by adding something that *destroys* its truth?"

Let us take Reverend Smyth's own principle and apply it here. "Rules exist," he says, quite rightly, "for a purpose, and the criterion of their efficacy—a criterion which must continually be applied—is their capacity to serve that purpose." This is a good, basic principle to keep in mind because it will force us to ask what preachers should seek to accomplish by means of a sermon. What is a sermon supposed to *do*? What is its *purpose*?

What Purposes Should a Good Sermon Serve?

At this juncture, it seems appropriate to examine Thomas's comments about a sermon's purpose, since we have been examining his sermons. And

---

[55] *Contra impugnantes*, pt. 3, ch. 5, ad 4 (Procter, *Apology*, 3.5.5).

according to Thomas, "The matter of preaching is twofold." Preachers should "preach all the things which are in this life useful for salvation [*in hac vita sunt utilia ad salutem*], either as regards God, or the neighbor or themselves," and they should also "preach about the things which we hope to have in the next life."[56] But the preacher must announce the Word of God "not with the desire for praise or profit, but for the salvation of men and the glory of God ['dum non intentione laudis aut lucri verbum Dei annuntiant, sed propter hominum salutem et Dei gloriam']."[57] Thus a preacher must have three qualities, says Thomas: "first, stability [*stabilitas*] to keep him from erring from the truth; second, clearness [*claritas*] that he may not be obscure in his teaching; and third, utility [*utilitas*] by which he seeks God's glory and not his own."[58] These three qualities, as many readers will know, are an echo of the Roman architect Vitruvius's three famous qualities of great architecture set forth in his *Ten Books on Architecture*: great buildings must have *firmitas* (be solid or durable), *utilitas* (be useful), and *venustas* (be beautiful).[59] Vitruvius's *firmitas, utilitas,* and *venustas* have become Thomas's *stabilitas, utilitas,* and *claritas*. And note, with Thomas, it is now not merely the work of art that must possess these qualities, *but the artist himself*. The preacher is the one who must possess "stability" or firmness to keep from wavering from the truth, even amidst the clamor of opposition. He must also possess the virtue of "clarity," which is not averse to the classical idea of beauty, but seeks first to communicate the truth without obscurity. And finally, the preacher must exhibit the virtue of "utility": what he must be "useful" for is preaching God's glory by proclaiming the Good News of our salvation won through the sacrificial death and Resurrection of Jesus Christ. The preacher, on this view, cannot build up the Body of Christ, the Church, unless he himself has been built as a firm, beautiful, and useful edifice. Preachers, says Thomas elsewhere, are to be "the mouth of Christ" (*praedicatores autem sunt os Christi*).[60]

---

[56] Aquinas, *Commentary on St. Paul's Epistle to the Romans*, ch. 10, lec. 2; this is my own translation from the Taurini edition, ed. Robert Busa (1953).

[57] Ibid.

[58] Aquinas, *Commentary on the Gospel of St. Matthew*, bk. 5, lec. 4 (taken from the material inserted from the commentary of Peter de Scala, a piece of information necessary for locating the reference in the Latin). This is my own translation from the Taurini edition, ed. Robert Busa (1953).

[59] See Vitruvius, *De architectura* 1.3.2.

[60] *Commentary on the Gospel of John*, ch. 12, lec. 4, Marietti no. 1633, trans. Fabian Larcher (Albany, NY: Magi Books, 1998); available also at http://dhspriory.org/thomas/John12.htm.

Likely Reverend Smyth would agree with all that. It is not my purpose to question his piety, his good intentions, or his desire to nourish good preaching. Allow me to suggest, rather, that the differences between what someone like Reverend Smyth would envision as an appropriate use of logic and an acceptable sort of rhetoric in preaching and what Thomas would, by contrast, be willing to allow are due largely to different sorts of cultural expectations. What seems clear historically, however, is that the *sermo modernus* style was not *forced* on medieval congregations; it was something they clamored for. It was a taste they developed, not an order of healthy vegetable puree forced down their throats every Sunday.

Why was it successful? I would suggest that it was because the style, at its best, offered a pedagogical ordering of discourse designed with the intent of moving both the mind and the heart. It provided clarity and a structure that aided memory and identifiably articulated the different parts. It provided the preacher with a reliable method of *inventio*, of sermon-making, that both was organized and, yet, allowed for a large amount of flexibility and, indeed, creativity. It also resulted in sermons that were not merely "exegetical," but "doctrinal" or "moral," while also seeming, at least, always to be heavily biblically grounded. The preacher of the *sermo modernus* style of sermon seemed to be steeped in the language of the Scriptures every bit as much as their earlier predecessors such as St. Bernard of Clairvaux.

But was its connection with the Word of God, as Reverend Smyth suggests, "purely superficial and purely formal"? In the end, this is perhaps the hardest criticism to defend against. What the *sermo modernus* approach to preaching does *not* do well, it must be admitted, is to examine the Scriptures *contextually*. That is to say, it is not merely an *exegetical* exercise, and as such, the method often loses some of the contextual analysis that purely exegetical homilies can provide.

CONSIDERING PREACHING IN ITS HISTORICAL AND PASTORAL CONTEXT

I would ask the reader to consider in this regard the cultural context in which such sermons were preached. Someone like Thomas Aquinas was usually preaching to friars or other clerics for whom the sermon was not their only time during the week to read the Scriptures. Most of them would have been steeped in the *bachelor biblicus*-sort of "cursory" reading of the Scriptures during their studies all week. Is this the sort of sermon to which they should have been treated on Sundays or other feast days? Did they need nothing more? So too we might make the same point about congregations in Cardinal Newman's day. Do learned audiences need nothing more than to hear another in a long line of "Bible study" classes? If not, then what should they hear? Thomas and his contemporaries believed that the sermon was a means for theological instruction, for praising God, and for changing people's lives.

Consider, for purposes of comparison, our current situation and the influence cultural factors can have on the nature of preaching. When Catholic preachers prior to the reforms of the Second Vatican Council preached more often than they do now on the Pauline epistles, there tended to be more "theological" and "doctrinal" content in their sermons and homilies. Now, however, preachers tend to focus attention solely on the Gospel (if they make any reference to the readings at all), although they will sometimes make use of the parallel Old Testament text selected for the day. In either case, when a contemporary preacher goes to the Scriptures for preaching material, he often enough will consider the Scriptures only as a source for potentially instructive *stories*—not, say, for example, as a source for potentially instructive *laws*, as a Jewish rabbi might do. Our current approach to preaching undoubtedly owes a great deal to the so-called "historical turn" of early nineteenth-century philosophy and with the revolutionary developments in historical-critical biblical scholarship that the "historical turn" helped make possible.[61] There is nothing intrinsically wrong with this approach, but there is still the question of what relevance the story has for forming a specifically Christian way of life. A story does not interpret itself.

Perhaps in reaction to the potential dryness of much contemporary historical-critical biblical scholarship, many contemporary preachers read Bible stories the way they read nearly every story they read or every movie

---

[61] Some trace the increased sensitivity to the historical dimension of thought to Hegel, others to Kant. See, e.g., Karl Ameriks, *Kant and the Historical Turn: Philosophy as Critical Interpretation* (Oxford, UK: Clarendon Press, 2006). *The Catholic Encyclopedia*, by contrast, has the following: "The Hegelian principle of evolution has undoubtedly influenced German criticism, and indirectly biblical criticism in general. Applied to religion, it has powerfully helped to beget a tendency to regard the religion of Israel as evolved by processes not transcending nature, from a polytheistic worship of the elements to a spiritual and ethical monotheism. This theory was first elaborated by Abram Kuenen, a Dutch theologian, in his *Religion of Israel* (1869–70)"; see "Biblical Criticism (Higher)," in *Catholic Encyclopedia* (New York: Robert Appleton Company, 1907–1912); available also at http://www.newadvent.org/cathen/04491c.htm. The particular sources of the shift are not so important for our purposes as simply the fact that they happened.

they watch: as exemplifying the importance of emotional love or of being nice to others or of the existential value of inner spiritual struggle.[62] Moreover, if sociologist Christian Smith is right, and the most prevalent form of religious conviction in the United States, at least among teens, is what he calls "moralistic therapeutic deism," then we should expect many (if not most) preachers to use Bible stories to teach the following lessons: There is a God, but he is caring, not judgmental; he wants people to be "good," which usually means "nice"; and he will help you in times of trouble.[63] These lessons are not necessarily bad, but we should recognize our own philosophical presuppositions and cultural limitations. Focusing attention on the things we do generally keeps us from focusing much (if any) attention on things medieval preachers were able to preach on regularly: the basic doctrinal elements of the Christian faith; the multiple layers of meaning in the biblical text (literal, allegorical, anagogical, and moral); and the virtues, both personal and civic, necessary for living a full Christian life, just to name three.

Let us suppose that good preaching should do at least three things well: first, teach sound Christian doctrine at the level of understanding appropriate to the congregation; second, engage in moral formation and exhortation appropriate to the Gospel call to love and holiness; and third, bring about a deepening engagement with the Sacred Scriptures, beginning with sound textual exegesis, but moving from there to an understanding and application of the biblical text to one's life as a whole, not only including one's duties and responsibilities in this life but also with an eye

---

[62] With regard to the last, inner spiritual struggle, note Reverend Smyth's complaint that medieval preaching did not seem to him as though it was a "dying man preaching to dying men." Perhaps this was because they lived in the face of death every day and did not need to be reminded constantly about death and because they were more interested in developing the virtues necessary for a long, flourishing, and indeed, *eternal* life.

[63] See Christian Smith and Melinda Lundquist Denton, *Soul Searching: The Religious and Spiritual Lives of Teenagers* (Oxford, UK: Oxford University Press, 2005), esp. ch. 4 ("God, Religion, Whatever: On Moralistic Therapeutic Deism," esp. 162–70). The basic elements of this "creed," according to Smith, are the following:

1. A god exists who created and ordered the world and watches over human life on earth.
2. God wants people to be good, nice, and fair to each other, as taught in the Bible and by most world religions.
3. The central goal of life is to be happy and to feel good about oneself.
4. God does not need to be particularly involved in one's life except when God is needed to resolve a problem.
5. Good people go to heaven when they die.

to the culmination of life in death and the life beyond. Undoubtedly no one method can accomplish all of these three goals equally well. I would argue, however, that the medieval manner of preaching—at least as we see it exemplified by Thomas Aquinas—does all three of these as well as most and better than many. Granted, its form and style owes much to the contemporary challenges of the influx of the Latin Aristotle into the West and the renewed emphasis in the newly formed universities of logic. If the older, line-by-line sort of textual exegesis was no longer moving the minds and hearts of the more literate and more sophisticated townspeople of the later Middle Ages, then this challenge had to be met; it could not simply be avoided. Preachers could not go on as though tastes and intellectual circumstances had not changed.

In addition, I would argue that the medieval sermon style—as practiced by its best preachers—succeeds admirably in communicating clearly and, above all, *memorably* the basic elements of the Christian faith. It excels in moral instruction and exhortation. And the encounter with the Sacred Scriptures it manages to bring about is, though not *contextual*, at least *repeated*. It is at least made clear to the congregation that the Christian Scriptures were *something important*, something worthy of their deep attention and respect, and not merely a historical artifact of interest largely only to specialists in archaic cultures. For medieval preaching of the sort we find in Thomas's sermons often enough forces a certain sort of moral and existential encounter with the text in that the medieval congregation was constantly being challenged to ask these questions as he or she listened to the preachers comments on the biblical text: not only "What does the text *say*?" but also "What (or in Whom) do I believe?"; "How should I live?"; and "to what end am I headed?" This, of course, is the value of medieval preachers being able to move easily from the literal level of the text to the allegorical or Christocentric meaning, and then finally to the anagogical and the moral. Again, there is a certain *flexibility* in this style of preaching (one can take any number of different approaches to the biblical text) within the context of a fairly clear *structure* (which allows for a more definite method of *inventio* and sermon construction, not to mention making it easier to follow and more memorable for listeners) that makes it worthy of our respect, even if not an object of our aesthetic taste.

I had mentioned in chapter 3 an old dictum among pharmacists about medications that goes something like this: a lot of things work some of the time, some things work a lot of the time, but nothing works all of the time. So too, we might say with sermons: a lot of them are effective some of the time, some of them are effective a lot of the time, but nothing works all of the time. For my part, I would place Thomas's sermons in the second of those categories, something that works a lot of the time, recognizing of course that nothing will work for everyone all of the time. I will allow the reader to decide for him- or herself which of these three categories he or she would put Thomas's sermons in and which of the three he or she would put most contemporary sermons in. Making the mental comparison would likely be instructive.

CHAPTER 6

Summary and Conclusions

THE QUESTION OF WHAT "BIBLICAL" PREACHING LOOKS LIKE IN VARIOUS HISTORICAL PERIODS

Some books set out to defend a very particular thesis, and the point of the examination of material is to provide evidence adequate to prove that thesis. In other books, the journey is as important as the destination and the learning comes not primarily from knowing what view the author is defending, such as "Thomas Aquinas is a biblical theologian," but from reviewing the material in such a way as to come to a better understanding of something, such as "What does it mean for Thomas Aquinas to be a biblical theologian?" or "What does being a biblical theologian look like in the thirteen century—what sort of forms does that take?" The upshot is not simply "Medieval theologians took the Bible seriously." It is, rather, "This is what taking the Bible seriously looked like in the Middle Ages."

As I hope will be clear by now, this book is of the latter sort rather than the former. There have been some partisans in the past who have claimed that theologians in the Middle Ages like Thomas Aquinas were not "biblical" or that they did not take the Bible seriously enough. I take it that such claims have not survived critical scrutiny and were effectively refuted long ago to such a degree that there's really no point arguing the point, any more than there would be any point in arguing whether Thomas Aquinas was a Dominican. He was a Dominican; now we can discuss (if we so choose) what being a Dominican meant during the time he lived and how it was different from being, say, a monk at Monte Cassino (if he had stayed there) during the time he lived or a Dominican today.

The attempt to clarify, as I have here, what being a biblical theologian meant for Thomas Aquinas and what role the Bible played in his preaching need not (and is not intended to) diminish the many other uses of Scripture throughout history. Aquinas is no John Henry Newman; but then, Newman was no Aquinas. And neither of them was quite the same as Augustine. All three have their virtues. No doubt all three have their limitations.

They also each had the benefits of a certain cultural background, as well as the challenges of their own historical moment. Newman had the benefit of the exalted language that characterized the King James Bible and the oratorical tradition of great poets and preachers from John Donne down to his own day. Newman also had a highly educated congregation willing to listen to very long orations. They could, however, also be petty, overly class conscious, and only "culturally Christian" in their convictions, as Kierkegaard suggested many in Europe were at the time. Augustine had the benefit of an unmatched classical education in the Ciceronian rhetorical arts, and he could depend upon his congregation knowing all sorts of classical references. These congregations also seem to have been willing to listen to long orations—even to enjoy them. But they were still highly susceptible (as many congregations are again today) to the blandishments of paganism, to doubt and unbelief, and to heresies of all kinds.

Aquinas, for his part, had the benefit of an unmatched education in philosophy and the arts of dialectic, and he was blessed to live in a culture that was thoroughly Christian in many respects, including much of its most important art, literature, and music, and to have congregations who were, in their own way, often deeply pious. By the same token, he also does not seem to have had congregations willing to stand for long orations or who cared much for fancy rhetorical flourishes. They were also, unlike many of the congregants in Newman's or Augustine's day, mostly illiterate, so whatever they knew of the Bible and of its teachings they were going to have to get from listening, and they were going to have to retain it in memory.

Indeed an issue I have not had the space to explore sufficiently, but which certainly merits more discussion, is the relationship between the challenges inherent in instructing a largely illiterate society and the "arts of memory" such as those described in Mary Carruthers's book *The Book of Memory: A Study of Memory in Medieval Culture*. We might re-state the question this way: What was the relationship between the "memory arts" and the largely "oral culture" of the Middle Ages?

In the modern world, "illiterate" often implies a lack of knowledge of key texts. Such has not always been the case, however. There are many "oral cultures" where plain persons who cannot read might still be expected to have memorized a great number of what we would call "texts." I am told that Ireland in the early part of the twentieth century was such a culture, where even those who could not read had memorized a large number of poems, song lyrics, and passages from Scripture. Homer's culture was another such fundamentally "oral" culture in which the vehicle of "literacy" was not reading written texts, but memorizing oral recitations.[1]

Thus even when Thomas was preaching to Dominican and Franciscan students at the University of Paris, he would have been preaching to those who were expected to go out and preach to a largely illiterate populace. Thomas was always aware of the fact that he was teaching future teachers: those who would be going out to preach and teach the Word of God to lay people in the churches. As he was always aware that he was teaching future teachers, so too he was aware that he preaching to future preachers—preachers who would be preaching to a populace that, although they might not have had the ability to read, might still have been expected to have committed to memory (if only by repeated hearing at the Mass) significant portions of the Scriptures. Perhaps we could say of such people that although they were "illiterate" (unable to read), they were not for that reason "unliterary" (unacquainted with important texts).[2]

---

[1] Centuries later, Plato would warn about the deleterious effects writing would have on memory, as for example in the scene from the *Phaedrus* in which Socrates tells the legend of how the king of Egypt, the god Thamus, scolded the god Theuth for inventing the art of writing, telling him: "now you, who are the father of letters, have been led by your affection to ascribe to them a power the opposite of that which they really possess. For this invention will produce forgetfulness in the minds of those who learn to use it, because they will not practice their memory. Their trust in writing, produced by external characters which are no part of themselves, will discourage the use of their own memory within them. You have invented an elixir not of memory, but of reminding; and you offer your pupils the appearance of wisdom, not true wisdom, for they will read many things without instruction and will therefore seem to know many things, when they are for the most part ignorant and hard to get along with, since they are not wise, but only appear wise." *Phaedrus*, 274c–275b, translated by Harold N. Fowler, in *Plato in Twelve Volumes*, vol. 9, Loeb Classical Library (Cambridge, MA: Harvard University Press; London, William Heinemann Ltd., 1925).

[2] A basic work exploring the fundamental issues surrounding "orality" and "literacy" within culture is Walter J. Ong, S.J., *Orality and Literacy: The Technologizing of the Word*, 2nd ed. (New York: Routledge, 2002). On "literacy" in the early Middle Ages, see, for example: Brian Stock, *The Implications of Literacy: Written Language and Models of Interpretation in the Eleventh and Twelfth Centuries* (Princeton, NJ: Princeton University Press, 1983).

Those of us in the modern world, by contrast, who exist in a culture that enjoys widespread "literacy," do not always experience one that is especially "literary." Most young people in our culture can read, but very few of them have memorized and thus can recite from memory any stories, poems, or biblical verses. We should not mistake our cultural expectations of "illiteracy," therefore, with the kind of congregations Thomas and his confrères were called upon to preach to.

Defending Thomas, But Only To Encourage Reading Him

Some readers will probably still not find Thomas's sermons "to their taste," but I hope they might at least gain some admiration for what these medieval preachers were able to accomplish within the forms that had become customary in their day, in the same way that some people who may not quite like what they consider to be the "stodginess" or "overly formal" character of the "Classical" period in music (as opposed to say the Baroque or the Romantic) could still admire the power and beauty a composer such as Mozart was able to achieve.

I admit to having tried to make as good a case as possible on behalf of the medieval practice of preaching, given my suspicion that many modern readers may find it strange, very much unlike what they are used to, and thus, perhaps, more than a bit suspect. Was this approach *really* "biblical"? Was it *really* an appropriate use of the Bible in preaching? Or did the categories of philosophy and logic ultimately overwhelm and thus deform the Gospel message? These are questions that the reader will ultimately have to decide for him- or herself. I have provided the evidence as fairly as I was able, although admittedly as someone who would be speaking as witness for the defense. I have not made any secret of my attitude towards the material, but any ultimate decision about the legitimacy of the practices I have discussed would have to await a direct encounter with a broader selection of Thomas's sermons, after which the reader can make up his or her own mind. My goal was primarily to drive the reader back to the sermons prepared as much as possible to read them with some appreciation of the historical, intellectual, and cultural context within which they were written.

Keeping all of this in mind, therefore, allow me in this concluding section simply to review some main points of the journey. This is a "conclusion" done by way of recapitulation or summary of the main points, not "conclusion" as propositions proven by preceding evidence.

Remembering the Sermons

In chapter 1, I pointed out that the biblical epigraph or *thema* verse that appears at the outset of a sermon by Aquinas is not really being "preached on" in the sense that the author intends to give a commentary on or interpretation of that particular verse. Rather, the *thema* verse is taken as a structured mnemonic device—the arts of memory and recollection being highly valued and generally well-developed in the Middle Ages—something that both provided form and helped inspire the content of the sermon that followed.

Indeed, let me ask the readers who have actually worked their way through chapter 1 this question: If I repeat the *thema* verse, "Behold/ your king/ comes to you/ meek," do you remember any of it? Do you remember, for example, that the word "Behold" was associated with the four "advents" or "comings" of Christ: (1) after death, (2) at the Incarnation, (3) into our minds, and (4) at the final resurrection of the dead? Do you remember that Christ comes to us as both king and friend, and thus that we find the combination "your king"? Do you remember that the word "king" suggests unity, fullness of power, abundant jurisdiction, and equity of justice? Do you remember that Christ is called "your" king—namely, the king of *man*—first, because man is made "in the image of God," second, because of God's special love for man beyond all other creatures, third, because of God's special solicitude toward man and his unique care for him, and fourth, because of Christ's conformity with our human nature? Do you remember that Christ is said to come "for you" (that is, for us) because he comes voluntarily, not under compulsion? And finally, do you remember that he comes "meekly," which is shown in four ways: in his conversion; in his gentle correction of sinners; in gracious acceptance of men; and fourth, in his Passion on the Cross, to which he was led "as a lamb"? If you find that any of those verbal and visual associations helped you to recollect the message and a good many of the details of the sermon, then you should understand why Thomas composed it the way he did.

Preached Words, Biblical Words, and the Word Made Flesh

I suggested at the end of chapter 1 that what made this sort of semiotic flexibility possible—that is to say, what made it possible for these medieval scholars and preachers to use biblical verses in multiple different ways and with various significations—was a Christocentric understanding of the Scriptures and the long tradition of interpreting the Scriptures in multiple figurative senses that this Christocentric understanding of the biblical texts made possible. There is no doubt, on one level at least, that using Matthew 21:5, "Behold, your king comes to you, meek," the way Thomas does in Sermon 5 (*Ecce rex tuus*) is a purely formal affair. It is an adventitious *usage* of the biblical text, not an interpretation of its inner meaning. And yet, what medieval theologians had learned from the long tradition of allegorical exegesis of the Scriptures was that the words of the sacred text could have multiple valences and several layers of meaning. What they learned, in other words, was that words could be used in many different ways, depending upon the context of meaning. (To use Wittgenstein's famous phrase, they learned that there were multiple sorts of "language games.")

What kept this potentially chaotic "play" of words and phrases from degrading into nonsense—the "glue" that held it all together—was that, behind all the various "words" of the Scriptures, was the "Word made flesh," the Incarnate Son of God, who was both the source and summit of all creation and, thus, of every human life. Semiosis, on this view, was fundamentally "incarnational," which is to say fundamentally "sacramental." That is to say, just as "things" were meant to draw the mind back to their Creator, so too, "words" were meant to draw the human mind and heart back to God. On this view, the "truth" that words convey, to the extent that bear any real truth, is going to be the truth of creation, which is also and crucially the truth of their reality established therein by their Creator. If, as Heidegger once suggested, language is the "house of Being,"[3] then the proper end of language is to bring greater openness to Being in all the various ways it discloses itself to us and thus enter into a deeper union and more profound communion with the one St. Thomas described as *Ipsum Esse Subsistens* ("Subsisting Being Itself"). Since all words have their ultimate referent in the Word, so too, all semiosis, all linguistic signification, is meant ultimately to bring us into closer contact with him who is both Creator and Redeemer.

It was not enough merely to preach the Bible; it was imperative that one preach Christ. The Bible was not merely a literary product to be interpreted as, say, Virgil's *Aeneid* was to be interpreted, but the Bible did need to be interpreted because it was written in actual human language. But beyond being a literary product, the Bible was thought to be the self-disclosure of the Creator who was also the Word made flesh. It was not suffi-

---

[3] The explicit reference occurs several times in Heidegger's *Letter on Humanism*. I am not suggesting, however, that Heidegger meant by "Being" what Aquinas did.

cient at the end merely to say, "This is what the text says and here is what I think it means." It was necessary, after saying *that*, to then be *changed* by those words in ways that brought one closer to the Triune God and, thus, into great loving communion with both God and neighbor.

My suggestion is that the medieval preacher asked himself the question "Am I using words in such a way as to direct the minds of my listeners to Christ? By listening to the words, do they know and love Christ more?" If the answer was yes, then the words had done their job. If not, the words had been "vain"—that is, empty. The signs had missed the thing. The arrow had missed its target. The question for the preacher about his sermon was "Will it build up an authentic faith in Christ? Does it communicate the truth of Christ? Does it exhort the listeners to works of charity and to become like Christ? Does it provision them with the sort of supernatural hope needed in the midst of the turmoil of the world to persevere in that faith and in that Christ-like love past these troubled times unto the end of time and into that period of a deeper communion?"

The question is not whether the Bible was at the center of medieval preaching—the Bible is nearly always at the center of Christian preaching, except during unfortunately corrupt periods—the question is *how*. How was the text viewed? What did people think it was meant to do to its reader or listener? How was it employed as a means of building up the faith, hope, and love of the People of God? Was it seen, for example, primarily as setting forth a series of wise laws to be followed, with commentaries on those laws that followed? Or was it viewed primarily as setting forth stories to be learned from, or as providing proverbs of wisdom to be heeded? Did readers believe that the words spoke forth the profound teachings of a wise mentor who both knew and loved much? Or did they take "the book" to be a great literary product and, thus, as spur to eloquent oratory with beautiful displays of verbal profundity? Was it, for example, understood as something to be *read* and understood and reflected on? Or was it taken to be something *heard* and repeated and remembered? Were the words thought to move the mind primarily, and the heart only after long and deep reflection on the words? Or were the words thought to be something to move the heart primarily, and the mind only in accord with the "language of the heart"? Or alternatively, were the words thought to be something that could and should move mind and heart in concert with one another because both were understood to be essential elements of the human soul and spirit?

All of these approaches have their benefits; undoubtedly, all too have their drawbacks. What should be clear, however, is that medieval preachers such as Aquinas took the Bible very seriously. Indeed, it was, I would argue, the controlling discourse that set the terms, both verbal and logical, within which all other reckoning and cognition was carried on. They were not, however, by the same token, unduly rigid in their understanding of the signification of the text. They believed it had many layers and many potential uses. It was for them, by necessity, as I have pointed out, something that had to be *heard* and *remembered*, given how little literacy existed among their congregations and how few books of any sort were in print.

THE PARTS OF THE SERMON: *DIVISIO* AND *DILATATIO*

I have found that much of what many people know about a book comes from the first chapter of that book. Thus I have very purposefully put in the first chapter the basic information I think a reader would need to be able to drop the book forever and go forth for a lifetime of reading the sermons of Thomas Aquinas and other later medieval preachers with some understanding and pleasure.

And yet, to provide a more thorough examination of the "nuts-and-bolts" of the *sermo modernus* style of preaching that originated in the mid-thirteenth century, which was the style adopted by Thomas Aquinas and his contemporaries, we moved on in chapter 2 to review the basic elements of the *sermo modernus* style: the *thema*, the "ante-theme" or "pro-theme," the "declaration of the parts" (or *divisio*), and finally the development of each of the parts of the sermon by a method described as *dilatatio* or "dilation." In this chapter, the goal was merely to make these basic elements clear so that the reader could return to Aquinas's sermons and, first, see more clearly the basic lineaments of their structure, and second, understand that Thomas did not construct his sermons this way accidentally or because of some bizarre logical obsession, but because it was the prevailing preaching style of the day.

At the end of chapter 2, I suggested that the two primary elements in the crafting of a *sermo modernus* style sermon were: (A) *divisio*—that is, the process of dividing the opening biblical verse or *thema* into various parts to facilitate their use as a mnemonic structuring device; and (B) *dilatatio*—that is, the methods by which the various parts were developed conceptually to create the content in the body of the sermon. Accordingly, in chapter 3, we examined the common methods of executing the *divisio* of the opening *thema*, using information derived from two popular medieval preaching manuals: the *Forma praedicandi* of Robert of Basevorn and the still-unattributed *Ars concionandi*, published sometimes among the works of St. Bonaventure, but probably not by him. And in chapter 4, we similarly examined the most common methods of *dilatatio*.

The Arts of Grammar, Rhetoric, and Logic and a Poet's Appreciation for Words

What the process of *divisio* and the subsequent methods of *dilatatio* demand of their users, I would suggest, is a very keen attention to words and how they signify. One has to distinguish very clearly between verbs and nouns, adjectives and adverbs, and the different ways in which they can be used, because each can be employed in a *divisio* only in its own particular ways. One can make a *divisio* or "dilate" a noun based on its properties, whereas one can make a *divisio* or "dilate" an adjective based on its comparative and superlative forms. Verbs can have different connotations—different ways of "coming" or "running" or "rising," whereas one preposition can suggest several different ways in which one thing can be related to another: *in* something or *on* something or *with* something else. And in a related vein, one has to know where it is appropriate to divide a sentence, and for that, one needs to understand the constituent parts of a sentence such that to divide it in one place or another makes sense, while another sort of division would be awkward or create confusion in the mind of the listener. Similarly there was the question of a word's various *connotations* and the various associations that might be made with it, each of which could spur various sorts of division or dilation of content.

One of the characteristics that makes the *sermo modernus* style so foreign to us, I would suggest, but that would make it much less so to, say, most poets, is that the authors of a "modern sermon" were accustomed to lavishing so much attention on the grammar, syntax, and each of the individual words of the opening *thema* verse. I can imagine many of the modern readers of Thomas's Sermon 5 (*Ecce rex tuus*), which we examined in chapter 1, would be inclined to say about Thomas's dilation of the word "Behold" (*Ecce*): "He has certainly made a lot out of one word." To which I would be inclined to reply: "Yes, he did. He certainly found that a great deal of meaning could be associated with that word." But notice, the sort of divisions and dilations that make sense with an interjection such as "Behold" are not the same as would be appropriate with a noun such as "king," with a pronoun such as "your" (in the phrase "your king"), or with a verb such as "comes." The effective medieval preacher had to be able to take all of these differences into account.

If the medieval preacher's command of the trivial arts of grammar, rhetoric, and logic was not proficient before he started his career of preaching, one imagines it had to improve rather drastically in fairly short order if he was to be successful. Simply preparing sermons in accord with the *sermo modernus* style would undoubtedly have gone a long way to helping him learn-through-use the principles of grammar, rhetoric, and logic he should have learned earlier in school, just as the prospect of preaching in the *sermo modernus* style would likely have forced the grim realization that he should have paid more attention earlier when he was a grammar-school student. Cultures that no longer study grammar will care less and less about words and what they do. And when that happens, they tend to become not only sloppier and less precise in their rhetoric, but also less poetic, given that a deep interest in words and their effects is crucial to both.

It was beyond the scope of this present work, but it would certainly have made an interesting and worthwhile study to compare and contrast the sort of education young clerics got, especially in grammar and rhetoric, with the sorts of guidelines that guided them in their composition of sermons.[4] So, for example, Suzanne Reynolds argues in her book *Medieval Reading: Grammar, Rhetoric, and the Classical Text* that:

> The twelfth century saw an increase in the production of classical texts, an expansion of education, and a series of crucial debates about language, signification and interpretation. All of these are part of a gradual shift in reading itself, broadly from the ruminative *lectio* of monastic meditation to the more public, structured reading processes of the classroom.[5]

---

[4] The key primary texts with which the interested student would have to acquaint him- or herself would be Cassiodorus's *Institutions of Divine and Secular Learning* and Martianus Capella's *The Marriage of Mercury and Philology*—from which the Middle Ages learned much of what they knew about the seven classical liberal arts of antiquity—as well as John of Salisbury's *Metalogicon*, a twelfth-century defense of the verbal and logical arts. For a good series of short selections from nearly all the major authors and an excellent introduction to the topic, however, see *Medieval Grammar and Rhetoric: Language Arts and Literary Theory, AD 300–1475*, ed. R. Copeland and I. Sluiter (Oxford, UK: Oxford University Press, 2012). Since the selections in this volume are necessarily fairly short to accommodate the number of authors covered (the book still comes in at 992 pages), in most cases, it will still be necessary to find these texts in their entirety somewhere else. And yet, what this book lacks in depth, it makes up for in breadth. In this book, one meets all the major players, even if sometimes only in passing. It is a great resource.

[5] Suzanne Reynolds, *Medieval Reading: Grammar, Rhetoric and the Classical Text* (Cambridge, UK: Cambridge University Press, 1996), 1.

What is interesting here is the extent to which, in a culture as dedicated to reading and especially to reading (or, more often, hearing) the Bible, changes in *the way people read* will have palpable results in *the way preachers preach*. Congregations (such as those in the nineteenth century) that read a lot of stories and novels will have certain expectations of sermons. Congregations who learn to read (and learn to read even the classic texts of Cicero and Aristotle) by first undergoing a rigorous course of structured study in grammar, rhetoric, and logic will likely have somewhat different expectations. We have glimpsed a bit of that vast territory from the vantage point offered by this book, but a more explicit examination would undoubtedly be fruitful and worthwhile.

Those unacquainted with the complexity of the historical context of the thirteenth century often speak as if rhetoric was put aside in the schools and universities and was replaced nearly *in toto* by logic. What this study shows, I would argue, among other things, is that a better way of approaching this particular question would not be to claim that logic *replaced* rhetoric, but rather to explore the various ways in which a new emphasis on logic *transformed* rhetoric. When it comes to medieval preaching, however, it is clear that all three of the trivial arts are still operating very much in tandem.

A New "Christian" Rhetoric

Indeed, one of the things I have argued in this book, specifically with regard to medieval rhetoric, is that the methods created and taught and promoted in conjunction with the *sermo modernus* style of preaching constituted a new sort of Christian rhetoric. I call it "Christian," in this context, because it was a rhetoric attuned very purposefully to the verbal patterns of the Christian Scriptures. The five classic canons for putting together an effective speech were:

1. *Inventio*: the "finding" of an appropriate topic and the suitable approach to the topic;
2. *Dispositio*: the arrangement of the arguments and various parts in a persuasive order;
3. *Elocutio*: perfecting the presentation and pronunciation of the speech;
4. *Memoria*: the memorization of the speech;
5. *Actio*: the actual delivery of the speech.

Medieval preachers knew these five canons, as they had all studied their Quintillian, Cicero, and the *Rhetorica ad Herennium*. What the *sermo modernus* style offered them was a new method of *inventio*—that is, of discerning one's topic and one's approach to the topic. It was an *inventio* that was guided by the structure of, and indeed by the nature of the word in, the opening biblical *thema* verse. The words of the verse suggested the topics to be covered, and the order of those words would determine the *dispositio*—or as the medievals called it, the *divisio*—of the parts of the speech. The *sermo modernus* style became popular, I would suggest, precisely because it provided not only a method of *inventio*, of finding a topic—and in this case, one keyed very purposefully to the scriptural reading for the day—but also a method of constructing and ordering the material of the sermon. The whole process, then, was designed to foster *memoria*, for the opening biblical verse functioned, as we have shown repeatedly, as an elaborate mnemonic device to help the listeners associate the topics covered with the words in the verse. The art of memory, then, was not only something that the preacher did for himself (indeed, medieval preachers rarely memorized their speeches). Rather, the arts of *memoria* were something the preacher used to help the *congregation* remember. This was, I would argue, a genuinely new development in the rhetorical arts, and at the center of this new sort of rhetoric stood the Christian Scriptures.

What is interesting in this regard is that, while scholars across the theological spectrum continued to differ on how the Bible was to be interpreted, especially with regard to what constituted the "literal sense" and the *sensus plenior* of the text, it remained the case that nearly *everyone* chose to preach using the *sermo modernus* style.[6] This new rhetoric of preaching united, in its own way, the disparate approaches to scriptural exegesis.

---

[6] There is, fortunately, an increasing bibliography of sources on medieval biblical exegesis. The two standard works in the area are still Beryl Smalley, *The Study of the Bible in the Middle Ages*, 2nd ed. (Notre Dame, IN: University of Notre Dame Press, 1989; orig. publ. Oxford, UK: Blackwell, 1952;), and Henri de Lubac, S.J., *Medieval Exegesis*, 4 vols. (Grand Rapids, MI: Eerdmans, 1998–), of which only three volumes are currently available in English translation. For a more current treatment and a good background to the whole area, see *The Practice of the Bible in the Middle Ages: Production, Reception, and Performance in Western Christianity*, ed. Susan Boynton and Diane J. Reilly (New York: Columbia University Press, 2011), and Frans van Liere, *An Introduction to the Medieval Bible* (Cambridge, UK: Cambridge University Press, 2014).

AN EVALUATION OF THE STYLE: SMYTH AND SMITH

In chapter 5, I attempted an accounting of some of the strengths and weaknesses of the *sermo modernus* style of preaching employed by St. Thomas and his contemporaries. There I suggested that the strength of the style was that it offered its listeners an ordered discourse designed both to instruct the mind and to move the heart. It was meant to provide clarity and a structure that aided memory and identifiably articulated the different parts of the oration. It provided the preacher with a reliable method of *inventio*, of sermon-making, that was organized and, yet, allowed for a large amount of flexibility and, indeed, even creativity. Its proper use resulted in sermons that were not merely "exegetical," but also "doctrinal" and "moral," while always remaining biblically grounded.

And yet, one of the weaknesses of the *sermo modernus* style of preaching was that, since it was not primarily an exercise in the exegesis and interpretation of the Scriptures, its ends being usually doctrinal teaching and moral exhortation, this sort of preaching was admittedly not usually well-suited to providing an overall contextual reading of Scripture. Such an overall contextual reading was supplied instead by the many biblical commentaries authored by theologians in the thirteenth century. But even fans of the style would have to grant, I think, that contextual exegesis was not the special strength of this particular style of preaching, although it did bring some knowledge of the Scriptures in a doctrinal and moral context that made it a living and important text for its listeners.

It is important to remember in this regard that the Scriptures were at this time a *public* book known mostly through *public* proclamation within the context of *public* worship and *public* teaching. The sort of preaching that would be most suitable in that context would not necessarily be most suitable to congregations in which the Scriptures are understood mostly as a *private* book and in which the preaching was seen primarily as fostering or informing *private* readings of that book by members of the congregation later, after the finish of the sermon. It is one thing to have to preach the Scriptures to a mostly-illiterate congregation (or alternatively, to a group of friars engaged in the *cursus biblicus* most of the week), as was Thomas's challenge; it is quite another thing altogether to be preaching the Scriptures to a mostly literate congregation of competent readers who might be expected to be dutifully reading their Bibles every night before bedtime, eager to know what sense they could make of it all, a state of affairs that was not common until centuries after Thomas's death.

There is no denying the challenges posed to the notion of the Bible as the ultimate source of wisdom by the philosophical writings of the ancient

Greek and Roman philosophers, especially, in Thomas's day, those of the newly-discovered Aristotle. As is well known, Thomas did not fail to take up that challenge and to face it head on, taking everything in it he could find of value and rejecting what did not accord with the wisdom of the revealed Word of God. And in the midst of all the struggles at the University of Paris and elsewhere over which sort of text would provide the controlling or "architectonic" sort of discourse for all the others—the ethics, physics, and metaphysics of Aristotle, the logic of the Organon, or the Christian Scriptures—Thomas continued to maintain the primacy and preeminence of the wisdom of the Scriptures, and he persistently taught his students the same.

It is my hope that this study has shown the reader that Thomas's sermons were remarkably well-organized, quite clever in their use of words and imagery, and above all, *memorable* for his listeners. They were crafted with a view towards teaching his listeners and exhorting them to *live biblically* by clarifying for them *what we should believe, the good that we should hope for,* and *the love that should animate us daily.*

Sermons on Sundays
(in the order of the liturgical calendar)

SERMON 1: *VENIET DESIDERATUS* (SERMON ON THE FIRST SUNDAY OF ADVENT)

Thema:

Veniet desideratus cunctis gentibus et implebit domum istam gloria. (Hag 2:8)
He who is desired by all the nations together will come, and he will fill this house with glory.

Division of the Thema:

All the saints always from the beginning of the world longed for and desired the coming of the Savior. And this is shown well and plainly in the saying mentioned in which the Prophet shows three things, in this order: (1) first, he shows it is God's Son himself who is coming down from the heavens: "**he will come**"; (2) second, he shows He is the one who mercifully fulfills the desires of the Fathers [Patriarchs]: "**who is desired by all the nations together**"; (3) third, he shows He is the one who freely bestows his pleasing benefit [upon us]: "**and he will fill this house with glory.**"

In the first part the lowliness of the coming one or of the coming is shown in view of the way ["he will come"]; in the second the necessity of the coming in view of the human race ["who is desired by all the nations together"]; in the third the utility of the coming in view of the gift offered ["and he will fill this house with glory"]. The first brings to the fore that we should prepare a warm welcome for him ["he will come"]; the second that we should focus our desire on him ["who is desired by all the nations together"]; the third, that we should receive the benefit offered ["and he will fill this house with glory"].

Analytical Outline:

I. **Veniet** (He will come): the Son's coming is absolutely necessary for us because:
   A) The world was imperfect,
   B) Man was cast down from his rightful honor, and
   C) Man offended God.

So Christ:
   A) Brought the highest grade of dignity,
   B) Led man back to his proper state, and
   C) Took away the offense and restored peace.

Further *dilatatio*:

A) The world was imperfect—so Christ restored the highest grade of dignity.
   The world fell short in:

   1. The grade of union
      We had:
      a) Union of corruptible with corruptible (natural things),
      b) Union of corruptible with incorruptible (humans), and
      c) Union of incorruptible with incorruptible (spiritual things),
      But not:
      d) Union of something temporal with something eternal (so "the Word became flesh").

   2. The manner of generation
      We had:
      a) Generation from Father without a mother eternally (the Son),
      b) Generation without a father or mother (Adam and Eve),
      c) Generation from father and mother,

But not:

d) Generation from a mother without a father in time (the Virgin Birth).

3. The grade of perfection (The creature is more perfect when it is united with its Creator)
We had:
a) Union with respect of strength (dependency for very existence),
b) Union with respect of grace in the just,
But not:
c) Union by essence, when the Son of God took on human nature in one person (and thus the whole world was taken on and perfected).

B) Man was cast down from his rightful honor—Christ leads man back to his proper state:

God's people were "scattered":
1. Subjected to different kings—Christ establishes one king
2. Adopted different laws—Christ establishes one law
3. Were corrupted by different errors—Christ is a single judge administering justice

C) Man offended God—Christ takes away the offense and establishes peace:

Because of his sin, man had to die—God's Son made satisfaction through mercy so that God did not fall short of justice in anything. And so it happened that there was, in the same man, justice to the full and infinite mercy, and so mercy and truth have met one another; justice and peace have kissed.

II. **Desideratus cunctis gentibus** (he who is desired by all the nations together): Christ is the one who fulfills the desire of the Fathers, for mankind was:

A) Weak through an incurable wound that corrupted the whole of human nature (thus, men desired the remedy of salvation),

B) Oppressed by an unbearable tyrant (thus, men desired a pleasing dominion), and

C) Thirsty with an unquenchable thirst because mankind lacked sacramental grace (thus, men desired the basin of a fountain, like a deer thirsts for running streams).

III. *Et implebit domum istam gloria* (and he will fill this house with glory): Christ bestows his gracious gifts on us, filling his house with glory:

A) The unique house is the Virgin Mary, which Christ filled with glory of divinity in the Incarnation;

B) The special house is the Church Militant, which Christ filled with the Holy Spirit; and

C) The general house is our heavenly homeland, which Christ filled with grace of happiness in the Ascension.

SERMON 2: *LAUDA ET LETARE* (ANOTHER SERMON ON ADVENT)

Thema:

Lauda et letare, filia Syon, quia ecce ego uenio et habitabo in medio tui, ait Dominus. (Zech 2:10)
Praise and rejoice, O daughter of Zion, for behold I come, and I will dwell in your midst, says the Lord.

Division of the Thema:

Here the prophet does three things: (1) First, he shows the affection of the holy fathers who preceded the coming of the Savior, continually persisting in their praises of him, where he says: **"Praise and rejoice, O daughter of Zion"**; (2) second, he shows the Son of God himself coming down from the heavens: **"Behold I come;"** (3) third, he shows him humbly appearing in human flesh: **"And I will dwell in your midst."**

Analytical Outline:

I. ***Lauda et laetare, filia Sion*** (Praise and rejoice, O daughter of Zion): These words suggest the joy of His coming:

For perfect gladness, three things are required:

A) That the mind is elevated to a divine benefit ("Daughter of Zion"),

B) That the affection is enlarged by spiritual joy ("rejoice"):

1. When it sees itself united with the divine partner,
2. When it experiences that it is placed in the community of the holy ones,
3. When it experiences the strength of heavenly help, and

C) That the tongue is excited to the favorable gift of divine praise ("sing praise")—praise for:

1. The power of the One who battles for us, leading us away from danger,
2. The justice of the Redeemer who, dying, destroyed our death, and

    3.   The benevolence of the Savior who has led us back to eternal life.

II. *Ecce ego venio* (Behold, I come): These words suggest the nearness of His coming:

    A) "Behold": he comes visibly in the form of humanity, which:

        1.   Excites our tepidity so that we may go and meet him,
        2.   Demonstrates its newness so that we may be attentive, and
        3.   Makes known that it is near at hand, so that we may organize a welcome place for him to stay.

    B) "I": he comes in a personal way in the substance of divinity; thus, his infinite sublimity is shown because:

        1.   He has eternal being and precedes all things,
        2.   He has immense power and has brought forth all things, and
        3.   He has perfect knowledge and thus governs all things.

    C) "Come": he comes as a friend, bringing what is useful; he comes because:

        1.   He was invited by the holy fathers,
        2.   He was moved by the push of piety,
        3.   He wished to undergo our weaknesses,
        4.   Since we were stripped of all honor, he has come as a leader of infinite dignity,
        5.   Since we were separated from the divine love, he has come as the peace of a love never heard of, and
        6.   Since we were deprived of light, he came as the light of infinite clarity.

III. *Habitabo in medio tui, ait Dominus* (I will dwell in your midst, says the Lord), whereby the humility of his coming is shown:

    A) "I will dwell"

1. With all people in a general way through the substance of the flesh
2. With the saints in a special way through infused grace
3. With good people in a familiar way by being present before their eyes

B) "In your midst" (like the middle person in a reconciliation)

1. To reconcile God and man and
2. To bring the fullness of joy

C) "Says the Lord": he was with us as the Lord to distribute favorable gifts.

Sermon 3: *Abiciamus opera* (summary only) (Sermon on the First Sunday of Advent)

Thema:

Abiciamus opera tenebrarum et induamur arma lucis. (Rom 13:12)
Let us throw off the works of darkness and put on the armor of light.

Division of the Thema:

The Apostle [Paul] ... with these words, or in these words, disposes us to two things: (1) A liberal abhorrence of all worldly stains and vices, and (2) an honorable love or pursuit of heavenly virtues. He does the first when he says, "**Let us throw off the works of darkness**," and the second, when he adds, "**and let us put on the armor of light.**"

Analytical Outline:

I. *Abiciamus opera tenebrarum* (Let us throw off the works of darkness)—
    The works and vices of the world are called "dark" and must be thrown off:

    A) For there is in them a lack of wisdom needed to arrive at the truth.

    B) In darkness there is a lack of foresight needed for preventing evil.

II. *Induamur arma lucis* (let us put on the armor of light):
    The works of the Gospel and the spiritual gifts of the Holy Spirit are, for us, the arms against the world, the flesh, and the devil, and make us stand firm in the light, because:

    A) Through the effect of enlightening grace, which is like light, they cause us to recognize the divine secret (*divinum secretum*), and

    B) Through the effect of the grace of honesty, which is like light, they make us beautiful, and in us, the whole universe.

SERMON 4: *OSANNA FILIO DAVID* (ANOTHER SERMON ON ADVENT)

Thema:

Osanna filio David. Benedictus qui venit in nomine Domini. Osanna in altissimis. (Matt 21:9)
Hosanna to the son of David : Blessed is he who comes in the name of the Lord. Hosanna in the highest.

Division of the Thema:

In these words we can consider three things to the praise of our Savior: (1) first, the task of our Savior ["**Hosanna**," which means "Save, I beseech"]; (2) second, the privilege of his origin ["**to the son of David; blessed is he who comes in the name of the Lord**"]; and (3) third, the highest point of his power ["**Hosanna in the highest**"].

Analytical Outline:

I. *Hosanna* (which means, "Save, I beseech"): the task of our Savior is human salvation, which was needed for three reasons:

    A) Because of the perversity of sin—
        Therefore salvation, that is, Jesus Christ, has drawn near to man, becoming like us, accepting human nature and suffering—"drawn near" to three kinds of people:

        1. Those who make peace with him (for God is the One who brings peace),
        2. Those who are devoted to God (for when our mind is dedicated to God, God dwells in it), and
        3. Those who are kind and merciful to their neighbors.

    B) Because of the oppression by enemies, enslaved by the devil through sin:
        Christ is the king by whose power the world is set free; as king he sent servants or messengers to save the people, the apostles; concerning whom we observe three characteristics:

        1. Their courage (though poor and illiterate, they invaded the whole world),

237

2. Their power (although earthly people, the Lord gave them power to cast out demons, cure the sick, raise the dead, and even forgive sins), and

3. Their justice (giving back to God what was his, namely glory, seeking not glory for themselves): they led the untied colt back to Christ.

*At this point in the sermon, since he has been discussing the "justice" of the apostles giving glory to the Lord, not themselves, there would have been an obvious and natural transition to his next point, that salvation is needed so that man would reject the glory of the world. Instead, Thomas inserts a rather long digression addressing various issues that arose in the conflict between the so-called "regulars" (those who lived by a rule, such as the Dominicans) and the secular masters at the University of Paris. He may especially have had in mind here the criticisms of Gerard of Abbeville, against whose various criticisms Thomas composed his *De perfectione spiritualis vitae*. These issues are:

1. That we should proceed from easier to more difficult things

2. Whether preachers prefer to convert rich people rather than poor

3. Whether those who live well in the world are more praiseworthy than those in religious life.

4. Defense of the life of poverty

(At this point, Thomas returns to his original order, continuing with the third point under "salvation was needed.")

C) So that men would reject the glory of the world—
Christ showed us the way of humility, riding on the donkey, carrying the cross, emptying himself of His divinity. A human being ought to humble himself in three ways [which Thomas relates to the scene of the crowd crying out during Christ's triumphal entry into Jerusalem, from which the day's Scripture reading is taken]:

1. His mind (the people cutting branches and spreading them before Christ means accepting the authorities and examples of the saints and placing them on the way of one's moral life),

2. His body, by fasting and vigils (the crowds spread out their garments on the road, which stands for throwing the body to the ground), and

3. His affection, giving it over completely to God (thus the crowds shouted "Hosanna" to the Lord).

II. ***Filio David. Benedictus qui venit in nomine Domini*** (to the son of David; blessed is he who comes in the name of the Lord): the privilege of his origin, which is twofold, human ("son of David") and divine ("in the name of the Lord"):

A) "son of David": calling to mind his humanity—
David bears the image of (is a type of) Christ in three respects:

1. His royal sovereignty,
2. His victory in wars, and
3. The grace and love he enjoyed from God.

B) "Blessed is he who comes in the name of the Lord": calling to mind his divinity—
Christ comes in the name of the Lord in a threefold manner:

1. In the truth of the divine name, since the generation of Christ from the Father was perfect and, thus, was "given the name that is above every name,"
2. In the strength of the divine name, and
3. In the manifestation of the divine name.

III. ***Osanna in altissimis*** (Hosanna in the highest): the highest point of his power—
"Hosanna" means "to save," and "in the highest" refers to salvation in the Triune God.
Our salvation consists in:

A) The stability of eternity,
B) The beauty of the divine light, and
C) The enjoyment of the divine delight.

SERMON 5: *ECCE REX TUUS* (WITH *COLLATIO*) (SERMON ON THE FIRST SUNDAY OF ADVENT)

Thema:

Ecce rex tuus venit tibi mansuetus [sedens super asinam]. (Matt 21:5)
Behold your king comes to you, meek, [sitting upon an ass].

Division of the Thema:

Now on this Sunday the Church celebrates the first coming of Christ, and we can see four things in the verse mentioned above: (1) first, the manifestation of the coming of Christ, where it says: "**Behold**"; (2) second, who the one is that is coming, where it says: "**your king**"; (3) third, the benefit of his coming: "**comes for you**"; and (4) fourth, the way of his coming, where it says: "**meek**."

Analytical Outline:

Preliminary Distinction: There are four advents of Christ:

1. The one in which He came in the flesh,
2. The one in which He comes into the mind,
3. The one in which He comes at death, and
4. The one in which He will come at the judgment.

The first advent of Christ—the one in which he came in the flesh—is touched upon in the aforementioned words, in which we are able to see four things:

I. A demonstration of the coming of Christ, where it says **Behold**.
II. The condition of His coming, where it says **your king**.
III. The humility of His coming, where it says **meek**.
IV. The utility of His coming, where it says **he comes for you**.
(Note that Thomas has mixed up numbers 3 and 4 in this listing. In the Latin epigraph, *venit tibi* comes before *mansuetus*. Thomas has listed them here in reverse order. He will treat them in their correct order, however, in the evening *collatio* that finishes off the sermon.)

I. *Ecce* (Behold): Which indicates a demonstration of Christ's coming—
We can understand four things when we say the word '**behold**':

A) First, we can be asserting something certain:
"Just as people doubt in some manner concerning the second coming of Christ, so some doubted His first coming." Thus, in the first sense, the prophet says "**behold**," surely the Lord will come.

B) Second, we can be indicating a determination of time:
"Although the time of Christ's coming at the final judgment is not at a time determined for us, because God wished us to always be vigilant in good works, yet His coming in the flesh was at a determined time, and thus it is said '**behold**.'"

C) Third, we can be indicating the manifestation of a thing:
"So, although the coming of Christ into the mind is hidden, yet Christ's coming in the flesh was manifest and visible."

D) Fourth, the word "behold" can be used for the comforting of men, and this in two ways:

1. First, in victory over their enemies.
2. Second, in the attainment of the good:
   We have obtained these two things in the coming of Christ: "we have peace and victory over the enemy, and we have joy from the hope obtained of future goods."

IIa. *Rex* (King)
There are four things that come with being a king:

1. First, a king suggests unity,
2. Second, a king has fullness of power,
3. Third, a king has an abundant jurisdiction, and
4. Fourth, a king brings equity of justice.

Each of these applies to Christ:

A) First, unity:
There must be unity for there to be kingship, otherwise, if there were many, dominion would not pertain to any one of them. Thus we must reject Arius, "who was positing many gods, saying that the Son was other than the Father."

B) Second, fullness of power:
Laws are not imposed *on* him; rather, he has authority *over* the law. Which is why he can say, "You have heard it said of old, but I say to you," as if to say, "I am the true king who can establish the law for you."

C) Third, abundance of jurisdiction:
Whereas other kings have dominion over this town or those cities, all creatures have been made subject to Christ.

D) Fourth, equity of justice:
Whereas tyrants submit all things for the sake of their own utility, Christ orders all things to the common good. (Thus, "he comes *for you*.")

[End of material in morning Sermon]

Collatio *(later that evening at vespers)*

IIb. *Tuus* (Your; Latin: *rex tuus*)
Christ is called "your king"—namely, the king *of man*—because of four things, namely:

1. Similitude of image,
2. Special love,
3. Solicitude of special and singular care, and
4. Conformity or society of human nature.

A) Similitude of Image between Christ and Man:
Every creature bears the image of God; nevertheless, man is more perfectly and especially was created in his image, not according to a corporeal likeness, but according to an intellectual likeness, in respect of the natural light impressed by God on the human mind. Thus, God sent His Son so that our image, deformed by sin, might be reformed by His grace.

B) Christ's Special Love for Man:
Although Christ loves all things that are, he nevertheless specially loves men, and he has transferred man to the level of and equality with the angels.

C) Christ's Solicitude and Singular Care for Man:
   Though God has care of all things, men are nevertheless specially subject to divine providence because they are ordered to life eternal.

D) Christ's Conformity or Society with Our Human Nature:
   God did not wish to give us a king who was of another kind—that is, of another nature—who would not be our brother.

III. **Venit Tibi** (He comes for you): Which deals with the utility of His coming—
He comes voluntarily, not under compulsion, not for his utility but for our need, for four reasons:

A) To manifest to us the divine majesty,

B) To reconcile us to God from whom through sin we were estranged as enemies,

C) To liberate us from slavery to sin, and

D) To give us a life of grace in the present and glory in the future.

IV. **Mansuetus** (meek): Which deals with the manner of His coming—
His meekness is shown in four ways:

A) In His way of life

B) In His correction of others

C) In His gracious acceptance of men (not only the just, but also sinners)

D) In His passion (to which He was led as a lamb)

Sermon 6: *Celum et terra transibunt* (summary only) (Sermon on the First Sunday of Advent)

Thema:

Celum et terra transibunt [verba autem mea non transibunt]. (Luke 21:22, Mark 13:31, Matt 24:35)
Heaven and earth will pass away [but my words will not pass away].

Division of the Thema:

Our most providential and meek Savior commended these words, like a most merciful shepherd out of care for his sheep's salvation in faith, to his disciples and in them to all believers for serious attention to the Last Judgment, without mentioning the term, because it is clear. (1) By the noun "**heaven**," the marvelous loftiness of the heavenly man is mentioned, and (2) by the noun "**earth**," the deserved lowliness of the worldly person is mentioned, and (3) by the verb "**will pass**," he carefully refers to a distinctive quality of each.

Analytical Outline:

I. *Caelum* (Heaven): "Heaven" describes the marvelous loftiness and the worthy eminence of the heavenly man, which is signified by the word "heaven" for four reasons:

A) The heavens are of a great brightness—
thus, a just man ought to be full of light by heavenly wisdom,

B) The heavens have a splendid appearance—
thus, the just man ought to be like a circle by a wide mercy or like an orbit by a broad devotion and perfect love,

C) The heavens set in motion—
thus, the just man ought to be moved always by a spiritual carefulness, and

D) The heavens are high in location—
thus, the just man ought to excel in holiness by eminence.

II. *Terra* (Earth): The worldly man is absolutely not comparable to the heavenly man; he is compared to earth as follows:

A) On the basis of his capacity of understanding ("The earth was void and empty"),

B) On the basis of the weakness of avarice ("Taste the things above, not those of the earth"),

C) On the basis of the aridity of wickedness ("And God called the arid land 'earth'"), and

D) On the basis of the immutability of the soul, or of the life, or opinion ("The earth truly stands forever").

III. **Transibunt** (Will Pass Away): Now that the most deserved disdain toward the worldly man and the marvelous loftiness of the just have been shown, the quality of the way of life of each of them must be distinguished, and "passing" (*transibunt*) is said of the just in a different way from the unjust:

A) The just man "passes":

   1. From sin to justice,
   2. From virtue to greater virtue, and
   3. From labor in the present life to eternal refreshment.

B) The unjust man "passes":

   1. From innocence to guilt,
   2. From guilt into greater guilt, and
   3. From guilt into eternal punishment.

SERMON 7: *ECCE EGO MITTO* (FRAGMENT ONLY) (SERMON ON THE SECOND SUNDAY OF ADVENT)

Thema:

Ecce ego mitto angelum meum ante faciem tuam. (Matt 11:10)
Behold I send my angel before your face.

Division of the Thema:

These words are taken from the last chapter of Malachi (3:1). In these words three aspects of the gracious arrival of the Savior are described: (1) the marvelous estimation of God the Father ["**Behold, I send**"], (2) the obliging ardor of the precursor ["**my angel**"], and (3) the marvelous kindness of the Savior ["**before your face**"].

[Editor's Note: Unfortunately, we do not presently have anything more than the introductory section of this sermon—the part *before* Thomas would have begun developing (or "dilating") each of the three elements of his opening *divisio*. What remain extant are merely some cursory comments about angels "who were sent to us in the name of God, in order to prepare the ways that lead to the heavenly dwelling places":

A) Because they disclose the secrets of the decrees of the divine will,

B) In order to fulfill their duty concerning the divine things coming down from heaven, and

C) In order to render examples and proofs of spiritual perfection.

Given the opening *divisio*, the structure presumably would have followed the outline given below. But until and unless we discover the full sermon, we do not know how Thomas would have developed it.]

Analytical Outline:

Three aspects of the gracious arrival of the Savior:

I. *Ecce ego mitto* (Behold I send): the marvelous estimation of God the Father

II. *Angelum meum* (my angel): the obliging ardor of the precursor

III. *Ante faciem tuam* (before your face): the marvelous kindness of the Savior

SERMON 8: *PUER JESUS* (WITH *COLLATIO*) (SERMON ON THE FIRST SUNDAY AFTER EPIPHANY)

Thema:
Puer Iesus proficiebat etate et sapiencia et gracia apud Deum et homines. (Luke 2:52)
The boy Jesus advanced in age and wisdom and grace before God and men.

Division of the Thema:
If we want to consider these words carefully, we will find in them four progresses of Christ: namely, (1) the progress of **age** in regard to the body, (2) the progress of **wisdom** in regard to the intellect, (3) the progress of **grace before God**, and (4) the progress also of **grace** in view of his living together **with men.**

Analytical Outline:
Preliminary consideration: We should be "amazed" regarding what is said of Jesus above that:

A) Eternity advances in age,

B) He who is the Truth advances in wisdom,

C) He who imparts grace advances in grace, and

D) The One who exceeds all people advances with people.

How, then, would Christ advance in these respects?

A) The eternal Son of God willed to become temporal, so that he could advance with age.

B, C, and D) Christ took on the full human nature. But from the beginning of his conception, his most blessed soul was full of every grace and truth. So we must say:

1. That he advances in wisdom, not only in acquiring a greater wisdom, but also when the wisdom in him is more evident;
2. That if he had shown his wisdom when he was seven years old, people could have doubted the truth of the assumed nature;

247

3. That Christ wanted to be similar to others, so he emptied himself, being made in the likeness of men, making himself little by taking on our littleness;

4. That at the time when a sign of wisdom normally appears for the first time in a human being, Christ manifested his wisdom for the first time, thus little by little; and

5. That he did not will to show his full wisdom so that:
   a) the truth of the human nature in him would be acknowledged, and
   b) we might have an example of advancing wisdom.

Christ's fourfold progress:

I. **Age** in regard to the body—
   If someone does not advance through a progress of the mind together with a progress of the body, four improper things would follow; it would be:

A) Monstrous:

   1. Imagine a body composed of various members that grows in one member but not others.
   2. Man is composed of body and soul: both must advance in concert.
   3. If only the body grows, then all attention will be given to it.

B) Damaging:

   1. Loss of Time: Someone who had time to acquire a great thing but wasted it doing nothing would consider this a great damage.
   2. Solomon says (Prov 5:9–10), "that you may not give your honor to others and your years to the cruel one; that foreigners may not take their fill of your strength, and that your labors may not be in a stranger's house":
      a) "That you may not give your honor to others":
         i. Honor is given when a man triumphs over his enemies.
         ii. Such honor is given to you if you triumph over the world.

iii. But when you give your natural strength for service to the devil, then you give your honor to a stranger.

b) "That you may not give your years to the cruel one": he is cruel because no matter how well you serve him, he will give you no rest.

c) "That your labors may not be in a stranger's house":

    i. If you are converted to the Lord, your good works will be in the Lord's house.

    ii. If not, your good works will be in a stranger's house.

C) Burdensome:

1. Doing something is easy for someone if he is accustomed to it from his youth, but difficult if he does not.

2. If you accustom yourself to doing your will and live in sins, either you despair about eternal life or you preserve yourself with great labor.

D) Dangerous:

1. The Lord demands from all people an account for how they spent their time.

2. If they have not spent their time well, they will be condemned.

[Editor's Note: So, the first point is that we must grow in mind as we grow in age. But how does a human being grow in mind? This means to grow "in wisdom and grace." And yet Thomas treats grace next because "the beginning of wisdom is fear of the Lord" (Sir 1.14).]

II. Grace—

Grace is something hidden because it is in the soul. It is known through its effects. Among all the effects, none is as manifest as peace. Peace is associated with grace. True peace is known by four characteristics:

A) High: "They went up into Jerusalem."

1. When the flesh consents with the spirit (not vice versa)

    2. Attained by means of "wearing out the flesh" and not indulging it

B) Customary: "[They went up to Jerusalem] according to custom for the feast day."

    1. Some practice abstinence when they want to bring about peace of the spirit with the flesh, but they do not comply with what is customary, preferring to distinguish themselves from others.

    2. Do not distinguish yourself, because God really seems to abhor attracting attention to yourself.

C) Persevering and Constant: "When the feast days were over, Jesus remained in the Temple"

    1. It is not enough that someone would not sin.

    2. If you have accustomed yourself to doing good, you ought not to abandon the good works.

D) Cautious: "His parents did not know."

    1. If you want to make peace with someone else and subject him to you, watch out for his friends.

    2. Watch out for "friends of the flesh."

Collatio *(later that evening at vespers)*

III. **Wisdom** in regard to the intellect—

As the progress of grace is shown in peace, so the progress of wisdom is shown in contemplation. Let us see what Christ has done in the Temple, and on the basis of these, we can know whether someone advances. Four things are necessary for man to advance in wisdom:

A) To listen open-heartedly:

    1. His parents found Jesus listening: So too, if you love and listen, you will be wise.

    2. Jesus had been in the Temple constantly for three days: So too, listen with perseverance.

3. Jesus is found listening to many: So too listen not to one teacher only, but to many, for one man has not advanced in all fields (e.g., Gregory vs. Augustine vs. Ambrose).
4. Listening to many while standing in their midst (the position proper to a just judge): So too, in a just way, one ought to form a judgment about the truth of what he hears.

B) To inquire diligently:

1. From a *magister* or from people wiser than you, including texts of those from previous generations (e.g., Augustine and Ambrose)
2. In contemplation of created things (for God has poured out his wisdom over all his works)
3. By sharing with other people (no one can advance in knowledge so well as when he shares with others what he knows himself)

C) To answer prudently: Christ gave answers and "all were amazed at his prudence"; prudence is required in an answer in three ways:

1. In proportion with the one who gives the answer (do not try to answer beyond your knowledge and strength)
2. In proportion with the listener (do not respond foolishly to foolish questions)
3. In proportion with the question, not with elegant epithets of words, but to the point

D) To meditate attentively—as did the Virgin Mary, who "kept all these words in her heart." Consider three things concerning Mary's meditation:

1. It was fruitful through frequent meditation.
2. It was complete, because she kept *all* the words.
3. It was profound, because she kept them in her heart.

Sum: There is no doubt that someone who listens open-heartedly, responds prudently, inquires diligently, and meditates with attention will advance much in wisdom.

IV. **Living together with people—**
If you want to advance in living together with people, you should have four characteristics:

A) Devotion: Reach out to others (just as "Jesus came down to be with them").

B) Purity: Some reach out to others, but too much, even to the point of sinning (Jesus came down to Nazareth, which means "flower," which stands for purity).

C) Humility: Avoid pride and learn obedience (Christ went down to Nazareth where "he was subservient to them").

D) Discretion, especially in being obedient: We should not be obedient to a superior if it would lead us away from God ("Did you not know that I had to be in these places that are my Father's?").

SERMON 9: *EXIIT QUI SEMINAT* (WITH *COLLATIO*)
(SERMON ON *SEXAGESIMA* SUNDAY, THE PENULTIMATE SUNDAY
BEFORE LENT)

Thema:
Exiit qui seminat seminare semen suum. (Luke 8:5)
He who was sowing went out to sow his seed.

Division of the Thema:
There are three things that must be considered here: (1) first, what the
seed is; (2) second, who the sower is [and his three ways of "going out"];
and (3) third, what and of what nature the sowing is [namely, what hinders
the sowing, and what is the fruit of the sowing].

Analytical Outline:
Preface: Holy Mother Church is a vineyard and a field. The wine-grower is
Christ. The fruits of the field are good works. The Father has sown peace
from heaven; the Son, truth; and the Holy Spirit, love. The angels have
also sown because they have stood by others who were falling. The martyrs
have sown strength; the confessors, justice; and the virgins, temperance.

I.   *Semen suum*: What is the seed?—
    "The seed is the word of God." How do we know it is the seed of
    God?

    A) It is *from* Christ: Whatever pertains to the heavenly wisdom
      that is in the highest is a word of wisdom or a seed of God.

      1. Wisdom which is not from above:
        a) Earthly: totally occupied with acquiring earthly
          things
        b) Beastly: totally focused on pursuing the pleasure of
          the body
        c) Diabolic: totally focused on being proud
      2. The quality of wisdom that is "in the highest":
        a) Modest
        b) Peaceful
        c) Leads to rectitude of the virtues

B) It is *in* Christ:
1. The splendors of the saints are the radiance of the virtues.
2. Every radiance of the virtues is derived from the Son of God, as an example is from the exemplar.
3. So if someone came and confronted you with a doctrine whose exemplar is not in Christ, it is not a seed of God—for example:
   a) Jovian preached that being married must be regarded as equal to virginity, although Christ had a virginal mother and loved the virginal disciple (John) to the highest extent.
   b) Vigilantius preached that the state of the rich who give alms is equal to poverty, which is also not in Christ who became very poor for our sake.
4. Thoroughly examine the things Christ said and did (in hope of achieving eternal life):
   a) Some run to divine things and do not care about temporal things.
   b) Others proceed by their virtues: they practice them and praise what they cannot fulfill.
   c) A few murmur and are tormented by too much envy, seeking after things for themselves in the Church, and are heretics, or not only do not do good things, but even counteract the good things in others.

C) It leads *to* Christ:
1. When you hear God's words with your ears and you love them with your heart and actually fulfill them with works, then God's words were spoken to you.
2. You ought to imitate Jesus Christ, so that you may become like him.

II. *Exiit qui seminat*: Who is the sower (and what are his three ways of "going out": *exiit*)?

A) Christ, who went out from the Father into the world, is the sower.

B) Preachers too must "go out" in a twofold way (two out of three total: see note below in the *collatio* accompanying this sermon):

1. By leaving the state of guilt, because a preacher must not preach to others what he is not doing himself:

   a) But where should we go out to when we leave sin? To the Passion of Christ.

   b) When should we go out? "Early in the morning": Do not hesitate to be converted to the Lord.

2. By leaving the world (cupidity) and the desire for earthly things behind in order to "come into the land:" the land of vision or contemplation, which is characteristic of the religious life:

   —When should we come into that land? Early in the morning (i.e., in youth): for example, Benedict left his nurse for the hermitage; John the Baptist grew up in the desert; and Jesus stayed in the Temple at twelve years old.

   —Three things warn me that I should not leave the world in my youth:

   a) One must gradually come to perfection; and yet:

      i. There is no one who eagerly desires a certain state without eagerly desiring it in his youth.

      ii No matter how much a person makes progress, he always grows.

      iii. It is easy to do the things that have become a habit for us from our youth.

      iv. "Adolescence and pleasure are empty" (Eccl 11:10).

      v. The conclusion of the foolish is "Rejoice, young man, in your adolescence . . . walk in the ways of your heart and in the sight of your eyes."

      vi. The conclusion of the wise is "Do not go after your lusts; remember your Creator in your youth."

   b) "I do not know whether the call is from the Holy Spirit."

      i. The Spirit blows where He wills. Will you block His path?

  ii. Objection: "It is not through the Holy Spirit that boys leave the world behind because many boys are converted, yet do not persevere in religious life; but if it had been from God, they would have stayed in the order." Reply: "God's works are thoroughly corruptible; it also happens that someone receives the grace of entering religious life but does not receive the gift to persevere—but this does not alter the fact that it comes from God."

 c) "I am a boy, so I cannot carry arms"—the arms of religion:

  The arms of religious life are not the arms of Saul (observances of the Old Law), but the arms of David—that is, the arms of Christ, whose "yoke is sweet and burden light" (observances of the New Law and religious life).

Therefore, early in the morning we ought to leave the world behind and come to Christ.

But what will be our fruit? Attainment of the kingdom of heaven.

Collatio *(later that evening at vespers)*

[Editor's Note: Thomas mentions above the preacher's "twofold" way of "going out." When he makes this comment, he is only referring to the first two of three. He covered the first two ways of "going out" in the morning's sermon. He begins the evening vespers with the third way of "going out."]

 3. Third *exitus* of the preacher: From contemplation to preaching

  a) This going out is very similar to the Savior's going out from the secret dwelling place of the Father to the public area of what is visible.

  b) God says, "Let *us* go out": I by inspiring you, and you by preaching.

  c) When shall we go out? Early in the morning:

   i. Gregory: Boys converted in the first period of life:

   Let your hand not be inactive in the evening: boys as well as old men must preach.

ii. Objection: "You must not summon such people nor lead them to religious life, according
to what the Lord says: 'You have gone through
sea and dry land to make one proselyte'" [Matt
23:15]. Reply: making converts is good. What
follows? What is the meaning of "And you make
him a son of Gehenna, twice as bad as yourselves" [Matt 23:15]? They led others to sinning
by examples.

—Chrysostom: A discipline sins more careless-
ly when he sees a teacher sinning, and, just as a
preacher who gives an example of a bad life is to
be condemned, so is the one who gives an example of a good life to be praised.

—Jerome: These words [Matt 23:15] concern
the scribes and Pharisees who, being under the
Old Law, converted others to circumcision.

iii. Objection: "It is good for boys to preach, so
that they let go of the secular world and come
to Christ in religious life, but it is not good to
attract or allure them with temporal benefits,
because Scripture says that the Jews are not
attracted to the faith by threats, terrors, and
benefits. But Scripture does not say that they
cannot be allured by flattery." Reply: Under the
Old Covenant, God promised temporal things,
promises that we make to little children who are
allured by benefits. But there were others who
clung to God because of God. Likewise, under
the New Covenant there, some perfect people
do not want to be allured by temporal things.
Others are imperfect men who are allured also
by temporal things. Therefore, regulations are
given in the Church so that they would be led by
the hand to come to the liturgy of the hours, not
that they go and pray because of these temporal
things, but that they become more kind-hearted
and lead a happier life.

iv. Objection: "It is allowed to attract boys to religious life, but not to let them take vows because

many who had taken vows returned into the world." Reply: Will the unbelief of those make the faith empty? The kingdom of heaven is like a dragnet thrown in the sea and gathering fish of every kind.

III. *Seminare*: What and of What Nature the Sowing Is (what hinders the sowing and the fruit of the sowing):

A) Threefold hindrance for the sowing on behalf of those for whom the seed is sown:

1. "The road where the seed does not bear fruit": emptiness of the affection; hearing the words but not doing them—twofold danger:
   a) trampled upon (by the bad examples of companions)
   b) eaten by the birds (by the evil plans of demons and so the fruit is lost)
2. "upon rock": hardness of heart
3. "in the thorns": cupidity

B) Fruits—a triple crop:
1. Thirty-fold (3 x 10 = 30): Faith in the Trinity and observance of the Ten Commandments are necessary for salvation (although there are alternate interpretations).
2. Sixty-fold (6 x 10): State of perfection comes by way of penitence, and the six counsels must be added to the Ten Commandments to produce a sixty-fold crop.
   —Counsels are not given in order to hinder the Commandments; counsels are safeguards to make sure that the Commandments are kept.
3. Hundred-fold: State of perfection comes by way of innocence (Isaac sowed and found a hundred-fold).
   —Everyone who left behind father or mother and others will receive a hundred-fold—that is, a pile of spiritual goods—and in the future he will possess eternal life.

SERMON 10: *PETITE ET ACCIPIETIS* (NOT ATTRIBUTABLE TO AQUINAS)

Thema:
Petite et accipietis ut gaudium vestrum sit plenum. (John 16:24)
Ask and you will receive, so that your joy may be complete.

Division of the Thema:
He touches in these words upon three things: (1) first, the Lord invites us to pray: **"Ask"**; (2) second, he assures us about our obtaining: "**and you will receive**"; and (3) third, so that we may rightly ask, he underlines what is necessary for us to have, when he adds: "**So that your joy may be complete.**" [The exegesis never gets beyond "Ask," after which it goes off on a tangent about various "hindrances" to prayer. Since Fr. Bataillon judged that this sermon could not be attributed to Aquinas, and since the "dilation" is incomplete, I have chosen not to provide an analytical outline.]

Sermon 11: *Emitte Spiritum* (with *Collatio*) (Sermon on Pentecost)

Thema:

Emitte Spiritum tuum et creabuntur et renouabis faciem terre. (Ps 104:30) Send forth your Spirit and they shall be created, and you will renew the face of the earth.

Division of the Thema:

We can consider four things in these words: namely, (1) the property of the Holy Spirit, (2) his mission, (3) the strength of the One sent, and (4) the receptive *materia* of this strength. For it says: "**Send out**" (the mission); "**your Spirit**" (the Person sent); "**and they will be created, and you will renew**" (the effect of the One sent); "**the face of the earth**" (the receptive *materia* of this effect).

I. *Spiritum tuum* (your Spirit): the property of the Holy Spirit (origin of living, being, and moving)—
"Spirit" seems to imply four things:

    A) Fineness of substance

    B) Perfection of life

    C) Incitement of a movement

    D) Hidden origin

"Let us inquire with regard to these four about the properties of the Holy Spirit, in reverse order."—

    D) Hidden origin:

       1. God did not make the world because he wanted to gain something.
       2. Rather, he created out of his loving will.
       3. The Spirit is the principle of being in all things.
       4. Thus, the Spirit had a hidden origin, the property of which is love.

C) Incitement of movement:

1. Love is the first movement of the will.
2. The principle of the movement of all things is life. Hence, the Holy Spirit is life, since he is the principle of movement of all things. He is the Giver of life. In him, we live and move and have our being.

[Editor's Note: Although Thomas had said above that he would consider the items in the list above in reverse order, he actually considers A before B. So we next get a consideration of the Spirit's "fineness" (*subtilitas*).]

A) Fineness of substance:

1. The Holy Spirit is the love of God and of the One who loves God; the Spirit is the love through which God loves God and the Father loves the Son.
2. The Spirit is God's Wisdom, which makes people understand.
3. The Spirit is love, but not for lower things. When love is connected with the highest things, it is pure and called "holy" love (thus, "holy" Spirit).
   a) Love of God, but also of neighbor
   b) Pure and holy, not deceitful
   c) Fine, because he makes a person draw back from coarse things and cling to God

B) Perfection of life: The Spirit not only gives us what we are (that we are, live, and move), but even more, makes us holy:

1. He refines them and makes them despise temporal things.
2. He bestows spiritual life.
3. He moves those whom he sanctifies through his incitement to do good.
4. He leads us back to the hidden origin, that we may be united with God.

II. *Emitte* (Send forth): the mission of the Holy Spirit— The Holy Spirit is sent:

A) Without necessity on his part—
The reason for his mission is our need:

1. Partly because of the dignity of our human nature (stretching out to God); partly because of the defect of it (clinging to honors, esteem in this world)
2. Things moved to a natural end are moved by something in nature, but things moved to a supernatural end—namely, the enjoyment of God—must have a supernatural mover
   a) Knowledge: "Eye has not seen and ear has not heard"; it transcends human knowledge.
   b) Love: "Nor did it come up in the heart of man" (what God has prepared for those who love him); it even exceeds the human desire.

B) Without change in Him—

1. When a messenger is sent from place to place, there is a change. But the Holy Spirit is sent without a change of place, since he is the true God and unchangeable.
2. He draws us to himself and is "sent" in the way we say that the sun is sent to someone when that person stands in the sunlight.
3. These missions spread throughout all nations and enter holy souls.
4. When the fullness of time had come, the Son of God was sent into the flesh, and thus it was right that the Holy Spirit would also be sent visibly, but not, however, that he would be received in the unity of a person as the Son in human nature.

C) Without subjection—

1. Slaves and servants are sent by their masters, since they are subjected to them; so too, some heretics believed that the Son and the Holy Spirit would be lesser than the Father since they are sent by the Father.
2. The Spirit sets people free.
3. The Spirit blows where he wills.

4. The term "being sent" is used because the Father is the originator:
   a) We find places where it says that the Holy Spirit is sent by the Father, while elsewhere it says that he is sent by the Son.
   b) The Greeks oppose strongly in this matter, but they argue in an unrefined way. For, where the Son speaks about the mission of the Holy Spirit, he connects the Son with the Father or the Father with the Son. Thus, the origination of the source comes from the Father.

D) Without separation—

1. The Spirit of unity is opposed to separation.
2. The Holy Spirit gathers together.
3. "That they may be one," in us, through the unity of the Holy Spirit, "just as we, too, are one." (John 17:22)
4. This union is begun in our time through grace and will be completed in the future through glory.

Collatio *(later that evening at vespers)*

III. *Et creabuntur et renovabis*: the twofold effects of the Holy Spirit, creation *(creabuntur)* and renewal *(renovabis)*:

A) Creation—
The "new creation": God *created* so that all things would exist in "the existence of nature"; and he willed to *re-create* them so that they would be in "the existence of grace." This re-creation is an effect of the Holy Spirit, and it consists in phases:

1. Grace of charity:
   a) When people are brought into existence, the first thing they obtain is that they live. This is so also when we are in grace, and it is love *(caritas)* that makes a man live when he is in grace.
   b) Love gives life to the soul. For, just as the body lives through the soul, so the soul lives through God, and God dwells in us through love.

    c) The day's Gospel: If someone loves me, then he will keep my word, and my Father will love him, and we will come, and we will make our dwelling in him.

    d) Gregory: Proof of love is the production of the work. You cannot fulfill the commandments by your own strength, but you can do so by means of the grace of God.

    e) This love (*caritas*) is from the Holy Spirit: "the love of God is spread in our hearts through the Holy Spirit."

2. Wisdom of knowledge:

    a) When people are made more loving, they get to know the will of God better. God reveals his secrets to his friends.

    b) The Holy Spirit will teach you everything, both outwardly and inwardly, by grace.

    c) He does not only teach; he also reminds us. The one who makes you believe and puts into practice what you hear is the one who reminds you. The Holy Spirit bends the heart so that it agrees and follows what it hears.

3. Peaceful harmony:

James 3:17: "The wisdom that is from above is chaste, peace-making, modest, gentle."

[Editor's Note: Thomas will dilate below on only the first two of these four adjectives: "chaste" and "peace-making." His discussion of "peace" causes him to go off into a different direction and dilate instead (but in a related vein) on a famous definition of peace by St. Augustine. Hence the secondary dilation builds upon the first.]

    a) "Chaste": earthly wisdom is not chaste, for it corrupts the affection through love of earthly things.

    b) "Peace-making": earthly wisdom makes people divided and full of strife, whereas the wisdom from above attracts us to God. Quarrels arise from three things:

        i. When someone is not modest

        ii. When someone is stubborn in their manner of thinking. Wisdom from above is "amenable"

   iii. The wisdom of the world does not allow its wise to agree with others, whereas this wisdom is agreeing with good people, hence "peace-making"

  c) The Holy Spirit's twofold peace:

   i. One is in the present, in which we live peacefully, although in such a way that we will still struggle against vices.

   ii. The other is the peace that we will have in the future, one without struggle.

  d) Some want peace in order to enjoy goods. But what is true peace? Augustine says, "Peace is security of mind, quietness of soul, simplicity of heart, a bond of love and the company of love." True peace, thus, is threefold:

   i. In relation to yourself—which requires:

    α) Your reason not be infected by errors or obscured by passions ("security of mind")

    β) Quietness in one's affection ("quietness of soul")

    γ) Simplicity in one's intention ("simplicity of heart")

   ii. In relation to your neighbor ("bond of love")

   iii. In relation to God ("the company of love")

  e) Hence, peace is certainly necessary for us: "No one can have peace with Christ who is at odds with a Christian."

 4. Constancy of strength (*firmitas*)

B) Renewal (in accordance with four things)—

 1. Cleansing grace: Renewal (which is from the Spirit) is liberation from sin.

 2. Progressing justice: A person is renewed when he is prepared to struggle against vices and when he will not cease to run on the way of God's commandments. (Who causes them to run? The Holy Spirit.)

 3. Illuminating wisdom: Someone who puts on a new garment by means of an exterior cleanness renews the mind internally through grace. Take off the old man (that is, the habit of the sinners with their deeds) and clothe

yourselves with the habit of virtue, which is not without deeds, with "the new man," with a rational mind. (From where is this wisdom? The Holy Spirit.)

4. Glory that makes complete: The body will be renewed, away from the old punishment and the old guilt (What is the source? The Holy Spirit, who leads us to the heavenly inheritance.)

IV. *Faciem terrae* (the face of the earth): whom or what it befits to receive these effects?

A) The whole world, which once was full of idolatry, is the "face of the earth."

B) "The face of the earth" is also the human mind. For, just as we see with our face in a corporeal way, so we see with the mind in a spiritual way. To receive this renewal, this "face" ought to have four characteristics:

1. Clean:
   a) "When you fast, anoint your head and wash your face"—with tears of a moved heart—and then you will be able to receive the renewal of the Holy Spirit.
   b) Create a clean heart in me, God.
2. Unveiled or uncovered:
   a) Some have the face of their mind covered by a mist of ignorance.
   b) Yet, we behold the glory of God with an unveiled face—meaning, free from attraction to earthly things.
3. Directed:
   a) Toward God:
      i. Through an upright intention
      ii. Through obedience
   b) Toward neighbor: "Do not turn away your face from your neighbor, for then, likewise, the face of the Lord will not be turned away from you." ("Therefore the apostles received the Holy Spirit while they were together."—Recall, it is the Feast of Pentecost.)
4. Stable and firm (e.g., "set your face"); persevering

SERMON 12: *SERAPHIM STABANT* (SERMON ON THE FEAST OF THE TRINITY)

Thema:

Seraphim stabant super illud; sex ale uni et sex ale alteri; duabus uelabant faciem eius et duabus uelabant pedes eius et duabus uolabant, et clamabant alter ad alterum et diceban: 'Sanctus, sanctus, sanctus Dominus Deus exercituum, et plena est omnis terra gloria eius.' (Isa 6:2–3)
The seraphim stood over him; the one had six wings and the other had six; with two they covered his face, and with two they covered his feet, and with two they flew; and they cried one to another saying: 'Holy, holy, holy Lord God of hosts; all the earth is full of His glory.'

Division of the Thema:

And thus, the excellent authority of the ones who reveal and of the things that are revealed was fitting, especially with regard to the things that pertain to the Holy Trinity.

Now the Prophet makes the authority of those who reveal the mystery of the Holy Trinity known for our day and age based on three things: (1) their task ["**Seraphim**"—that is, "those who glow and set on fire"], (2) their dignity ["**above it**"], and (3) their unanimity ["**cried to one another**"].

[Further along in the sermon] Now it remains to look at what they revealed when they said: "Holy, holy, holy. . ." In these words they make known three things to us: first, the mystery of the sacred Trinity ["**Holy, holy, holy**"]; second, that the image of the Trinity itself is impressed upon rational creatures ["**Lord God of Hosts**"]; third, that a trace of the same Trinity is reflected in all other creatures ["**all the earth is full of His glory**"].

Part 1: The authority of those who reveal the mystery of the Holy Trinity

I. *Seraphim*—their task:

A) "those who glow with fire": the apostles (Editor's Note: Pentecost was a week earlier)

B) The Son, who comes from the Father makes the Father known, therefore it was becoming that the mystery of the

Trinity was revealed to us by seraphim, that is, through the apostles, who were taught by the Son and set on fire by the Holy Spirit.

II. *Super illud* (above it)—their dignity

A) "Above it" (that is, above the Temple)

B) "With two [wings] they covered their head, and with two they covered their feet, and flew with two wings":

1. It is granted to the apostles to reveal some things and to keep other things hidden from the people.
2. They flew by teaching, but by hiding, they covered the head, since the first principle of all things itself cannot be examined, and since the very principle is also the end, they covered their feet as well.
3. The things in the middle were not covered because the things that are from the beginning to the end—namely the divine effects—are manifest to us.

III. *Clamabant alter ad alterum* (cried out to one another)—the source of the apostles' authority (their unanimity)

Part 2: What they revealed when they said, "Holy, holy, holy . . ."

I. *Sanctus, sanctus, sanctus* (Holy, holy, holy): the mystery of the sacred Trinity—
As Dionysius says, no way is as successful for getting to know God as the way of removal (*via remotionis*, part of the *via negativa*, saying what God is not): this way of removal is understood by the term "holiness," for "holy" is the same as what is pure and "pure" is what is separated from other things. We find in creatures three most excellent things (but in each case, no one can achieve the purity the way these are in God):

A) Essence—
In the essences of created things, we find a threefold defect that keeps them completely remote from God:

1. The weakness of corruption
2. The defect of composition
3. The defect of mutability

Hence God is incorruptible, simple, and immovable. Three are names given in order to exclude the defects mentioned:

1. Power (excludes weakness)
2. Unity (excludes composition)
3. Eternity (excludes mutability)

B) Knowledge—
In creatures, we find a threefold defect in knowledge:

1. Defect of the knowledge of material and singular things,
2. Defect of knowledge through appearances, and
3. Defect of knowledge insofar as it is diminished; that is, they cannot see God in his essence.

But above the knowledge of these three is the knowledge of the Word of God, which contains all things, knows all things (Wis 1:7). (Hence, the Arians are foolish because, if they had been right, God would not have known himself.) And since the Word of God is free of these defects, three things are attributable to him:

1. Wisdom: to exclude singular knowledge
2. Beauty, splendor: to exclude obscure knowledge
3. Equality: to exclude diminishment

C) Affection—
There is a similar threefold defect of holiness:
1. When our affection is deprived
2. When our affections are held back and closed, not sharing their goods because they love themselves
3. When our affection is disquieted, not at peace in view of the ultimate end ("Our hearts are restless until they rest in Thee.")

Holy affection is above these:

1. Not deprived, for it loves all things that are
2. Not closed, filling all with goodness
3. Not disquieted, since it is the love of the ultimate end, which loves itself and all things because of itself

Therefore three things are attributed to him:

1. Union (so that it may be clear that he is not lacking anything, for deprived love causes discord but the Holy Spirit is the One who binds together.)
2. Goodness: so that it may be clear that the Holy Spirit is not closed
3. Use: so that it may be clear that he is peaceful and that he concerns the end

Question: But are these three holinesses ("Holy, holy, holy…")? No. For in us, being, willing, and understanding are three different things; thus, the holiness of being is different from the holiness of will and of understanding. But in God, being, understanding, and willing are the same, and so the holiness of these three is the same. But it is repeated three times not in order to show a triple holiness, but rather the holiness of three.

II. **Dominus Deus exercituum** (Lord God of hosts)—the image of the Trinity impressed upon rational creatures

A) "Lord": God has special providence with regard to them, by punishing, instructing, and by rewarding (thus "Lord")

B) "God": God is their end and their reward (thus "God")

C) "Of Hosts": in respect of freedom (for they are soldiers)

III. **Plena est omnis terra gloria eius** (full is the whole earth with your glory)—a trace of the same Trinity reflected in all other creatures

A) We find in the creation account:

1. The power of God, so that the Father may be recognized
2. The art of God, who forms all things so that the Son may be recognized

   3. The good pleasure of God, who approves so that the Holy Spirit may be recognized

B) The properties of creatures show a trace of the three Persons, for every creature:

   1. Subsists through the power of the Father
   2. Has an appearance because it is formed by the Word of God
   3. Is ordered through the love of the Holy Spirit towards its end

Sermon 13: *Homo quidam fecit cenam magnam* (with *collatio*) (Sermon on the Second Sunday after the Feast of the Trinity)

Thema:

Homo quidam fecit cenam magnam et vocavit multos. (Luke 14:16)
A certain man made a great supper and invited many.

Division of the Thema:

Just as the body cannot be maintained without physical refreshment, so also the soul is in need of spiritual refreshment for its maintenance. . . . Concerning this spiritual refreshment, the Lord makes a comparison in today's Gospel. We can see two things: first, the preparation of this refreshment, where he says "**A certain man made a great dinner**"; second [in the *collatio*], the announcement of the feast when it was prepared, where it says, "**and he invited many.**"

Analytical Outline:

I.   *Homo quidam fecit cenam magnam* (A certain man made a great dinner)—the preparation of the refreshment; regarding which there are three aspects to be considered: First, the man who made the dinner; second, the kind of dinner it is; and third, how it is great.

[Editor's Note: Notice, in what follows, that after discussing who the "certain man" (*homo quidem*) is who made the dinner (namely, Christ), Thomas will discuss "what kind of dinner it is" and "how great it is" together. Thus, I have listed both in the outline below under "B" (*fecit cenam magnam*) rather than trying to make two categories, one for "he made a dinner" (*fecit cenam*) and another for "great" (*magnam*), as Thomas's threefold division might suggest. The reader will find that, for each of the three types of "refreshment" provided by the dinner, Thomas offers three reasons for its greatness.]

    A) Who the man is who made the dinner (*Homo quidam*: "a certain man")

        1. The man is the Son of God, who is truly a man in view of his assumed human nature,

        2. It indicates a "certain" man, as if to say some particular

things are in him that are not in others; he is distinct, since he has:

a) The fullness of divinity
b) The fullness of truth
c) The fullness of grace
[Editor's Note: These three will show up in reverse order below under the threefold "refreshment."]

B) What kind of dinner it is and its greatness (*fecit cenam magnam*: "he made a great dinner")—Christ (who is "the certain man") has made a triple refreshment:

1. Sacramental refreshment (since Christ has the fullness of grace)
   a) Early meal: sacramental refreshment in the Old Testament (according to the First Law)
   b) Dinner: sacramental refreshment in the New Testament (Last Supper)
   c) The dinner is called "great" because of:
      i. The magnificent provision—by reason of:
         α) The place where it comes from: bread from heaven
         β) The dignity of the ones who eat it: the angels are refreshed by the Word of God (now set before you)
      ii. The greatness of the delight in taste—delight is caused by three things:
         α) Memory of things past: calling to mind that man is redeemed by the blood of Christ
         β) Hope of future things: hope of future happiness
         γ) Experience of things present: the body of Christ and the unity of the Church
      iii. The greatness of the effect: virtue, for it unites us with God and makes us live in God
2. Intellectual Refreshment (since Christ has the fullness of truth)
   a) Early meal: teaching of the philosophers, who gather truths from creation
   b) Dinner: refreshment of the Sacred Scripture

    c) The dinner is called "great" because of:

        i. The magnificent provision, for it is taken from the best things, which exceed every sense

        ii. The greatness of delight in taste, whose sweetness is above that of every other science, for a consideration is called delightful in two ways:

            α) Because of the consideration itself (e.g., a demonstration concerning a triangle is delightful in itself, but "no one really cares about a triangle")

            β) Because of the thing considered (when, for example it is loved, which is the case with Sacred Scripture, since in it there is not only delight about getting to know the truth, but even concerning beloved things)

        iii. The greatness of effect: it gives life, brings people to faith, and incites them to love

    3. Refreshment for our affection (since Christ has the fullness of divinity)

      a) Early meal: grace in the present

      b) Dinner: glory in the future

      c) The dinner is called "great" because of:

        i. The magnificent provision: that man would sit at the table of God, enjoying God himself

        ii. The greatness of delight in taste: something is delightful insofar as it is good; but if things that participate in the good are delightful, how much more delight is caused by infinite goodness

        iii. The greatness of effect: the eternity of life

Collatio *(later that evening at vespers)*

"Today we have spoken about the preparation of this dinner; now we must speak about its announcement. For the 'certain man' certainly has not prepared the dinner for no one to sit at the table, but in order to make it known to others. See that this dinner is not made known to anyone but to one who is called to it."

II. *Vocauit multos* (he called many)—

Section 1: Two kinds of calling:

A) Interior:

1. The calling through which the Lord addresses man internally is never in vain.
2. The grace infused in human hearts by divine abundance is not repelled by any hard heart.

B) From the Outside (e.g., from an angel or a human being):

1. Not as effective as the one that is directly from God; thus, although he "called many," he sent his servant to say to the ones who were invited, "Come!"
2. But who is the servant? The Apostle Paul and the other preachers, prelates, and teachers are the servants; all such people who remind us of the good that God has done for us are called servants of God.

Section 2: Those who are called and how they are called:

A) Who are called?

1. Those who were invited to the dinner (who received the privilege of a divine office) but did not come because of a triple hindrance (related to loving the world more than God):
   a) Pride ("I have bought a house and I need to see it"): Often those who are proud of the gifts given to them by God think of the gifts, not of the One from whom the gifts came.
   b) Concupiscence of the eye ("I have bought five yoke of oxen"): the five senses which completely enslave someone to sensory things:
      i. Some have obtained the grace of eloquence or the gift of wisdom, with which they ought to serve God, but turn them around and use them for concupiscence and the acquisition of earthly things.

ii. Not only cupidity but also curiosity is repudiat-
ed. Some are very curious about external things
about what others do, so that they try to find
out what others do and neglect their own deeds.

c) Concupiscence of the flesh ("I have married a wife
and therefore cannot come to the dinner"):

    i. Some turn themselves to pleasures when they
have been exalted through the gifts of God.

    ii. There is a difference between the sin of pride
and of cupidity (first two above), on the one
hand, and lustfulness, on the other.

    iii. For, the proud and the ones who desire to com-
mit a sin intentionally and do not want to come
to the dinner.

    iv. But those who sin through the sin of the flesh
sin because of weakness and incapability.

2. Others called were downtrodden citizens ("Go out into
the streets and call the weak, the blind, and the lame"):

a) Those who are poor in temporal things but rich in
spiritual things are chosen.

b) Concerning those who are rich in temporal things
but poor in spiritual things, they fail in:

    i. Knowledge ("blind"):

      α) Blinded by sin, they suffer a defect of
knowledge because they disdain what is
good and choose what is evil.

      β) Those who love pleasures more than God
are swollen and blind.

      γ) Because of this blindness, rich people de-
spise divine things and would rather have
temporal things.

    ii. Strength of mind and virtue through sin ("the
weak")

    iii. Rectitude ("the lame"): that is, in their inten-
tion. These are the lame; from the outside they
seem to follow the Lord, but if anyone sees their
intention, it becomes clear they are lame.

3. Others who were strangers—(When the servant had led
those people in, he said to his lord, "There is still room,"
by which predestination is indicated, for not only the

great and the faithful are called. Therefore, the Lord says: "I have other sheep, which are not from this flock, and I must lead those to me, and it will be one flock, one shepherd" (John 10:16). The people who are outside signify the unbelievers, among whom there is a triple distinction ("And the master said to the servant, 'Go out to the highways and hedges ["exi in vias et sepes"] and compel people to come in, that my house may be filled.'"):

a) Those in the dark roads (*viis tenebrosis*) are the Gentiles and pagans who do not share in the faith at all.
b) Those in the scattered roads (*vias dissipatas*) are the Jews, who share something with us—namely the sacred doctrine of the Old Testament.
c) Those in the hedges (*in sepibus*) are the heretics because hedges divide and their thorns sting.

B) How are they called?
There is a triple manner of calling:

1. The first group is called by a simple summons (the ones invited).
2. The second group must be led inside (the poor and downtrodden).
   —Some have taken up the plan to come to God in baptism; they have renounced the devil, but now they need someone to instruct them and lead them in and make them acquainted with the King.
3. The third group (the unbelievers and heretics) must be compelled in two ways:
   a) By the evidence of miracles
   b) By means of punishment

Those who were in the roads and hedges (those in the second and third groups) did not excuse themselves; only those who were invited did. In this is signified that cold sinners are converted more quickly than ones who stray from the way on which they were going.

Sermon 14: *Attendite a falsis prophetis* (with *Collatio*) (Sermon on the third Sunday after the Feast of Peter and Paul; 14 July 1269)

Thema:

Attendite a falsis prophetis qui ueniunt ad uos in uestimentis ouium, intrinsecus autem sunt lupi rapaces ; a fructibus eorum cognoscetis eos. (Matt 7:15) Beware of false prophets who come to you in sheep's clothing; inside they are ravenous wolves: by their fruits shall you know them.

Division of the Thema:

The Lord advises us in the words above to be careful against Satan's servants. In these words he teaches us four things: (1) First, he teaches of what kind the enemies are, where he says: "**Beware of the false prophets.**" (2) Second, he teaches what ambushes they make, where he says: "**They come to you in sheep's clothes.**" (3) The third thing is that it threatens to damage us, where he says: "**Inside they are ravenous wolves.**" (4) Fourth, he teaches how to recognize them, where he says: "**By their fruits you will know them.**" These enemies are false prophets, and they are very dangerous, and therefore we must watch out for them, for they are as dangerous for us as good angels are necessary and useful.

Analytical Outline:

I. *Attendite a falsis prophetis* (Beware of the false prophets)— What kind of enemies they are:

    A) Definition of a prophet—four things can identify a prophet:

        1. Divine revelation

        2. Understanding: Sometimes things are divinely revealed to a person but he does not understand it, for example, Nebuchadnezzar, Pharaoh; interpretation is required to understand the visions.

        3. That the things revealed and that he understands are made known by him to others: For, if a person had a revelation and understood it but kept it to himself, it would be of no avail.

        4. The working of miracles: Some things that are revealed and made known from God are above human perception. But people do not believe unless things are proven, and this proof is the working of miracles.

Thus:

1. At times, someone who receives a divine revelation is called a prophet.
2. Yet, sometimes we call someone a prophet not because he has received a divine revelation, but because it is given to him to understand the things revealed.
3. Sometimes we call people prophets who recite the revealed things.
4. Sometimes those who work miracles are called prophets.

How is "prophet" conceived here and now? Chrysostom says that those who prophesy about Christ are not called prophets now, but rather those who interpret a prophecy about Christ, since no one can interpret the prophetic meanings unless through the Holy Spirit.

B) Why someone is a *false* prophet—four ways a prophet can be false:

1. Falseness of the teaching—prophets must teach truth, not false and stupid things, such as:
   a) Saying things merely to please people (not revealing iniquity or calling people to repentance)
   b) Calling "good" what is evil and "evil" what is good
   c) Having false assumptions and making false statements
   d) Profane language and a worldly life (e.g., if someone says it is better to fast without a vow than with a vow)
2. Falseness of the inspiration—true inspiration is always from God; false inspiration is from either:
   a) The devil
   b) Their own spirit (rather than God's), for example:
      i. Those who speak according to Platonic ways of thinking, which cannot arrive at truth
      ii. Those who say that the world is eternal
      iii. Those who study philosophy and say some things that are not true according to the faith (And when someone tells them that this is opposed to the faith, they answer that the Philosopher says this, but they themselves do not main-

tain this; yes, that they only repeat the words of the Philosopher. Such is a false prophet, or a false teaching, because causing doubt and not solving it is the same as giving way to it. It is like digging a pit and leaving it open for someone to fall into.)

    iv. "The scandal of the philosophers":

        α) There have been many philosophers, and they have said many things that pertain to the faith, and yet, you will scarcely find two of them who harmonize in one conclusion.

        β) Any philosopher who has said something that belongs to the truth has not said it without a mixture of falseness.

        γ) An old woman [instructed in the faith] knows more about these things that pertain to the faith than all philosophers heretofore. Pythagoras, for example, left everything to give himself over to the study of philosophy when he heard a *magister* disputing about the immortality of the soul. But which old woman nowadays would not know the soul is immortal? Faith is capable of much more than philosophy is.

3. Falseness of the intention—true intention is for the benefit of the people:

    a) For the sake of their advancement, to render them devout

    b) For the sake of exhortation, to render them ready and willing in good works

    c) For the sake of their consolation, to render them patient in adversities

    d) Example of falseness of intention: a bishop who takes up the task of governing and preaching not for the benefit of the people but for temporal gain or empty glory

4. Falseness of the life: teaching one thing but living another

Collatio *(later that evening at vespers)*

II. **Qui veniunt ad vos in vestimentis ovium** (who come to you in clothes of sheep)—What kind of ambushes they make (the hiding place of false prophets is hypocrisy):

A) The clothes of sheep: the sheep are Christians who obey Christ, having double garments:

1. Virtues of the soul
2. Good works

B) The clothing of Christ's sheep is fourfold (put on falsely by hypocrites):

1. Worship—hypocrites put on this garment for:
   a) Empty glory: praying out *in public* so that they may be seen:
      i. "In public" is not so much a place, as the soul: The one who has his soul not with the people, but with God, prays in a hidden place.
      ii. If someone prays alone in his room, but wants to be seen by the people, he prays in public.
      iii. Hence, Chrysostom says, "Let the one who prays not do anything new, so that he could not be seen by the people. . . . But when you pray with others, pray as the others. . . . Seeking new gestures and ways pertains to what Christ calls praying in the synagogues. A man in his praying ought to be in conformity with others."
   b) "For gain":
      i. Some seek in a most scandalous way gain from little old ladies: they say "long prayers," in order to make them devout and receive gifts from them.
      ii. Is it bad, then, to pray abundantly? Augustine says, "Let much speech be absent from prayer, but let praying much not be missing—more by signs than by spoken words, more by tears than by addressing."
2. Righteousness and mercy—hypocrites always pretend to wear this garment:

a) Doing acts of justice before the people
b) Giving alms to be seen
3. Penance—hypocrites simulate penance and an austere life:
   a) To be seen by the people
   b) Beware ostentation not only in the splendor of physical things, but also in vulgar things. Beware of being boastful of oneself by having a poorer way of life than his position requires.
   c) Be content with moderate things and do not seek the low things too much.
4. Innocence—hypocrites simulate piety and purity; whereas outside they wear clothes of sheep, inside they are grasping wolves.

III. *Intrinsecus autem sunt lupi rapaces* (inside they are grasping wolves)—How they threaten to damage us—Hypocrites are compared to wolves because of four things:

A) Wolves grasp (seize) sheep:

1. Hypocrites grasp the goods of soul and body.
2. They lead people to err.
3. They persecute people physically and rob them of things.

B) Wolves disperse the sheep
—Someone disperses when he deviates from what the Church teaches.

C) Wolves do not spare the sheep:

1. A person who would kill someone and would not spare him unless one silver coin could be gained is called very cruel. Hypocrites act in such a way.
2. Hypocrites seduce souls in order to have followers and honors, even though the life of the soul is better than that of the body.

D) Wolves persevere in their malice—until the end.

IV. *A fructibus eorum cognoscetis eos* (from their fruits you will know them)—How to recognize them: *by their fruits.*

—Augustine says that many are deceived because they mistake the clothes of a sheep for the fruits. Some simple people see others doing good exterior works—fasting, praying, and the like—which are the clothes of the sheep, but these are not their own clothes.

—Yet, the sheep of Christ should not hate their own clothes if wolves disguise themselves with these.

—What, then, are the fruits that sheep produce, on the basis of which wolves or hypocrites can be detected?

A) The first occurs in the affection and concerns the heart:
    1. The sheep of Christ, the saints, have their proper fruit in the heart, which is the love of God and neighbor.
    2. But hypocrites have another fruit, ambition, because they love honor (the first places at the table).
    3. If someone wants to be received with full honors while he shows humility on the outside, the garment does not correspond with the fruit.

B) The second occurs in the speech and concerns the mouth:

    1. Good people say good things and speak about good things.
    2. If someone says something that is not in tune with his works, he does not have clothes that are like his fruit. For example, it is difficult for a heart full of jealousy not to utter something of this sort.

C) The third occurs in the operation and concerns work:

    1. In good people, there is good fruit.
    2. The fruit of a godless person leads to sinful work.
    3. You can know a person by his works (through consistency).
    4. The road on which we are ordered to walk is laborious; hypocrites do not choose to work hard.

5. Furthermore, hypocrites show themselves moderate, but when they have a chance to pursue their desires, they pursue them to the highest extent.

D) The fourth occurs in times of trouble and concerns patience and strength:

1. There will be disquiet for the fruits of the godless; the teaching of a man is known through patience.
2. As soon as, through some temptations, they begin to withdraw or negate the things that follow from that clothing or pursue what they desire, it becomes clear whether it is wolf in a sheep skin or sheep in its own skin.

SERMON 15: *HOMO QUIDAM ERAT DIVES* (WITH *COLLATIO*) (SERMON ON THE NINTH SUNDAY AFTER THE FEAST OF THE TRINITY)

Thema:

Homo quidam erat dives qui habebat villicum et diffamatus est apud illum quia dissipasset bona illius. (Luke 16 :1)
There was a rich man who had a steward and he was discredited before him because he had squandered his goods.

Division of the Thema:

Two persons are presented here: (1) the person of the lord,* where it says: "**There was a rich man**"; and next (2) the person of the steward, where it says: "**who had a steward.**"

So first the person of the lord is presented to us, where it says: "**There was a man**, etc.**"** Three things are mentioned concerning the person of the lord: (1) what he is, where it says "**a man**"; (2) his wealth, where it says that "**he was rich**"; and (3) how he takes care of his wealth, where it says "**who had a steward.**"

[At the beginning of the *collatio* later in the day] "There was a rich man, etc." As it was said today, in these words two persons are introduced: the person of the lord and the person of the steward. Some things have been said about the lord; now we will speak about the steward. And concerning the steward we can consider three things: (1) his task, (2) his abuse, and (3) the danger threatening him. We can consider his task because **he was a steward**, his abuse because **he squandered the goods of his lord**, and his peril because **he was discredited**. [Editor's Note: In the body of the *collatio* itself, there is a fourth entry dealing with the *remedy*. See Section II.D below.]

[*Editor's Note: I have used the lowercase "lord" to indicate that the parable is about a master and his servant. In Thomas's sermon, the "certain man who was rich" (the earthly lord) will allegorically signify *the Lord*, Jesus Christ. But we start with a parable about an earthly lord.]

Analytical Outline:

Introduction: The parable is proposed to take away the haughtiness from our heart, since some believe that they are without a yoke, and to them it seems that whatever they like is allowed to them.

I. Person of the Lord:

A) *Homo quidam* (There was a certain man)—What he is:
He is God-man on account of three things:

1. Similarity of God with man:
   a) Man is made in the image and likeness of God.
   b) If the image of God were carved in wood and some-one threw mud on it, would he not be called blasphemous? Much more so is the one who corrupts the image that is created in God's likeness because much more excellent is the image of God in the soul than the image of Christ in wood.
2. Intimacy of God with man:
   a) If someone lived with the French, we could say that, by contact with the French, he has become a Frenchman. So too, by a certain intimacy and contact with us, God can be called a man because it is delightful for him to be with people, not merely in a spiritual way, but by taking on our flesh and dwelling with people in a physical way.
   b) It would be ungrateful if a king sought friendship with a poor man and the latter refused the king's friendship. If God is so intimate with us, we ought to apply ourselves to being intimate with him, opening the affection of our hearts for Christ.
3. What is proper to man—man is by nature a social being:
   a) Wild animals live alone, but humanity is characterized by "kindness" (*benignitas*).
   b) Someone who is destructive and harmful is called inhumane, as though he had taken on the nature of a wild animal.
   c) This property of *benignitas* befits God to the highest extent because his merciful deeds are over all his works and he saved us not on the basis of works of justice that we have done, but according to his mercy.

B) *Erat dives* (who was rich)—His wealth:
He is "rich" in three respects:

1. By reason of the perfection of his nature:
   a) Some are rich in things owned, but poor inside, like those who do not have wisdom.
   b) Someone was to give his daughter in marriage. There were two men courting her: one rich in possessions but poor in wisdom; the other wise but not rich. He went to a wise man and asked to whom he should give his daughter. The wise man answered, "I prefer a man lacking in riches over riches that lack a man."
   c) God is rich in himself, for every good whatsoever that is found in a creature comes from him.
   d) If you seek knowledge or goodness, all of it is in the most excellent and original way in God.
   e) If you have these riches that are in God, you will not lack anything. God alone can fulfill our desire.
2. By reason of an affluence and abundance of gifts:
   a) God "gives affluently" and still his treasure is not diminished.
   b) If someone gives abundantly, many would thrust themselves forward in order to receive. But if you want to receive, God is ready to give. So you ought to thrust yourself forward in order to receive.
   c) Man ought always to long more and more for the possession of spiritual things:
      i. The appetite for an end has neither manner nor measure. But the appetite for the things that are *for* an end is regulated according to the measure of the end. For example, a doctor does not set a measure to the goal of health, but he sets a measure to the medicine he gives to bring about health.
      ii. The goods of the soul are an end; the goods of the body are *for* an end. Hence, with regard to temporal goods, we ought to seek according to a measure, but with regard to goods of the soul, we ought to seek as much as we can.
      iii. Some want to limit their virtue, saying, "It is enough for me to do this," but do not want to limit their riches.

      iv. We ought always to approach God for spiritual goods; as for temporal goods, we ought to leave it up to him that he may give us from these in accordance with what seems best to him.

3. By reason of the multitude of things he possesses (all things are his):

    a) If a man sees someone else's servant, and if that servant promises to serve him, he must not trust in that servant's promise because his lord could stop him. But if the lord of the servant promises that this servant will serve this man, then he can trust him.

    b) Therefore, we ought to trust in God because he can give all things.

C) *Qui habebat villicum* (who had a steward)—How he takes care of his wealth

By means of his power, God could do all things by himself, but he did not will this.

Instead:

1. Whereas God reserved the governance for himself, he has commissioned some to be keepers, and he willed that the beauty of the order and the perfection of the universe be preserved.[1]

2. Furthermore, God wanted to govern all things by himself because of the usefulness, because he did not want anything to be superfluous.

    a) Why has God made the sun? So that we would not lack its warmth and light. If it had no use, it would have been superfluous.

---

[1] *Editor's Note: Thomas's text is not entirely clear here, but I take it his meaning is that, as Fr. Hoogland rightly suggests in a footnote in his translation, and as Thomas says elsewhere, "the order of things to each other makes up the good of the universe" ("ordo rerum ad invicem est bonum universi"). Thus Thomas goes on to add: "Imagine that we would not need one another; this would not be the beauty of the universe." Thus, I take his meaning to be that, while God governs all creation in that he continually (eternally) keeps all things in order, he also wills that we *keep* the order he has created. God willed the order himself; it does not depend upon us. But it is also his will that we keep the order he has willed. This interpretation helps make sense of Thomas's next point: we should not be superfluous servants because God has not created anything that was not to be useful.

b) You would be superfluous in the world if you do not do something useful. And the Lord judges that a "useless servant" should be thrown into the "outer darkness."

3. Moreover, God willed to commission some to be managers out of liberality. God willed that the goodness of a thing would go over onto other things.

a) Dionysius says that nothing is more divine than becoming a co-operator with God

b) When you [i.e., the young Dominican friars to whom he is preaching] preach for the salvation of the soul or do other good things, you co-operate with God.

4. Who are stewards? God has appointed stewards on different levels in an order:

a) Angels—to manage the things that are above creation

b) Men—set over earthly things

   i. But know that the Lord is God. Hence, Chrysostom says, "You are a stranger, and the things commissioned to you are only of a transitory and short use," and gives two examples:

      α) You have a field or estate: How many owners has it had before you? Infinite, and it barely contains so many clods of earth.

      β) Likewise, it is with you as with someone who rests in the shade: you pass away and someone else comes who rests there as you did.

   ii. Things come and go for you in the world according to divine providence, not according to yours. You are a steward, not the lord.

c) Leaders and managers—mediating instruments between people and angels—appointed to lead the people

d) Servants such as St. Dominic and St. Francis—who work with care for the salvation of the people

Collatio *(later that evening at vespers)*

II. Person of the servant *(villicum)*

A) *Villicum*—his task or "office": he was a steward. Stewards are managers, like angels and men. And since we are men, let us say that the care for the regulation of the goods is commissioned to man, to whom the Lord entrusts three things:

1. Himself
   a) If you have entrusted something to someone, you demand an account of him.
   b) But God has entrusted man to himself. Therefore, we must render account to him of both intellect and will.
2. Spiritual goods—which can be used in a good or in an evil way, depending upon whether you have love
3. Exterior things (If a certain lord has entrusted his goods to you, you ought to render account of those by the end of the year; so too God demands at the end of your life an account of the things granted to you.)

B) *Dissipasset bona illius*—his abuse [of his office]: he squandered the goods of his lord in three ways:

1. By using them for himself—God has entrusted you to yourself not in order to be your own, but that you may be his and that you seek God's glory, not your own:
   a) Gifts of knowledge
   b) Gifts of riches, which are meant to be used for the honor and glory of God
2. By keeping back things that did not belong to him:
   a) Taking care of yourself does not mean that you think about only yourself and care about only yourself. Just as the eye is not made for itself alone, but so that it is of service to the whole body, so a certain old man has said, "Because I am a human being, I consider nothing human alien to me."
   b) Grace from God: Not for yourself alone, just as the sun does not have brightness for itself alone, but in order to pour it out for others.

    c) Temporal goods: Are you not a looter by keeping for yourself the things entrusted to you to be distributed? It is the bread of the poor that you hold in your hand, the tunic of the nude which you keep in your room, the shoe of the unshod, and so on.

3. By superfluous and prodigal diversion:

    a) By giving himself up to the devil for a mediocre delight

    b) By selling his grace if he has it for a favor of the public

C) *Diffimatus est*—the danger threatening him, which is threefold:

1. *Diffimatus est* ("he was discredited")—after death, your sins do not remain hidden.

2. *Iam non poteris amplius villicare* ("You cannot be a steward any more")—loss of function: after death you cannot have knowledge and money anymore.

3. *Fodere non valeo, mendicare erubesco* ("I do not have the strength to dig, and I am ashamed to beg")—impossibility of aid: there is no work, no thought, no knowledge, and no wisdom with the inhabitants of the netherworld, just as the foolish virgins wanted to beg but were given nothing.

D) What is the remedy [for the steward] from the danger?
    —Christ's recommendation: "Make friends for yourselves with the mammon of iniquity, so that, when you are wanting, they may receive you in eternal tents" ("Facite vobis amicos de mammona iniquitatis ut cum defeceritis recipiant vos in aeterna tabernacula")—

1. But what is this counsel about "the mammon of iniquity"? We usually explain or understand this in four ways:

    a) When someone has riches that one of his ancestors has not acquired justly (St. Basil)

    b) When an unjust man values these riches highly (St. Augustine)

    c) Because they lead to iniquity

d) When a man kept the riches for himself unjustly (Chrysostom)

2. What is the meaning of "so that when you are wanting they may receive you in eternal tents" ("ut cum defeceritis recipiant vos in aeterna tabernacula")?

   a) St. Augustine: Who else are those of whom the eternal tents are than the saints of God?

   b) Who else are the ones that are received by them in the eternal tents than they who serve their needs and give to them with gladness what they lack?

   c) Must alms be given to sinners?

      i. All other things being equal, it is better to give to a just man than to a sinner because, by giving to a just man, you do a work that is meritorious and, in a similar way, so is the work of the one who receives.

      ii. But this is not so in the case of a sinner; only the work you do is meritorious, but not what he does.

Sermons on Feast Days

SERMON 16: *INVENI DAVID* (IN LEONINE VOLUME, BUT NOT IN TORRELL'S LIST) (SERMON ON THE FEAST OF ST. NICHOLAS, DECEMBER 6)

Thema:

Inveni David servum meum, oleo sancto meo unxi eum, manus mea auxiliabitur ei et brachium meum confirmabit eum. (Ps 88:21)
I have found David my servant; with my holy oil I have anointed him. My hand will assist him and my arm will make him firm.

Division of the Thema:

From these words we can learn four praiseworthy things of this holy bishop [St. Nicholas]: (1) first, his wondrous election; (2) second, his unique consecration; (3) third, the effective execution of his task; and (4) fourth, his immovable and firm stability. His wondrous election is shown in the words: "**I have found David, my servant.**" His special consecration is shown where it says: "**I have anointed him with my sacred oil.**" The effective execution of his task is shown in the words: "**My hand will help him.**" His stable firmness is shown where it says: "**and my arm will make him firm.**"

Analytical Outline:

I. *Inveni David servum meum* (I have found David my servant): his wondrous election

    A) Four things concerning the meaning of "finding"; it implies:

        1. Rarity [e.g., in English idiom, we might say of a rare deal on a laptop computer, "What a *find*!"]
        2. Inquiry: we speak of being found when things are sought after [e.g., "Seek and ye shall find"].
        3. Appearance: finding implies that it appears clearly to you [e.g., in English idiom, we sometimes say, "I found the movie to be delightful," or "I find this painting to be very ugly."]
        4. Experimental proof: When someone doubts about something and later on he knows it for sure, he says: "I have found [or "I have found out": *inveni*] that this is how it is."

B) In these four ways, the Lord "found" St. Nicholas—the Lord found in St. Nicholas:

1. Something rare: a "matured," "seasoned," "suitable" (*tempestivum*) virtue, rare in young men:
   a) Because St. Nicholas was preserving his sanctity in his youth, we say that he was "found."
   b) Figs ripen later than other fruits, and if they ripen at the right time, they are called "found." In this sense, boys who preserve their sanctity in their boyhood are called the first fruits of the gift tree and are called "found"—and that is pleasing to God. Hence, Micah 7:1 says: "My soul has desired early-ripening figs."
   c) Fish of the season and fruits of the season are in great demand; similarly, great is God's demand that man carries the yoke of the Lord in his youth.
2. Something he, the Lord, sought after: a devout mind— for instance, St. Nicholas was constantly in the church and in devout prayer.
3. Appearance: the Lord found in St. Nicholas something that shone clearly, a dedicated affection
   a) Nothing makes a man so radiant as dedication and kindness (*benignitas*) to others
   b) God is hidden in himself. Still he is revealed to us through his works of kindness (*opera beneficientia*).
   c) St. Nicholas was to the highest extent compassionate, and he felt deeply for the afflicted.
   d) A servant is someone who carries out the operation of the Lord. The pre-eminent operation of the Lord is mercy. So a servant of the Lord is someone who tries to carry out his mercy towards the poor.
4. Experimental Proof: the Lord found in St. Nicholas something proved through experience, faithfulness:
   a) A servant ought to be faithful so that he refers everything he has and does to God. This is St. Nicholas, and because of this it says, "my servant."
   b) If you do good in order to have allowances (*prebenda*), you serve yourself, not God.
   c) A good bishop should not be like this, but ought to

be innocent as for himself, devout in his relation to God, and merciful in his relation to his neighbors, as well as faithful in everything and having respect for everything.

II. *Oleo sancto meo unxi eum* (I have anointed him with my sacred oil): his special consecration (The sanctification of bishops is done with oil; indeed, there is hardly any sanctification in which oil is not used.)

A) In order to signify the power of oil, we must notice that we use oil for four purposes:
1. For the healing of a wound
2. As fuel for a light
3. To season the taste of food
4. To soften

B) In Saint Nicholas:
1. For healing of a wound: which is understood as healing grace, as St. Nicholas was anointed with the oil of healing grace because he was so full of health that he could pour out for others "wine and oil"—the wine of correction and the oil of mercy and comfort
2. As fuel for a light: by which is signified the study of wisdom
3. To season the taste of food: by which spiritual joy is signified:
    a) Spiritual joy makes it easier to do good works, for with sadness, even ordinary work is difficult.
    b) Hence, priests are anointed with oil, namely with the oil of joy.
4. To soften: by which mercy and kindness (*benignitas*) of heart are signified:
    a) St. Nicholas was completely filled with mercy and devotion.
    b) Oil flows, and in a similar way, mercy flows over all good works. So unless you have mercy, your works are nothing. Just as, in St. Francis, the marks of Christ's Passion were in his body because he was intensely affected by the Passion of Christ, the marks

of mercy reflect in St. Nicholas, for oil dripped from his tomb as a sign that he was a man of great mercy.

III. *Manus me auxiliabitur ei* (my hand will help him): the effective execution of his task
God does not have a physical hand, but his power is called his hand, and this "hand" helped Nicholas in four ways:

A) By drawing Nicholas to himself and tearing him away from evil things

B) By leading him

C) By comforting or strengthening him

D) By filling him with the power to perform miracles:

    1. The Lord has adorned him with miracles because he was most merciful.
    2. Mercy made St. Nicholas wondrous, and the Lord strengthened him until he achieved the goal of eternal life.

IV. *Brachium meum confirmabit eum* (my arm will make him firm): his stable firmness

[Editor's Note: This fourth division is missing. Why this is so is not clear. Fr. Bataillon gives three possible reasons, which span the logical possibilities: (1) the copyist did not write it down or copy it for some reason such as that he ran out of ink; (2) this fourth topic was a part of the *thema* Thomas dilated upon in the evening *collatio*, but this has not come down to us; or (3) Thomas simply ran out of time and did not get to develop his fourth point. He does seem to be rushing a bit at the end of Section III above. But that might simply be because he was finishing the morning sermon and wanted to get to a natural breaking place to set up for the evening's *collatio*. Those seem to be the three most logical possibilities. But the truth is that we do not know. All we know at the moment is that we do not have anything more.]

Sermon 17: *Lux orta est* (with collatio) (Sermon on the Feast of the Birth of the Blessed Virgin Mary, September 8; not attributable to Thomas)

Thema:
Lux orta est justo, et rectis corde laetitia. (Ps 96:11)
Light is risen for the just, and joy for the upright of heart.

Division of the Thema:
Now two things in particular are brought to our attention in this verse: (1) first, the rising of the Virgin's glory, when it says, "**A light has gone up**"; and (2) second, the fruits of the birth: "**for the just, and joy for the upright of heart.**"

[Restatement at the beginning of the *collatio*] "A light has gone up for the just, and joy for the upright of heart." Today it was said in what way the Blessed Virgin in her rising is a brilliant light. It remains to see in what way she is joy for [righteous or] upright people, since it is written in this verse, "and joy for the upright of heart."

[Editor's Note: The statement of the division of the parts of the *thema* does not show up until well into the sermon. Indeed, the structure of this sermon is very sloppy and disordered compared to Thomas's others. In addition, the sources this author cites (e.g., Bernard is quoted frequently) are also rather different from the sources cited in Thomas's other sermons. It is, in other words, altogether odd and uncharacteristic. It is for this reason easy to agree with the Fr. Bataillon's judgment in the Leonine volume: "Sermon inauthentique."]

Sermon 18: *Germinet terra* (Sermon on the Feast of the Birth of the Blessed Virgin Mary, September 8)

Thema:

Germinet terra herbam virentem et proferentem semen, lignumque pomiferum faciens fructum. (Gen 1:11)
Let the earth sprout forth the green plant that brings forth seed, and the fruit tree that bears fruit.

Division of the Thema:

These words reflect the divine disposition to provide for each and every thing according to what befits it. Hence God in his providence gave to man, because he is earthly, a remedy from the earth [*humanus*, earthly; derived from *humus*, from which is also derived "human"]. . . . Now a twofold medicine is put forth from the earth: the green plant and the fruit-bearing tree. The green plant is the Blessed Virgin, whose birth the Church is celebrating these days. [Editor's Note: Thomas does not, at this point, tell his audience what the "fruit-bearing tree" signifies. Later, in the evening *collatio*, however, he will make clear that "the fruit-bearing tree" is the Cross of Christ. See directly below.]

[From the *collatio*] The Most High has raised from the earth two remedies for us: **the green plant** and **the fruit-bearing tree**. We have spoken about **the plant**, which is the Blessed Virgin. Now it remains to speak about **the fruit-bearing tree**, the tree of the Cross of our Lord, which is to be venerated.

Analytical Outline:

I. *Herbam virentem et proferentem semen* (the green plant that brings forth seed): the Virgin Mary

    A) *Herbam* (plant)—regarding plants, we can consider three things:

        1. A plant is short in height:
        a) Signifies humility
        b) A tree is highly elevated from the earth (signifying pride) and yet most firmly fixed in the earth. A plant, however, only clings a little to the earth, and its roots are just under the surface.

   c)   In a similar way, a proud man's heart is pinned to the earth, and he cannot come loose from the earth, although he makes himself very big and is elevated high. On the other hand, a humble man does not have anything on earth; therefore, his heart is easily removed from the earth. So in this way Mary is compared with a plant in regard to her moderation.

   d)   In the littleness of a humble plant the humility of Mary is commended.

2. A plant is pliant in slenderness:

   a)   A heart is called pliant when it easily gives in (a virtuous and natural pliability of heart, as opposed to a vicious and unnatural one).

   b)   The natural order requires that a lower thing gives in to an action of a higher thing; so too, the will or the heart of a human being is set between two:

      i.   Something above itself: God

      ii. What is below it: the concupiscence of the flesh or the cupidity of the world

   c)   The Virgin was obedient to the divine will and teaches obedience

   d)   Obedience is a special virtue:

      i.   Gregory: "It is the only virtue that plants the other virtues in the mind and protects the ones that have been planted."

      ii. Some whisper that it is better to be obedient with a spontaneous will rather than on the basis of a vow. This is not true.

   e)   By the disobedience of one man, we are all sinners. So, it was becoming that we would be saved by obedience and that, just as the obedience of the Son began in the mother, so the Blessed Virgin was obedient.

3. A plant has medicinal strength:

   a)   The human race was weak because of sin, and God wanted to apply the remedy of a medicine.

   b)   Doctors show that their medicine works by first applying it to serious weaknesses.

   c)   The whole human race was feeble, and as for the woman, it seemed that it was completely corrupted.

    d) And so the Lord, willing to show that his medicine was good, showed it in a woman first, in order to distribute it through a woman to others.

    e) "The medicine of all people is in the swiftness of a cloud" (Sir 43:22): the strength of this medicine appeared swiftly in that the Blessed Virgin obtained grace in the maternal womb because she was sanctified in the womb from original guilt.

B) *Virentem* (green)—through virginity:

  1. Moisture (since moisture is the cause of greenness):

    a) Just as every plant withers because of fire or the sun, so the concupiscence of the flesh makes the greenness of virginity wither.

    b) The greenness of virginity is nurtured by heavenly love: virginity is the result of God's grace with the freedom of the free decision.

    c) Because Mary had the fullness of the moisture of grace, it was her strongest resolution to live as a virgin forever.

  2. Beauty (we see in greenness a beauty that delights):

    a) Order is what properly delights.

    b) The natural order of humankind is that the flesh is subject to the spirit.

    c) In the Virgin, nothing was disordered, neither in action nor in affection.

  3. Utility (as long as a plant is green, there is hope that it will produce fruit):

    a) Similarly, someone who is green through virginity produces the fruit of love, but when he shrivels through concupiscence, his works are fruitless in view of eternal life.

    b) Because Mary had the greenness of virginity in an excellent way, she produced an amazing fruit: not only spiritual fruit, but also the fruit of her womb.

C) *Proferentem semen* (producing seed)—seed of three kinds:

  1. Holy seed:

a) It is holy because of its origin, God.

b) It is characteristic of seed that it produces what is similar to that form from which it comes forth: children of God are brought about by the seed of God's Word.

2. Virtuous seed:

   a) The mustard seed is the tiniest and yet produces a great tree.

   b) The little seed is Christ, who was little on the Cross and grew so big that he filled heaven and earth.

3. Necessary seed:

   a) There is no salvation in anything else.

   b) This earth is the human nature destitute of the moisture of grace. Then how could it bring forth a plant? It was:

      i. Arid because of the concupiscence of sin.

      ii. Lowest because earth is below heaven.

   c) "And God said: Let the earth put forth the green plant":

      i. "He said" the word, meaning that he put forth the word that produced a fruit. "Wisdom has built a house for herself" in the Blessed Virgin.

      ii. Because it was arid, the Holy Spirit made it moist [cf. the discussion of virtuous seed above].

      iii. Because the earth was lowest, he gave himself to it and entered it, so as to make it the heavenly seed [cf. the discussion of holy seed above].

Therefore, if someone is empty through sin, let him ask for this plant, and he will be filled with good things. Likewise if someone is arid, let him take refuge with that Word, and he will be moistened. Likewise, if someone is downhearted, let him take refuge with that Word, and he will be led back to the heavenly light.

Collatio *(later that evening at vespers)*

We have begun the solemn days of his Cross. It is very suitable to connect these two remedies, because the green plant has brought forth our salvation, whereas the fruit-bearing tree has sustained the plant and has exalted it. Hence it says that Jesus's mother stood at the foot of the Cross. Let us look at this tree.

II. *Lignumque pomiferum faciens fructum* (and the fruit tree bearing fruit)—the tree of the Cross of Christ

Concerning the tree, Moses describes three things: (1) its appearance [*eius speciem*]: it is wood; (2) its adornment: it is fruit-bearing [*pomiferum*)]; and (3) what it produces: it produces fruit [*faciens fructum*].

A) *Lignum* (wood, tree)—It befits our remedy for three reasons:

1. It befits the wound: Just as "the human race is wounded because of disobedience, since the first man stole a fruit from the forbidden wood," so also "the new man has placed himself, as a salutary fruit so to speak, back onto the wood." The "forbidden tree" in the Garden is described as (a) good to eat from; (b) beautiful to the eyes; and (c) delightful to look at. The Cross is the medicine to each:

   a) Good to eat from: The wood of the Cross teaches the mortification of the flesh by which we are made alive. If you live according to the flesh, you will die (Rom 8:13).

   b) Beautiful to the eyes: There was worldly beauty in the forbidden tree. But the beauty of the first tree is completely changed into shame, whereas the shame of the Cross is completely changed into glory.
   Excursus: "See how the wood of the Cross is exalted." [Editor's Note: This comment allows Thomas to recount briefly the story of how the Byzantine emperor Heraclius re-captured the Cross from the Persians in the year 628 and eventually returned it to Jerusalem.]

   c) Delightful to look at: The delight of the flesh is not a true delight, since it has more about bitterness than about delight. If the just suffer adversities, the wood of the Cross makes these sweet. The Cross even makes one glory in adversity. Thus, the wood of the Cross befits the wound.

2. It befits the healing of the wound:
   a) The first evil of man occurred when Adam was thrown out of Paradise (Gen 3:22–24). What was

the remedy? The Tree of Life. But because Adam was not permitted to approach the Tree of Life, he could not have the remedy. Christ has taken up the wood for us: the Cross has become for us the "Tree of Life."

b) The second danger was the flood (Gen 6–8). The remedy came by means of the wood of Noah's ark.

c) The third danger came when the people of Israel were oppressed by the Egyptians (Exod 1:8–22). The remedy came by means of wood, since Moses struck the sea with a rod, dividing it and then reclosing it over the Egyptians.

d) It says in 1 Samuel 4:7 that the children of Israel fought against the Philistines and that the Ark of the Lord, which was made of wood, was brought into the camp. So, the wood befits the wound and the healing.

3. It befits the healer because Christ is exalted by the wood of the Cross:

a) He is like a warrior and the Cross is his "triumphant chariot": this is the thing that elevates Christ.

b) It is like the sedan chair of Solomon (see Song 3:9).

c) It also is like the rod that guides the people.

d) Moreover, he is exalted as a *magister* in his (wooden) seat of instruction.

B) *Pomiferum* (fruit-bearing)—the adornment of the tree: it is loaded with fruit (*onusta pomis*).

What are its fruits ["et quae sunt eius poma"]?

* In Deut 33:13–15, in the blessing of Joseph, mention is made of three fruits: (1) the fruits of heaven, (2) the fruits of sun and moon, and (3) the fruits of eternal hills.

1. Which are the fruits of heaven? The members of Christ: not only the physical members of Christ's body, but those of his mystical body.

2. Which are the fruits of sun and moon? The examples of virtue which Christ has shown on the Cross:

a) Love (No greater love than to lay down one's life for his friends; John 15:13)

      b)   Humility (Humbled himself to death on a cross; Phil 2.8)

      c)   Patience (when he was cursed but he did not curse; 1 Pet 2:23)

3. Which are the fruits of the eternal hills? The writings of teachers who are imbued with wisdom. On the Cross, Christ teaches:

      a)   Faith: "My God, my God, why have you abandoned me?" (Matt 27:46)

      b)   Hope: "Today you will be with me in paradise." (Luke 23:43)

      c)   Patience: "Father, forgive them, for they know not what they do." (Luke 23:34)

      d)   Devotion: "Father, into your hands I commend my spirit." (Luke 23:46)

      e)   How to live a human life together: "Woman, behold your son"; "Behold your mother." (John 19:26–27)

C) *Fructum faciens*: fruit continually held by the wood
Now there are trees that have flowers and fruits all the time [*continue habent flores et fructus*]. In a similar way, the tree of the Cross has flowers all the time [*continue habet flores*]. See that the wood of the Cross has produced a triple fruit [*fructum*]:

1. The fruit of cleansing [*fructum purgationis*]: Through the Cross we are liberated from sins.

2. The fruit of sanctification: Man, alienated from God through sin, is reconciled through Christ. Thus we make the sign of the cross to sanctify ourselves.

3. The fruit of glorification: Through sin, humankind is excluded from paradise, and therefore, Christ has suffered on the Cross so that, through the Cross, the gate from the earthly things to the heavenly things would be open. Hence, the Cross of Christ is signified by the ladder that Jacob saw whose top reached the heavens. All the saints go up to the heavens by the power of the Cross.

SERMON 19: *BEATI QUI HABITANT* (SERMON ON THE FEAST OF ALL SAINTS, NOVEMBER 1)

Thema:
Beati qui habitant in domo tua, Domine, in secula seculorum laudabunt. (Ps 83:5)
Blessed are those who dwell in your house, O Lord; they will praise you forever and ever.

Division of the Thema:
[Editor's Note: The division of this sermon is not as clear-cut as others. One can discern a rough outline structured according to the *thema* verse above, but the sermon is more loosely constructed and the various parts of the *thema* verse frequently appear at the end of a section rather than at the beginning.]

The entire sermon is related to the first word in the *thema* verse, *Beati*, which is often translated "blessed," but which can also be translated "happy." Thus, the entire sermon is about happiness or "blessedness" (*beatitudo*). There are three major sections.

In the first section of the sermon (under Roman numeral I below), Thomas discusses three ways in which people err with regard to happiness:

(1) Some people err, he says, concerning the abode of happiness, which he relates to the words *qui habitant in domo tua* ("who live in your house").
(2) Others err concerning the duration of happiness, which he relates to the words *in secula seculorum* ("forever and ever").
(3) And finally, there are those who err concerning the occupation or operation of the happy ones (the *beati*), which he relates to the word *laudabunt* ("they will praise [you forever and ever]").

As I mentioned above, this structure is not stated clearly at the beginning of each section; it is stated at the end, as though providing an answer to the question posed by the discussion.

In the second section of the sermon (under Roman numeral II below), Thomas discusses how we can arrive at the sort of true happiness enjoyed by the "blessed" (the *beati*, the happy ones). This section is organized around the three types of happiness—worldly, political, and contemplative—and the answer to the question of how we can arrive at happiness is given in terms of the eight Beatitudes from the Sermon on the Mount recounted in Matthew 5:3–11, each of which begins in Latin with the word *beati*, "blessed [are] . . ." (the poor, the meek, those who mourn, etc.).

In the third section of the sermon (under Roman numeral III below), Thomas brings together the three types of happiness from section II—worldly, political, and contemplative—with each member of his original threefold division of the *thema* verse. Thus we can say of the happiness of the saints (the *beati*), that:

(1) Compared to earthly happiness, the happiness of the saints has an abundant abode. Hence, it says, "**Happy are those who live in your house.**"

(2) Compared to the happiness that belongs to the political life, the saints have continuity, for the ruler of a city ought to apply himself to preserve the good of the city all the time. Hence, it says: **forever and ever.**

(3) Compared to the happiness that belongs to contemplation, the saints live with the divine things, since contemplative happiness consists particular in contemplation, which the saints enjoy. Hence, it says: **They will praise you.**

[Editor's Note: Needless to say, the structure of the whole is remarkably ingenious. While it employs the opening *thema* verse as a structuring device, it does so in a novel and fascinating way.]

Analytical Outline:

Introduction:

—"There is no one with a correct understanding who does not know that the community of God and angels and people is one community. . . . This is a community insofar as they share the same end, namely, happiness [*beatitudine*]."

—"Now, people who live together, in the sense that they have the same end, must share with one another what they are doing in such a way that those who have not yet reached the end are led to it. . . . Whereas the ones who have already achieved the end help others to achieve it. And this is the reason why we celebrate the feasts of the saints who have already attained happiness."

—"Therefore, since we have come now to the festivities of the community of the saints [*de beatorum societate*], we are to speak about happiness [*beatitudine*]."

Beati: So we must know that, although the affect of all people is directed towards happiness ("omnium hominum affectus ad beatitudinem tendat"), but still there are some people with a different idea about happiness.

I.   Thus, with regard to beatitude, the many err in three ways:

A) They err with regard to the abode of happiness, placing it
    in this world, either in corporeal things or in virtues or in
    knowing things (*scienciis*). But this opinion is at odds with:

1.   The perfection of happiness
     a)   Happiness is the perfect good, and since it is the ul-
          timate end, it must quiet desire.
     b)   This would not be the case if, after these things have
          come into our possession, some desire would remain.
          Such is the case with all things in this world.
2.   The purity of happiness
     a)   Since happiness is the highest good, it cannot be
          mixed with evil.
     b)   Yet, in this life, no one can be found who is not sub-
          ject to a particular misery.
3.   The stability of happiness
     a)   Happiness would not quiet our desire unless it were
          stable.
     b)   The more we love the goods we possess, the more af-
          fliction they bring about as we fear losing them.
     c)   Exterior things and the human body are subjected
          to various events, and no one is safeguarded against
          this, so that, from experience, we can learn that, in
          this life, there is no stability.

Therefore, if you ask the Psalmist where the true abode of happiness is, he
answers: *Beati **qui habitant in domo tua domine** ("Happy are **those who
live in your house, Lord**").

B) Concerning the duration of happiness, some people err in
    saying that the souls that have left the body attain happiness
    and that, after a long course of years, they return to a body
    and subsequently stop being happy because they are subjected
    again to the miseries of our present life. This is the error of
    Plato and his followers. But this idea seems reprehensible for
    three reasons:

1. It is contrary to natural desire:
   a) For, there is naturally in everything an appetite by which it conserves itself in being and in its perfection.
   b) But there is a difference:
      i. In things that lack the ability to consider the universal, their appetite is directed towards the here-and-now, so that their perfection is preserved in this way.
      ii. But a rational nature, knowing the universal, naturally has the appetite to conserve its perfection all the time.
   c) So, if the soul has not reached everlasting happiness, it is not satisfied by natural desire.
2. It is contrary with the perfection of grace:
   a) Everything that is totally filled with its own perfection is immovably preserved in it.
   b) Thus, the intellect truly remains immovable in its thinking according to the first principles because, through them, the intellect is filled insofar as it concerns that truth.
   c) It is not, however, completely filled with probable chains of reasoning, and so it does not think in an immovable way.
   d) But a happy soul is totally filled with happiness; otherwise, happiness would not be a perfect good.
3. It is contrary to the equity of divine justice:
   a) Through love a human being clings to God with the intention never to recede from him.
   b) "Who will separate us from the love of Christ?"
   c) Hence, it is not fully satisfying love if it is, at times, removed from the enjoyment of God.

If you ask the Psalmist, he responds: *in saecula saeculorum* (forever and ever) *laudabunt te* (they will praise you).

C) Concerning the occupation of the blessed, Jews and Sarracens err, saying that the blessed abandon themselves to excessive eating, drinking, and unions with women. Their opinion is justly rejected for it is:

1. Contrary to the privilege of humankind:
   a) If happiness were according to the use of food and sensual things that are found in other living creatures, not only humankind but even animals ought to have happiness.
   b) But this is the privilege of humankind, that among the lower creatures, only the human being is capable of happiness.
2. Contrary to the nature of joy of humankind:
   a) A higher nature is not made happy by something lower.
   b) If the happiness of humankind consisted in eating and drinking, then someone would also be made happy by the food he eats, and thus these goods would be worth more than a human being.
   c) Humankind, however, is placed above all other lower natures.
3. Contrary to zeal for the virtues (*virtutis studium*):
   a) For a human being, virtue consists in being torn away from pleasures.
   b) Hence, the virtues that concern pleasure are named by what restricts them, like abstinence, temperance, and the like.
   c) Other virtues concern wearisome and difficult things, as with fortitude.
   d) Now, if the happiness of humankind consisted in the pleasures of the flesh, then virtue, which is the way of happiness, would not tear us away from the pleasures of the flesh, but would imply the pleasures.

So if we ask David what he thinks the occupation and action of the happy ones, the saints, he would answer: "They will praise you" (*laudabunt te*).

II. How can we arrive at this happiness? There are three types of happiness:

A) Worldly happiness, which consists in possessions and the enjoyment of worldly things, such as honors [dignity], riches, and delights:

1. Ambitious people strive after dignity by means of arrogance and money.
   a) The Lord teaches us, however, to arrive at dignity by the opposite way: by poverty and humility.
   b) Thus he says: "**Happy the poor in spirit**, for the kingdom of heaven is theirs."
2. People of this world arrive at riches by quarrels (*litigia*) or warfare or by somehow using violence in matters (*saltem in causis decertando*).
   a) But God teaches the opposite way, the way of mildness.
   b) Thus he says: "**Happy the meek**, for they will inherit the earth."
   c) This happiness befits the martyrs, who were not angry with their persecutors, but rather prayed for them.
3. People strive to attain delights (*delectaciones*) by various comforts (*solacia*).
   a) But the Lord teaches us the opposite way, mourning.
   b) Thus he says: "**Happy they who mourn**, for they will be comforted."

B) Happiness that belongs to the political realm, which consists in acting well, governing one's actions with prudence:

1. The maximum of his ability is reached when he governs not only himself, but even a city and a kingdom. Hence this happiness befits in particular kings and princes.
2. But there is a difference [actually two differences] between a king and a tyrant:
   a) First difference:
      i. A king is someone who is intent upon the good of the people by his reign. So, what a king issues is not discordant with the order of his wisdom.
      ii. However, a tyrant is, by his own wish, intent upon being discordant with the divine order of wisdom, for he aims at the satisfaction of his own desire, so that he accomplishes everything as he pleases and is intent to arrive at this through greed, by plundering others unjustly.

iii. But the Lord teaches us to arrive at happiness by the contrary way: by justice.

iv. Thus he says: "**Happy are those who hunger and thirst for justice**, for they will be filled."

b) Second difference:

i. A tyrant is intent upon not being punished for the evils he has done.

ii. The tyrant does so by means of cruelty: he exerts himself so that he may be feared so much that no one would contradict him.

iii. But the Lord teaches a contrary way: the way of mercy.

iv. Thus he says: "**Happy are the merciful,** for they will obtain mercy."

C) Contemplative happiness, which is proper to those who apply themselves to acquiring the truth, and especially divine truth:

1. Philosophers can only obtain this happiness if they are intent upon two things: learning the truth and obtaining authority.

a) They will only get to know the truth by studying.

i. But God teaches a shorter way: by the cleanness of the heart.

ii. So he says: "**Happy the clean of heart**, for they will see God."

iii. And this happiness befits, in particular, the virgins who preserved a cleanness of mind and body.

b) Philosophers want to acquire authority by contentious debates.

i. But the Lord teaches us to arrive at divine authority through peace.

ii. Thus he says: "**Happy the peacemakers**, for they will be called children of God."

iii. This happiness befits the apostles.

D) "**Happy they who suffer persecution for the sake of righteousness, for theirs is the kingdom of the heavens**":

1. This is said in order to strengthen the ones mentioned before (A, B, and C).
2. If someone is pulled away from happiness because of persecution, he is not strong in poverty, mildness, and the other virtues.
3. Therefore, all the rewards mentioned before ought to be included in this happiness—and so he returns to what he said at the beginning of the Beatitudes, saying: "for theirs is the kingdom of the heavens."
4. And we should understand "because they will possess the earth" in a similar way, and likewise the other sayings.

III. So, the happiness of the saints contains whatever is found praiseworthy in any of the others mentioned:

A) Compared to earthly happiness, the happiness of the saints has an abundant abode. Hence, it says: "**Happy are those who live in your house.**"

1. In this house he will obtain whatever he may desire.
2. There will be enough riches present there.
3. There will be delights that refresh the total human being.

B) Compared to the happiness that belongs to the political life, they have continuity, for the ruler of a city ought to apply himself to preserve the good of the city all the time. Hence, it says: "**forever and ever.**" This continuity comes forth from three things:

1. From living together with good people,
2. From the removal of condemnable behavior, and
3. From the immunity to all evils and miseries.

C) Compared to the contemplative happiness, they will live in a way with the divine things, since contemplative happiness consists particularly in contemplation. Hence, it says: "**They will praise you.**"

1. For, they will see without an intermediary and clearly.

2. And, like sons and daughters, they will love him incessantly.

3. And, as good sons and daughters, they will honor God by praising him (the Psalmist need only mention "praise" because what is praised is known and loved).

Sermon 20: *Beata Gens* (with *Collatio*) (Sermon on the Feast of All Saints, November 1)

Thema:

Beata gens cuius est Dominus Deus eius, populus quem elegit in hereditatem sibi.(Ps 33:12)
Blessed the nation whose God is the Lord, the people whom he has chosen for His inheritance.

Division of the Thema:
By the mouth of David the Holy Spirit commends this company of the saints in four ways: (1) first, based on their dignity; (2) second, based on their leader; (3) third, based on how they are arranged; and (4) fourth, based on their election. He commends that group of the saints based on their dignity where it says: "**Blessed the nation**"; based on their leader where it says: "**whose Lord* is its God**"; based on how they are arranged, he calls them a people, when he says "**people**"; based on their election, when he says: "**whom the Lord has chosen for His inheritance.**"

[*Editor's Note: I have followed Fr. Hoogland's precedent of using lower case "lord" for Thomas's first use of *dominus* in the *divisio* and upper case "Lord" for the second because there is an interesting ambiguity in the Psalm worth noting. Instead of translating the Latin "Blessed the nation whose God is the Lord," we could render it, as Fr. Hoogland does, "Blessed the nation whose lord is its God." Indeed, this second translation preserves the Latin *eius* ("its") which is missing from the first. Understood this way, the Psalm would be suggesting that a nation is blessed if its "lord" (its ultimate ruler) is God. And yet, it is also possible (and indeed, more likely) that the Psalm should be rendered "Blessed the nation for whom its god is the LORD" ("the LORD" here standing in for the sacred tetragrammaton, or "Yahweh"), which would imply that Judah is blessed because, instead of a pagan god or gods, it has Yahweh as its god. Let us presume for the moment that the second of these ("the LORD") is more likely the meaning intended in the original context in which the Psalm was written. And yet, given Thomas's discussion below of "lord" as a word "calling to mind their leader," we might suppose he was thinking of the first (earthly) sense of "lord." Indeed, the imagery of "kingdom," "crown," and "lord" suffuses the first part of the sermon. By the same token, since he is talking about the angels, it is clear he also means to refer to the LORD God. Note, however, that whether it is a "lord" or "the LORD," Thomas would have understood it as referring ultimately to Christ. That this is the ultimate reference Thomas has in mind is made clear by the fact that the latter part of the sermon is organized around the beatitudes from Christ's Sermon on the Mount. Thus Thomas is able to put to good use the full range of potential meanings present in the word *dominus* ("lord").]

Analytical Outline:
Prothema: The Church recollects the glory of the saints to provoke in us heavenly desire.

Introduction:
The verse "Happy the nation . . ." is meant for the souls of the people all together, so that they hear with delight the praises of their heavenly homeland and of their parents ("laudes patriae suae et parentum suorum"): of their heavenly homeland, so that we hasten to return to it; of their parents—the saints in the homeland—so that by following their example, we will not lapse.

By the mouth of David, the Holy Spirit calls to mind this company of the saints in four ways:

I. **Beata Gens** (Happy the nation): calling to mind their dignity, which consists in three things:

A) They have arrived at the place for which we strive: the kingdom where there is no end:

1. In Sacred Scripture, the end of humankind is compared to three things (which is appropriate because every action of ours is reduced to these three):
    a) A crown (*corona*): the goal for those in the active life—some struggle. Those who have struggled according to the rules deserve a crown because, as it is written in 2 Timothy 2:5, "no one will be crowned unless he struggles according to the rule."
    b) A prize (*bravium*): the goal for contemplatives—some run. Contemplatives run fast because no earthly things hinder them. And those who compete in a race deserve a prize.
    c) A reward (*mercedi*): the goal for "the workers" (*lab-*

orantes), such as prelates (*praelati*), who bring about salutary works among the ordinary people (*in plebe*). "Everyone will receive a proper reward [*propriam mercedem*] in accordance with his work [*secundum laborem suum*]."

2. What is the glory of the saints in the homeland?
   a) They have sought after a crown as good strugglers—an incorruptible crown.
   b) They have pursued a prize as runners.
   c) They have sought after a reward as good workers.

B) They possess everything we desire and even more—
Consider what you can desire among the pleasures and delights. All of these the saints have, but only as for spiritual delights, not for worldly ones:

1. Riches: If you desire riches, the saints are the wealthiest, for nothing is missing for those who fear the Lord.
2. Honors: If you desire honors, the saints are invested with the greatest honor.
3. Knowledge (*scientia*): If you seek knowledge, the saints have that too because they drink knowledge from the very fountain of wisdom.

C) They are invested above what we can understand:

1. "Eye has not seen, O God; you alone have seen the things you have prepared for those who love you" (Isa 64:4).
2. The saints in the homeland have all their desires fulfilled because they have come to the fountain of every good.
3. You cannot fully enjoy every good unless you come to the fountain of every good, which is God himself.
4. Since God is great and above every intellect, the saints who enjoy God are elevated so high that no one can reach them.

II. *Cuius dominus deus eius* (whose Lord is its God): calling to mind their leader

A) The dignity of the saints depends on their leader, God, in whom is our beatitude:

    1. It is most miserable, degrading, and terrible that a human being would be subordinate to someone inferior to himself or to a villain.

    2. Someone who has a worthy master whom he serves is happy.

    3. It is just to be subordinate to God, for the highest perfection of a thing is that it is subordinate to what is more perfect than it.

    4. As *materia* is not perfect unless it is subordinate to a *forma*, so the soul is not perfect unless it is subordinate to God.

    5. Thus, our happiness lies in being subordinate to God—a subordination often mediated by angels, prelates, and those who educate us, who guide us where we ought to go in order to arrive at happiness.

    6. But the saints in the homeland are not subjected to educators. Thus, it says: "Happy the nation whose Lord is its God"

B) But there were and are some people that have said that our happiness is in earthly things:

    1. But all things pass like a shadow.

    2. Moreover, they do not fill themselves because "the greedy will never have enough money."

C) So too, there were and are some, like the Stoics, who say that happiness is found in internal goods, such as virtues and knowledge:

    1. "The wise will not take pride in his wisdom" (Jer 9:23).

    2. Everything that is within you is subordinate to your nature. But what makes you happy ought to be above you, not subjected to you.

D) Still others say that happiness is found in things that are [not above or within us, but] next to us; they put their trust in humankind. But there are two objections:

1. "Do not put your trust in princes" (Ps 146:3).
2. Nor can we put our trust even in angels because our intellect is made for the vision of the Highest Cause.

E) "Happy the nation whose Lord is its God." How are we to understand this "its"? It means that God is to be:

1. Known: the saints in the heavenly homeland know God; two things accompany this knowledge.
   a) A clear and direct vision—
      i. We see God only indirectly, through created things; the saints see God clearly, not in a mirror darkly.
      ii. In order to see God clearly, we must have pure eyes, but our eyes are darkened by the fire of concupiscence, the fire of anger, and the fire of desiring evil things.
   b) A perfect similarity with God—
      i. Knowledge does not come about unless through an assimilation of the one who knows with the thing known.
      ii. The saints in heaven have a perfect similarity with God, seeing him as he is.
      iii. Thus, if you want to arrive at similarity with God in heaven, you must apply yourself to becoming similar to him in good works here.
      iv. Christ came to give peace to the world; thus it says: "**Happy the peacemakers**, because they will be called children of God."
2. Possessed: The saints have God as their possession and this is enough for them.
   a) In what way do the saints possess God? "Happy the one who fears him" (John 4:14).
   b) How have they arrived at possessing him? Through love.
   c) What do you possess in possessing God? What is in God: "Glory and riches are in his house" (Ps 112:3).
      i. Glory (as of kings), which is promised to the humble: "**Blessed the poor in spirit**, because theirs is the kingdom of the heavens."

      ii. Riches: The saints have anything that someone can desire. But to whom is this given? Not to those who quarrel about earthly things. Heavenly riches are acquired by mildness: "**Happy are the meek**, for they will possess the earth."

3. Enjoyed: The saints have God to enjoy and delight in.

    a) The saints in heaven do not delight in temporal things, but in God, the fountain of every good. Thus it says in Luke 22:30: "that you may eat and drink at the table in my Kingdom."

        i. What is eating at God's table? To delight in and to be refreshed by the same thing by which God is refreshed.

        ii. And what is the thing by which God is refreshed? His goodness.

        iii. Thus, when you are refreshed by the goodness of God, you eat at God's table—and this is the happiness of the saints.

    b) The delight of the saints has three characteristics:

        i. This joy gives consolation.

        ii. This joy is complete (Augustine says. "No one can arrive at this satisfaction except by hungering for justice"): "**Happy those who hunger and thirst for justice**, for they will be satisfied."

        iii. This joy is not mixed with mourning and anxiety: "**Happy the merciful**, for they will receive mercy."

Collatio *(later that evening at vespers)*

III. ***Populus*** (people): calling to mind how they are arranged:
What is a people? Augustine says, "A people is a multitude of men and women together, united by a consensus of law and by a common purpose" (*De civitatae Dei* 19.31). Thus, three things are meant:

A) A numerous multitude, which pertains to:

1. The dignity of a king, especially this king; only God knows how big the multitude of the saints is (see Rev 7:9).

2. Joyfulness: the more people who are freed from corruption, the more joy.
3. Our security: "Fear not, for there are many more with us than with them" (2 Kings 6:16).

Thus, the multitude of saints in heaven brings:
1. Honor to God,
2. Joy to the saints, and
3. Safety to us.

[Editor's Note: At this point in the *collatio*, Thomas says: "We must speak about the election of the saints." This is the topic he proposed for the fourth part of his division (associated with the phrase *quem elegit in hereditatem sibi*, "whom he has chosen for His inheritance"). The problem is that he has finished only the first of the three subdivisions of his third division (associated with the word "people"). Indeed, he proceeds below to dilate upon the second subdivision—the ordered distinction among the saints—after which, however, he concludes without having discussed in any substantive way his third subdivision under "people," on the "harmonious union" of the saints, or saying anything on their election (which was to be the topic of division IV).

It is unknown why the *collatio* was cut short. Nor is it entirely clear why Thomas says at this point that he must discuss next the "election of the saints." Some people have speculated that, realizing he was running short on time, Thomas united divisions III and IV so as to wrap up more quickly.

It is not evident to me from the actual content in the *collatio* that this is what Thomas does. Rather, it seems more likely that Thomas may have misspoken or that the scribe made an error. Either way, Thomas proceeds to discuss, in what follows, the "ordered distinction" among the saints. And strangely (if it was the case that he knew he was running short on time), he even goes into a rather long digression about the proper understanding of the Aristotelian "mean."

If Thomas thought that he might skip the rest of his dilation of division III and go directly to division IV, it is clear he reconsidered immediately and did not in fact do so. Rather, he finished his dilation of the second subsection of division III and then wrapped up with a conclusion. This, at least, is how I understand the structure of what remains, as my outline below indicates.]

B) The ordered distinction:
1. The distinction of the saints is handed down to us on the basis of the knowledge in the epistle, but that diversity [in the epistle reading] is in the world, not in heaven.
2. Therefore, we hear in the Gospel about a difference between the saints that will be in heaven among the glorious people.
   a) Some will be kings: the apostles. How have they acquired their reign? Through poverty: "**Happy the poor in spirit**, for theirs is the kingdom of the heavens."

   [Editor's Note: This statement about "poverty" inspires a digression about the proper understanding of Aristotle's account of virtue as a "mean." Can *poverty*, for example—giving away all one's goods (such as Thomas and his Dominican confreres have done)—ever be considered a "mean"?]

Digression on virtue as a mean:
1. Some say that virtue consists in keeping the middle and in such a way that every renouncement, even virginity, does not belong to the virtues.
2. Virtues should not keep the middle according to quantity, but according to a right way of reasoning.
3. For example, magnanimous men do great things, but in accordance with the mean proper to them: where they ought to, in accordance with what they ought, and because of what they ought to be.
4. So too, philosophers have laid aside all their belongings so that they can make themselves free for philosophy and live moderately.
5. If this was the case with the Gentiles, it is also true for Christians.
6. But note that, if a man wanted to renounce his wife when she asked him for what he owes her, renouncement would be a vice, even though we find the highest virtue in virginity.

[End of digression; resuming the outline from where we left off above]

   b) There are also victorious martyrs: "**Happy are the meek**, for they will possess the earth."
   c) There are also some who live in solace, like the holy confessors who mourned while they were in the world and did great penance, such as Anthony of the

Desert and Benedict, who lived in tears and great, austere penance, and who now have joy and consolation: "**Happy are those who mourn**, they will be consoled."

d) There are also most righteous judges—namely, the prophets—who preached justice: "**Happy those who hunger and thirst for justice**, for they will be satisfied."

e) Patriarchs who fervently applied themselves to the work of mercy (e.g., Abraham) received everyone who came to him and now receives at his bosom all who are chosen. [Editor's Note: "**Blessed are the merciful**" is implied, not stated.]

f) Virgins, who preserved their purity are also there: "**Blessed are the pure of heart**, for they will see God."

g) Likewise, we find in heaven the choir of angels who strive for peace: "**Happy the peacemakers**, for they will be called children of God."

Summary: It is clear now how the poor have acquired the kingdom; the meek, the earth; the mourning, consolation; those who hunger after justice, satisfaction; the merciful, mercy; the clean, the vision of God; and the peacemakers, becoming "children of God."

[Editor's Note: Thomas did not have time to discuss the final divisions he had set out above:

III. C) The harmonious union of the saints.

and

IV. *Quem elegit in hereditatem sibi* (whom he has chosen for His inheritance): calling to mind their election.]

Sermon 21: ***Beatus vir*** (with *collatio*) (Sermon on the Feast of St. Martin, November 11)

Thema:

Beatus vir cuius est auxilium abs te; ascensiones in corde suo disposuit in valle lacrimarum in locum quem posuit. (Ps 83:6-7)
Happy the man whose help is from you; he has set his heart on ascending while in the valley of tears, in the place which he has built.

Division of the Thema:

This day St. Martin is promoted to the highest dignity and the highest place, namely, to the kingdom of the heavens. Therefore, Mother Church commemorates his happiness. Concerning his happiness three things come up that we must consider based on the words proclaimed. First, we can consider the beginning of his happiness; second, the progress; and third, its endpoint. The origin or cause of his happiness was divine help, which is mentioned when it is said: "**Happy the man whose help is from you.**" He has made progress in ascents: he advances from one virtue to another, which is mentioned when it says: "**He has set his heart on ascending**." The endpoint of his happiness is the gain of eternal happiness, which is mentioned when it says: "**in the place which he has built.**"

Analytical Outline:

Prothema: Martin has arrived at the glory of highness through divine help. That help is ready for all people. And just as St. Martin needed divine help in order to arrive at the glory of highness, so we too need divine help so that we can arrive at glory.

Introduction: This day St. Martin is promoted to the highest dignity and the highest place, to the kingdom of heaven. Therefore, Mother Church commemorates his happiness, concerning which three things must be considered: the origin of his happiness; the progress; and the end.

I.   *Beatus vir cuius est auxilium abs te* (Happy the man whose help is from you): divine help as the origin or cause of his happiness—With our reason, we find in creatures that, when something reaches something by its own nature, it is the cause of it. As for those things that it does not reach by its own nature—like fire: it is warm by its own nature, and therefore it is the cause of the heating in other things not warm by their own nature. God is happy by his own nature and, thus, is the cause of happiness in others. So, no one can arrive at happiness unless by divine help. The Lord grants us a triple help:

A) God chides mankind (a correction that is not worth anything unless one becomes more intimate with God's grace) in three ways:

    1. By inspiring fear,
    2. By forgiving him his sins, and
    3. By drawing him away from sins.

B) God teaches man in three stages:

    1. He enlightens the intellect through faith,
    2. He raises up the mind through hope, and
    3. He changes the affection through love.

C) God takes us up—
God magnified St. Martin in three steps:

    1. Through the holiness of his works
    2. Because of the greatness of his miracles:
       a) He raised up three dead people.
       b) His garments and letters cured those who were ill.
       c) He made him great in the fear of his enemies.
       d) His enemies sent peace negotiators.
    3. In the spreading of his fame over all the earth

Collatio *(later that evening at vespers)*

II. *Ascensiones in corde* (he has set his heart on ascending): the progress of his happiness in ascents (advancing from one virtue to another)—

A) Threefold ascent:

    1. Through the sacrament of regeneration
    2. According to his state—Martin ascended in three ways:
       a) From the military state to the clerical,

    b)   From the clerical to the religious ("ruled" or "regular" clergy), and

    c)   From the religious state to the pontifical.

  3. According to merit—Martin ascended three times according to merit:

    a)   In the military state (he applied himself to advance in mercy and devotion),

    b)   In the clerical state (he applied himself to obedience),

    c)   In religious life (he excelled in poverty and austerity), and

    d)   In the pontifical state (he maintained the same humility).

B) How St. Martin ascended:

  1. With prudence,

  2. With humility, and

  3. With fervor.

III. *In locum quem posuit* (in the place which he has built): the endpoint of his happiness, which is gaining eternal happiness, eternal glory.

[Editor's Note: As was the case with Sermon 20 above, Thomas seems to have run out of time, so he sums up with only one line on the topic of the endpoint of happiness: "So, because the saint we celebrate today has well prepared his ascent in the progress of happiness, he has arrived at the endpoint of happiness, which is eternal glory, to which may we be led by him who with the Father and the Holy Spirit . . ." And with this, he brings his *collatio* to its end.]

APPENDIX 2:
THOMAS'S SERMONS AND
THE MEDIEVAL DOMINICAN LECTIONARY

I HAVE LISTED EACH OF THE SERMONS BELOW, numbered as they appear in the Leonine edition and in Fr. Hoogland's translation. This list is meant to indicate whether the *thema* verse for the sermon was taken from the lectionary reading for the day.

I have indicated "YES" if the *thema* verse corresponds with the readings assigned for the day in the Dominican lectionary, "NO" if it does not, and "PERHAPS" if the answer is unclear. There are several instances in which Thomas may have used verses from a reading in the Franciscan lectionary. Since the lectionary seems not to have specified which Psalm was to be used, when Thomas preaches on a verse from a Psalm, I have merely noted "PSALM," suggesting that this Psalm verse *may* have been used during the liturgy but that this remains unclear. Although sermons without a *collatio* may or may not have been university sermons, when a sermon was given "with *collatio*," it is certain these *were* university sermons.

It may be worth noting that, in most of his sermons for special feast days, Thomas used a Psalm verse as the *thema*, whereas he never used a Psalm verse as a *thema* in any of his extant Sunday sermons.

The list of lectionary readings for the liturgical year was taken from M. O'Carroll's "Table of Mass Pericopes for the Temporal Cycle," in "The Lectionary for the Proper of the Year in the Dominican and Franciscan Rites of the Thirteenth Century," *Archivum Fratrum Praedicatorum* 49 (1979): 79–103 (esp. 85 ff).

Sermon 1 (*Veniet desideratus*): Haggai 2:7—NO
Sermon on the First Sunday of Advent
    Romans 13:11–14
    Matthew 21:1–9

Sermon 2 (*Lauda et letare*): Zechariah 2:14—NO
Another Sermon on Advent

(There is no Sunday in Advent within the Dominican lectionary where the reading is from Zechariah.)

Sermon 3 (*Abjiciamus opera*): Romans 13:12—YES
Sermon on the First Sunday of Advent
    Romans 13:11–14
    Matthew 21:1–9

Sermon 4 (*Osanna filio David*): Matthew 21:9—YES
Sermon on the First Sunday of Advent
    Romans 13:11–14
    Matthew 21:1–9

Sermon 5 (*Ecce rex tuus*): Romans 21:5—YES
Sermon on the First Sunday of Advent
    Romans 13:11–14
    Matthew 21:1–9
    With *collatio*

Sermon 6 (*Celum et terra transibunt*): Luke 21.33—PERHAPS*
Sermon on the First Sunday of Advent
    *This Gospel verse is within the readings for the First Sunday of Advent in the Franciscan calendar, not the Dominican.

    Franciscan Readings for I Advent
        Romans 13:11–14
        Luke 21:25–33

    Dominican Readings for I Advent
        Romans 13:11–14
        Matthew 21:1–9

Sermon 7 (*Ecce ego mitto*): Matthew 11:10—PERHAPS*
Sermon on the Second Sunday of Advent
    *This Gospel verse is within the readings for the Second Sunday of Advent in the Franciscan calendar, not the Dominican.

    Franciscan Readings for II Advent
        Romans 15:4–13
        Matthew 11:2–10

Dominican Readings for II Advent
    Romans 15:4–13
    Luke 21:25–33

Sermon 8 (*Puer Jesus*): Luke 2:52—YES
Sermon on the First Sunday after Epiphany (within the Octave of Epiphany)
    Romans 12:1–5
    Luke 2:42–52
    With *collatio*

Sermon 9 (*Exiit qui seminat*): Luke 8:5—YES
Sermon on Sexagesima Sunday (penultimate Sunday before Lent)
    2 Corinthians 11:19–12:9
    Luke 8:4–15
    With *collatio*

Sermon 10: (*Petite et accipietis*) *dubia* (not by Thomas)

Sermon 11 (*Emitte spiritum*): Psalm 104:30—PSALM
Sermon on Pentecost
    With *collatio*

Sermon 12 (*Seraphim stabant*): Isaiah 6:2–3—PERHAPS*
Sermon on the Feast of the Trinity
    *The text in Isaiah 6:2 is the *Veni sancte spiritus*, which was likely to have been chanted.

Sermon 13 (*Homo quidam fecit cenam magnam*): Luke 14:16—YES
Sermon on the Second Sunday after the Feast of the Trinity
    1 John 3:13–18
    Luke 14:16–24
    With *collatio*

Sermon 14 (*Attendite a falsis*): Matthew 7:15–16—PERHAPS*
Sermon on the Third Sunday after the Feast of the Apostles Peter and Paul (or the Seventh Sunday after the Feast of the Trinity, according to Nürnberg MS)
    * This verse would *not* have been read on the Seventh Sunday after the Feast of the Trinity, but it *would* have been read on the Eighth Sunday after the Feast of the Trinity.

VII Post Trin
    Romans 6:19–23
    Mark 8:1–9

VIII Post Trin
    Romans 8:12–17
    Matthew 7:15–21
    With *collatio*

Sermon 15 (*Homo quidam erat dives*): Luke 16:1—YES
Sermon on the Ninth Sunday after the Feast of the Trinity
    1 Corinthians 10:6–13
    Luke 16:1–9
    With *collatio*

Sermon 16 (*Inveni David*): Psalm 89:21-22—PSALM
Sermon on the Feast of St. Nicholas, December 6

Sermon 17 (*Lux orta*): Psalm 97:11—PSALM
Sermon on the Feast of the Birth of the Virgin Mary, December 8

Sermon 18 (*Germinet terra*): Genesis 1:11—PERHAPS*
Sermon on the Feast of the Birth of the Virgin Mary, December 8 (or
within the octave of the feast)
    * I do not have access to information on readings for the special
    feasts. It is unclear whether this reading from Genesis would have
    been used or not.
    With *collatio*

Sermon 19 (*Beati qui habitant*): Psalm 84:5—PSALM
Sermon on the Feast of All Saints, November 1

Sermon 20 (*Beata gens*): Psalm 33:12—PSALM
Sermon on the Feast of All Saints, November 1
    With *collatio*

Sermon 21 (*Beatus vir*): Psalm 83:6-7—PSALM
Sermon on the Feast of St. Martin, November 11
    With *collatio*

Comments:

1. In the case of those sermons for which the biblical *thema* appears to have been taken from the lectionary reading for the day, one might ask whether Fr. Bataillon identified them as having been given on that particular day precisely because the *thema* verse corresponded with the lectionary reading identified in Professor O'Carroll's article. If Bataillon identified the date of the sermon based on its correspondence to O'Carroll's list, then we would have something of a "feedback loop." This scenario seems unlikely, however, given the variations from that pattern, especially the readings that appear to have been taken from the Franciscan lectionary rather than the Dominican.

2. For those sermons for which the biblical *thema* has been taken from the Old Testament, I am presuming that, since an Old Testament reading was generally not specified in the medieval lectionary, these verses may have been chosen by Thomas himself *ad hoc*.

3. The reader should also note the following confusions surrounding Sermons 6, 7, and 14:
   A) **Sermon 6**: Fr. Bataillon has identified the sermon *Celum et terra transibunt* as being a "Sermon on the First Sunday of Advent." The *thema* Thomas chose was from Luke 21:33, which was *not* part of the reading for the First Sunday of Advent in the Dominican lectionary, but it *was* part of the reading for the First Sunday of Advent in the Franciscan lectionary (Luke 21:25–33). The question is whether Thomas might have been preaching somewhere where the Franciscan readings were being used?[1]

---

[1] Fr. Torrell (Torrell, *Sermons*, 18) points out that, according to the statutes of the University of Paris, the obligation for the faculty of theology to preach extended both to Sundays and to nonworking feast days. In the latter case, the sermon would be delivered at the house of either the Franciscans or the Dominicans. University statutes also specified that if the master designated to preach on a certain day was not able to fulfill his obligation, he could be replaced by another master. It is not clear whether a Dominican master could stand in for a Franciscan master or vice versa. When the

B) **Sermon 7**: Fr. Bataillon has identified the sermon *Ecce ego mitto* as being a "Sermon on the Second Sunday of Advent." The *thema* Thomas chose was from Matthew 11:10, which was *not* part of the reading for the Second Sunday of Advent in the Dominican lectionary, but it *was* part of the reading for the Second Sunday of Advent in the Franciscan lectionary (Matt 11:2–10). This usage prompts the same question posed above: was there a reason Thomas would have used the Franciscan lectionary rather than the Dominican? Or was the usage of both more fluid at Paris than O'Carroll's list might lead us to expect?

C) **Sermon 14**: The issues surrounding Sermon 14 (*Attendite a falsis*) are yet more complicated. Fr. Bataillon suggests that this sermon was preached "on the Third Sunday after the Feast of the Apostles Peter and Paul," or (what I take it amounts to the same thing), "the Seventh Sunday after the Feast of the Trinity." According to the note in Hoogland's translation, this last identification is actually in one of the manuscripts of the sermon. The confusion arises from the fact that the verse Thomas has chosen for his *thema* is Matthew 7:15–16. This, if I am reading the calendar correctly, is *not* from the readings for the day for the Seventh Sunday after the Feast of the Trinity (which would be Rom 6:19–23 and Mark 8:1–9). But Matthew 7:15–16 *would* correspond to the reading for the *Sixth* Sunday after the Feast of the Trinity in the Franciscan lectionary (Matt 7:15–21), *or* it might corre-

---

morning sermon was scheduled for one of the mendicant houses, the evening *collatio* had to be given there as well. But if the morning sermon was delivered elsewhere, preachers were not bound by the obligation to preach the evening *collatio*. Hence it may be relevant that neither Sermon 6 nor Sermon 7 has an accompanying *collatio*. And yet it is also worth noting that the preaching schedule for the year was set by a commission composed of four regent masters. One presumes the commission was made up of representatives from both the Franciscans and the Dominicans. What is not yet clear is how this commission would have reconciled the readings from the different Franciscan and Dominican lectionaries when it came time to assign preaching duties for the year. Given the differences, was there, for example, some sort of compromise according to which Dominicans sometimes had to preach on the readings in the Franciscan lectionary, and vice versa? At this point, we do not know. The situation may have been much more fluid than our simple list of lectionary readings might suggest.

spond to the *Eighth* Sunday after the Feast of the Trinity in the Dominican lectionary (Matt 7:15–21). Is it possible that the manuscript identification is incorrect—that the attribution is off by a week, one way or the other?

SELECTED BIBLIOGRAPHY OF SOURCES CITED

Ameriks, Karl. *Kant and the Historical Turn: Philosophy as Critical Interpretation.* Oxford, UK: Clarendon Press, 2006.

Aquinas, Thomas. "Les *Opuscula fratris Thomae* chez Ptolémée de Lucques." Edited by A. Dondaine *Archivum Fratrum Praedicatorum.* Vol. 31. Rome: Istituto Storico Domenicano, 1961.

—————. *Catena Aurea: Commentary on the Four Gospels Collected out of the Works of the Fathers by S. Thomas Aquinas.* Translated by John Henry Newman. Vol. 4. Oxford: Parker, 1841–45. http://dhspriory.org/thomas/CAJohn.htm.

—————. *The Commandments of God: Conferences on the Two Precepts of Charity and the Ten Commandments.* Translated by L. Shapcote. London: Burns & Oates, 1937.

—————. *Commentaries on Aristotle's "On Sense and What Is Sensed" and "On Memory and Recollection."* Translated by Kevin White and Edward Macierowski. Washington, DC: Catholic University of America Press, 2005.

—————. *Commentary on Galatians.* Translated by Fabian Larcher, O.P. Albany, NY: Magi Books, 1966. http://dhspriory.org/thomas/SSGalatians.htm#56.

—————. *Commentary on the Gospel of St. John.* Translated by James A. Weisheipl and Fabian R. Larcher, O.P. Aquinas Scripture Series 4. Albany, NY: Magi Books, 1980 (part 1), 1998 (part 2). http://dhspriory.org/thomas/SSJohn.htm.

—————. *Commentary on the Letter of St. Paul to the Romans.* Translated by Fabian Larcher, O.P. Edited by J. Mortensen and E. Alarcón. Lander, WY: Aquinas Institute, 2012. For a Latin version on-line, see http://www.corpusthomisticum.org/cro00.html.

—————. *Commentary on the Second Epistle to the Corinthians.* In *Commentary on the Letters of Saint Paul to the Corinthians.* Translated by Fabian Larcher, O.P., Beth Mortensen, and Daniel Keating. Edited by John Mortensen and Enrique Alarcón. Lander, WY: The Aquinas Institute for the Study of Sacred Doctrine, 2012. http://dhspriory.org/thomas/SS2Cor.htm#41.

—————. *Liber contra impugnantes Dei cultum et religionem.* In *An Apology for the Religious Orders.* Translated by John Procter. London: Sands, 1902; reprint, Westminster, MD: Newman Press, 1950. http://dhspriory.org/thomas/ContraImpugnantes.htm#35.

———. *On the Power of God.* Translated by Lawrence Shapcote. Westminster, MD: The Newman Press, 1952.

———. *Puer Jesus.* Translated by Athanasius Sulavik. http://www.dhspriory.org/thomas/Serm08PuerIesus.htm

———. *Responsi ad lectorem Bisuntinum.* In *Sancti Thomae de Aquino Opera Omnia.* Vol. 42. Rome: Commissio Leonina, 1979. See also "Responsio de 6 articulis ad lectorem Bisuntinum." Quaestio 3. http://www.corpusthomisticum.org/os5.html.

———. *The Sermon-Conferences of St. Thomas Aquinas on the Apostles' Creed.* Translated by N. Ayo, C.S.C. Notre Dame, IN: University of Notre Dame Press, 1988.

———. *Sermones.* In *Sancti Thomae de Aquino Opera Omnia.* Vol. 44.1. Edited by L. J. Bataillon, O.P., et al. Paris: Commissio Leonina, Éd. du Cerf, 2014.

———. *St. Thomas's Commentary on the Psalms.* Translated by Hugh McDonald, Stephen Loughlin, et al. http://www4.desales.edu/~philtheo/loughlin/ATP/Proemium.html.

———. *Summa Theologica.* Translated by the Fathers of the English Dominican Province. 2nd rev. ed. London: Burns, Oates & Washbourne, 1912–1936; reprinted in 5 vols. Westminster, MD: Christian Classics, 1981. http://dhspriory.org/thomas/summa/index.html.

———. *Super Evangelium s. Matthaei lectura.* Edited by R. Cai. Turin: Marietti, 1951.

———. *The Three Greatest Prayers.* Translated by L. Shapcote. London: Burns, Oates, 1937; reprinted, Manchester, NY: Sophia Institute Press, 1997.

———. *Thomas Aquinas: The Academic Sermons.* Translated by Mark-Robin Hoogland, C.P. The Fathers of the Church: Mediaeval Continuation 11. Washington, DC: Catholic University of America Press, 2010.

———. *Thomas d'Aquin: Sermons.* Traduction française, introduction et commentaire de J.-P. Torrell, O.P. Paris: Cerf, 2014.

———. *Thomas d'Aquin, Sermons sur les dix commandements (Collationes de decem preceptis).* Traduction française, introduction et commentaire de J.-P. Torrell, O.P. Paris: Cerf, 2015.

Augustine. *Confessions.* Translated by J. G. Pilkington. *A Select Library of the Nicene and Post-Nicene Fathers of the Christian Church*, 45–207. Vol. 1. Edited by Philip Schaff. New York: Scribner's, 1907.

———. *De doctrina christiana* ("St. Augustin's Christian Doctrine"). Translated by J. F. Shaw. *A Select Library of the Nicene and Post-Nicene*

Fathers of the Christian Church, 513–597. Vol. 2. Edited by Philip Schaff. New York: Scribner's, 1907.

———. *Eighty-Three Different Questions*. Translated by David L. Mosher. Fathers of the Church. Vol. 70. Washington, DC: Catholic University of America Press, 1982.

———. *Quaestionum in Heptateuchum libri VII*. Corpus Christianorum Series Latina, 33. Eds. J. Fraipont, D. De Bruyne. Turnhout, Belgium: Brepols, 1958.

Bataillon, L. J., O.P., "*Similitudines* et *exempla* dans les sermons du XIIIe siècle." *Prédication*. Étude 10, 192–193.

Benedict XVI. Regensburg Lecture: "Faith, Reason and the University." September 12, 2006. http://w2.vatican.va/content/benedict-xvi/en/speeches/2006/september/documents/hf_ben-xvi_spe_20060912_university-regensburg.html.

Bériou, Nicole. "Les Sermons Latins Après 1200." In *The Sermon*. Edited by Beverly Mayne Kienzle. Typologie Des Sources Du Moyen Age Occidental 81. Turnhout, Belgium: Brepols, 2000.

———. *L'avènement des maîtres de la Parole. La prédication à Paris au XIIIe siècle*. 2 vols. Paris: Institut d'Études augustiniennes, 1998.

Biblia Sacra Vulgata. 5th ed. Stuttgart: Deutsche Bibelgesellschaft, 1983.

Bonaventure. *Collationes in Hexaemeron et Bonaventuriana quaedam selecta ad fidem codicum mss*. Edited by F. M. Delorme, O.F.M. Bibliotheca Franciscana scholastica Medii Aevi 8. Florence: Collegium S. Bonaventurae, 1934.

———. *Collations on the Ten Commandments*. Translated by Paul J. Spaeth. Works of Saint Bonaventure 6. St. Bonaventure, NY: The Franciscan Institute, 1995.

———. *Sancti Bonaventurae Sermones dominicales*. Edited by J. G. Bougerol. Grottaferrata: Collegio S. Bonaventura, Padri Editori di Quaracchi, 1977.

——— *Sermones de Tempore, de Sanctis, de B. Virgine Maria et de Diversis*. Doctoris Seraphici S. Bonaventurae Opera Omnia 9. Ad Claras Aquas (Quaracchi): Collegium S. Bonaventurae, 1901.

———. *The Sunday Sermons of St. Bonaventure*. Translated by Timothy Johnson. Works of Saint Bonaventure 12. St. Bonaventure, NY: Franciscan Institute, 2008.

Bonelli, Benedetto. *S. Bonaventurae operum omnium supplementum*. In *Tria Volumina Distributum*. Vol. 3. Tridenti: Monauni, 1774.

Bougerol, Jacques. *Introduction to the Works of Saint Bonaventure*. Translated by J. Guy De Vinck. Paterson, NJ: St. Anthony Guild Press, 1964.

Boyle, John F. "The Theological Character of the Scholastic 'Division of the Text' with Particular Reference to the Commentaries of Saint Thomas Aquinas." In *With Reverence for the Word: Medieval Scriptural Exegesis in Judaism, Christianity, and Islam*. Edited by J. D. McAuliffe, B. D. Walfish, and J. W. Goering. Oxford, UK: Oxford University Press, 2003.

———. "Thomas Aquinas and Sacred Scripture." *Pro Ecclesia* 4 (1995): 92–104.

Boynton, Susan and Diane J. Reilly, eds. *The Practice of the Bible in the Middle Ages: Production, Reception, and Performance in Western Christianity*. New York: Columbia University Press, 2011.

Caplan, Harry. "A Late Medieval Tractate on Preaching." In *Studies in Rhetoric and Public Speaking in Honor of James Albert Winans*. New York: Century, 1925.

Carruthers, Mary. *The Book of Memory: A Study of Memory in Medieval Culture*. New York: Cambridge University Press, 1990.

Cassiodorus. *Institutions of Divine and Secular Learning and On the Soul*. Translated by James W. Halporn. Liverpool, UK: Liverpool University Press, 2003.

[Cicero]. *Rhetorica ad Herennium*. Translated by Harry Caplan. Loeb Classical Library. Cicero I. Cambridge, MA: Harvard University Press, 1954.

Collins, J. B. tr. *The Catechetical Instructions of St. Thomas Aquinas*. New York: J. F. Wagner, 1939; reprinted, New York: Scepter, 2002.

Copeland, R. and I. Sluiter, eds. *Medieval Grammar and Rhetoric: Language Arts and Literary Theory, AD 300–1475*. Oxford, UK: Oxford University Press, 2012.

Crane, T. F. *The Exempla of Jacques de Vitry*. London: T. F. Crane, 1890.

D'Avray, David L. *The Preaching of the Friars: Sermons Diffused from Paris before 1300*. Oxford, UK: Oxford University Press, 1985.

Davy, M. M. *Les sermons universitaires parisiens de 1230–1231: contribution à l'histoire de la prédication médiévale*. Paris: J. Vrin, 1931.

De Basevorn, Robert. *Forma praedicandi*. In *Artes Praedicandi: contribution à l'histoire de la rhétorique au moyen âge*. Edited by Thomas Charland. Publications de l'Institut d'Etudes Medievales d'Ottawa 7 Paris/ Ottawa: J. Vrin / Institute of Medieval Studies, 1936.

———. *The Form of Preaching*. Translated by Leopold Krul, O.S.B. In *Three Medieval Rhetorical Arts*, 109–215. Edited by James J. Murphy. Berkeley: University of California Press, 1971.

De Bourbon, Étienne. *Tractatus de diversis materiis praedicabilibus.* Edited by Jacques Berlioz and Jean-Luc Eichenlaub. *Corpus Christianorum. Continuatio Mediaevalis* 124. Turnhout, Belgium: Brepols, 2002.

De Lubac, Henri, S.J. *Medieval Exegesis.* 4 vols. Grand Rapids, MI: Eerdmans, 1998–2009.

De Tocco, William. "From the First Canonisation Enquiry." In *The Life of St. Thomas Aquinas: Biographical Documents.* Translated and edited by Kenelm Foster, O.P. London: Longmans and Green, 1959.

The Divine Comedy of Dante Alighieri: Paradiso. Translated by Allen Mandelbaum. New York: Bantam Books, 1984.

Donne, John. "Preached upon the Penitentiall Psalmes." In *The Sermons of John Donne.* Edited by George Potter and Evelyn Simpson. Vol. 5. No. 17. Berkeley: University of California Press, 1959. See also http://contentdm.lib.byu.edu/cdm/compoundobject/collection/JohnDonne/id/3200/rec/1, "Preached upon the Penitentiall Psalmes," 20.

Gilson, Étienne. "Michel Menot et la Technique du Sermon Médiéval." In *Les Idées et Les Lettres,* 109–54. Paris: Vrin, 1932; and *Revue d'Histoire Franciscaine* 2.3 (1925): 301–60.

Gomperz, J. J. "The Speech Community." In *The International Encyclopedia of the Social Sciences,* 381–86. New York: Macmillan, 1968. Reprinted in *Linguistic Anthropology: A Reader,* 66–73. Edited by Alessandro Duranti. 2nd ed. Oxford, UK: Wiley-Blackwell, 2009.

Gui, Benardo. "The Life of St. Thomas Aquinas." In *The Life of St. Thomas Aquinas: Biographical Documents,* ch. 32. Translated and edited by Kenelm Foster, O.P. London: Longmans and Green, 1959.

Hazel, Harry Charles. "A Translation, with Commentary, of the Bonaventuran '*Ars Concionandi.*'" PhD diss., Washington State University, 1972.

———. "The Bonaventuran '*Ars Concionandi.*'" *Western Journal of Speech Communication* 36.4 (1972): 241–50.

Heidegger, Martin. "Letter on Humanism." In *Basic Writings.* New York: Harper & Row, 1977.

Humbert of Romans. *De eruditione praedicatorum.* In *B. Humberti de Romanis opera de vita regulari.* Edited by J. J. Berthier. Rome: Typis A. Befani, 1888–1889.

———. *Treatise on Preaching.* Translated by the Dominican Students Province of St. Joseph. Edited by Walter M. Conlon, O.P. Westminster, MD: The Newman Press, 1951.

John of Salisbury. *Metalogicon.* Translated by Daniel McGarry. Philadelphia, PA: Paul Dry Books, 2009.

Joinville, Jean de. *Life of St. Louis*. In *Chronicles of the Crusades*. Edited and translated by Margaret Shaw. Baltimore, MD: Penguin Classics, 1963.

Kienzle, Beverly Mayne, ed. *The Sermon*. Typologie Des Sources Du Moyen Age Occidental 81. Turnhout, Belgium: Brepols, 2000.

Langlois, M. Ch.-V. "L'éloquence sacrée au moyen age." *Revue des Deux Mondes* 115 (1893): 170–201.

Leclerq Jean. "Un sermon inédit de Saint Thomas sur la royauté du Christ." *Revue Thomiste* 46 (1946): 152–66.

———. *The Love of Learning and the Desire for God: A Study of Monastic Culture*. Translated by Catharine Misrahi. 3rd ed. New York: Fordham University Press, 1961.

Leo XIII, Pope. *Aeterni Patris*. "On the Restoration of Christian Philosophy." August 4, 1879. http://w2.vatican.va/content/leo-xiii/en/encyclicals/documents/hf_l-xiii_enc_04081879_aeterni-patris.html.

———. *Iampridem Considerando*. October 15, 1879. https://w2.vatican.va/content/leo-xiii/it/letters/documents/hf_l-xiii_let_18791015_iampridem.html.

Liere, Frans van. *An Introduction to the Medieval Bible*. Cambridge, UK: Cambridge University Press, 2014.

Little, A. G. *Studies in English Franciscan History*. New York: Longmans and Green, 1917.

Markus, R. A. *Saeculum: History and Society in the Theology of St. Augustine*. Cambridge, UK: Cambridge University Press, 1970.

Martianus Capella. *The Marriage of Philology and Mercury*. Martianus Capella and the Seven Liberal Arts. Vol. 2. Translated by William H. Stahl, et al. New York: Columbia University Press, 1977.

Minnis, Alistair. *Medieval Theory of Authorship: Scholastic Literary Attitudes in the Later Middle Ages*. 2nd ed. Philadelphia, PA: University of Pennsylvania Press, 2010.

Mulcahey, Michèle. *First the Bow is Bent in Study: Dominican Education Before 1350*. Toronto, ON: Pontifical Institute of Medieval Studies, 1998.

Murphy, James J. *Rhetoric in the Middle Ages: A History of Rhetorical Theory from Saint Augustine to the Renaissance*. Berkeley: University of California Press, 1974.

Neale, J. M. *Mediaeval Preachers and Mediaeval Preaching*. London: J. C. Mozley, 1856.

Newman, John Henry. *An Essay in Aid of a Grammar of Assent*. London: Longmans and Green, 1903.

————. *Fifteen Sermons Preached Before the University of Oxford Between 1826 and 1843*. 3rd rev. ed. Reprinted by Notre Dame, IN: University of Notre Dame Press, 1997.

————. *The Tamworth Reading Room: Letters on an address delivered by Sir Robert Peel, Bart., M.P., on the establishment of a reading room at Tamworth*. London: J. Mortimer, 1841.

O'Carroll, Maura, S.N.D. "The Lectionary for the Proper of the Year in the Dominican and Franciscan Rites of the Thirteenth Century." *Archivum Fratrum Praedicatorum* 49 (1979): 79–103.

Ong, Walter J., S.J. *Orality and Literacy: The Technologizing of the Word*. 2nd ed. New York: Routledge, 2002.

Origen. "A Letter from Origen to Gregory." In *Ante-Nicene Fathers*, 393–394. Vol. 4. Edited by Philip Schaff. Edinburgh: T&T Clark.

Owst, G. R. *Literature and Pulpit in Medieval England*. Cambridge, UK: Cambridge University Press, 1933.

————. *Preaching in Mediaeval England: An Introduction to Sermon Manuscripts of the Period c. 1350–1450*. Cambridge, UK: Cambridge University Press, 1926.

Philo of Alexandria. *On the Creation of the World*. In *The Works of Philo: Complete and Unabridged*. Translated by C. D. Yonge. Peabody, MA: Hendrickson Pub., 1993.

Plato. *Phaedrus*. Translated by Harold N. Fowler. Plato in Twelve Volumes. Vol. 9. Loeb Classical Library. Cambridge, MA: Harvard University Press, 1925.

Prümmer, D., O.P., et al., eds. *Fontes Vitae S. Thomae Aquinatis*. Toulouse, FR: Revue Thomiste, 1912–1934.

Reynolds, Suzanne. *Medieval Reading: Grammar, Rhetoric and the Classical Text*. Cambridge, UK: Cambridge University Press, 1996.

Roberts, Veronica. "Augustine's Ciceronian Response to the Ciceronian Patriot." *Perspectives on Political Science* 45.2 (2016): 113–24.

Rouse, Richard H. and Mary A. Rouse. *Preachers, Florilegia and Sermons: Studies on the "Manipulus Florum" of Thomas of Ireland*. Studies and Texts 47. Toronto, ON: Pontifical Institute of Mediaeval Studies, 1979.

The Second Vatican Council's Dogmatic Constitution on Revelation (*Dei Verbum*). Translated by Walter J. Abbott, S. J. http://www.vatican.va/archive/hist_councils/ii_vatican_council/documents/vat-ii_const_19651118_dei-verbum_en.html/.

Septuaginta. Edited by Alfred Rahlfs and Robert Hanhart. Stuttgart: Deutsche Bibelgesellschaft, 2007. https://www.academic-bible.com/en/online-bibles/septuagint-lxx/read-the-bible-text/.

Smalley, Beryl. *The Study of the Bible in the Middle Ages.* 2nd ed. Notre Dame, IN: University of Notre Dame Press, 1989; orig. publ. Oxford, UK: Blackwell, 1941.

Smith, Christian and Melinda Lundquist Denton. *Soul Searching: The Religious and Spiritual Lives of Teenagers.* Oxford, UK: Oxford University Press, 2005.

Smyth, Charles. *The Art of Preaching: A Practical Survey of Preaching in the Church of England, 747–1939.* New York: MacMillan, 1940.

Sparks, H. F. D. "Jerome as Biblical Scholar." In *The Cambridge History of the Bible.* Vol. 1. *From the Beginnings to Jerome.* Edited by P. R. Ackroyd and C. F. Evans. Cambridge, UK: Cambridge University Press, 1970.

Stock, Brian. *The Implications of Literacy: Written Language and Models of Interpretation in the Eleventh and Twelfth Centuries.* Princeton, NJ: Princeton University Press, 1983.

Tolomeo of Lucca. *Historia ecclesiastica.* In *Rerum Italicarum Scriptores.* Vol. 11. Edited by L. A. Muratori. Milan, IT: Ex typographia Societatis Palatinae in Regia Curia, 1724.

Torrell, Jean-Pierre., O.P. "Les *Collationes in decem preceptis* de saint Thomas d'Aquin. Edition critique avec introduction et notes." *Revue des sciences philosophiques et théologiques* 69 (1985).

———. *Initiation à Saint Thomas d'Aquin: Se Personne et Son Oeuvre.* Paris: Cerf, 2015.

———. *Saint Thomas Aquinas, Vol. 1. The Person and His Work.* Translated by Robert Royal. Washington, DC: Catholic University of America Press, 2005.

Waleys, Thomas (Thomas of Wales). *De modo componendi sermones.* In *Artes Praedicandi: contribution à l'histoire de la rhétorique au moyen âge.* Edited by Thomas Charland. Publications de l'Institut d'Etudes Medievales d'Ottawa 7 Paris/Ottowa: J. Vrin / Institute of Medieval Studies, 1936.

Welter, Jean Thiebaut. *L'Exemplum dans la littérature religieuse et didactique du moyen age.* Paris: Occitania, 1927.

Yates, Frances. *The Art of Memory.* London: Routledge, 1966.

Zier, Mark. "Sermons of the Twelfth Century Schoolmasters and Canons." In *The Sermon.* Edited by Beverly Mayne Kienzle. Typologie Des Sources Du Moyen Age Occidental 81 Turnhout, Belgium: Brepols, 2000.